The Routledge Handbook of Accounting in Asia

As the centre of world economic development has shifted towards Asia over the last two decades, many Asian countries have witnessed rapid growth in economic and business operations. In light of these recent changes, accounting has played a significant role in assisting economic transition and advancement in Asian countries. However, although the general trend over recent decades towards convergence in financial reporting standards and practices has dramatically improved the comparability of accounting information, considerable variances remain in practices between countries.

This handbook therefore provides an up-to-date review of contemporary accountancy across Asia, illustrating how standards have been reshaped to accommodate the needs of economic and social trends. As well as providing an overview of standards in the larger Asian economies of China, India and Japan, contributions to the *Handbook* also include studies of countries such as Sri Lanka, Nepal, Cambodia and Mongolia. In particular, this handbook analyses:

- financial accounting and reporting
- management accounting
- auditing and accounting professionalization
- governmental and public-sector accounting
- accounting education
- accounting development in Asian emerging economies.

The Routledge Handbook of Accounting in Asia offers students, academics, regulators and practitioners an essential reference guide to the current scholarship and practice in the field of accountancy in Asia. It will be a useful resource in particular for students of accountancy, business studies and Asian studies.

Zhijun Lin is Professor, Associate Vice President and Dean at the School of Business, Macau University of Science and Technology.

The Routledge Handbook of Accounting in Asia

Edited by Zhijun Lin

Routledge
Taylor & Francis Group

LONDON AND NEW YORK

First published 2018
by Routledge
2 Park Square, Milton Park, Abingdon, Oxon OX14 4RN

and by Routledge
52 Vanderbilt Avenue, New York, NY 10017

First issued in paperback 2020

Routledge is an imprint of the Taylor & Francis Group, an informa business

British Library Cataloguing-in-Publication Data
A catalogue record for this book is available from the British Library

Library of Congress Cataloging-in-Publication Data
Names: Lin, Zhijun, 1955– editor.
Title: Routledge handbook of accounting in Asia / [edited by]
    Zhijun Lin.
Description: Abingdon, Oxon; New York, NY: Routledge, 2018. |
    Includes bibliographical references and index.
Identifiers: LCCN 2017004564| ISBN 9781138189034 (hardback) |
    ISBN 9781315641867 (ebook)
Subjects: LCSH: Accounting—Asia—History.
Classification: LCC HF5616.A78 R68 2018 | DDC 657.095—dc23
LC record available at https://lccn.loc.gov/2017004564

ISBN 13: 978-0-367-66002-4 (pbk)
ISBN 13: 978-1-138-18903-4 (hbk)

Typeset in Bembo
by Swales & Willis Ltd, Exeter, Devon, UK

Contents

Contents

Figures

Tables

Contributors

Pawan Adhikari is a Lecturer in Accounting at the Essex Business School, University of Essex, UK. He has been engaged in research in various aspects of accounting, in particular public-sector accounting in emerging economies, for the last 15 years and has contributed to both academic and practitioners' journals. Previously, Dr Adhikari held the position of chief executive officer (CEO) at the Accounting and Auditing Standards Board in Nepal, where he was involved in enforcing IFRSs in Nepalese enterprises.

Saiful Azam is currently a Lecturer in Accounting at RMIT University, Australia. His primary research interests are in financial accounting and reporting. His research papers appear in several international journals.

Imtiaz Badshah is currently an Associate Professor in the Faculty of Business, Languages, and Social Sciences, Østfold University College (HiØ), Norway. Earlier, Badshah worked as an Assistant Professor in NUST Business School (NBS), National University of Sciences and Technology, Islamabad. He has obtained his PhD in Accounting from Bodø Graduate School of Business, University of Nordland (renamed as Nord University), Norway. His research areas are in management accounting, financial accounting, governance and reform. Dr Badshah has worked with several renowned journals as a reviewer. He is an expert in various committees with the Higher Education Commission of Pakistan and the Security Exchange Commission of Pakistan.

Kashi Balachandran is a former editor-in-chief of the *Journal of Accounting Auditing and Finance*. He has served as distinguished institute professor of the G.D. Goenka World Institute and is executive director of Glocal University in India. He has taught at the Stern School of Business, New York University; the University of Wisconsin; the Georgia Institute of Technology; the University of Kentucky; SDA Bocconi University, Italy; the University of Rome-Tor Vergata; Tunghai University in Taiwan; and the International University of Japan. He is on the editorial boards of several prestigious academic journals including the *Journal of Applied Management Accounting Research*.

Sainjargal Banzdai is a Professor of Accounting and Head of the Department of Accountancy at the School of Business of the Mongolian National University. His research areas are financial, economic and investment analysis and asset valuation. He is a certified public accountant and a leading property appraiser in Mongolia. Professor Sainjargal has published seven textbooks and more than 30 journal articles.

Juliet Cadungog-Uy is a Professor and Lecturer at CamEd Business School and a research and M&E adviser for an NGO in Phnom Penh, Cambodia. She is the former dean of the College of Business and Accountancy of Negros Oriental State University, the Philippines, and a graduate school lecturer. She has conducted research in the fields of health, education and business.

C.B. Chan is working in Phnom Penh, Cambodia. She received her PhD from Latrobe University, Australia, in 2008. Dr Chan has several papers published in high-ranking accounting journals.

Parmod Chand is an Associate Professor of Accounting at Macquarie University in Sydney, Australia. He is also a member of CPA Australia. Dr Chand has published extensively in the area of international accounting, including articles in leading scholarly journals such as *The European Accounting Review, The International Journal of Accounting, Accounting and Finance, Journal of International Accounting Research* and *Critical Perspectives on Accounting.* Dr Chand has also regularly been a keynote presenter at technical conferences of professional accounting bodies.

Wen-Ching Chang is an Accounting Professor at National Changhua University of Education, Taiwan. Her research interests include audit quality, auditor choice and earnings quality. She has papers published in the *Journal of Accounting and Public Policy, Asia Pacific Journal of Accounting and Economics* and *The International Journal of Accounting.*

Zhibin Chen is Professor of Accounting, Chair of the Department of Accounting and Associate Dean of the School of Economics and Management, Southeast University, China. Professor Chan is a PhD student supervisor and his research interests include governmental accounting, corporate finance and internal control. Professor Chan has published many academic articles and books in related fields in China.

Battuya Demberel is an Associate Professor of Accounting at the School of Business of the Mongolian National University. He earned his DBA from Chungnam National University, South Korea, in 2011. Dr Battuya has published several academic papers in international journals, as well as three textbooks and other research projects. Dr Battuya is also a project consultant for several government-funded projects in Mongolia. He is a member of the Mongolian Institute of CPA with a licence for auditing.

Shoichiro Hosomi is a Professor of Management Accounting at the Graduate School of Social Science, Department of Business Administration, Tokyo Metropolitan University, Japan. He completed his doctoral programme at Waseda University, Japan. He has been a Visiting Researcher at the Department of Education, University of Oxford, UK (April 2013–March 2014). Professor Hosomi is a senior director of the Asia-Pacific Management Accounting Association (APMAA) and an editorial board member of *The Journal of Management Accounting Japan* (JMAJ) of the Japanese Association of Management Accounting (2014–). He is also an associate research fellow of SKOPE (skills, knowledge and organizational performance) at the Department of Education, University of Oxford (2013–). Professor Hosomi is the co-author of *Management Accounting for Intangibles* (Chuo-keizaisha, 2012).

Guoqiang Hu is a Lecturer at the Business School, Tianjin University of Finance and Economics, China. He has taught financial accounting and internal control. His research interests are in corporate governance and financial and accounting issues in the Chinese capital market.

He has led research projects sponsored by the National Natural Science Foundation of China and the Philosophy and Social Science Foundation of the Education Ministry. He has published in such journals as *The European Journal of Finance*, *Accounting Research*, *Auditing Research* and the *Journal of Audit & Economics*.

Guiru Hua is an Associate Professor at the Department of Accounting at the East China University of Science and Technology and a visiting scholar at the University of Texas Rio Grande Valley, USA. He has published extensively in top finance and accounting journals in China, such as *Financial Research*, *Accounting Research* and *Managerial Accounting Research*.

Bing Huang is a Lecturer in Accounting at the Business School, Xiangtan University. She teaches financial accounting and auditing theory. Her research interests are in accounting and corporate governance issues in China. She has published a number of papers in academic journals in China.

Kerry Jacobs is Professor of Accounting at UNSW Canberra, Australia. His research interests are focused on issues of public-sector accountability, governance, audit, financial management and reform, particularly the relationship between accounting and politics. He received his PhD from the University of Edinburgh in Scotland and has been honoured as a fellow of the New Zealand and the two Australian professional accounting associations. Professor Jacobs has published over 40 papers and contributed to five different books about different aspects of public-sector accountability and governance. He is an ACT council member of the ICAA and is on the Audit and Risk Committee for the Victorian and the Queensland Auditor General's Offices, Australia.

Johnny Jermias worked for several years as an auditor in Indonesia before continuing his education at the University of Waterloo, Canada, where he earned his PhD in 1996. He has taught both undergraduate and graduate courses in Canada, Singapore and Indonesia. Before working as an academic, Dr Jermias worked as a senior executive at a multinational company. Dr Jermias has published articles in leading accounting journals including *Journal of Accounting Research*, *Accounting, Organizations and Society*, *European Accounting Review*, *British Accounting Review*, *International Journal of Accounting*, *Accounting and Finance*, *Journal of International Accounting Research*, *Accounting Perspectives* and *Management Accounting Research*. Dr Jermias currently sits on the editorial board of *Contemporary Accounting Research*.

Prem Lal Joshi is a Professor of Accounting and the Chair of CEBP at Multimedia University, Malaysia. He has taught in India, Kenya, Turkey, Bahrain and Malaysia. He has presented papers at more than 35 international conferences and has published over 90 research papers in international and regional journals. He has also conducted several researches in interdisciplinary areas. He was the founding editor-in-chief of two international journals in accounting and is currently an associate editor of IJFAS, Australia. He is on the editorial boards of several academic journals.

Chan Yoke Kai is currently an Associate Professor of Accounting and the head of the accountancy programme at Singapore University of Social Sciences. He has previously been a faculty member of the business schools at both the National University of Singapore and Nanyang Technological University, and a visiting scholar at the University of Sydney. His current research interests are accounting education and corporate social responsibility. He has published several academic papers in high-ranked international journals such as *Accounting, Organisations and Society*, *ABACUS* and *Financial Management*.

Saleha B. Khumawala is the Robert Grinaker Professor of Accounting and the founding director of the SURE (stimulating urban renewal through entrepreneurship) microfinance program at Bauer College of Business, University of Houston. She is a CPA and CGMA, and teaches and does research in the field of government and non-profit accounting. She has published in *The Accounting Review*, *Journal of Accounting and Public Policy* and other academic journals.

Anbalagan Krishnan started his career as a consultant and worked as a cost accountant in the manufacturing sector. After a few years of industrial experience, he moved to academia and was appointed a vice principal-cum-registrar at a higher learning institution. Currently he is an Associate Professor at Xiamen University Malaysia. He has vast teaching experience in a number of accounting and managerial accounting units. He has also presented a number of research papers in accounting at reputable international conferences. He was a paper reviewer for *Contemporary Management Research*. He also possesses experience in contract dealing and negotiation training in industry. He is a certified financial accountant of CPA Malaysia and CPA Australia.

Jay Junghun Lee is an Assistant Professor of Accounting at the University of Massachusetts (UMass), Boston, USA. Prior to joining UMass Boston, he was an Assistant Professor at Hong Kong Baptist University. Dr Lee received his bachelor's, master's and PhD degrees in business administration from Seoul National University in Korea and his master's degree in accounting from the University of Illinois at Urbana–Champaign. He has published his research on financial accounting, auditing and corporate governance in top-tier academic journals such as *Contemporary Accounting Research*, *Review of Accounting Studies*, *Auditing: A Journal of Practice and Theory*, *Journal of Accounting and Public Policy* and *Journal of Banking and Finance*.

Allene Ng Bee Lian is an Associate Faculty Member with the accountancy programme at Singapore University of Social Sciences. She is currently a consultant with an international professional services firm and the director of Procolony, a Singapore-based start-up. With over 20 years' industry experience, she previously held various finance management roles at Hewlett-Packard and the National Healthcare Group in Singapore.

Z. Jun (Zhijun) Lin is a Professor, an Associate Vice President and the Dean of the School of Business at Macau University of Science and Technology, Macau. He is an accounting professor and has taught in several universities before joining MUST, including Xiamen University, China; the University of Lethbridge, Canada; the University of Hong Kong; and Hong Kong Baptist University. Professor Lin has published more than 50 academic papers in internationally refereed journals, as well as several textbooks and monographs. Professor Lin is a member of the American Institute of CPAs, the Chinese Institute of CPAs and CPA Australia, and he is also a CGMA, CMA (Australia).

Uantchern Loh is the former chief executive of the Singapore Accountancy Commission (SAC), a statutory body under the Ministry of Finance. He joined the SAC prior to its formation and was responsible for building a team from scratch in establishing the SAC. He helped in formulating the SAC's mission, vision and strategic plan and the SAC Act, which lead to the creation of the SAC on 1 April 2013. Uantchern was instrumental in the development of the Singapore QP, which was launched in June 2013.

Naranchimeg Lombodorj is an Associate Professor of Accounting at the School of Business of the Mongolian National University. He is interested in research on the foundations of accounting and analysis of financial statements and is a member of the Mongolian Institute of Certified Public Accountants and the Mongolian Institute of Certified Appraisers. Dr Naranchimeg has published several textbooks and research papers in national academic and professional journals.

Agus Fredy Maradona is a Lecturer in the Faculty of Economics and Business at Universitas Pendidikan Nasional in Denpasar, Indonesia. He holds the chartered accountant qualification from the Institute of Indonesia Chartered Accountants. He is currently pursuing his PhD in the Department of Accounting and Corporate Governance at Macquarie University, Sydney, Australia, under the Australia Awards Scholarships programme.

Frode Mellemvik is the Director of the High North Center for Business and Governance, and a professor at Nord University Business School, Bodø, Norway. Professor Mellemvik has published books and articles on management, government, education, research and Arctic-related topics. He has worked at academic institutions in Europe and the US and is an honorary doctor and honorary professor at several universities. Professor Mellemvik has been rector/president at Bodø University College (Nord University) for 10 years. He has participated in several boards and councils, including as chairperson of the Norwegian Government's High North Council, chair of the board of the Nordic Academy of Management, member of the board of the European Accounting Association and member of the board of CIGAR (Comparative International Government Accounting Research network).

Nguyen Cong Phuong is an Associate Professor of Accounting at the School of Economics, Danang University, Vietnam. He received his PhD in management science from the University of Paris Dauphine. His primary research interests are in the regulation of accounting, especially accounting regulation in the developing countries, corporate governance and earning quality. He has published articles in academic journal such as *European Accounting Review* and *Journal of Accounting & Organizational Change*. He has recently co-authored a book, *IFRS in a Global World*.

Janek Ratnatunga is an Adjunct Professor at Swinburne University, Australia, He has held senior academic appointments at the University of Melbourne and Monash University in Australia and the Universities of Washington, Richmond and Rhode Island in the USA. He is currently the editor of the *Journal of Applied Management Accounting Research*. He has worked in the profession as a chartered accountant with KPMG. He has been awarded the prestigious joint American Accounting Association, AICPA (USA), CIMA (UK) and CMA (Canada) Impact on Management Accounting Practice Award for a publication that has the greatest potential impact on management accounting practice.

Paul Scarbrough is an Associate Professor of Accounting at Goodman School of Business, Brock University, Canada. He received his PhD from Virginia Polytechnic Institute and State University (Virginia Tech), USA. He has been at Brock since 1995 and has held several positions in the Faculty of Business, including accounting department chair. Prior academic appointments in the USA include Boston University and Bentley University. His international teaching experience includes appointments at Waseda University (Tokyo) and Linnaeus University (Sweden).

Professor Scarbrough is a vice-president of the Asia-Pacific Management Accounting Association. He is the author of several management accounting books and has published his research in various journals, including *Accounting, Organizations and Society*, *Journal of Business Venturing*, *Journal of Business Ethics*, *Accounting Horizons*, *Asia-Pacific Management Accounting Journal*, *Journal of International Accounting, Auditing and Tax*, *The International Journal of Accounting* and *Management Accounting Research*.

Arpita Shroff is an Assistant Professor at the University of Houston–Downtown, USA. She worked extensively with not-for-profit organizations in India before she came to the USA for further studies. Besides accounting for governmental and not-for-profit institutions, her research interests include capital market research and research on the accounting standards updates released by the FASB. Dr Shroff is also a certified public accountant.

Satoshi Sugahara is a Professor in Accounting at Kwansei Gakuin University, Japan. His recent research interests are accounting education and International Financial Reporting Standards (IFRS). He completed his PhD at Yokohama National University, Japan, in 2000. Professor Sugahara has also studied and completed master's degrees in commerce at the Australian National University in 2003 and in education at the University of Sydney in 2011.

Michael Tse is a Professor and Head of Accounting at the Holmes Institute, Australia. He is also the global chair of the Institute of Certified Management Accountants. He has taught at Monash University, Deakin University and Charles Sturt University in Australia, and at Jubilee University in Papua New Guinea. He holds a PhD from La Trobe University and is a member of Chartered Accountants Australia and New Zealand, the Institute of Certified Management Accountants and the Australian Computer Society. He has published extensively and is the web editor of the *Journal of Applied Management Accounting Research*.

Susumu Ueno is Professor Emeritus of Accounting at Konan University, Japan. He received his MBA from the University of Maryland and his DBA from Southern Illinois University. Professor Ueno is the chair of the board of directors of the Asia-Pacific Management Accounting Association (APMAA) and the chief editor of *Asia-Pacific Management Accounting Journal* (APMAJ, 2010–). He served as the APMAA president from January 2010 to December 2013. Professor Ueno is a member of the Japanese Association of Management Accounting (JAMA) and was the editor-in-chief of the *Journal of Management Accounting, Japan* (JMAJ) from April 2014 to March 2017. At JAMA he served as vice president (2008–2011) and has been an executive director since 2002. The association gave Professor Ueno its Special Award in 2014, recognizing his contributions to both research and education and his history of service to the academic community. Professor Ueno has published many management accounting books and published his research in various journals, including *Asia-Pacific Management Accounting Journal*, *The Journal of International Business Studies* and *The International Journal of Accounting Education and Research*.

Yan Wang is a postgraduate student at the School of Economics and Management, Southeast University, China. Her research fields include governmental accounting and corporate finance.

Ying Wang is a faculty member at the School of Economics and Management, Southeast University, China. Her research fields include governmental accounting and corporate finance.

Jason Xiao is a Professor of Accounting and the Director of the China Business Research Centre at Cardiff Business School, Cardiff University, UK. He has taught accounting and finance in China, AIS, business finance and international accounting. His research interests are in accounting and corporate governance issues in China. He was a founding joint editor of the *China Journal of Accounting Studies*. He has published in leading academic journals such as *Abacus, Accounting and Business Research, Accounting Horizons, Accounting, Organizations and Society, British Journal of Management, European Journal of Accounting, European Journal of Information Systems, Journal of Accounting and Public Policy, Journal of Banking and Finance, Journal of Corporate Finance* and *Journal of Management Accounting Research*.

Qin Xu is a Lecturer in Accounting at the School of Business, University of International Business and Economics, China. She teaches enterprise accounting practices, financial statement analysis and professional accounting. Her research interests are in finance and accounting issues in listed companies and the role of institutional investors in corporate governance and she has published papers in these areas in China. She has also published a book titled *The Role of Institutional Investors in Corporate Governance*.

P.W. Senarath Yapa is an Associate Professor and has extensive experience in research, teaching and consultancy in accountancy projects. Presently he works at the School of Accounting at RMIT University, Melbourne, Australia. He has taught in several universities in different countries, including Sri Lanka, Belgium, Brunei, the Netherlands and China. Professor Yapa has more than 70 research papers in high-quality international academic journals such as *Accounting, Auditing & Accountability, International Journal of Accounting, Critical Perspectives on Accounting, Accounting Education – An International Journal, Accounting History* and *Australian Tax Forum*. He is a member of CPA Australia.

Han Yi is an Associate Professor of Accounting at Korea University Business School. He earned his PhD from Michigan State University in 2006 and was a faculty member at the University of Oklahoma until 2011. He teaches financial reporting classes and his research interests are in financial reporting and auditing issues. He served as an editorial board member at *Auditing: A Journal of Practice & Theory* (2013–2014) and has published articles in *The Accounting Review, AJPT* and *Accounting Horizons*. Professor Yi recently served both the Korea Accounting Standards Board and the Financial Supervisory Service as an academic fellow.

Dehui Yu is a Lecturer in Accounting at the School of Management, China Women's University. She has taught financial management, cost and management accounting, the application of EXCEL in financial management and financial management simulation software and provided comprehensive training for industry and commerce. She has published several papers in China. She has published a book titled *A Study of Influence Factors and Usefulness of Fair Value Disclosure: The Case of Financial Instruments*.

Haiyan Zhou is a Professor at the School of Accountancy at the University of Texas Rio Grande Valley, USA. She currently serves as editor-in-chief of *Asian Review of Accounting* and also on the editorial boards of the *Journal of International Accounting, Auditing and Taxation* and *Review of Accounting in Emerging Markets*. Some of her recent publications can be found in top accounting and auditing journals such as *Journal of Contemporary Accounting and Economics, Auditing: a Journal of Theory and Practice, Journal of Accounting and Public Policies, International Journal of Accounting, Journal of International Accounting, Auditing and Taxation, Asian Review of Accounting* and *Journal of International Financial Management and Accounting*.

Preface

The centre of world economic development has shifted to Asia over the last two decades, as many Asian countries have witnessed fast growths in economic and business operations. International communities have paid increasing attention to the investment environment and opportunities in Asia, the most dynamic and energetic region, which has the largest population and potential for economic growth. Since accounting is a common business language that assists international investors to assess corporate performance and make efficient investment decisions, we prepare and publish this *Routledge Handbook of Accounting in Asia*.

Given the pace of recent rapid economic growth and social change in Asia, accounting has played a significant role in assisting economic transition and development in most Asian countries. This is because accounting is an important information system for supplying relevant and useful financial data to governments' economic planning and administration at the macro level and to business financing decision makers and financial management at the micro level. The advancement of accounting is directly associated with the efficient functioning of capital markets and economic and social development in individual countries.

Currently, accounting internationalization has gained momentum in the course of economic globalization, cross-border capital market integration and the new Industrial Revolution based on high-tech innovations around the world. Accounting standards and practices in all countries were originally shaped by specific national influences owing to the different social, economic, political, cultural and legal systems being installed in each country, but most countries have now, more or less, engaged in the international convergence of accounting standards and practices aiming at adopting or fully converging on the international accounting standards or norms set out by international professional bodies such as the International Accounting Standards Board (IASB) or the International Federation of Professional Accountants (IFAC) in the movement of economic globalization. Asian countries have embarked on the international convergence journey in recent years, bringing about significant changes, to varied extents, in accounting and auditing standards and practices in these countries. Thus, an updated introduction of accounting and auditing development in Asian countries is highly desirable to the international business community to gain an insightful understanding of the development in order to facilitate cross-country capital flows and to assist international investors to make rational investment and credit decisions towards one of the most prominent economic regions in the world, Asia. The *Handbook* should serve this purpose.

There are three distinct characteristics of this *Routledge Handbook on Accounting in Asia*. First, the *Handbook* is a collection of the most up-to-date accounting developments in Asian countries, an in particular it illustrates how Asian countries have responded to the current international convergence of accounting standards and practices in restructuring or reshaping their domestic accounting systems to accommodate the needs of their economic and social transitions in recent years. Second, this *Handbook* elaborates on the development of accounting in most of the Asian countries with a wider scope of coverage. Unlike similar previous publications, this *Handbook* does not only include the updated accounting development in the major economies of Asia, but also presents the evolution and progress of accounting in some small economies with relatively slow economic growth and social change. For instance, in Sri Lanka, Nepal, Cambodia and Mongolia, relatively weak financial infrastructure or accounting systems were in place and little exposure of their accounting development is currently available in Western literature. Coverage of these relatively small or emerging Asian economies in the *Handbook* should assist international communities to obtain first-hand descriptions of the accounting frameworks and recent changes that have taken place in these Asian countries. Third, the *Handbook* presents several subsystems of accounting by themes in different sections, such as financial accounting and reporting, management accounting, accounting and auditing professionalization, governmental and public-sector accounting, accounting education and accounting development in Asian emerging economies, to outline the related practices and experiences in the selected countries on these different dimensions of accounting development. Such an introduction of major accounting subsystems or themes with separate sectional highlights should obviously assist readers to have a more constructive or informative understanding of accounting developments in Asian countries.

The *Handbook* is suitable for a variety of reader groups, including libraries in educational institutions, corporations and other economic entities, accounting professionals, business executives, market regulators and general investors. The *Handbook* can also be a textbook or supplementary readings for undergraduate or postgraduate accounting courses or training programmes offered through various educational platforms.

It is acknowledged that the publication of this *Handbook* is attributed to the strong commitment and support from many persons. First of all, we are grateful to all of the contributors, who have prepared and submitted their manuscripts on time, thus making the *Handbook* publication possible. Second, we really appreciate the editorial team at Routledge (UK), especially Leanne Hinves, Stephanie Rogers and Rebecca Lawrence, for their advisory support for the initiative and for all editorial assistance for this *Handbook*. It would have been impossible to publish this *Handbook* on time without their continuing support and hard work.

Zhijun Lin

Part I

Financial accounting and reporting

Financial accounting derived from the traditional accounting system is a process of recognition, measurement, recording, classification, summarization and reporting of the operating activities of an economic entity, and it aims to provide accounting information, on a regular basis, about the entity's financial position and operating results to external users (mainly investors, creditors, government regulatory authorities and others) to assist their decision-making (FASB, SFAC, No. 1). To ensure the comparability of the reported information (i.e. financial statements), financial accounting and reporting must follow the authoritative accounting standards (e.g. the generally accepted accounting principles, GAAP) in each country; thus, financial accounting and reporting practices are subject to the influences and constraints of the specific political, economic, social and legal systems in each country, which results in the evolution of substantial differences in accounting standards and practices in different countries over a long period.

However, internationalization of accounting standards has become a new trend of financial accounting and reporting since the early 1980s owing to cross-border capital flows and the increase of multinational business activities. In particular, following the rapid growth of economic globalization and the international integration of capital markets around the world, the process for the internationalization of financial accounting and reporting has sped up dramatically since the early 2000s. With the endorsement and support of international associations of capital market regulators (e.g. the International Organization of Securities Commissions, IOSCO) and some intergovernmental organizations (including the United Nations and the European Union), the International Accounting Standards (IAS) and the International Financial Reporting Standards (IFRS) developed by the International Accounting Standards Board (IASB) have been widely recognized and accepted since 2005. Most countries in the world have now engaged in international convergence with IAS/IFRS, albeit by varied approaches or to different extents. The progress of international accounting convergence has a significant impact on financial accounting and reporting in Asian countries. Some countries have fully accepted IAS/IFRS to replace their national accounting standards and some have adopted IAS/IFRS with modifications to accommodate local conditions, while other countries intended to take the adoption gradually. Nonetheless, almost all Asian countries have embarked on the journey of international accounting convergence at varied pace in the last decade.

This section provides an updated description of the development of financial accounting and reporting in four Asian countries: Indonesia (Chapter 1), South Korea (Chapter 2), China (Chapter 3) and Pakistan (Chapter 4).

As explained in Chapter 1, Indonesia was historically under Dutch rule and its traditional accounting system has stemmed from the Dutch commercial codes but it has shifted to the American accounting models owing to the rapid growth of the domestic capital market over the recent two decades. Thus, Indonesia is a pioneer in the adoption of IAS/IFRS in the region, as its national accounting associations made a commitment in 2008 to full convergence with IAS/IFRS in the country. However, unlike the 'big bang' adoption approach in EU member countries, Indonesia has followed a gradual adoption process, in which some selected IAS/IFRS have been adopted each year as the Indonesian equivalents of IFRS. There are two major phases in the IAS/IFRS convergence process in Indonesia. In Phase I (2008–2012), the first batch of 35 IAS/IFRS and 20 interpretations were issued by the Indonesian standards setter with varied effective dates over the period. In Phase II (2012–2015), the convergence aimed to reduce the differences between Indonesian accounting standards as of 1 June 2012 and the IAS/IFRS, with another set of IFRS-equivalent Indonesian accounting standards being issued and implemented. Interestingly, Indonesia has also developed a set of Shari'a accounting standards to cater for businesses (mainly financial institutions) that operate according to Islamic norms, a unique feature of Indonesian financial accounting and reporting. Readers can also learn from this chapter about the economic and business environment, capital market development and regulatory framework for accounting and reporting in Indonesia.

South Korea is an economy with a high growth rate in Asia and it has exercised significant economic influence in the region and the world. However, as pointed out by the authors of Chapter 2, contrasting with its rapid and steady economic growth, Korea received the lowest ever score for its accounting transparency before 2011. Accounting and reporting practices in Korea were inherited from the German-style commercial civil law systems owing to a history of Japanese annexation before World War II. Chapter 2 explains that the massive aid plans from the US after the Korean War led to the creation of dominant government-controlled banks, which required accounting information mainly for government capital allocation and banks' credit analysis. Therefore, the initial accounting and reporting standards in Korea were framed mainly to facilitate government economic development policymaking and banks' credit rationing instead of the information needs of capital market participants in the country. In addition, two sets of accounting standards were formulated for publicly traded companies and non-traded companies, respectively, in Korea. Such an accounting system resulted in less transparent and reliable corporate reporting, which, indirectly, induced or exacerbated the financial crisis in the country in 1997. After the bailout by the International Monetary Fund (IMF) and the World Bank following the financial crisis, significant accounting and auditing reforms have been implemented to shift to US-style accounting and reporting systems in Korea. With the establishment of the Korea Accounting Standards Board (KASB) in 1999, Korea has actively participated in the international convergence process, aiming at fully adopting IAS/IFRS (renamed as K-FRS) in the country. However, a unique feature of KASB is that it allows companies to submit IFRS-related interpretation enquires (i.e. local interpretations). As pointed out by the authors of Chapter 2, Korea has not rejected any accounting policy option permitted by IAS/IFRS, but KASB has added some presentation and disclosure requirements following requests from local users and regulators. Thus, some concerns have emerged about whether K-FRS is essentially identical to IFRS since a few discrepancies do exist in current Korean accounting and reporting practices. An accounting scandal is also analysed to show how and why IRFS adoption alone does not necessarily improve accounting transparency. The authors have thus offered some recommendations for immediate changes to improve accounting transparency and financial reporting quality in Korea, which should also be relevant to other countries in the region.

China is one of the fastest-growing economies in the world. Although the former Soviet-style centrally planned economic administrative system was installed after the civil war in 1949, when the main objectives of accounting and reporting were to serve the government's economic administration and specific policy needs, the economic reforms started at the beginning of the 1980s have brought about significant changes in the Chinese economy. Public ownership has been diluted, with most state-owned enterprises (SOEs) being privatized and converted into share companies when two major stock markets reopened in the country. As a result, the user group of business accounting and reporting has been expanded to include outside investors and creditors, with substantial change in the format and content of financial accounting and reporting in light of the adoption of international norms. Under the current movement of economic globalization and internationalization of the Chinese capital market, the Chinese government has actively promoted accounting reforms to speed up the process of international convergence of Chinese accounting. In particular, the new Chinese accounting standards (CAS), implemented on 1 January 2007, have achieved the recognized status of 'equivalent' to IAS/IFRS, and substantially improved the understandability and international comparability of Chinese accounting and reporting practices.

As outlined in Chapter 3, a significant change in the new CAS has been the adoption of 'fair value accounting (FVA)' in Chinese accounting, which is a standard practice in IAS/IFRS. Departing from the long tradition of 'historical accounting' in Chinese accounting, FVA requires businesses to revalue holding assets and liabilities on the reporting date with market-value benchmarks. Thus, revaluation gains or losses must be recognized and measured under FVA and they must be recognized in either balance sheet or income statement in terms of the classification purposes of the assets or liabilities concerned. Not only is FVA a new practice in Chinese accounting; it may also leave room for accounting judgement or accounting number manipulation subject to the less-developed valuation market and insufficient market regulation in China. Chapter 3 presents a study of the FVA application for both publicly listed financial firms and non-financial companies in the Chinese context, with an analysis of the pros and cons of adopting FVA in both CAS and practice, as well as its application implications, thus providing some empirical evidence to demonstrate the necessity and actual effect of the convergence of Chinese accounting with international norms.

Chapter 4 introduces accounting and reporting developments in Pakistan. Pakistan is unique in this book as it is a Muslim-majority country and Islam has been officially declared the state religion. The country has been of central importance at the international level since its independence in 1947. It played an important role in 1979 during the Soviet–Afghan war and in the war against terrorism after the 9/11 attacks. The history of Pakistan has witnessed both civil and military regimes. It is interesting to analyse the role of politics in initiating accounting reforms during various civilian and military regimes.

After independence in 1947, Pakistan inherited accounting practices from Britain. Moreover, several institutions have since been established to strengthen the accounting profession in the country. The accounting profession in Pakistan has grown and corporate accounting and reporting practices developed relatively rapidly in the recent few decades, keeping pace with economic growth and the global convergence of accounting standards and practices, including the formation of a national professional association (the Institute of Chartered Accountants of Pakistan (ICAP)) and the establishment of a legal and regulatory framework to promote better accounting and financial reporting practices in the country.

In Pakistan, the basic requirements for accounting and financial reporting for companies are set by the Company Ordinance 1984, which mandates that all companies operating in Pakistan prepare, present and publish their financial statements.

Recently, Pakistan has also followed the global wave of reforms initiated in developed countries and commenced to partially adopt International Accounting Standards (IAS/IFRS), which resulted in a hybrid accounting system in Pakistan since the early 2000s. That is, country-specific accounting and reporting processes gradually harmonized with international norms. As pointed out by the authors of Chapter 4, the institutional set-up in Pakistan may not fully support IFRS in their original shape, or the accounting rules coming from developed countries may not be applicable to developing countries in their exact form as developing countries may not have supporting institutional arrangements for their implementation. Therefore, changes in institutional settings should be considered when adopting International Accounting Standards in developing countries.

Overall, financial accounting and reporting practices in Asian countries have moved towards convergence with international accounting and reporting standards, although there are some differences in the convergence approaches or extents. The differences are attributed to the specific historical and institutional settings in the social, political, economic, cultural and legal systems of individual countries. However, Asian countries will more actively participate in accounting internationalization alongside the continuing progress of economic globalization and cross-border capital market integration. It is to be fully expected that financial accounting and reporting standards and practices in all Asian countries will become more transparent and comparable, which should assist domestic and international users of financial statements to make more efficient and effective economic decisions.

1

Development of financial reporting standards and practices in Indonesia

Agus Fredy Maradona and Parmod Chand

Introduction

Indonesia, the largest economy in South East Asia, is one of the emerging economies currently engaged in the process of converging their national accounting standards with the International Accounting Standards (IAS) or the International Financial Reporting Standards (IFRS). Unlike the 'big-bang' adoption approach in the European Union member countries and Australia, IFRS adoption in Indonesia follows a gradual process in which some selected IFRS are adopted each year and published as the Indonesian equivalents of IAS/IFRS which are promulgated by the International Accounting Standards Board (IASB). Indonesia provides an interesting example of how IAS/IFRS are adopted in an emerging economy, as the country has a unique history in the development of national accounting structures and has experienced a rapid expansion in its financial systems.

Indonesia was colonized by the Dutch, thus early Indonesian accounting practices were heavily influenced by the Dutch accounting system (Diga and Yunus, 1997). When the accounting system was later changed to the Anglo-American model, the influence of Dutch accounting remained apparent. More recent accounting standards setting in the country has been oriented towards the IFRS.

Indonesia has pledged its support for the global convergence with IAS/IFRS, and in 2008 the Indonesian Institute of Accountants, the national body of the accounting profession, which oversees the setting of accounting standards, formalized its commitment to full convergence with IAS/IFRS in the country (Deloitte Touche Tohmatsu, 2009). Over the last decade, the Indonesian accounting standards-setting body has worked towards the gradual adoption of IAS/IFRS, with the intention of ensuring that Indonesian accounting standards will be fully converged with IAS/IFRS in the near future.

This chapter examines the development of accounting standards and practices in Indonesia since its early stages to the current period of convergence of the country's national accounting standards with IFRS. We first provide an overview of Indonesia's economy and business environment, followed by a description of the regulatory framework that governs financial reporting and auditing in the country. We then outline the development of the Indonesian accounting profession since the 1950s. This section is followed by a detailed examination of the development of Indonesian accounting standards. The last section presents a brief summary and conclusions.

An overview of Indonesia's economy and business environment

Economic development

Indonesia is an archipelagic country of more than 13,000 islands, spanning the equator between the Asian mainland and Australia and between the Indian Ocean and the Pacific Ocean. With a total land area of 1,811,570 square kilometres, Indonesia is ranked fifteenth in the world in terms of land area. Indonesia had a population of 254.5 million in 2014, making it the fourth most populous country in the world, just behind China, India, and the US (World Bank, 2016). Of the total population, 67 per cent falls within the working-age category and about 49 per cent constitutes the country's labour force. Indonesia has a multicultural society that comprises numerous ethnic groups with different traditional languages, all united by a single national language, Bahasa Indonesia.

Historically, Indonesia was colonized by the Dutch, who first came to the archipelago in the sixteenth century in search of spices and to establish trade in this commodity. An early Dutch settlement was marked by the establishment in 1603 of the first permanent trading post of the Dutch East India Company (Vereenigde Oost-Indische Compagnie – VOC), a Dutch government-backed company that monopolized the spice trade in the region. The Dutch colonial government formally took control of the region in 1800 following the demise of the Dutch East India Company (Ricklefs, 2001). After a prolonged national revolutionary struggle, Indonesia eventually proclaimed its independence as a United Republic in 1945.

While the Indonesian economy in the early period after independence was heavily weighted towards the agricultural sector, its economic structure began to change in the late 1960s when the Indonesian government commenced a gradual process of industrialization. This process accelerated in the 1980s when the government decided to diversify into manufactured exports instead of solely focusing on oil exports (Goeltom, 2007; Wie, 2012). Indonesia's economy has expanded substantially ever since the beginning of the industrialization era, although this economic expansion was interrupted by a significant economic downfall in the late 1990s when the country was severely affected by the East Asian financial crisis. Being the largest economy in South East Asia and the sixteenth largest in the world, Indonesia's GDP in 2014 stood at 888.5 billion US dollars, which is more than three times the country's 2004 GDP (World Bank, 2016). As an emerging industrialized country, Indonesia relies heavily on the industrial sector to support its economy. In fact, output from this sector accounted for 42.9 per cent of the 2014 GDP, in contrast to the agricultural sector, which contributed only 13.7 per cent to the economy.

Indonesia has also been increasingly integrated into the global economy over the last five decades, and the proportion of foreign trade in its GDP rose from 28 per cent in 1970 to 49 per cent, on average, over the last five years (World Bank, 2016). Countries such as Japan, China, Singapore, the US and Australia are among Indonesia's main trading partners, and they account for a significant volume of the country's export and import of raw materials and primary products. Indonesia's main export commodities include palm oil, petroleum gas, coal and rubber, while the top import commodities are refined petroleum, machinery and engines, electronic equipment, iron and steel, and plastics, among others.

The Indonesian economy, in general, demonstrates a strong foundation and a promising outlook. Unlike other Asian countries and most of the world's developed economies, Indonesia suffered only mildly from the effect of the 2007–2008 global financial crises. Between 2007 and 2014, Indonesia enjoyed steady economic growth at an average annual rate of 5.74 per cent (World Bank, 2016), and this growth is predicted to continue (OECD, 2015). Furthermore, as the only South East Asian member of the G20 group of countries, Indonesia is considered likely to play an increasingly significant role in promoting economic development and ensuring political stability, both in the region and globally.

Business enterprises

Based on their legal status, business enterprises in Indonesia can be classified into two broad categories: non-incorporated businesses and incorporated businesses. Non-incorporated businesses may take the form of sole proprietorships and partnerships. A sole proprietorship is owned and managed by a single person; there is no financial or legal separation between an owner and his/her business, and the owner is personally liable for any debts or lawsuits against his/her venture. Similarly, partnerships are characterized by a lack of financial or legal separation between owners and their businesses, although for taxation purposes the partnership will be considered a separate entity from the owner.[1] Both sole proprietorships and partnerships are relatively straightforward to establish and are governed by uncomplicated business regulations, hence they are common among small and micro-sized enterprises.

Incorporated businesses in Indonesia are limited liability companies (*perseroan terbatas* – PT), which are subject to the Limited Company Act.[2] A limited liability company is seen as a separate legal entity from its shareholders (i.e. the company's owners), hence the liability of the shareholders is limited to the amount of capital they have invested in the company. This type of company may be either a privately held company or a public company. A privately held company is one whose shares are held by a small group of shareholders and will not be traded to the public on the stock exchange. A public company in Indonesia refers to a company that has raised capital from the general public through an initial public offering (IPO) and has its shares traded on the stock exchange.

Limited liability companies are subject to extensive regulations and stringent corporate governance principles, hence this type of business is common only among medium or large enterprises. The corporate governance structure of Indonesian companies follows a dual board (two-tier) governance system, with a board of directors retaining the management function and a board of commissioners retaining the supervisory function. A limited liability company, whether privately or publicly held, can be classified as a state-owned enterprise (SOE) if the majority shareholder of the company is the Indonesian government or its agencies. Foreign investors who wish to invest in Indonesia through foreign direct investment can only do so by establishing or taking over a limited liability company.

The capital market

The first stock exchange in Indonesia was established in Jakarta by the Dutch colonial government in 1912, largely to raise capital for the colonial government-controlled plantations.[3] After independence, the newly formed Indonesian government took control of the financial sector and re-established the Jakarta Stock Exchange in 1952. Poor economic conditions and political instability in the first two post-independence decades severely disrupted the functioning of the capital market, and the stock exchange became inactive in the late 1950s (Sunariyah, 2010).

Economic reforms introduced by the government in the late 1960s brought about a capital market reactivation programme. With the preparation steps that started in 1970, the government finally reactivated the Jakarta Stock Exchange in 1977. However, the capital market only began to gain popularity in the late 1980s, marked by increasing number of public offerings and the establishment of a second stock exchange, the Surabaya Stock Exchange, in Surabaya. To strengthen governance in the capital market, the Indonesian government passed the Capital Market Act in 1995.

In an effort to foster efficiency in the Indonesian capital market, and to ensure that the market would be able to compete with stock markets in other countries, the Jakarta Stock Exchange and the Surabaya Stock Exchange amalgamated in 2007 into a single stock exchange, the Indonesia Stock Exchange (IDX), based in Jakarta. The IDX is a private company whose shares are owned by securities companies that are registered members of the exchange. Since its establishment, the IDX has expanded steadily, and the number of companies listed on the exchange grew from 393 in 2007 to 511 in 2014 (IDX, 2015). Furthermore, between 2007 and 2014, market capitalization of securities traded on the IDX grew from 211.7 billion US dollars to 422.1 billion US dollars (World Bank, 2016). Both domestic and foreign investors actively participate in the stock market.

The Indonesian capital market is overseen by the Financial Service Authority (Otoritas Jasa Keuangan – OJK), an independent, legislation-backed institution that reports directly to the Indonesian Parliament. Established in 2013, the OJK took over both the capital market and financial institution supervisory function, which was previously held by the Capital Market and Financial Institution Supervisory Agency of the Ministry of Finance (Badan Pengawas Pasar Modal dan Lembaga Keuangan – BAPEPAM-LK), and the banking industry supervisory function, previously held by the central bank, the Bank of Indonesia. The OJK has the authority to promulgate regulations governing the capital market, to oversee the implementation of capital market regulations and conduct investigations into suspected violations, and to impose sanctions on individuals or institutions suspected to have violated the regulations. In January 2016, the OJK published a master plan for the financial services sector, which provides, among other things, guidance for further development of the Indonesian capital market.

Regulatory frameworks in Indonesia

Regulatory frameworks for financial reporting

The regulations that govern financial reporting in Indonesia can generally be classified into two categories, namely those applying to businesses in general (both non-incorporated and incorporated) and those applying only to limited liability companies. The financial reporting requirements for all Indonesian business enterprises are mainly prescribed in the Indonesian Commercial Code and the tax laws. The Commercial Code, which is based on the 1838 Dutch Commercial Code (Silondae and Ilyas, 2011), requires every business enterprise to keep accounts about its business activity so that the rights and obligations of the enterprise can be determined at any time. The Code also requires an enterprise to prepare a balance sheet within six months of the financial year end. However, the Code does not have specific requirements concerning the procedures or standards that should be followed in preparing the accounts and presenting the balance sheet. The tax laws, meanwhile, primarily require businesses to submit, along with their tax return documents, annual financial statements, consisting of a balance sheet, a statement of profit and loss, and other necessary information, to the Indonesian tax office, for the purpose of determining taxable income. The tax laws also prescribe certain accounting methods that are applicable in the preparation of financial statements for tax purposes, which may differ from the accounting methods for preparing general-purpose financial statements.

The financial reporting regulations for limited liability companies are primarily prescribed in the current Limited Company Act, published in 2007.[4] The Act requires Indonesian limited liability companies to present a set of financial statements to the annual shareholder meeting no later than six months after the end of the financial year. These financial statements must consist of a balance sheet, a statement of profit and loss, a statement of cash flow, a statement of changes in equity, and notes to the financial statements, and the preparation of these statements must be based on the accounting standards set by the authorized professional accounting organization in Indonesia.

In addition to the Limited Company Act, several other regulations impose further requirements on financial reporting by certain types of limited liability companies. For example, the 1995 Capital Market Act and capital market regulations issued by the OJK specify financial reporting requirements that should be met by companies that plan to conduct an IPO or whose shares have been listed on the IDX. Furthermore, OJK regulations governing the finance industry stipulate specific financial reporting requirements for banks and other financial institutions.

Auditing requirements

The regulations that govern corporations in Indonesia require certain types of incorporated businesses to have their financial statements audited by public accountants. For example, the Limited Liability Act stipulates that audit by independent auditors is compulsory for: 1) companies that receive deposits from the general public and manage the funds on behalf of the depositors (e.g. commercial banks and investment companies); 2) companies that issue bonds to the general public; 3) public listed companies; 4) companies whose majority shareholder is the Indonesian government or its agencies; 5) companies with total assets and/or annual revenues of 50 billion rupiah; and 6) other companies whose financial statements are required by regulations to be audited. The audited financial statements must be submitted to the Ministry of Law and Human Rights. The Act also requires these companies to publish their audited balance sheets and statements of profit or loss in a national newspaper no later than seven days after their financial statements have been authorized by their annual shareholder meetings.

The auditing requirements for public listed companies are stipulated in the OJK regulations. In particular, these regulations require public listed companies to submit audited annual financial statements to the OJK and to publish them to the general public no later than three months after the financial statement date. The publication of the audited financial statements must be done through at least one national newspaper and include at least the balance sheet, the statement of profit or loss, the statement of cash flows and the independent auditor's report. The OJK regulations also require public companies to submit audited interim or half-year financial statements no later than three months after the date of the financial statements. Apart from the OJK regulations, public listed companies are required to submit audited annual and half-year financial statements to the IDX based on similar prescriptions included in IDX regulations.

The accounting profession in Indonesia

The development of the Indonesian accounting profession

During the colonial period, the accounting profession in Indonesia was dominated by Dutch accountants and accounting firms, which conducted their professional practices in line with the systems in the Netherlands (Tuanakotta, 2007). After national independence, the emergence of the Indonesian accounting profession was marked by the enactment of the Accountant Designation Act in 1954. This Act prescribes the broad criteria for the use of the designation of professional accountant and the provision of public accounting services by Indonesian professional accountants. In 1957, the first Indonesian professional accounting association, the Institute of Indonesian Accountants (Ikatan Akuntan Indonesia – IAI), was founded, to advance the accounting profession and accounting practice in Indonesia, which at the time was still in its initial stage. To foster the growth of the public accounting profession, the IAI established its Division of Public Accountants in 1977 (Tuanakotta, 2007). In 1997, the IAI became a member of the International Federation of Accountants (IFAC).

Prior to 2007, there were four divisions within the IAI: the Division of Public Accountants, the Division of Management Accountants, the Division of Academic Accountants and the Division of Public Sector Accountants. In 2007, following a major organizational restructuring process within the IAI, the Division of Public Accountants was liquidated. This division, which formerly oversaw the public accounting profession, changed its organizational status to that of a separate professional association under the new name of the Indonesian Institute of Certified Public Accountants (Institut Akuntan Publik Indonesia – IAPI). A second spin-off in the IAI organizational structure occurred in 2009. The management accountant division was dismissed and a separate professional body, called the Indonesian Institute of Management Accountants (Institut Akuntan Manajemen Indonesia – IAMI), was established. Both the IAPI and the IAMI were initially institutional members of the IAI. However, this institutional membership status was terminated in 2012 when the IAI decided to limit its membership to individuals.

The two organizational restructures within the IAI left the Institution with two divisions: the Division of Public Sector Accountants, which focused on the development of public-sector accounting practices, and the Division of Academic Accountants, which focused on administering accounting academia and promoting academic research. In March 2014, IAI established a third division, called the Division of Tax Accountants, which focuses on advancing professional, education and research activities in the field of taxation. In December 2014, the IAI altered its international name from the Indonesian Institute of Accountants to the Institute of Indonesia Chartered Accountants. The change in name reflects the IAI's strategy to signify its current professional accounting qualification programme, i.e. Chartered Accountants (CA) of Indonesia, which was firstly introduced by the Institute in December 2012.

Professional memberships

The dynamic within the Indonesian accounting profession in recent years has resulted in the existence of three professional accounting associations: the Institute of Indonesia Chartered Accountants (IAI), the Indonesian Institute of Certified Public Accountants (IAPI) and the Indonesian Institute of Management Accountants (IAMI). Each association has its own professional examination programme and other criteria for admitting members. While some of their roles may overlap, the three professional associations do not have equal authority regarding the provision of services through public practice.

Institute of Indonesia Chartered Accountants (IAI)

IAI has three categories of membership: 1) student members, comprising accounting students at the undergraduate level; 2) associate members, who are graduates of undergraduate or postgraduate programmes in accounting; and 3) chartered members. To qualify for a chartered membership, a person must have an accounting educational background (either undergraduate, postgraduate or professional), successfully pass the chartered accountant examinations and satisfy a minimum three-year professional experience requirement. A chartered member of the IAI is granted the professional designation of chartered accountant by the Institute and is eligible to be registered on the State Register of Accountants, administered by the Indonesian Ministry of Finance. A person who is registered on the State Register of Accountants is regarded as a registered accountant and is eligible to use the title 'accountant' (*akuntan* – Ak.), as prescribed in the 1954 Accountant Designation Act.

In accordance with Ministry of Finance regulations, registered accountants are permitted to provide professional services to the public through accounting services firms (*kantor jasa akuntansi* – KJA), provided that those firms have been licensed by the Ministry. The firms can only provide non-assurance services such as financial statement preparation, financial statement compilation, management accounting services, management consulting, taxation services, agreed-upon procedures and information technology services. An accounting services firm cannot provide assurance services such as the audit of financial statements.

IAI members are required to follow a code of professional ethics set by the Institute. Chartered members are also required to undertake continuing professional education courses and attain the required minimum number of participation credit points if they want to maintain their chartered membership status.

Indonesian Institute of Certified Public Accountants (IAPI)

The IAPI is a specialized public accountant association that supervises the public accounting profession in Indonesia. According to the Indonesian Public Accountant Act, assurance services such as the audit of financial statements can only be provided by public accountants through public accounting firms (*kantor akuntan publik* – KAP).[5] To qualify as a public accountant, a person must have an accounting education background (either undergraduate or postgraduate level) and pass all levels of certified public accountant examinations administered by IAPI. There are three levels of examination: basic, professional and advanced. A candidate who has passed the basic and professional levels will be granted the certified professional accountant of Indonesia (CPAI) designation by the Institute and will be able to proceed to the advanced level. The certified public accountant (CPA) qualification will only be granted if a candidate has passed the advanced level of the examinations, satisfied a minimum three-year professional experience requirement and is registered as a member of the IAPI. After attaining the CPA qualification, a CPA can engage in public practice provided that he or she has obtained a practice licence from the Ministry of Finance. Apart from providing assurance services, public accountants can also provide non-assurance services through their public accounting firms.

While IAPI members primarily constitute public accountants or those with a CPA qualification, its membership is also open to individuals without these qualifications who work for public accounting firms. Members with a CPA qualification and/or a public accountant licence are required to undertake continuing professional education courses and satisfy the minimum participation credit point requirement. The IAPI publishes the Indonesian Professional Standards of Public Accountants (Standar Profesional Akuntan Publik – SPAP), consisting of a code of ethics, auditing standards and other related assurance service-related pronouncements, which should be applied by individuals working for public accounting firms, whether they are members or non-members of the IAPI. These standards have been adopted from the professional standards published by the IFAC. The IAPI is currently an associate member of the IFAC.

Indonesian Institute of Management Accountants (IAMI)

The IAMI is a professional association that specializes in management accounting practices. The membership base of the IAMI is quite large because it is not limited to those who hold professional accounting qualifications. Individuals without a formal accounting education background who work in management accounting-related areas can also be members of this professional organization. The IAMI organizes the certified professional management accountants (CPMA) examination, a certification programme that focuses on the competency of professionals in management accounting field. The Institute grants the CPMA qualification to candidates who have passed the examination and satisfied certain minimum work experience requirements. Under current professional accounting regulatory frameworks, a CPMA qualification does not lead to a professional licence to engage in public practice.

Supervision of public practice

Public practice by professional accountants in Indonesia, through either accounting services firms or public accounting firms, is overseen by the Ministry of Finance. The Ministry is responsible for setting government policies related to the accounting profession, as well as setting government strategies for the development of the profession. Apart from issuing practice licences, the Ministry has the authority to conduct investigations into potential violations of laws and regulations concerning the accounting profession, impose administrative sanctions and even revoke the practice licences of registered accountants and public accountants.

In addition to the supervision by the Ministry of Finance, the OJK oversees the provision of professional services by public accounting firms in the capital market and financial services industry. The OJK in particular has the authority to license public accountants (and thus public accounting firms) who are authorized to provide assurance services for listed public companies and commercial banks.

Accounting standards in Indonesia

Accounting standards setting

The formulation of accounting standards in Indonesia is a task for the IAI. A special committee for the establishment of accounting standards was appointed by the IAI in the early 1970s, when there was a need to develop a set of Indonesian accounting standards as a part of the government's initiative to reactivate the capital market. This led to the publication of the first codified accounting standards in the country, the Indonesian Accounting Principles (PAI), by the IAI in 1973. As these standards were largely based on the US GAAP, their publication marked a shift in the country's financial reporting orientation away from the Dutch system, which had been applied since colonization, to the US system (Diga and Yunus, 1997; ADB, 2003). Following this publication, the IAI established a permanent standard-setting body, called the Indonesian Accounting Principles Committee (Komite Prinsip Akuntansi Indonesia – KPAI), in 1974. A second edition of the PAI was published in 1984 as a response to the government's intention to accelerate Indonesian capital market reform in the mid-1980s.

The accelerated growth of the capital market that started in the late 1980s prompted several developments in the standards-setting process. First, the KPAI was reorganized into the Indonesian Financial Accounting Standards Committee (Komite Standar Akuntansi Keuangan – KSAK) in 1994. Second, the IAI transformed the basis of accounting standards setting in the same year from the US GAAP to the International Accounting Standards

(IAS) and made a formal decision to support the harmonization programme initiated by the International Accounting Standards Committee (IASC). This move was evident from the formulation of a new set of Indonesian Financial Accounting Standards in 1994, which was adapted from IAS standards. This new set of codified standards included direct adoption of the IASC Framework for Preparation and Presentation of Financial Statements. Nevertheless, the influence of the US accounting standards remained notable in the 1994 accounting standards pronouncement and its subsequent revisions, since several standards continued to be based on the US GAAP.

Another major change in the institutional structure for standards setting took place in 1998, when KSAK was restructured into the Indonesian Financial Accounting Standard Board (Dewan Standar Akuntansi Keuangan – DSAK) (ADB, 2003). The newly established standards setter has greater power than its predecessor because it has been granted authority to set and endorse the statements and the interpretations of financial accounting standards. This authority makes the DSAK an autonomous accounting standards setter within the IAI's organizational structure. In addition, the new standards setter has a stronger structure than ever before, since the board comprises representatives from the public accounting profession, academia, industry, the central bank and government (ADB, 2003). In 1998, the IAI also established the Indonesian Financial Accounting Standards Advisory Council (Dewan Konsultatif Standar Akuntansi Keuangan – DKSAK), which serves as the advisor for the DSAK. Both the DSAK and the DKSAK continue to be the main players in Indonesian accounting standards development, including in the current process of converging Indonesian accounting standards with the IFRS.

Convergence with the IFRS

Since 1994, the development of Indonesian accounting standards has been influenced by the dynamics in the international accounting standard-setting arena. Consequently, the recent trend towards the global convergence of IFRS has inevitably affected the DSAK's strategy in formulating Indonesian accounting standards. In 2004, the IAI indicated its early intention to support the IASB convergence programme, and this, to some extent, was reflected in the Indonesian codified accounting standards issued in 2007. However, it was not until 23 December 2008 that the IAI publicly made a formal statement that Indonesian accounting standards would fully converge with IFRS, with an expected completion date of 1 January 2012 (Deloitte Touche Tohmatsu, 2009), and this process is still progressing in 2016.

Chand and Patel (2011, p. 15) suggest that there are five different convergence approaches a country can choose to adopt the IFRS: 1) full adoption of the IFRS; 2) selective adoption of the IFRS or adoption with a time lag; 3) IFRS adoption with modification to account for country-specific characteristics; 4) preservation of national accounting standards but in harmony with the IFRS; and 5) continuation of national accounting standards. Of these five approaches, IFRS convergence in Indonesia follows a mixture of the second and third approaches, whereby the IFRS are adopted gradually into domestic accounting standards and minor modifications are made to align the standards with the Indonesian regulations and business environment.

The IFRS convergence strategy adopted by Indonesian accounting standards setter means that there are several phases in the IFRS convergence process in the country. The first phase covers the period between 2007 and 2012 (Sinaga, 2011). The Indonesian codified accounting standards published on 1 September 2007 reflect the beginning of this phase, in which a number of Statement of Financial Accounting Standards (Pernyataan Standar Akuntansi Keuangan – PSAK) in the pronouncement signified a full adoption of the IFRS/IAS. For example, IAS 16 (*Property, Plant and Equipment*), IAS 32 (*Financial Instruments: Presentation*) and IAS 39 (*Financial Instruments: Recognition and Measurement*) were among the first batch of standards to be fully adopted in Indonesia, and soon gained wide attention from the public. Major changes in accounting practice have been brought about by IAS 16, which was adopted as PSAK 16 (*Fixed Assets*), because it allows companies to choose either the cost model or the revaluation model in the valuation of properties, plants and equipment. Similarly, IAS 32 and IAS 39, which were adopted as PSAK 50 (*Financial Instruments, Presentation and Disclosure*) and PSAK 55 (*Financial Instruments: Recognition and Measurement*), respectively, also sparked controversy, particularly in the financial industry, owing to their complexity.

The gradual approach to IFRS convergence means that the newly adopted IFRS have different effective implementation dates. Between 1 January 2008 and 1 January 2012, DSAK endorsed 35 PSAKs adopted from the IFRS, along with 20 interpretations of financial accounting standards. Specifically, there is one PSAK with an effective date of 1 January 2009, 16 PSAKs that became effective on 1 January 2011, and 18 PSAKs that were implemented on 1 January 2012. The completion of the first phase of the IFRS convergence process was marked by the publication of the codified Indonesian accounting standards on 1 June 2012. In general, Indonesian accounting standards in 2012 were equivalent to the IFRS as at 1 January 2009 (Sinaga, 2011), although two standards, IFRS 1 (*First-time Adoption of International Financial Reporting Standards*) and IAS 41 (*Agriculture*), had yet to be adopted in Indonesia. As with IAS 41 (*Agriculture*), the DSAK's position was that it would wait for the IASB to finalize the standard before adopting it in Indonesia (Sinaga and Wahyuni, 2012). Meanwhile, IFRS 1 (*First-time Adoption of International Financial Reporting Standards*) would not be adopted until Indonesian accounting standards had fully converged with IFRS (Sinaga, 2011).

The second phase of IFRS convergence covered the period between 2012 and 2015, aiming to reduce the differences between Indonesian accounting standards as of 1 June 2012 and the IFRS. During this period, the DSAK amended nine IFRS-equivalent PSAKs, replaced one IFRS-equivalent PSAK, issued four newly adopted IFRS-equivalent standards and modified the remaining standards to align with the IFRS as of 2014. The progress of the second phase of the IFRS convergence was marked by the publication of the codified Indonesian accounting standards on 1 January 2015, making the Indonesian accounting standards in 2015 equivalent to the IFRS as at 1 January 2014 (IAI, 2014). This progress means that the lagged gap between Indonesian accounting standards and IFRS has been narrowed from three years in the first phase to one year in the second phase. During the second phase of IFRS convergence, neither IFRS 1 nor IAS 41 had been adopted. These standards, along with other IFRS standards issued or revised after 1 January 2014, will be addressed in the ensuing phases of the Indonesian IFRS convergence programme.

The present structure of accounting standards

The current Indonesian IFRS-equivalent accounting standards are codified in the Indonesian Financial Accounting Standards pronouncement of 1 January 2015, which consists of accounting standards that are self-developed by DSAK to cater for certain financial reporting issues not covered under IFRS. As mentioned above, Indonesia adopted a convergence strategy that allows its standards setter to modify the IFRS slightly to accommodate country-specific characteristics. As a result, there are several minor modifications in the Indonesian accounting standards compared to the IFRS, although the differences between the two sets of standards are not considered substantial. For example, in PSAK 1 (*Presentation of Financial Statements*), adopted from IAS 1 (*Presentation of Financial Statements*), the DSAK provides additional explanations of the definition of financial accounting standards to bring them into line with Indonesian capital market regulations (IAI, 2014). Table 1.1 provides a list of Indonesian accounting standards as of 1 January 2015, along with their comparison with IFRS as of 1 January 2014.

Table 1.1 Indonesian accounting standards as at 1 January 2015 and their comparison with IFRS

Indonesian accounting standards (PSAK)	IAS/IFRS equivalent	Differences
PSAK 1 Presentation of Financial Statements	IAS 1	PSAK 1 is substantially consistent with IAS 1 as of 1 January 2014. Minor differences relate to the scope of the application of the standard and adjustments that have been made in PSAK 1 to align it with Indonesian regulations and the accounting standards structure.
PSAK 2 Statement of Cash Flows	IAS 7	PSAK 2 is substantially consistent with IAS 7 as of 1 January 2014.
PSAK 3 Interim Financial Reporting	IAS 34	PSAK 3 is substantially consistent with IAS 34 as of 1 January 2014.
PSAK 4 Separate Financial Statements	IAS 27	PSAK 4 is substantially consistent with IAS 27 as of 1 January 2014. Exceptions include: 1) PSAK 4 allows only parent companies to present separate financial statements, and the financial statements must be as a supplement to the consolidated financial statements; 2) PSAK 4 requires all parent entities to present consolidated financial statements and, unlike IAS 27, no exception is provided; and 3) other minor modifications to align PSAK 4 with Indonesian regulations and the accounting standards structure.
PSAK 5 Operating Segments	IFRS 8	PSAK 5 is substantially consistent with IFRS 8 as of 1 January 2014. Minor modifications were made to maintain its consistency with other accounting standards (e.g. PSAK 4).
PSAK 7 Related Party Disclosures	IAS 24	PSAK 7 is substantially consistent with IAS 24 as of 1 January 2014. Minor modifications were made to maintain consistency with other standards such as PSAK 4 and PSAK 65.
PSAK 8 Events after the Reporting Period	IAS 10	PSAK 8 is substantially consistent with IAS 10 as of 1 January 2014. However, PSAK 8 does not specify disclosures of owners or other parties who have the power to amend published financial statements, since legally no one in Indonesia has the power to make an amendment.
PSAK 10 The Effects of Changes in Foreign Exchange Rates	IAS 21	PSAK 10 is substantially consistent with IAS 21 as of 1 January 2014. Minor modifications were made to align PSAK 10 with the local context (e.g. local currency).
PSAK 13 Investment Property	IAS 40	PSAK 13 is substantially consistent with IAS 40 as of 1 January 2014. Minor differences are associated with issues on biological assets, because Indonesia has not adopted IAS 41.
PSAK 14 Inventories	IAS 2	PSAK 14 is substantially consistent with IAS 2 as of 1 January 2014. Minor differences are associated with issues on biological assets, because Indonesia has not adopted IAS 41.

(continued)

Table 1.1 (continued)

Indonesian accounting standards (PSAK)	IAS/IFRS equivalent	Differences
PSAK 15 *Investments in Associates*	IAS 28	PSAK 15 is substantially consistent with IAS 28 as of 1 January 2014. Minor differences include: 1) PSAK 15 stipulates that the board of commissionaires is part of the governing body of entities, because Indonesian companies adopted a dual board system; 2) PSAK 15 does not adopt certain paragraphs that refer to IFRS 9 because Indonesia has not adopted IFRS 9; and 3) PSAK 15 does not adopt certain paragraphs that concern parent companies exempted from presenting consolidated financial statements and companies that present standalone financial statements.
PSAK 16 *Fixed Assets*	IAS 16	PSAK 16 is substantially consistent with IAS 16 as of 1 January 2014. Minor differences relate to: 1) issues on biological assets (since IAS 41 has not been adopted); 2) PSAK 16 does not prescribe the change of accounting policy from a cost to revaluation model; and 3) PSAK 16 provides additional explanations on the depreciation of land consistent with the Indonesian context.
PSAK 18 *Accounting and Reporting by Retirement Benefit Plans*	IAS 26	PSAK 18 is substantially consistent with IAS 26 as of 1 January 2014. Minor modifications were made to align the standards with local regulations.
PSAK 19 *Intangible Assets*	IAS 38	PSAK 19 is substantially consistent with IAS 38 as of 1 January 2014.
PSAK 22 *Business Combinations*	IFRS 3	PSAK 22 is substantially consistent with IFRS 3 as of 1 January 2014. Minor differences exist as PSAK 22 does not adopt the stipulation concerning business combination of mutual entities, and provides additional stipulation related to goodwill resulting from business combination before the effective date of the accounting standard.
PSAK 23 *Revenue*	IAS 18	PSAK 23 is substantially consistent with IAS 18 as of 1 January 2014. There are minor differences in relation to the scope of the standard, as IAS 41 has not been adopted.
PSAK 24 *Employee Benefits*	IAS 19	PSAK 24 is substantially consistent with IAS 19 as of 1 January 2014.
PSAK 25 *Accounting Policies, Changes in Accounting Estimates, and Errors*	IAS 8	PSAK 25 is substantially consistent with IAS 8 as of 1 January 2014.
PSAK 26 *Borrowing Costs*	IAS 23	PSAK 26 is substantially consistent with IAS 23 as of 1 January 2014. Minor differences exist because IAS 41 has not been adopted.
PSAK 28 *Accounting for Casualty Insurance*		There is no standard in IFRS which is equivalent to PSAK 28. PSAK 28 complements the stipulations in PSAK 62 (*Insurance Contracts*).
PSAK 30 *Leases*	IAS 17	PSAK 30 is substantially consistent with IAS 17 as of 1 January 2014. Minor differences relate to issues on biological assets because IAS 41 has not been adopted.

PSAK 34 *Construction Contracts*	IAS 11	PSAK 34 is substantially consistent with IAS 11 as of 1 January 2014.
PSAK 36 *Accounting for Life Insurance*		There is no standard in IFRS which is equivalent to PSAK 36. PSAK 36 complements the stipulations in PSAK 62 (*Insurance Contracts*).
PSAK 38 *Business Combination of Under-Common-Control Entities*		There is no standard in IFRS which is equivalent to PSAK 38.
PSAK 45 *Financial Reporting in Not-for-Profit Organizations*		There is no standard in IFRS which is equivalent to PSAK 45.
PSAK 46 *Income Taxes*	IAS 12	PSAK 46 is substantially consistent with IAS 12 as of 1 January 2014. Certain modifications have been made to align PSAK 46 with Indonesian tax regulations.
PSAK 48 *Impairment of Assets*	IAS 36	PSAK 48 is substantially consistent with IAS 36 as of 1 January 2014. Minor modifications were made to maintain the consistency between PSAK 48 and other standards (e.g. PSAK 4), and because IAS 41 has not been adopted.
PSAK 50 *Financial Instruments: Presentation*	IAS 32	PSAK 50 is substantially consistent with IAS 32 as of 1 January 2014.
PSAK 53 *Share-based Payment*	IFRS 2	PSAK 53 is substantially consistent with IFRS 2 as of 1 January 2014.
PSAK 55 *Financial Instruments: Recognition and Measurement*	IAS 39	PSAK 55 is substantially consistent with IAS 39 as of 1 January 2014.
PSAK 56 *Earnings per Share*	IAS 33	PSAK 56 is substantially consistent with IAS 33 as of 1 January 2014. Minor modifications were made to maintain the consistency between PSAK 56 and other standards.
PSAK 57 *Provisions, Contingent Liabilities, and Contingent Assets*	IAS 37	PSAK 57 is substantially consistent with IAS 37 as of 1 January 2014.
PSAK 58 *Non-current Assets Held for Sale and Discontinued Operations*	IFRS 5	PSAK 58 is substantially consistent with IFRS 5 as of 1 January 2014.
PSAK 60 *Financial Instruments: Disclosures*	IFRS 7	PSAK 60 is substantially consistent with IFRS 7 as of 1 January 2014. Minor modifications have been made because IFRS 9 has not been adopted.
PSAK 61 *Accounting for Government Grants and Disclosure of Government Assistance*	IAS 20	PSAK 61 is substantially consistent with IAS 20 as of 1 January 2014. Minor differences concern the scope of the standard as IAS 41 has not been adopted.

(continued)

Table 1.1 (continued)

Indonesian accounting standards (PSAK)	IAS/IFRS equivalent	Differences
PSAK 62 Insurance Contracts	IFRS 4	PSAK 62 is substantially consistent with IFRS 4 as of 1 January 2014. Differences exist as PSAK 62 does not adopt the stipulations concerning the measurement of insurance liabilities on an undiscounted basis, because it is not consistent with PSAK 28 and PSAK 36.
PSAK 63 Financial Reporting in Hyperinflationary Economies	IAS 29	PSAK 63 is substantially consistent with IAS 29 as of 1 January 2014.
PSAK 64 Exploration for and Evaluation of Mineral Resources	IFRS 6	PSAK 64 is substantially consistent with IFRS 6 as of 1 January 2014.
PSAK 65 Consolidated Financial Statements	IFRS 10	PSAK 65 is substantially consistent with IFRS 10 as of 1 January 2014. Exceptions include: 1) PSAK 65 does not adopt stipulations regarding the exception for parent companies to not provide consolidated financial statements; 2) PSAK 65 does not adopt stipulations that refer to IFRS 9 because this standard has not been adopted; and 3) other minor modifications to maintain the consistency between PSAK 65 and other PSAKs.
PSAK 66 Joint Arrangements	IFRS 11	PSAK 66 is substantially consistent with IFRS 11 as of 1 January 2014. Minor modifications were made to align PSAK 66 with Indonesian business regulations and to ensure PSAK 66 would be consistent with other PSAKs.
PSAK 67 Disclosure of Interests in Other Entities	IFRS 12	PSAK 67 is substantially consistent with IFRS 12 as of 1 January 2014. Minor modifications were made to align PSAK 67 with Indonesian business regulations and to ensure PSAK 67 would be consistent with other PSAKs.
PSAK 68 Fair Value Measurement	IFRS 13	PSAK 68 is substantially consistent with IFRS 13 as of 1 January 2014. Minor modifications were made to align PSAK 68 with the local business environment and to ensure PSAK 68 would be consistent with other PSAKs.

Based on the Indonesian Financial Accounting Standards Pronouncements as at 1 January 2015 (IAI, 2014)

Apart from a set of accounting standards that are equivalent to IFRS, the current Indonesian accounting standards consist of two other pronouncements, namely: 1) accounting standards for small and medium-sized enterprises; and 2) Shari'a accounting standards. The set of standards for SMEs is entitled the Financial Accounting Standards for Non-publicly Accountable Entities (Standar Akuntansi Keuangan Entitas Tanpa Akuntabilitas Publik – SAK-ETAP), which were published in July 2009 and came into effect on 1 January 2011. The SAK-ETAP were developed based on the IFRS for SMEs, although the two sets of standards are not identical owing to the modifications made by the DSAK to make the SAK-ETAP applicable to the Indonesian context. These standards are applicable to: 1) companies that are not listed in the stock exchange or in the process of being listed in the exchange; and 2) companies outside the financial industry.[6]

The Shari'a accounting standards have been developed to cater to businesses that operate according to Islamic norms. Examples of such businesses include Shari'a commercial banks and other Shari'a financial institutions. The Indonesian Shari'a accounting standards are developed by the Shari'a Accounting Standard Board (Dewan Standar Akuntansi Syariah – DSAS), another standards-setting body under the IAI in Indonesia.

Concluding remarks

Early accounting rules and practices in Indonesia were significantly influenced by the Dutch system as a result of the country's former status as a Dutch colony. A shift towards the Anglo-Saxon accounting systems started in the 1970s, marked by the publication of the first codified Indonesian accounting standards, which were based on the US GAAP. Over the last four decades, these accounting standards have developed extensively, in parallel with rapid growth in the Indonesian economy and the advancement of the country's capital market. Recent developments of Indonesian accounting standards have marked substantial changes in standards-setting orientation away from the US GAAP towards the standards issued by international accounting standards-setting bodies. This has led to the decision to fully converge the IFRS and Indonesian accounting standards. Indonesia has adopted a gradual approach to IFRS convergence, a strategy that aims to achieve a full convergence of Indonesian accounting standards with IFRS in sequential stages.

Alongside the development of accounting standards, the Indonesian accounting and auditing profession has also grown rapidly since its inception in the 1950s. The initial structure of the profession, which was characterized by the Dutch accounting professional schemata, has now developed into that which is widely implemented in Anglo-Saxon countries such as the US and the UK. This includes the existence of specialized accounting professional associations, the requirement to pass professional examinations to become a qualified member of an association, the formal licensing procedures for public practice, and the requirement to undertake continuing professional education. The progressively established accounting profession is a major advantage for Indonesia, as it serves as a foundation for achieving high-quality financial reporting practices in the country.

While accounting standards and the accounting profession have advanced significantly, some issues remain to be dealt with by the Indonesian accounting standards setter, the accounting profession and stakeholders in financial reporting practice, particularly in relation to the current IFRS convergence programme. The most crucial issues are the implementation of the newly issued IFRS-equivalent standards and the settlement of residual differences between the IFRS and the Indonesian accounting standards. The implementation of IFRS-equivalent standards requires the readiness of professional accountants in Indonesia to apply the standards in the preparation of financial statements or to conduct audits on financial statements prepared on the basis of these standards.

It has been argued that the IAS/IFRS are principles-based standards which provide only broad principles, rather than detailed rules, to guide their implementation (Nobes, 2005; Bennett et al., 2006; Bradbury and Schröder, 2012). The lack of detailed rules in the IAS/IFRS means that accountants are required to exercise professional judgement when interpreting and applying the standards (Bennett et al., 2006; Bradbury and Schröder, 2012). This can be a major challenge to Indonesian accountants, because under the previous accounting standard regime they were accustomed to applying a more rules-based set of accounting standards. This issue in turn raises the need for appropriate training programmes to familiarize accountants with the new accounting standards, and more importantly to equip accountants with the skills required to make appropriate judgements under IAS/IFRS. This necessity has been recognized by Indonesian professional accountant bodies such as the IAI and the IAPI, and a number of continuing professional education programmes, workshops and seminars have been organized by the professional associations to increase accountants' aptitude for implementing the Indonesian equivalent of the IAS/IFRS.

The residual differences between the current Indonesian accounting standards and the IFRS pose a challenge to the Indonesian accounting standards setter. When the IAI formalized its commitment in 2008 to support the IFRS convergence programme, it stated that Indonesia intended to achieve full convergence with the IFRS by 2012. Nevertheless, although two stages of IFRS convergence have been completed, Indonesian accounting standards as of 31 December 2015 have not fully reflected the most recent version of IFRS. These residual differences are inevitable owing to the gradual and selective approach to IFRS convergence adopted by IAI, thus a delay in the adoption of most recent standards issued by the IASB is unavoidable.

The continuing revision of the IFRS and the publication of new accounting standards by the IASB, as well as the need for Indonesian standards setter to adhere to the designated phases in formulating and implementing new standards, have resulted in the Indonesian equivalents of the IFRS failing to reflect subsequent amendments to the IFRS. Nevertheless, the DSAK of the IAI has shown effort in dealing with this issue, since the standards-setting body has been able to reduce the time gap between the Indonesian accounting standards and the IFRS from three years in the first stage of convergence to one year in the second stage. As the DSAK continues to follow the development of the IFRS in updating the Indonesian accounting standards, full convergence between the two sets of standards is likely to be achieved in the subsequent stages of the IFRS convergence programme.

Notes

1 There is a form of partnership called CV (Commanditaire Vennootschap). In this partnership form, there are two different kinds of partner: active partners and silent partners. Silent partners are not involved in managing the business, and are liable for any debts or lawsuits against their business up to the amount of capital they have invested in the business.
2 Apart from limited liability companies, incorporated businesses in Indonesia can also take the form of cooperatives. However, this form of enterprise is common only among small and micro-sized entities and does not have to follow complicated financial reporting regulations; thus, it is not discussed in this chapter.
3 During colonization, Jakarta was known by its previous name, Batavia.
4 The Limited Company Act was first introduced in 1995.
5 A certified public accountant (CPA) with a practice licence from the Ministry of Finance has the authority to lead an assurance engagement and sign an independent auditor's report. Professional accountants without this qualification may work in the audit area but they are not qualified to lead an audit engagement or sign an auditor's report.
6 Micro commercial banks (*bank perkreditan rakyat* – BPR) are allowed to use the SAK-ETAP based on regulations of the OJK.

References

ADB (Asian Development Bank) (2003) *Diagnostic Study of Accounting and Auditing Practices (Private Sector): Republic of Indonesia.* Retrieved from www.adb.org/publications/diagnostic-study-accounting-and-auditing-practices-indonesia.
Bennett, B., Bradbury, M. and Prangnell, H. (2006) Rules, principles and judgments in accounting standards. *Abacus, 42*(2), 189–204.

Bradbury, M.E. and Schröder, L.B. (2012) The content of accounting standards: Principles versus rules. *The British Accounting Review*, *44*(1), 1–10.

Chand, P. and Patel, C. (2011) *Achieving Global Convergence of Financial Reporting Standards: Implications from the South Pacific Region*. London: Emerald.

Deloitte Touche Tohmatsu (2009) *Point of View*. Retrieved from www.iasplus.com/en/binary/asia/0909pointofview1.pdf.

Diga, J. and Yunus, H. (1997) Accounting in Indonesia. In N. Baydoun, A. Nishimura and R. Willett (Eds), *Accounting in the Asia-Pacific Region* (pp. 282–302). Singapore: John Wiley & Sons.

Goeltom, M.S. (2007) *Essays in Macroeconomic Policy: The Indonesian Experience*. Jakarta: Gramedia.

IDX (Indonesia Stock Exchange) (2015) *IDX Fact Book 2015*. Retrieved from www.idx.co.id/id-id/beranda/publikasi/factbook.aspx.

IAI (Ikatan Akuntan Indonesia/Institute of Indonesia Chartered Accountants) (2014) *Financial Accounting Standards Effective as of 1 January 2015 (Standar Akuntansi Keuangan per efektif 1 Januari 2015)*. Jakarta: IAI.

Nobes, C.W. (2005). Rules-based standards and the lack of principles in accounting. *Accounting Horizons*, *19*(1), 25–34.

OECD (Organisation for Economic Co-operation and Development) (2015) *Indonesia – Economic Forecast Summary (November 2015)*. Retrieved from www.oecd.org/eco/outlook/indonesia-economic-forecast-summary.htm.

Ricklefs, M.C. (2001) *A History of Modern Indonesia since c. 1200*. Basingstoke: Palgrave.

Silondae, A.A. and Ilyas, W.B. (2011) *Essentials of Business Law (Pokok-pokok Hukum Bisnis)*. Jakarta: Salemba Empat.

Sinaga, R.U. (2011) *Konvergensi IFRS*. Retrieved from www.iaiglobal.or.id/tentang_iai_download.php.

Sinaga, R.U. and Wahyuni, E.T. (2012) Out of the shadows. *Accounting and Business International*, *July 2012*, 55–56.

Sunariyah (2010) *Introduction to Capital Market (Pengantar Pengetahuan Pasar Modal)*. Jakarta: UPP STIM YPKN.

Tuanakotta, T.M. (2007) *Half-Century of the Accounting Profession (Setengah Abad Profesi Akuntansi)*. Jakarta: Salemba Empat.

Wie, T.K. (2012). *Indonesia's Economy since Independence*. Singapore: ISEAS.

World Bank (2016) *World Development Indicators*. Retrieved from http://databank.worldbank.org/data/reports.aspx?source=2&country=IDN&series=&period=.

2

Transparency at the crossroads

Contemporary accountancy in Korea

Jay Junghun Lee and Han Yi

Introduction

South Korea has been continuously praised for its steady economic growth and accurate eco-nomic data.[1] However, in recent reports Korea has also received the lowest-ever scores on accounting transparency from two respectable economic analysis agencies, the World Economic Forum (WEF) and the International Institute for Management Development (IMD).[2] The purpose of this chapter is to offer some insights into this conflicting scene by describing the current landscape of accountancy in Korea. We define accountancy as the activities of all par-ties that are explicitly or implicitly involved in the value chain of producing and consuming accounting information.[3] These parties include the controlling owners, management, audit committees, external auditors, regulators (including standard setters), and outside investors, as shown in Figure 2.1.

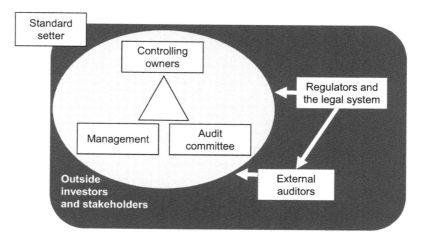

Figure 2.1 The parties in Korea's accounting landscape

In the next section, we briefly describe the history of economic development and accounting/ auditing standard changes in Korea. It is important to note that the Korean economy has migrated from a government-controlled, planned economic system to a market-driven one. Similarly, accounting and auditing practices have not been developed by market forces but shaped by the government's initiatives and external economic shocks.

The third section summarizes the key institutional features of Korean accounting practices after the adoption of the International Financial Reporting Standards (IFRS) in 2011. We discuss accounting institutions and practices related to the following constituencies:

1   The Korea Accounting Standards Board and the IFRS
2   External auditors and regulatory requirements
3   Controlling owners, management, and audit committee
4   Regulators and investors.

The fourth section describes the recent accounting scandal of Daewoo Shipbuilding & Marine Engineering to illustrate how and why the adoption of the IFRS does not necessarily improve accounting transparency in Korea. The final section concludes the chapter.

Historical background

Economic development and the Generally Accepted Accounting Principles in Korea[4]

Although Korean merchants are known to have used a systematic double-entry bookkeeping system, the first set of modern financial statements based on the double-entry bookkeeping system emerged only in the late nineteenth century for commercial banks (e.g., the financial statements of Daehan Chunil Bank, currently Shinhan Bank, for 1899–1905). The Chosun dynasty in Korea collapsed in 1910. Japan annexed the Korean Empire and colonized it until 1945. During this period, Japanese institutions, influenced largely by German institutions, penetrated Korea and therefore accounting rules in Korea were a part of commercial civil law system. That is, as in other civil law countries, accounting information was more important for fixed-income claimants and taxation authorities than for equity investors. After the unconditional surrender of Japan in 1945, which ended World War II, Korea was divided into the Soviet-controlled northern part and the US-controlled southern part, leading to the Korean War, which lasted from 1950 to 1953. The massive US aid plan to support South Korea led to the creation of government-controlled banks and their capital allocation, which requires accounting information for credit analyses. As a result, the Korean government initiated the formulation of the first set of Generally Accepted Accounting Principles (GAAP) in 1958. Note that, unlike Western countries, where GAAP evolved as a social contract, Korea treated GAAP as part of the commercial civil law system.

As the Korean economy rapidly grew, the government realized the important role of the equity market in allocating capital resources. To meet the information demands of investors for publicly traded companies, the Korean government, specifically the Securities Review Committee, issued a set of detailed accounting rules in 1975. These rules created two sets of GAAPs: one for publicly traded companies and the other for nontraded companies. The era of dual accounting standards was ended by the External Audit Law in 1980, which delegated the standards-setting function to a government agency, the Securities Operation Committee under the Ministry of Public Finance, and required not only publicly held companies but also privately held companies exceeding a size threshold to have their financial statements audited by certified public accountants (CPAs). This system continued to survive until the Asian financial crisis and the International Monetary Fund's (IMF) bailout of Korea in 1997.

The Korean economic development was driven primarily by her government until 1997. The key strategy was to fund profitable businesses with foreign loans. Under this development plan, the Korean government screened a small number of promising projects and entrepreneurs, and subsidized them intensively in the form of sovereign debt guarantees and credit rationing through banks. As a result, the role of accounting information in capital markets was limited. Publicly traded companies focused on the fixed assets on their balance sheets as collateral for bank loans (e.g., land for nonoperating purposes) because the primary source of funding was banks rather than stock markets. The tragedy of the 1997 financial crisis and the IMF bailout was the inevitable consequence of this government- and bank-driven development strategy. No matter how carefully the government screened projects, the failure rate of funded projects was higher than the corresponding rate under the market screening system. A major problem was that the Korean government and government-owned banks took over the nonperforming loans of unsuccessful projects but the managers of the failed projects did not suffer any serious consequences. This distorted system encouraged managers to expand capacity beyond the optimal level, leading to a big bust, as happened in 1997. A classic example is the massive accounting fraud, and collapse, of the Daewoo Group.[5] Accounting information had little role in the allocation of financial resources because the government selected projects and restructured industries on a regular basis.

Following the 1997 financial crisis and the IMF bailout, the World Bank requested that Korea delegate the accounting standards-setting function to a private-sector body. Korea accepted this request and established the Korea Accounting Standards Board (KASB) as a private-sector standards-setting body in 1999. The KASB issued a series of local accounting standards (K-GAAP), which were replaced by the IFRS in 2011.[6] These changes reflected the rapid growth of stock markets and the increasing demand of equity investors for high-quality accounting information. Note that some companies that survived the 1997 financial crisis grew to become global players and they no longer welcomed local regulatory intervention. These large companies, as well as some information technology (IT) companies that were founded during the IT boom in the early 2000s and survived the subsequent IT bust, became more dependent on the equity markets than on banks as a source of finance. These global and young companies strongly supported the adoption of the IFRS. However, the adoption of the IFRS was not a preferred choice for a majority of local companies that relied heavily on bank financing.

External audits and audit committees

The Korea Institute of Certified Public Accountants (KICPA) was founded on December 11, 1954, long before the Law of Certified Public Accountants became effective in 1968. Prior to 1981, when the External Audit Law was promulgated, the KICPA matched audit teams and their auditees using a three-year mandatory rotation. This system (non-contract audit assignment) was justified by the idea of auditor independence. Under the assignment system, however, audit quality deteriorated because auditors had little incentive to make efforts to improve audit quality. At the same time, audit risk increased as an audit team (typically four auditors) could not provide an effective assurance service for large and complex entities. The External Audit Law in 1981 introduced contract-based voluntary audit engagements in Korea, although regulators maintained the "auditor designation" rules for firms with high audit risk (the rules specify 13 conditions, as of 2015).

The audit committee (AC) was introduced in 1999 by the Commercial Law after both the IMF and the World Bank requested that Korea secure accounting transparency at the firm level as a condition of the bailout. A set of internal control (IC) rules was introduced by the Corporate Restructuring Promotion Law in 2001. Note that it was not Korean companies but the government that introduced both the AC and IC systems. Therefore, managers had little economic incentive to increase the monitoring power of the AC and IC systems voluntarily, leaving many commentators to believe that neither system functioned as effectively as in many Western countries.[7]

Unique "auditor retention" rules were introduced in 1997 following the revision of the External Audit Law. Under the rules, publicly listed companies were not allowed to switch auditors for at least three years after the initial audit engagement. Policymakers believed that a minimum contract period would increase the bargaining power of auditors, thereby increasing auditor independence. However, market participants observed serious unintended consequences. Some companies took advantage of a three-year minimum contract period and obtained deep discounts in the initial year (i.e., lowballing). After the three-year contract period, they abandoned the incumbent auditor for another deep discount from a new auditor. Statistics from the Financial Supervisory Service (2013) indicate a huge fee discount from auditor switches, especially when the switch was from a Big Four to a non-Big Four firm (22.8 percent discount). Nevertheless, the rules are still in place. Another unique feature, the "mandatory auditor rotation" rule, was experimented from 2006 to 2010 in Korea. The idea behind this rule was that the auditor rotation would cut off the plausible long-term collusive ties between auditors and their clients. However, the intended positive effect was not observed, and the rule was finally nullified.

Section summary

Whereas Western countries developed accounting rules on the basis of voluntary contracts, Korea introduced accounting rules as a part of the legal system. Similarly, while financial markets have been the main driver for project selection and economic growth in Western economies, government planning was the key driver of economic growth in South Korea before the 1997 financial crisis. Therefore, the role of accounting information in Korea for contracting and valuation was restricted. Accounting and audit reforms have been, in part, enforced by foreign entities (i.e., the World Bank and the IMF) after the financial crisis, but many corporations argue that the adoption of the IFRS and global compliance rules are burdensome.

Key institutional features of current Korean accounting practices

The Korea Accounting Standards Board and the IFRS

The Korea Accounting Standards Board

As discussed in Section 2.1, the Korea Accounting Standards Board (KASB), which is nested within the Korea Accounting Institute (KAI), was established in 1999 as an independent accounting standard setter. Following External Audit Law, Article 13, and the Law's enforcement decree, Article 7-3, the FSC (equivalent to the US SEC) delegates to the KASB the power to establish Korean accounting standards. The KAI is a research center that supports the KASB with its research activities. Currently, the KASB plays the following two roles depending on the category of company to which accounting standards are enforced:

1   Facilitating the IFRS endorsement: the KASB facilitates the Korean government's endorsement of every standard issued by the International Accounting Standards Board (IASB) for the Korean companies that apply the IFRS.
2   Setting the local accounting standards: the KASB sets the accounting standards for non-IFRS-applying companies, typically nonlisted companies that are subject to external audits as well as small and medium-sized companies that are not subject to external audits.

Thus, the KASB deals with three tiers of accounting standards, as shown in Table 2.1.[8]

Since the adoption of IFRS in 2011, the KASB has actively participated in various IASB activities. As of 2015, the KASB has at least one representative on the IFRS Advisory Council, the IFRS Interpretations Committee, the Accounting Standards Advisory Forum, the IASB, the IFRS Foundation Trustees, and the IFRS Foundation Monitoring Board, as depicted in Figure 2.2.

One unique feature of the KASB is that it allows companies to submit IFRS-related interpretation questions (that is, questions relating to local interpretations of the IFRS). The External Audit Law explicitly requires the KASB to answer such questions even though the IASB has its own IFRS Interpretations Committee and is known to discourage local interpretation activities.[9] Because accounting standards are regarded as part of the legal system, the violation of which would lead to criminal charges in Korea, the Law accordingly grants citizens the right to reduce accounting-related uncertainties. It is slightly different from the "no-action letter" activities that are carried by the FSS (the enforcement agency of the FSC). Once IFRS-related questions are submitted, both the KASB and the FSS set up a meeting for deliberation. Conclusions, if any, are delivered privately to the company that raised the question (i.e., they are not publicly disclosed).

Korean IFRS (K-IFRS)

All domestic companies whose securities are traded in public markets, as well as all financial institutions (both public and private), in Korea are required to use the IFRS in their consolidated financial statements. Specifically, these companies follow the IFRS that are issued by the

Table 2.1 The KASB and its three-tier accounting standards

Accounting standards	Coverage	No of firms (as of 2014)	External audit requirement	Related laws
1 K-IFRS	All publicly traded companies and financial firms	3,878	Required	The External Audit Law
2 Local Korean GAAP	Private companies that are subject to the External Audit law	20,180		
3 Local Korean GAAP for small/medium-sized firms	Private companies that are NOT subject to the External Audit Law	466,062	Exempted	The Commercial Law
4 Local Korean GAAP for nonprofit organizations	All forms of nonprofit organizations	Unknown	Exempted	In progress (Draft published)

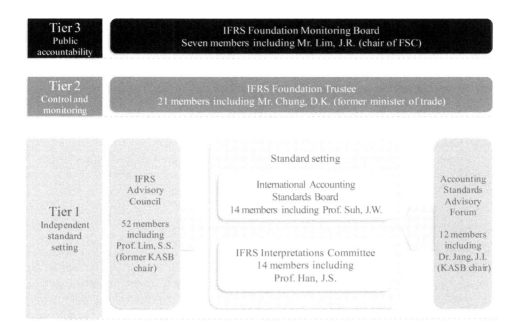

Figure 2.2   KASB activities

IASB, translated into Korean, and endorsed by the Korean government (namely, the K-IFRS). The Korean translation and its process were endorsed by the IFRS Foundation. The auditor's report and the footnotes on the basis of presentation should state that financial statements have been prepared in conformity with the IFRS. Korea has not rejected any accounting policy option permitted by the IFRS, but has added some presentation and disclosure requirements following requests from local users and regulators. Such additions have been permitted under written agreement with the IFRS Foundation and do not affect full compliance with the IFRS as issued by the IASB.

These additions are:

1   An IAS 1 requirement to present operating profit or loss on the face of the statement of profit or loss and other comprehensive income.
2   An IAS 1 requirement to present the statement of appropriation of retained earnings. This requirement was added to IAS 1 for the consistency with the Commercial Law.
3   An IAS 11 requirement to disclose the stage of completion of a contract, the gross amount due from customers for contract work, construction receivables, and the allowance account by major construction sites of "cost-to-cost"-method firms.

In addition, the KASB has renumbered the K-IFRS as follows:

- IAS XX → K-IFRS 10XX
- IFRS XX → K-IFRS 11XX
- SIC XX → K-IFRS 20XX
- IFRIC XX → K-IFRS 21XX

To summarize, one view might be that the Korean IFRS are essentially identical to the original IFRS (apart from the Korean translation and a few additional disclosure and presentation requirements).

Subtle differences between the K-IFRS and the IFRS in the applications[10]

On the other hand, some might not agree that the Korean IFRS are essentially identical to the original IFRS. Korean IFRS users, preparers, and auditors have expressed concerns that there are some local interpretations that seem to deviate from the strict application of the IFRS. Some commentators have also pointed out that there have been a few occasions in which regulatory agencies have attempted to distort the neutral applications of the IFRS to achieve some policy goals. Two representative cases are illustrated below.

REVENUE RECOGNITION OF APARTMENT COMPLEX CONSTRUCTION PROJECTS

Most apartment complex construction projects in South Korea go through the following procedures. First, construction companies and buyers enter into sales contracts and buyers pay about 10 percent of the apartment price as a deposit. Second, buyers pay 40–60 percent of the apartment price in installments during the construction process. Third, construction companies complete the project. Fourth, buyers pay the remaining amounts of the apartment price. Finally, buyers move into the new apartments.

One question is whether or not companies can use the percentage-of-completion method (IAS 11 (*Construction Contracts*)) in this case. Obviously, construction companies prefer to use the percentage-of-completion method to smooth earnings over time. However, some criticize this view because IFRIC 15.12 (*Agreements for the Construction of Real Estate*) dictates that IAS 11 (*Construction Contracts*) does not apply if consumers do not have an option to specify the major structural elements of the design of the real estate before construction begins and/or to specify major structural changes once construction is in progress. Then, the next question is whether or not IFRIC 15.17 is applicable. This states that "The entity may transfer to the buyer control and the significant risks and rewards of ownership of the work in progress in its current state as construction progresses. In this case, if all the criteria in paragraph 14 of IAS 18 are met continuously as construction progresses, the entity shall recognize revenue by reference to the stage of completion using the percentage-of-completion method."

A majority of the Big Four offices in Korea informally concluded that this was not the case where a percentage-of-completion method is applicable. Specifically, the Seoul offices of two global Big Four firms expressed such opinions during the deliberation process of a local interpretation. However, the KASB, the FSS, and related industries strongly supported the idea that conditions (a) and (b) of IAS 18.14 (*Revenue*) are met and that conditions (c) through (e) of the standard could be continuously met during the project.[11] Finally, the KASB and the FSS concluded in 2011 that a percentage-of-completion method is suitable for local contractors, despite strong opposing views from the Big Four firms.

BONDS WITH DETACHABLE WARRANTS WHERE THE EXERCISE PRICE IS
MODIFIED WHEN STOCK PRICES DROP

A relatively simple question has been submitted: Are bonds with detachable warrants debt or equity if the bonds have a condition that the exercise price is modified when stock prices drop? Because the instrument in this case does not meet the fixed-for-fixed condition for equity under IAS 32, the bonds were more likely to be classified as debt than as equity. When the KASB–FSS meeting was held, therefore, the majority (seven out of 10, including all five accounting firms, the KICPA, and the KASB) viewed the instrument as debt. However, regulatory agencies were concerned that if the instrument were classified as debt as opposed to equity, about eight billion US dollars of unexercised amount, held by 492 firms, would have a big impact on the prudence regulation. Both companies and financial regulatory agencies strongly opposed the debt classification, distorting the deliberation process. Finally, the FSC and its Accounting Ruling Board concluded in 2011 that the instrument must be classified as equity.

Overall, the aforementioned two cases clearly illustrate that the interests of both industries and regulatory agencies could substantially influence the deliberation process of local interpretations in Korea. Given that the IASB discourages local interpretations owing to the potential influence of interested parties, some constituencies might question whether the Korean IFRS are fully compatible with the IFRS as issued by the IASB.

Other cases of this sort are as follows:

1 the presentation of operating income (which now is officially solved by modifying the K-IFRS)
2 consolidation rules for special purpose entities in the construction industry
3 book versus fair value assignment from spinoffs
4 whether or not to recognize the control premium when block share sales are viewed as a forward contract
5 the application of fair value hedge accounting for USD/THB currency swaps.

External auditors and regulatory requirements

External auditors

Recently, investors and stakeholders questioned the reputation of major audit firms in Korea because they failed to detect a series of accounting frauds. These frauds include Hyosung (one billion US dollars in 2014), six member firms of the Dongyang Group (six billion US dollars in 2014), STX (two billion US dollars in 2014), Moneual, Inc. (2.5 billion US dollars in 2014), and Daewoo Shipbuilding & Marine Engineering (seven billion US dollars in 2015). Auditors argue that the audit environment is not as friendly as in the advanced economies. Specifically, they argue that audit fees are low, legal liabilities have increased, and the merits of the auditing job have diminished.

The number of new CPAs has been strictly controlled by the national uniform CPA exam. A series of transparency reforms after the 1997 financial crisis increased the demand for CPAs, and the FSS, which is in charge of the CPA test, has almost doubled the number of new CPAs since 2001. For example, the number of new CPAs has increased from 505 in 1999 to 917 in 2015.

Table 2.2 depicts the number of auditors employed by each audit unit category as of March 2013. There are about 16,000 actively licensed CPAs in Korea. Of these, 55.7 percent are employed by audit firms while the others are sole practitioners (36.5 percent) or CPAs in small offices (7.8 percent).

Korean auditors argue that audit fees are significantly lower than those in the US, Japan, and China. Table 2.3 shows the trend in the number of audit clients, average assets of audit clients, and audit fees. An interesting observation is that both the number of auditees and their sizes increase over time but audit fees remain relatively flat. One interpretation of this is that auditors work efficiently and thus make audit fees competitive. An alternative interpretation is that

Table 2.2 Number of licensed CPAs by auditor category

Category	March 2011		March 2012		March 2013	
	Number of auditors	%	Number of auditors	%	Number of auditors	%
Audit firm	7,956	56.5	8,468	56.5	8,888	55.7
Audit team	1,175	8.4	1,208	8.1	1,237	7.8
Individuals	4,939	35.1	5,310	35.4	5,820	36.5
Total	14,070	100.0	14,986	100.0	15,945	100.0

Source: FSC

audit firms compete for a larger number of auditees (or for a greater amount of client assets) and are willing to compromise audit quality (i.e., using the same level of time and efforts to audit an increased amount of client assets). Consistent with the latter view, audit fees per audit hour have been uniformly decreasing over the past 10 years (see Figure 2.3). A sharp decline of audit fees per hour since 2011 coincides with the transition to IFRS.

Table 2.3 Number of clients, asset sizes and audit fees

Year	2009	2010	2011	2012	2013	Percentage change over five years
Number of auditees	15,747	17,868	18,287	19,642	20,472	*30%*
Average Assets (billion KRW)	202	197	214	216	238	*18%*
Audit Fees (million KRW)	28.0	26.4	27.7	27.8	28.0	*0%*

Source: FSC

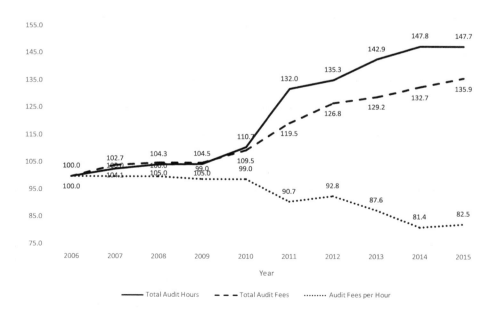

Figure 2.3   Audit hours, audit fees and audit fees per hour, 2006–2015

Table 2.4 shows an increasing trend of lawsuits filed against auditors. This in part reflects the aftermath of the global financial crisis of 2007–2008 and related corporate failures. However, the trend also mirrors the government's attempts to protect investors at the enforcement and litigation levels.

Additionally, Figure 2.4 shows an increasing time-series trend of inactive CPAs, implying that the merits of partitioning in assurance services might have decreased over time. This interpretation makes sense when one also looks at the downward trend of the number of uniform CPA test takers in Figure 2.5. Overall, all these statistics imply that the net benefits for an average CPA might have decreased, suggesting that the working environment has become unfavorable to the audit profession.

Regulatory requirements

ISA and revised ISA

In 1999, Korea first adopted the International Standards on Auditing (ISA), issued by the International Auditing and Assurance Standards Board, to replace the local audit standards. Korea also adopted the revised ISA in 2014 to meet the changing audit environment and to

Table 2.4 Number of lawsuits filed against auditors

Court	Year								
	2006	2007	2008	2009	2010	2011	2012	2013	Sum
Daegu Regional				1					1
Supreme	2		1						3
Busan Regional						1			1
Seoul High		1			1		1	2	5
Seoul Southern Regional				1	1	1			3
Seoul Eastern Regional						1			1
Seoul Western Regional				2			1	1	4
Seoul Central Regional		1	1	2	4	10	7	1	26
Total	2	2	2	6	6	13	9	4	44

Source: KICPA

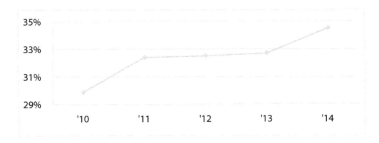

Figure 2.4   Percentage of inactive CPAs

Source: FSC

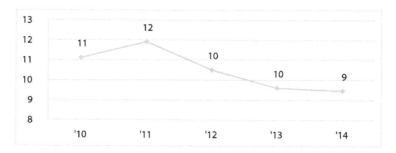

Figure 2.5 Number (in thousands) of uniform CPA test applicants
Source: FSC

improve audit quality. An important feature of the revised ISA is to encourage a long-form report that can increase the legal liability of auditors. Unlike in the UK, which had already adopted a long-form report, the Korean legal system recognizes the auditor's legal liability to a third party. In many Western countries, audit contracts are voluntary contracts between auditors and clients, and an auditor can terminate a contract if the client is not cooperative. However, in Korea audits are mandatory by law, and audit opinions are often crucial to a firm's listing or delisting status. Thus, terminating an engagement with a client is easier said than done in Korea, given the need for the acquisition of new clients and the retention of existing clients. Nevertheless, the FSS plans to introduce a long-form report including "key audit matters."

Auditor conformity in the consolidated financial statements of large business groups

Korea has one unique audit feature for consolidated financial statements. When two auditors engage in the audits of the consolidated financial statements of a large business group, the primary auditor, who provides the audit opinion in the consolidated financial statements, has the option to separately disclose its own legal liability and that of the other auditor. This is not the case in other ISA jurisdictions.

Unique regulatory experiments

Korea adopted mandatory auditor rotation rules in 2004 and, subsequently, abandoned the rules in 2010. Mandatory auditor rotation was introduced to resolve the auditor independence problem associated with long auditor tenure. The rationale is that if a long-term auditor–client relationship induces the auditor to compromise its independence, the mandatory rotation of auditors will improve audit quality by enhancing auditor independence. Many researchers explored evidence supporting the claimed benefits of the rules, but most failed to find such evidence (e.g., Kwon *et al.*, 2014).

In addition, Korea currently has auditor designation and retention rules in effect. The FSS *designates* an auditor to a specific client for the following cases: No auditor appointed at the end of the audit engagement period, inappropriate auditor changes, the FSS review cases, high-risk firms in terms of weak financial position and performance, and private firms planning IPOs. Studies provide evidence that auditor designation improves audit quality by lowering abnormal accruals, increasing conservatism and market reaction to earnings announcements (e.g., Kim and Yi 2009). In contrast, the rule requiring auditor retention for the first three years is intended to enhance auditor independence by discouraging opinion shopping by clients. However, commentators argue that this rule works against auditors in that the rule forces auditors to provide an audit opinion even when auditors should walk away by exercising an exit option. Given that the audit is not so effective in the early stage of the learning curve, the auditor retention rule may diminish rather than enhance the audit quality, especially in the first-year audit (Ji *et al.*, 2006). Moreover, some clients may exploit the rule to obtain a discount on audit fees (i.e., lowballing).[12]

Disclosures/others

The FSS requires audit firms to provide annual reports that include various audit firm characteristics regarding financial status, human capital, and client characteristics. Thus, external users can assess the resource constraints and monitoring capacities of audit firms.

Auditees should disclose both audit fees (along with other non-audit service fees) and audit hours in their annual reports. New disclosure rules, implemented since 2015, require the breakdown of audit hours into partner audit hours, rank-specific audit hours (i.e., directors, managers, associates, etc.), and quality control review hours at the client level. This requirement also includes the disclosure of hours spent for each audit function (i.e., planning, field hours, review, etc.)

Since 2015, all publicly listed companies should file preaudit financial statements to the Korea Exchange (the major stock exchange in Korea), even though they are not yet publicly disclosed. Future research may use the data to assess what adjustments auditors actually make in the audit process.

IFRS and audit effectiveness

After the adoption of IFRS in 2011, the audit focus shifted from individual financial statements to consolidated financial statements. The focus on the consolidated financial statements, along with the expanded disclosure requirement in IFRS, dramatically increased audit hours. However, the rise in audit fees fell short of the rise in audit hours, resulting in decreased audit fees per hour. These factors not only reduced audit quality but also increased audit risk.

The adoption of IFRS also changed the importance of the quality control group (or the review group) in audit firms. Prior to the adoption of the IFRS, each quality control group had only one or two members. The number has increased to about 30 staff members since IFRS adoption. The adoption of the IFRS has also increased the dependence of local audit firms on the global networks. Overall, these factors appear to have contributed to audits that are more effective.

Controlling owners, management, and audit committee

Controlling owners

Many Korean business groups, the so-called *chaebols*, have controlling owners among founders and their family members. Using convoluted cascades or stock pyramiding schemes, these owners typically exercise significant voting rights (in many cases, more than 50 percent), whereas their cash flow rights are only fractional (in many cases, less than 15 percent). Therefore, there is rare traditional agency problem between controlling owners and management agents (the type I agency problem) in many Korean firms. Instead, the (noncontrolling) outside shareholders of these companies suffer from the type II agency problem (e.g., tunneling or expropriation by controlling shareholders). Because these private benefits of control are huge, controlling owners and management have weak incentives to increase the monitoring power of external auditors or audit committees.

In addition, Korean companies have been dependent on bank loans as their financing sources (owing mainly to the main banking tradition from German/Japanese institutions), rather than relying on the fixed-income or equity securities markets. This stems from the tradition of project selection by the government and the government's preference for corporations with proven records for its capital rationing. Thus, except for a few truly global players, who are currently listed on the US and Japanese capital markets, as well as some IT companies that were established during the IT boom in the early 2000s, Korean companies have not benefited from the capital market reward for transparent accounting (e.g., a low cost of capital). Overall, these factors lead to weak incentives to improve accounting transparency.

Management

Tenure for senior management is relatively short in Korea. Except in cases where chief executive officers (CEOs) are controlling owners, most corporations have internally promoted CEOs with three-year renewable terms. Therefore, CEOs seeking another term face strong incentives to manage earnings. In addition, Korean judicial authorities are quite lenient on criminal charges against white-collar crimes, especially for the management of large business groups (Choi *et al.* 2016). For example, Mr. Woo-Choong Kim, the founder and CEO of the Daewoo Group, was charged with masterminding an accounting fraud of 43 billion US dollars, but he served only two years in prison and walked out with a special pardon from the president of Korea. As a whole, these factors contribute to weak incentives for accounting transparency at the firm level.

Audit committee

As discussed above, neither the controlling owners nor management has strong incentives to improve accounting transparency. Thus, the audit committee (AC) system, which was introduced by a series of reforms following the 1997 financial crisis, does not function well. Ms. Yu Kyoung Kim, the KPMG Audit Committee Institute leader, points out the following weaknesses of audit committees in Korean firms (Kim 2016).

Independence: Currently, the FSC advises only financial institutions to adopt the requirements for independence, the limitation of tenure, and related AC disclosures. However, this advice should be extended to all listed companies.

Expertise: Currently, the FSC requires only financial institutions to satisfy the qualification requirements for AC members, internal audit team formation, and access to internal management information. But this requirement should be extended to all listed companies.

Engagement with external auditors: Currently, the AC does not fully exercise the power of attorney in terms of audit engagement (i.e., auditor selection and audit hour/fee determination). An amendment plan to force the power to belong to the AC has been drifting into the National Assembly (the legislative body in Korea) since 2014.

Liability: There was recently the first court ruling to acknowledge the liability of AC members in accounting fraud. The problem is, however, that the AC members in this case did not have proper support from management and access to corporate resources, and thus could not function as expected.

Overall, controlling owners and management have little incentive to build a strong AC and thus tend to fill the committee with close friends, alumni and former colleagues. As a result, the AC does not have the independence, expertise, and skill sets required for effective AC functions.

Regulators and investors

Regulators

Regulators appear to have two conflicting motives regarding IFRS implementation. On the one hand, both the FSC and the FSS would like to strongly enforce the IFRS so that Korean companies improve financial reporting quality and reduce the cost of capital. Both agencies experimented with various accounting and auditing policy options in this regard (e.g., auditor retention, designation, and rotation rules). Reacting to the demands of local investors, they also require companies to present operating income as a timeline (which the IFRS do not require) and to disclose contracting information in detail for the percentage-of-completion method. At the same time, both agencies actively participated in international regulatory meetings to improve collaboration with foreign capital market regulators.

On the other hand, however, neither agency does not yet completely respect companies' and auditors' own judgments in the accounting and auditing process because financial accounting is regarded as part of the legal system. The FSS still reviews financial accounting cases and uses "no-action letters" to guide local accounting practices. The FSS also works with the KASB to provide local IFRS interpretations on important accounting issues. A problem is that both the FSC and the FSS are regulatory bodies on financial systems and their focus is, in many cases, biased toward prudent regulation for financial institutions (see the detachable warrant case above). The agencies' involvement in accounting interpretations thus exposes them to the political influences of interest groups (see the revenue recognition case of apartment complex construction projects above).

Moreover, the capacity of the FSS in reviewing the annual reports of all listed companies on a regular basis is quite limited. The number of review and inspection teams is fewer than 50 in total. According to 2015 statistics, the FSS reviewed and inspected only 3 percent of listed companies annually. In other words, each firm can expect to receive a regular review from the FSS about every 30 years. This resource constraint is in stark contrast with the resources deployed by the US Public Company Accounting Oversight Board and the Japanese Certified Public Accountants and Auditing Oversight Board. Combined with weak incentives for controlling owners, management, and ACs, this low capacity of ex post monitoring reduces the quality of enforcement.

Investors

Han *et al.* (2016) assessed the capital globalization of Korean firms after the adoption of IFRS. They used a survey instrument and reported the following responses:

1   More foreign funds flew into small KOSDAQ (the Korean equivalent of NASDAQ) firms after the IFRS adoption (potentially owing to less information asymmetry for small firms).
2   There was no evidence supporting the increased raising of capital from overseas markets.[13]
3   The usefulness of financial reporting in terms of international comparability and reliability has increased.
4   The Korea discount (i.e., the systematic underpricing of Korean stocks) has been mitigated.

In contrast to this survey result, Song and Jeong (2016) found no discernible pattern in the empirical proxies of accounting quality and market perception (i.e., earnings persistence, abnormal accruals, the earnings response coefficient, and the cost of capital) over the period of 2006–2015 surrounding the IFRS adoption. Therefore, whereas the market participants and investors see benefits of IFRS adoption in Korea, there is no strong evidence to support the claimed benefits.

Another survey by the KASB (2015) assesses the costs and benefits of IFRS adoption in Korea for both preparers and investors. About a half of the respondents stated that the costs of IFRS adoption exceeded the corresponding benefits. Only 10 percent of survey respondents agreed that the benefits were greater than the costs. Likewise, most respondents did not observe significant changes in accounting transparency, creditworthiness (including credit ratings), the cost of capital, and the usefulness of accounting information following the IFRS adoption in Korea. Overall, there is no strong evidence that investors and market participants are rewarded from IFRS adoption in Korea.

The Case of Daewoo Shipbuilding & Marine Engineering

Daewoo Shipbuilding & Marine Engineering (DSME), which, along with Hyundai Heavy Industries and Samsung Heavy Industries, was one of Korea's top three shipbuilders, reported losses of about three billion US dollars in the second quarter of 2015. After the announcement of the loss, the company experienced "stock price crash" over two weeks. As of July 2016, both the Prosecutors' Office and the FSS are closely investigating the case. The former CEO, Mr. Jae-Ho Ko, was arrested for committing accounting fraud of about 4.6 billion US dollars from 2012 to 2014. Several other managers and external auditors of the company are under investigation for participating in the accounting fraud. This case clearly demonstrates the following weaknesses of the accounting value chain in securing transparency.

Controlling owners: Although the Korea Development Bank (KDB), a government-owned bank, held the controlling ownership of DSME, it did not properly monitor the management of DSME owing to its lack of accountability. Both government officials and KDB officers were interested in creating new positions in DSME for their former colleagues, but never closely monitored the performance of DSME.

Management: Since the CEO's tenure was only three years and their reappointment was based on the size of new contracts (not profitability), the incumbent CEO focused on winning new contracts and increasing expected sales. Internal accountants used the percentage-of-completion method to record revenues even when contracts were highly risky and the costs were unprojectable.

Audit committee: AC members lacked independence, expertise, and incentives to oversee the financial reporting of DSME effectively. They held meetings every few months, but did not check the effectiveness of internal controls or question the accounting numbers behind the projects.

External auditors: The Seoul office of Deloitte audited DSME during the fraud period but never issued a warning for the abnormally profitable DSME when other similar shipbuilders reported a sequence of losses. Only after DSME's financial troubles emerged to the public, in March 2016, did DSME release its restated financial statements. Deloitte argued that they could not request the restatement in a timely manner because they did not receive supporting evidence from DSME. The market watchers viewed this restatement as a preempting excuse for future litigation.

Regulators and standard setters: The FSS failed to detect the high risk of earnings manipulation in the shipbuilding industry. The FSC overreacted to the DSME case by requiring additional disclosures over and above the current IFRS requirements for the percentage-of-completion method. In doing so, the FSC required engineering/procurement/construction companies to disclose strategic information, which cannot be effectively enforced by the FSS.

Investors: Investors are the true losers in this case because all related parties, such as controlling owners, management, AC, auditors, and regulators, did not function well in protecting the interests of outside investors.

This case shows that accounting transparency cannot be achieved by simply adopting high-quality accounting standards. As many prior academic studies indicate, accounting quality is a function of the incentives of managers and controlling owners, the monitoring power of ACs and auditors, high-quality accounting standards, and the enforcement mechanisms, including regulators and the legal system. The DSME case shows that, although Korea has adopted high-quality accounting standards such as IFRS, all other factors need significant improvement to secure transparent accounting.

Conclusion

Korea adopted the IFRS successfully in 2011, but still remains at the bottom of the global rankings for accounting transparency. This irony arises from the weak incentives of accounting constituencies to improve transparency. First, constituencies have a weak demand for transparent accounting for contracting and valuation purposes. Accounting did not evolve as a contracting device in Korea, but was introduced for the government's credit rationing. Because Korea pursued economic growth through the government's coordinated planning rather than relying on the market mechanisms, the role of accounting for contracting and valuation is quite limited. Second, controlling owners and managers receive few benefits from transparent accounting. Korean companies were dependent on the main banks (through government intervention) as their sources of finance rather than on equity markets. As a result, controlling owners of large companies did not enjoy or experience the capital market reward for accounting transparency through the low cost of capital and a high level of liquidity.

The market liberalization in the early 1990s and the financial crisis in the late 1990s substantially changed the accounting environment in Korea. Both the IMF and the World Bank, which bailed out Korea during the crisis, strongly encouraged Korea to adopt many financial reforms, including accounting reforms. This set the ground for the independent standard setter (the KASB), IFRS adoption, and advanced institutions including ACs. However, the ex post effect of new rules and regulations is quite limited because reporting entities do not feel a strong need for accounting transparency and all monitoring mechanisms do not function effectively.

Accounting transparency in Korea is currently at the crossroads. Accounting transparency is key to financial development and economic growth, but the adoption of high-quality standards cannot on its own guarantee accounting transparency in Korea. Hence, we recommend four immediate changes to improve transparency. First, the cost of committing accounting fraud for both controlling owners and managers should increase significantly compared to the current level of the cost. Second, AC members should have all the rights to oversee internal controls and external audits, accompanied by increased legal liabilities and compensation. Third, regulators should not interrupt the judgments of preparers and auditors in the financial reporting and auditing process. Regulators should maintain the congruence of the Korean IFRS to the IFRS in their original form. Finally, regulators should increase their ex post review power to the level of US and Japanese regulators.

In an exhaustive historical survey, Soll (2014) showed that the economic success of a society is sustainable if and only if transparency, accountability, and good government work together. We all know that without political will and imagination, financial accountability remains toothless. South Korea is a democratic country. Her political will and imagination for transparency and accountability will be determined by her people. Therefore, the real question for the Korean people is whether or not they really believe and act on the presumption that prosperity only builds upon transparency and accountability.

Notes

1 Lucas (1993) describes the continuing transformation of Korean society as "a miracle." Similarly, Sharma (2012) ranks Korea as "the gold medalist" in terms of her fast growth and accurate economic data.
2 The WEF's 2015 report ranked South Korea as seventy-second in terms of auditing and accounting practices among the 141 countries surveyed. Similarly, IMD's 2016 global competitiveness report placed South Korea at the bottom of the 61 countries surveyed.
3 In contrast, we use "accounting" to describe activities surrounding an accounting system.
4 See Cho and Jeong (2011) for the detailed chronology of Korean GAAP development. They classify its history into seven stages: 1) before the influence of modern Western culture (pre-1876); 2) the introduction of modern Western culture after a commercial treaty with Japan (1876) but before the annexation by Japan (1910); 3) under the coercive rule of Japan (1910–1945); 4) after liberation from Japan, during the Korean War, and up to the first Korean accounting standards (1945–1958); 5) the era of multiple accounting standards (1959–1980); 6) the period of single accounting standards (1981–1998); and 7) after the financial crisis (1999–2010).
5 Woo-Choong Kim founded the Daewoo Group in 1967 and made it Korea's second-largest conglomerate through a series of mergers and acquisitions, aided by the Korean government. The aggressive M&As led to a severe liquidity shortage in the aftermath of the 1997 financial crisis. Kim committed accounting fraud to the value of 41 trillion won (US$43.4 billion) during the crisis period.
6 See KASB and FSS (2013) for the details of migration from the local Korean GAAP to the IFRS.
7 See comments from Yoon (2014), the leader of the PwC Seoul Assurance Group.
8 Note that the External Audit Law requires the following types of firms to be audited by CPAs: 1) companies whose assets exceed 12 billion Korean won (approximately 10 million US dollars); 2) companies whose assets exceed seven billion Korean won, with either a total debt of seven billion Korean won or at least 300 employees; and 3) publicly traded companies or private companies planning initial public offerings (IPOs).
9 Mr. Wayne Upton, chairman of the IFRS Interpretations Committee, made this point at various meetings.
10 This part is based largely on conversations with local practitioners.
11 IAS 18.14 states that:
    Revenue from the sale of goods shall be recognized when all the following conditions have been satisfied: (a) the entity has transferred to the buyer the significant risks and rewards of ownership of the goods; (b) the entity retains neither continuing managerial involvement to the degree usually associated with ownership nor effective control over the goods sold; (c) the amount of revenue can be measured reliably; (d) it is probable that the economic benefits associated with the transaction will flow to the entity; and (e) the costs incurred or to be incurred in respect of the transaction can be measured reliably.
12 Prior studies indicate the first-year audit quality is the worst owing to the learning curve effect (e.g., Johnson et al., 2002; Myers et al., 2003). The first-year audit is also characterized by low audit fees owing to the bidding competition (Craswell and Francis, 1999; Ghosh and Lustgarten, 2006). To exploit the cheap initial audit and lax monitoring in the first year, clients may prefer to switch auditors every three years.
13 Similarly, the survey reveals that Korean firms cross-listed to the US stock markets were exempted from the 20-F reconciliation requirement if they submitted IFRS-based financial statements to the SEC, but the cost of financial reporting increased after the adoption of the IFRS.

References

Cho, I.S. and Jeong, S.W. (2011) Chapter 6: Republic of Korea. In G. Previts and P. Walton (Eds), *A Global History of Accounting, Financial Reporting and Public Policy: Part C: Asia and Oceania*. Sydney: University of Sydney.

Choi, H., Kang., H-G., Kim, W., Lee, C. and Park, J. (2016) Too big to jail? Company status and judicial bias in an emerging market. *Corporate Governance: An International Review*, *24*(2), 85–104.

Craswell, A.T. and Francis, J.R. (1999) Pricing initial audit engagements: A test of competing theories. *The Accounting Review*, *74*(2), 201–216.

Financial Supervisory Service (FSS) (2013) *Review Statistics*. Seoul: FSS.

Ghosh, A. and Lustgarten, S. (2006) Pricing of initial audit engagements by large and small audit firms. *Contemporary Accounting Research*, *23*(2), 333–368.

Han, B., Yi, J., Park, I-H. and Seo, Y. (2016) *IFRS Adoption and Capital Globalization in Korea. KASB Research Report No. 38*. Seoul: KASB.

Ji, H.M., Park, H.J. and Moon, S.H. (2006) Auditor independence under auditor non-switching system. *Study on Accounting, Taxation & Auditing*, *44*, 1–26 (in Korean).

Johnson, V.E., Khurana, I.K. and Reynolds, J.K. (2002) Audit-firm tenure and the quality of financial reports. *Contemporary Accounting Research*, *19*(4), 637–660.

Korea Accounting Standards Board (KASB) (2015) *Costs and Benefits of IFRS Adoption in Korea – Preparers' Perspectives*. Seoul: KASB.

Korea Accounting Standards Board (KASB) and Financial Supervisory Service (FSS) (2013) *IFRS Adoption and Implementation in Korea and the Lessons Learned*. Seoul: KASB and FSS.

Kim, J-B. and Yi, C.H. (2009) Does auditor designation by the regulatory authority improve audit quality? Evidence from Korea. *Journal of Accounting and Public Policy*, *28*(3), 207–230.

Kim, Y.K. (2016) *Is It Possible to Have the Audit Committee from Advanced Countries Work for Korea?* Seoul: KPMG.

Kwon, S.Y., Lim, Y. and Simnett, R. (2014) The effect of mandatory audit firm rotation on audit quality and audit fees: Empirical evidence from the Korean audit market. *Auditing: A Journal of Practice & Theory*, *33*(4), 167–196.

Lucas, R.E., Jr. (1993) Making a miracle. *Econometrica*, *61*(2), 251–272.

Myers, J.N., Myers, L.A. and Omer, T.C. (2003) Exploring the term of the auditor–client relationship and the quality of earnings: A case for mandatory auditor rotation? *The Accounting Review*, *78*(3), 779–799.

Sharma, R. (2012) *Breakout Nations: In Pursuit of the Next Economic Miracles*. New York: W.W. Norton.

Song, M.S. and Jeong, J.H. (2016) IFRS adoption and its impact on financial reporting quality. KASB Working Paper. Seoul: Korea Accounting Standards Board.

Soll, J. (2014) *The Reckoning: Financial Accountability and the Rise and Fall of Nations*. New York: Basic.

Yoon, H-C. (2014) Strengthening Role of Audit Committee. *Korea Times*, March 23, 2014.

3

De jure adoption and *de facto* implementation of FV accounting in China[1]

Guoqiang Hu, Bing Huang, Jason Xiao,
Qin Xu and Dehui Yu

Introduction

This chapter aims to examine the extent of fair value accounting (FVA) adoption in the new Chinese Enterprise Accounting Standards (CEAS), issued in 2006, and its implementation in practice in China's listed firms. Following a study by Peng and Bewley (2009), we use the term "adoption" to refer to the extent to which FVA is adopted in the 2006 EASs (i.e., *de jure* adoption), and the term "implementation" to refer to the extent that the adopted FVA in the 2006 CEAS have been effectively implemented (i.e., *de facto* implementation).

Based on the setting of China, a stream of recent studies empirically investigates the economic consequences of FVA adoption. For example, He *et al.* (2012) document several unintended effects of mandatory IFRS adoption in China by focusing on FVA adoption. Li Jing and Li (2010) find evidence on the relevance of FV measurement for Chinese commercial banks. Qu and Zhang (2015) explore the suitability of FVA in China and do not find evidence that FVA contributes to the improvement of value-relevance of earnings and book value owing to IFRS convergence and the consequent application of FVA. Closely related to our study, Zhang *et al.* (2012) use a qualitative approach to explore the implementation of FVA in China as part of a global process of neoliberalization and financialization of political and economic systems, and argue that FVA institutionalizes a technical commitment to the ideals of neoliberalism. Zhang *et al.* (2012) argue that FVA practice is imbued with assumptions about the state and the market that have little bearing on the realities of Chinese capital markets. Peng and Bewley (2010) investigate the implementation of FVA in China using aggregated data in government reports, and their findings are based on preliminary outcomes two years after CEAS implementation. Peng *et al.* (2013) provide a theory-based analysis of the process that eventually led to the acceptance of FVA in China. These studies suggest that China's institutions are in many respects incompatible with FVA, which thus causes unintended economic consequences (He *et al.*, 2012). This study attempts to expand the literature by investigating the implementation issues of FVA in practice using hand-collected data from annual reports of China's listed firms.

To pursue our research objectives, we first identify the adoption of FVA in 38 CEAS issued in 2006 by the Ministry of Finance (MoF), China's standards setter. We find that more than 23 of the 38 CEAS require or permit FVA. However, our observation shows:

1) that the adoption of FVA for investment property is *voluntary*, that is, firms can opt to use the cost model or the FV model to subsequently measure investment property when there is an active property market and reliable market prices and other relevant information of identical or similar property can be continuously obtained; 2) that the use of FVA is *partially mandatory*, that is, firms are required to use FV measurement and disclose FV information in particular circumstances for debt restructurings, revenue, government grants, leases, and identifiable tangible and intangible assets acquired through business combinations not under common control; 3) FVA is *conditionally mandatory* for biological assets and exchanges of nonmonetary assets, and they should be measured using the cost model unless any well-established evidence indicates that the FV of relevant assets can be obtained in a reliable and continuous manner; and 4) FVA is *mandatory* for such assets or transactions as share-based payments, enterprise annuity funds, financial instruments, the transfer of financial instruments, and the recoverable amounts in asset impairment tests.

We then empirically investigate the implementation of FVA in practice by China's listed firms, using a hand-collected data set on FV measurement and disclosure extracted from the annual reports of listed financial and nonfinancial firms for the period between 2007 and 2011. We obtain several findings by analyzing this data set. First, both financial and nonfinancial firms complied well with the mandatory or partially mandatory requirements of CEAS in their use of FV to measure assets, liabilities, or transactions (ALTs), but they disclosed little FV information in the notes to financial statements. Meanwhile, while FV measurement is mandatory, the sample firms were more likely to recognize impairment losses on fixed assets than on intangible assets or goodwill, probably because the FV of intangible assets and goodwill is more difficult to obtain and measure. Second, although firms are required to conditionally use FVA to measure ALTs, such as the exchange of nonmonetary assets, few firms had such ALTs and, if they did have them, they preferred not to use FV to measure them. Third, few sample firms (especially nonfinancial firms) preferred the FV model for the subsequent measurement of investment property even though they are allowed to opt to use it when reliable market prices and other relevant information of identical or similar assets can be continuously obtained. Even if they adopted FV measurement, the quality of their FV information disclosure was low. Fourth, the sample firms largely depended on external asset appraisers to estimate the FV (Level 3 FV) of nonfinancial assets or liabilities. Some even directly used the carrying value to represent the FV of relevant assets or liabilities. In contrast, most firms used Level 1 FV, represented by quoted prices of identical assets or liabilities in the active markets, or Level 3 FV, such as an appraisal value from asset appraisers, as the FV of financial assets or liabilities. Moreover, the firms also disclosed more detailed FV information on financial assets or liabilities. Finally, the impact of FVA implementation on the financial statements of sample nonfinancial firms was insignificant between 2007 and 2011 except for a few firms. In contrast, the financial impact of FVA implementation in measuring financial instruments was considerately more significant for financial firms.

Overall, these findings indicate that FVA is widely applied not only in CEAS but also in practice in Chinese accounting. However, while the level of implementation of FVA for nonfinancial instruments by listed firms was low, it was relatively high for financial instruments. We believe that the results indicate important implications for standards setters and the regulators of listed firms in the country.

The remainder of this chapter is organized as follows. The next section outlines the adoption of FVA in the 2006 CEAS. The third section describes our data sources and research methods. In the fourth and fifth sections, we analyze the extent of implementation of FVA by China's nonfinancial listed firms and financial listed firms, respectively. The final section concludes this study with a discussion of our findings and their policy implications.

The adoption of FVA in China's accounting standards

The development of FVA in China

The first adoption of FVA in China can be traced back to 1998, when the *Enterprise Accounting Standard – Debt Restructurings* was released by the Ministry of Finance (MoF). Before this, historical cost was the dominant measurement basis in Chinese accounting systems, whereas FV was strictly prohibited. Since the reform and opening-up policy initiated in 1979, China's economy has experienced rapid development and integrated more fully with international markets. The Shanghai Stock Exchange (SHSE) and the Shenzhen Stock Exchange (SZSE) were established in 1990 and 1991, respectively. These developments presented challenges to the traditional accounting systems based purely on historical cost (Peng and Bewley, 2009). In order to meet the needs of economic development and bring Chinese accounting standards more into line with IFRS, the MoF successively issued 10 accounting standards between 1997 and 2000. Among these standards, FVA was required in *Debt Restructurings* (1998), *Investments* (1998), and *Non-monetary Transactions* (1999). For example, the debt restructurings standard defines FV as the amount for which an asset could be exchanged, or a liability settled, between knowledgeable, willing parties in an arm's length transaction. The standard further stipulates that assets surrendered or received by debtors or creditors in debt restructurings should be measured at FV, and, meanwhile, any gain or loss owing to debt restructuring should be recorded as net income in the current period. Additionally, FVA was indirectly used in impairment tests of assets in 1998.

However, these three standards were hastily revised and their application of FVA was suspended in 2000, only one year after the release of the nonmonetary transactions standard and two years after the release of the debt restructurings and investment standards. The main reason for this abandonment was that many Chinese listed firms used FV for earnings management, and the inactive markets and a shortage of valuation experts made it difficult to measure FV (Feng, 2001). In a speech to the Symposium of the Issues on Accounting and Finance under the New Economic Environment in 2002, Feng (2003), an official of the MoF, observed that lacking active markets in China at present caused extreme difficulties for FVA adoption in practice; as the use of FV largely depends on the subjective judgment and estimates of accountants, the reliability of FV information was questioned, and FVA provided substantial room for enterprises to manipulate earnings. Indeed, Wang (2005) found that the adoption of FVA in nonmonetary transactions caused significant earnings manipulation, but the abuse of FV was promptly inhibited by the revised standard on nonmonetary transactions where FV was replaced by carrying value. Dai *et al.* (2007) provided evidence on earnings management in accounting for impairment of assets.

Nonetheless, in the 2000 Chinese Enterprise Accounting System, which entirely abandoned the use of FVA, the MoF further expanded the scope of asset impairment tests from only four types of asset (that is, inventories, accounts receivables, and short-term and long-term investments) to virtually all assets except cash. Despite the broader move away from FV, the use of asset impairment tests illustrates the continuing convergence of Chinese accounting standards with international ones (Peng and Bewley, 2010).

When China entered the WTO in 2001, the resulting increase in foreign direct investment and cross-border trade created a stronger demand for convergence with international standards. On November 8, 2005, China Accounting Standards Committee (CEASC) representatives signed a convergence strategy agreement with the IASB. The MoF then issued the 2006 CEAS based on the IFRS on February 15, 2006. The 2006 CEAS consist of a revised conceptual framework and 38 specific standards, taking effect for listed firms from January 1, 2007, and for nonlisted financial firms and central and local state-owned enterprises (SOEs) from January 1, 2008. Other enterprises were also encouraged to apply the 2006 CEAS. A major feature of the 2006 CEAS is that FV measurement or disclosure, which was previously banned in the Enterprise Accounting System stipulated by the MoF in 2000, became required or permitted in over 20 standards. The 2006 CEAS covered almost all aspects of FVA, including initial measurement, subsequent measurement, impairment recognition, and disclosures.

Nevertheless, "[c]onsidering the realistic situation of an emerging market and transition economy, the [2006] CEAS mainly adopt historical cost accounting and set strict conditions for the application of FVA" (MoF, 2010). The restrictions or conditions are set out in the specific standards. For example, the FV model is allowed for the subsequent measurement of investment property and biological assets only when the FV can be continuously and reliably obtained. The 2006 CEAS also prohibits the reversal of impairment losses of fixed assets, intangible assets, and other assets.

The adoption of FVA in the 2006 CEAS

As noted above, FVA is required or permitted in over 20 standards of the 2006 CEAS. There are four forms of *de jure* adoption across standards, including voluntary, conditionally mandatory, partially mandatory, and mandatory adoption.

First, voluntary adoption of FVA is allowed. That is, a firm can opt to use FV to measure some assets or transactions. For example, a firm can use the FV model for subsequent measurement when there is conclusive evidence that the FV of an investment property can be reliably determinable on a continuing basis (CEAS 3 (*Investment Property*)). However, when the FV model is chosen, the firm is also required to disclose the basis and method used to determine the FV and the impact of FV changes on earnings.

Second, the adoption of FVA may be conditionally mandatory, that is, relevant assets or liabilities should be measured at FV when specified conditions are met. For example, when an exchange of nonmonetary assets meet both of the following conditions, the cost of the asset received should be measured at FV plus any related taxes, and the difference between the FV used and the carrying amount of the asset given up should be recognized in profit or loss for the current period: 1) the exchange transaction has commercial substance and 2) the FV of either the asset received or the asset given up can be reliably measured (CEAS 7 (*Exchange of Non-monetary Assets*)).

Third, the adoption of FVA can be partially mandatory. This means that a firm must use FV measurement for some transactions in particular circumstances. For instance, when a debt is repaid by a transfer of noncash asset(s) to the creditor in a debt restructuring, the debtor should recognize the difference between the carrying amount of the debt and the fair value of the noncash asset(s) transferred in profit or loss for the current period (CEAS 12 (*Debt Restructurings*)). Similarly, an enterprise shall determine the cost of business combination at FV when the business combination does not involve enterprises under common control (CEAS 20 (*Business Combinations*)).

Finally, if the adoption of FV is mandatory, it requires a firm to use FV, rather than other measurements, to measure relevant assets or liabilities. For example, financial assets or liabilities shall be initially measured at FV according to CEAS 22 (*Recognition and Measurement of Financial Instruments*). Similarly, liquid financial products that are acquired in the operation of an enterprise annuity fund should be measured at FV on initial acquisition and on subsequent valuations (CEAS 11 (*Enterprise Annuity Fund*)).

Table 3.1 shows the adoption of FVA in the 38 specific CEAS as of December 31, 2013. Two new CEAS issued by the MoF after 2013 are related to the adoption of FV accounting but are not included in our analysis. The MoF released CEAS 39 (*Fair Value Measurement*) in January 2014, which became effective on July 1, 2014, for entities adopting CEAS. CEAS 39 is based on IFRS 13 (*Fair Value Measurement*), which standardizes the definition of FV, clarifies valuation techniques and the fair value hierarchy, and specifies the disclosures of relevant information of FV measurement. CEAS 41 (*Disclosure of Interests in Other Entities*), issued by the MoF in March 2014, stipulates that a business entity that becomes an investment entity shall disclose the effect of the change of status on the financial statements for the reporting period, including the total amount of FV, as of the date of change of status, of the subsidiaries that cease to be consolidated, and the total gain or loss related to the change of the total amount of FV. In addition, the MoF also released four revised accounting standards in 2014 that are related to FVA, that is, CEAS 2 (*Long-term Equity Investment*), CEAS 9 (*Employee Benefits*), CEAS 30 (*Presentation of Financial Statements*), and CEAS 37 (*Presentation of Financial Instruments*). However, the amendments do not affect the adoption of FVA in the four standards.

The overall adoption of FVA in EASs reported in Column (5) of Table 3.1 shows that 23 standards require or permit FV measurement or disclosure. Columns (1), (2), (3), and (4) indicate the extent of FV adoption in initial measurement, subsequent measurement, impairment tests, and disclosure, respectively.

Table 3.1 Adoption of FVA in the 2006 China Enterprise Accounting Standards

CEAS	(1) Initial measurement	(2) Subsequent measurement	(3) Impairment tests	(4) Disclosure	(5) Overall
CEAS 1 *Inventories*	PM				Yes
CEAS 2 *Long-term equity investments*	PM		M		Yes
CEAS 3 *Investment property*		V	CM	CM	Yes
CEAS 4 *Fixed assets*	PM	PM	M	PM	Yes
CEAS 5 *Biological assets*	PM	CM	M		Yes
CEAS 6 *Intangible assets*	PM	PM	M		Yes
CEAS 7 *Exchange of nonmonetary assets*	CM			CM	Yes
CEAS 8 *Impairment of assets*			M	M	Yes
CEAS 10 *Enterprise annuity fund*	M	M		M	Yes
CEAS 11 *Share-based payment*	M	M		M	Yes
CEAS 12 *Debt restructurings*	PM			M	Yes
CEAS 14 *Revenue*	PM				Yes
CEAS 16 *Government grants*	PM				Yes
CEAS 20 *Business combinations*	PM			PM	Yes
CEAS 21 *Leases*	PM			PM	Yes
CEAS 22 *Recognition and measurement of financial instruments*	M	PM	M	PM	Yes

CEAS 23 *Transfer of financial assets*	M	M			Yes
CEAS 24 *Hedging*	M	M			Yes
CEAS 27 *Extraction of petroleum and natural gas*		PM	PM		Yes
CEAS 30 *Presentation of financial statements*				M	Yes
CEAS 31 *Cash flow statements*				M	Yes
CEAS 37 *Presentation of financial instruments*				M	Yes
CEAS 38 *First-time adoption of EAS for Business enterprises*	M		M	M	Yes
Total (M/PM/CM/V)	17 (6/10/1/0)	10 (4/4/1/1)	9 (7/1/1/0)	14 (8/4/2/0)	23

Notes: M, PM, CM, and V indicate the four different levels of FVA adoption requirements across standards: mandatory, partially mandatory, conditionally mandatory, and voluntary.

Methodology and data

To capture the current situation of FVA implementation well, we collected data by hand on FV measurement and disclosure from the annual reports of a sample of listed financial and nonfinancial firms. The process of collecting data began with the identification of the adoption of FVA in initial measurement, subsequent measurement, impairment tests, and disclosures by going through all the 2006 CEAS and related application guidance issued during 2006–2012. Then we distinguished the four forms of FV adoption in specific 2006 CEAS: mandatory, partially mandatory, conditionally mandatory, and voluntary, as shown in Table 3.1. Finally, we designed two checklists for picking up data from the annual reports of the sample firms. After discussion by the research team members a few times and a trial data collection using 100 annual reports of five financial firms and 15 nonfinancial firms for 2007–2011, the two checklists were finalized.

We randomly selected 120 nonfinancial firms from 2,415 listed A-share firms that were listed as of December 31, 2011, and obtained 600 firm-year observations for 2007–2011. The sampling process and the industry distribution of the sample are shown in Panels A and B of Table 3.2, respectively. As shown in Panel C, our sample of financial firms included all listed A-share financial firms (making up 135 firm-year observations) as of December 31, 2011, excluding financial firms listed after 2007 because we wanted all sample firms to fall into the same time period. The annual reports of all sample firms for the sampling period were downloaded from www.cninfo.com.cn, a website on which listed firms publish their annual reports and other firm information as required by the China Securities Regulatory Commission (CSRC). From the annual reports, FV measurement and disclosure data were manually collected by one PhD student in accounting and three accounting lecturers at Chinese universities.

Implementation of FVA in listed Chinese nonfinancial firms

Based on the regulatory framework of FVA in China and hand-collected data from Chinese listed nonfinancial firms, this section first reports the extent of China's implementation

Table 3.2 Sample selection and distribution

Panel A: Listed nonfinancial firms	Number
Listed A-share firms on December 31, 2011	2,415
Minus: listed firms with special treatment or particular transfer (ST/PT) status	192
Listed financial firms	40
Delisted firms	34
Firms listed in the Small and Medium Enterprises Board (SMEB) and Growth Enterprises Board (GEB)	939
Firms listed after 2007	79
Listed firms used for random selection	1,131
Randomly selected firms	120
The total observations of listed nonfinancial firms for 2007–2011	600

Panel B: Distribution of sample listed nonfinancial firms by industry			
Industry	Obs	Industry	Obs
Farming, forestry, animal husbandry, and fishery (A)	1	Manufacture (C) Including:	54
Extraction (B)	7	Food and beverages (C0)	9
Electric power, steam and hot water generation and supply (D)	11	Textile, garment, leather, and feather (C1)	3
Construction (E)	1	Timber and furniture (C2)	0
Transportation and warehousing (F)	8	Paper and printing (C3)	0
Information technology (G)	7	Petroleum, chemical, rubber, and plastics (C4)	6
Wholesale and retail trade (H)	7	Electronic(C5)	3
Real estate (J)	18	Metallic and nonmetal (C6)	7
Social services (K)	2	Machinery, equipment, and instruments (C7)	19
Media and culture services (L)	1	Medicine and biological (C8)	7
Conglomerates (M)	3	Other manufacturing (C9)	0
Total	66	Total	54

Panel C: Listed financial firms	Number
Listed A-share financial firms on December 31, 2011	40
Minus: firms listed after 2007	13
Listed financial firms for data collection	27
Including: Banking (I01)	14
Insurance (I11)	3
Securities and Futures (I21)	8
Financial trusts (I31)	2
Total observations of listed financial firms for 2007–2011	135

of FVA in practice, including initial and subsequent measurement, impairment tests, and disclosure, in the first four parts. As FVA is widely adopted in CEAS 22 (*Recognition and Measurement of Financial Instruments*), CEAS 23 (*Transfer of Financial Assets*), CEAS 24 (*Hedging*), and CEAS 37 (*Presentation of Financial Instruments*), we focus on them in the fifth part of this section.

Use of FV for initial measurement

Implementation of the mandatory requirements of FV use for initial measurement

Apart from the financial instruments standards, three other standards require enterprises to use FV in initial measurement, that is, CEAS 10 (*Enterprise Annuity Fund*), CEAS 11 (*Share-Based Payment*), and their relevant requirements in CEAS 38 (*First-Time Adoption of Accounting Standards for Business Enterprises*).

Table 3.3 displays the descriptive statistics on the implementation of mandatory requirements of FV use for initial measurement in the 600 nonfinancial firm-year observations. We find that 56 out of the 600 firm-year observations presented the amounts of annuity funds in the notes to financial statements, involving 21 firms. This suggests that these firms established enterprise annuity fund schemes and recognized annuity funds. Further, four out of the 21 firms disclosed that they established annuity fund schemes but did not provide any detail about them. The level of disclosure was well below what is prescribed in the standards. According to CEAS 10 (*Enterprises Annuity Fund*), listed firms should disclose the following information in the notes: the kinds of investment, amounts, and methods for the recognition of the FV; the proportion of each kind of investment within total investment funds; and any other event that is likely to cause important influence on the investment value.

Table 3.3 also indicates that only 17 out of the 600 nonfinancial firm-year observations experienced share-based payment, involving eight firms. On December 31, 2005, the CSRC issued *Administrative Regulations on the Effect of Stock Incentives of Listed Firms (trail implementation)*, marking the beginning of a new era in China's system of equity-based compensation. By the end of 2011, 299 listed firms in China's A-share market issued draft equity incentive schemes, but few firms officially implemented them (e.g., they were later cancelled or suspended for various reasons). Further, all 17 observations used FV to initially measure share-based payment, and most of them chose the binomial model or the Black–Scholes option pricing model to identify the FV of share-based payment. However, few firms disclosed detailed information on how to estimate FV, such as assumptions and parameters for estimation.

Table 3.3 Implementation of mandatory FV requirements for initial measurement by nonfinancial firms

		CEAS 10 Enterprise Annuity Fund	CEAS 11 Share-Based Payment
No. of observations involving mandatory FV requirements for initial measurement (% of 600 observations)		56 (9.33)	17 (2.83)
Whether use FV for initial measurement	Yes	—	17
	No	—	0
	Undisclosed	56	0
Implementation by the FV hierarchy	Level 1	—	2
	Level 2	—	0
	Level 3	—	14
	Undisclosed	56	1

Implementation of partially mandatory requirements of FV use for initial measurement

The partially mandatory use of FV for initial measurement is applicable to the following cases: 1) the cost of assets invested by investors should be recognized as the initial value in accordance with the value as stipulated in the investment contract or agreement, but the FV of the assets should be initially recorded when the value stipulated in the investment contract or agreement is deemed to be unfair; and 2) for assets acquired through an exchange of nonmonetary assets (CEAS 7), debt restructurings (CEAS 12), government grants (CEAS 16), or business combinations (CEAS 20), the FV of the assets should be recognized as the initial cost when these transactions are measured with FV. The assets involving these transactions may include inventories, long-term equity investment, fixed assets, biological assets, and/or intangible assets, and these are reflected in CEAS 1 (*Inventories*), CEAS 2 (*Long-Term Equity Investments*), CEAS 4 (*Fixed Assets*), CEAS 5 (*Biological Assets*), and CEAS 6 (*Intangible Assets*). In addition, the use of FV is also partially mandatory for initial measurement of some special transactions as prescribed in CEAS 4 (*Fixed Assets*) and EAS 14 (*Revenue*). For example, CEAS 4 (*Fixed Assets*) stipulates that if a certain payment is made for purchasing several fixed assets not priced separately, the cost of each fixed asset should be recognized by allocating the payment according to the proportion of FV of each fixed asset to the total cost of all assets acquired.

Table 3.4 reports the descriptive statistics on the implementation of partially mandatory requirements of the use of FV in initial measurement by nonfinancial firms. The results show that 29 out of the 600 firm-year observations involved the partially mandatory requirements of FV use for initial measurement of inventories, which was largely because of business combinations (25 observations). Further, 14 out of the 29 sample observations used FV, two used carrying value, to measure the value of inventories, and three did not disclose relevant information. Among the 14 nonfinancial firm-year observations, eight used Level 3 FV by employing asset appraisers to estimate the FV of inventories, but six did not disclose this information.

Eleven nonfinancial firm-year observations reported how they dealt with initial measurement of long-term equity investment when required to use FV measurement by CEAS 2 (*Long-Term Equity Investment*).[2] Five out of the 11 observations used the appraisal value as the FV of long-term equity investment, four did not adopt FV measurement but used the carrying value instead, and two did not disclose this information. Notice that this standard is closely related to CEAS 20 (*Business Combinations*), which stipulates that for a business combination not under common control the combination cost should be the acquisition-date FV of the assets paid, the liabilities incurred or assumed, and the equity securities issued by the acquirer in exchange for the control over the acquiree; and, the acquirer should recognize goodwill as of the acquisition date measured as the positive balance of the combination cost over the FV of the net identifiable assets it obtains from the acquiree. Table 3.4 shows that 79 out of the 600 observations used FV to initially measure the long-term equity investment owing to business combinations not under common control. In particular, 59 of the 79 observations used the appraisal value as Level 3 FV to initially measure the long-term equity investment, while 19 directly used the carrying value to represent the FV.

Table 3.4 also shows that 42 out of the 600 nonfinancial firm-year observations involved partially mandatory requirements of FV use for the initial measurement of fixed assets, which was largely because of the business combinations not under common control, which made up 37 observations. Twenty-eight out of the 42 observations used FV to initially measure fixed assets, most of which relied on an appraisal value (Level 3 FV), and 14 of which directly used the carrying value. Few firms disclosed relevant information on how to identify the FV of fixed assets. Similar results can be found for the implementation of the partially mandatory requirements of using FV to measure intangible assets. Table 3.4 shows that 34 of the 600 observations involved the partially mandatory requirements of FV use for initial measurement of intangible assets, largely owing to business combinations not under common control. Most of them adopted the FV measurement, in particular Level 3 FV, by using an appraisal value. Two observations accepted intangible assets from government grants but did not disclose any relevant information.

Concerning the use of CEAS 12 (*Debt Restructurings*), Table 3.4 reveals that 99 out of the 600 observations experienced debt restructurings in our sample period, but few of them (only nine observations) used FV for the initial measurement of related assets or liabilities. Sixty-one observations disclosed only the total amount of the gains or losses on debt restructurings without revealing any further details. The nine observations using the FV measurement relied on an appraisal value. We also find that the partially mandatory requirements of FV use for the initial measurement of lease transactions were applicable to 21 of the 600 observations, but only two stated in the notes that they used the FV of the leased assets and the present value of the minimum lease payments to initially measure the leased asset, and did not disclose detailed information. Four observations used the carrying value as the FV. Most of the 21 observations did not disclose any information on whether the firms used FV measurement or how to identify the FV. In addition, none of the sample firms involved applied FVA to biological assets, had government grant transactions, or used FV to recognize revenue.

The implementation of conditionally mandatory FV requirements in initial measurement

The implementation of conditionally mandatory FV requirements in initial measurement only involves CEAS 7 (*Exchange of Non-monetary Assets*). The standard stipulates that the FV of the assets and relevant payable taxes should be recognized as the cost of assets received when the exchange of nonmonetary assets satisfies the following two conditions simultaneously: 1) the transaction has commercial substance; and 2) the FV of the assets received or surrendered can be measured reliably. In practice, only 14 out of the 600 observations undertook the exchange of nonmonetary assets, and only seven of them used FV, while the others did not disclose relevant information. This suggests that few firms had exchanges of nonmonetary assets and adopted FV measurement. The firms also had quite low quality of information disclosure.

Implementation of FV requirements in subsequent measurement

Implementation of mandatory FV requirements in subsequent measurement

Mandatory FV requirements for subsequent measurement are prescribed in CEAS 10 (*Enterprise Annuity Fund*) and CEAS 11 (*Share-Based Payment*). Showing results similar to those reported in Table 3.3, 56 out of the 600 observations established enterprise annuity fund schemes but did not provide any detailed information on subsequent measurement. Unlike annuity funds, most firms with share-based payment complied well with the requirements of CEAS 11 by using FV to recognize expenses on share-based payment.

Table 3.4 Implementation of partially mandatory FV requirements for initial measurement by nonfinancial firms

	CEAS 1 Inventory	CEAS 2 Long-term Equity Investment	CEAS 20 Business Combinations	CEAS 4 Fixed Assets	CEAS 5 Biological Assets	CEAS 6 Intangible Assets	CEAS 12 Debt Restructur-ings	CEAS 14 Revenue	CEAS 16 Government Grants	CEAS 21 Leases
Panel A: Whether the standard was used										
No. of observations involving partially mandatory FV requirements for initial measurement	29	11	79	42	0	34	99	0	0	21
(% of 600 observations)	(4.83)	(1.83)	(13.17)	(7.00)	(0)	(5.67)	(16.5)	(0)	(0)	(3.50)
Panel B: The way the asset was acquired										
Invested by investors	0	0	2	0	0	3	—	—	—	—
Exchange of nonmonetary assets	0	3	0	1	0	2	—	—	—	—
Debt restructurings	2	4	0	1	0	1	—	—	—	—
Business Combinations	25	2	—	37	0	25	—	—	—	—
Issuing equity securities	—	1	2	—	—	2	—	—	—	—
Government grants	0	0	—	0	0	—	—	—	—	—
Financing leases	—	—	—	3	—	—	—	—	—	—
Purchasing several fixed assets not priced separately	—	—	—	0	—	—	—	—	—	—
Cash	—	—	70	—	—	—	—	—	—	—
Others	2	1	5	0	0	1	—	—	—	—
Panel C: Whether FV was used for initial measurement										
Yes	14	5	59	28	0	23	9	0	0	2
No	12	4	19	14	0	7	29	0	0	4
Undisclosed	3	2	1	0	0	4	61	0	0	15
Panel D: Implementation by the FV hierarchy										
Level 1	0	0	0	0	0	0	0	0	0	0
Level 2	0	0	0	0	0	0	0	0	0	0
Level 3	8	5	49	24	0	23	6	0	0	0
Undisclosed	6	0	10	4	0	4	2	0	0	2

Implementation of partially mandatory FV requirements in subsequent measurement

CEAS 4 (*Fixed Asset*), CEAS 6 (*Intangible Assets*), and CEAS 27 (*Extraction of Petroleum and Natural Gas*) stipulate a partially mandatory use of FV for subsequent measurement. The former two may involve FV measurement when firms have fixed assets or intangible assets held for sale. For example, EAS 4 specifies that fixed assets being classified as held for sale are carried at the lower of the carrying amount or FV less relevant disposal costs. In practice, few firms had noncurrent assets held for sale. We found that only eight out of the 600 nonfinancial firm-year observations held fixed assets for sale, and only one observation had intangible assets held for sale. Although seven out of the eight observations with fixed assets held for sale had adopted FV measurement, only one had hired an asset appraiser to estimate the FV and two had used the carrying amount less depreciation, while the others did not disclose relevant information. The one observation with intangible assets held for sale used the appraisal value as the FV. In addition, no sample firm was involved with CEAS 27 (*Extraction of Petroleum and Natural Gas*).

Implementation of conditionally mandatory FV requirements in subsequent measurement

CEAS 5 (*Biological Assets*) requires enterprises to use FVA when meeting specific conditions. It prescribes that, if there is conclusive evidence that the FV of a biological asset can be reliably obtainable on a continuing basis, the biological asset shall be measured at FV. Further, both of the following conditions shall be satisfied if FV is to be used for measurement purposes: 1) there is an active market for the biological assets; and 2) the market price and other relevant information regarding the same or similar types of biological asset can be obtained from the market so that the FV of the biological asset can be reasonably estimated. We found that only seven out of the 600 nonfinancial firm-year observations held biological assets, involving two listed firms. However, the two firms did not adopt the FV model, probably because it was difficult to satisfy the two conditions.

Implementation of voluntary FV requirements in subsequent measurement

CEAS 3 (*Investment Property*) stipulates that firms should use the cost model in subsequent measurement, but can opt to use the FV model when there is an active property market and reliable market prices and other relevant information of identical or similar property can be continuously obtained. When the FV model is adopted, it also requires the disclosure of the basis and method used to determine the FV and the impact of FV changes on earnings. Our results show that 316 out of the 600 observations engaged in investment property, involving 73 nonfinancial listed firms. However, only two firms (or eight observations) chose the FV model for subsequent measurement, while the others used the cost model. Interestingly, this suggests that most listed firms were unwilling to adopt the FV model even though they could do so. More importantly, the two adopting firms disclosed inadequate information on how to determine the FV of an investment property.

The use of FV in asset impairment

The third type of FV adoption in CEAS relates to the process of asset impairment testing. The adoption includes three forms: mandatory, conditionally mandatory, and partially mandatory.

First, the mandatory adoption of FVA in impairment tests involves the impairment of long-term equity investment (CEAS 2), fixed assets (CEAS 4), biological assets (CEAS 5), intangible assets (CEAS 6), and goodwill (CEAS 8). For the impairment of long-term assets, one of the oldest accounting principles is that an asset must not be carried at more than the recoverable amount of the asset. FV plays an important role in estimating the recoverable amount because a business entity can recover such assets by selling them. EAS 8 specifies that the recoverable amount of an asset is the higher of its FV less selling costs and the present value of the future cash flows expected to be derived from the asset.

Table 3.5 presents the statistics on the practical implementation of FV requirements for impairment tests. Panel A of Table 3.5 shows that 60 out of the 600 nonfinancial firm-year observations recognized impairment losses of long-term equity investments, involving 40 listed firms. Most of them used a kind of appraisal value as the receivable amount to estimate the amount of impairment by comparing it with the carrying amount of long-term equity investment. However, these firms did not disclose information on how to identify the recoverable amount. In the notes to the financial statements, they briefly stated that the recoverable amount of assets is the higher of FV less selling costs and the present value of the expected future cash flows, but did not disclose detailed information on the values and on how they were estimated. Instead, some firms disclosed the reasons for the impairment of long-term equity investment, such as the investing entity's involvement in a lawsuit, bad performance, loss, or going out of business.

With regard to fixed assets, Table 3.5 shows that 135 observations recognized impairment losses of fixed assets, involving 63 nonfinancial firms. Thirty-eight out of the 135 observations only disclosed the method of impairment testing, such as net realizable value or appraisal value, but did not provide any detailed information. Ninety-seven observations did not disclose relevant information. Two firms with biological assets did not recognize any impairment. We also found that, compared with fixed assets, firms were less likely to recognize any impairment losses of intangible assets given the greater difficulty in obtaining their FV, and that the quality of disclosure on the impairment of intangible assets was lower as well. Table 3.5 shows that 4 percent of all 24 observations recognized impairment losses of intangible assets, involving 14 listed firms. However, only six observations disclosed even the method of impairment testing, such as the difference between recoverable value and carrying value or appraisal value, while the other 18 observations did not disclose any information. Similar results can be found for the impairment of goodwill. Table 3.5 shows that 17 out of the 21 observations recognizing the impairment losses of goodwill did not disclose relevant information on impairment testing, and only four disclosed the method of impairment.

Second, CEAS 3 (*Investment Property*) requires firms to conduct impairment testing of the balance sheet data when using the cost model for the subsequent measurement of investment property. Although 73 sample firms chose the cost model, only five (involving nine observations) recognized an impairment loss of investment property. Further, we find that the impairment amount was largely due to the transfer from impaired fixed assets or inventories to investment property. The low probability for investment property impairment is largely related to the continuous rise of China's real estate prices in recent years.

Finally, CEAS 27 (*Extraction of Petroleum and Natural Gas*) specifies that an entity shall recognize impairment losses on mineral interests in properties under one of the following two circumstances: 1) impairment of mineral interests in proved properties shall be accounted for in accordance with EAS 8; and 2) mineral interests in unproved properties shall be tested for impairment at least annually. An impairment loss on a mineral interest in an unproved property shall be recognized in profit or loss for the current period at the amount by which its FV is less than

Table 3.5 Implementation of FV requirements in impairment tests by nonfinancial firms

	No. of observations involving FV use in impairment (% of 600 observations)	Use of FV by the FV hierarchy			
		Level 1	Level 2	Level 3	Undisclosed
Panel A: The implementation of mandatory FV measurement for impairment tests					
CEAS 2 *Long-Term Equity Investments*	60 (10.00)	0	0	48	12
CEAS 4 *Fixed Assets*	135 (22.50)	0	0	38	97
CEAS 5 *Biological Assets*	0 (0)	0	0	0	0
CEAS 6 *Intangible Assets*	24 (4.00)	0	0	6	18
CEAS 8 *Impairment of Assets (Goodwill)*	21 (3.50)	0	0	4	17
Panel B: The implementation of conditionally mandatory FV measurement for impairment tests					
CEAS 3 *Investment Property*	9 (0.15)	0	0	0	9
Panel C: The implementation of partially mandatory FV measurement for impairment tests					
CEAS 27 *Extraction of Petroleum and Natural Gas*	0 (0)	0	0	0	0

its carrying amount. This suggests that FVA is partially mandatory in the impairment of mineral interests in properties in China. Nevertheless, as the extractive transactions are largely concentrated on the industry of oil and gas, none of the 120 sample firms was involved with CEAS 27.

Further, Table 3.6 presents statistics on the impact of FVA implementation in impairment testing during 2007 to 2011 on listed nonfinancial firms' reported net incomes, owners' equity and total assets. The raw data for the analysis are extracted from the CSMAR database. The impacts are calculated as total amount of impairment loss relating to a total of fixed assets, long-term equity investment, intangible assets, investment property, and goodwill. The results show that the mean (median) proportion of impairment losses to net income was 21.89 (4.58) percent, with the maximum proportion being 1773.86 percent, suggesting that the impairment loss had a large effect on reported earnings of Chinese listed firms, and the impacts were different across firms. On the balance sheets, the mean proportion of impairment losses to total assets (owners' equity) was 0.56 (1.13) percent, and the median proportion of impairment losses over total assets (owners' equity) was 0.14 (0.30) percent, with the maximum being 25.32 (48.46) percent. This indicates that the impact of impairment losses on the balance sheets is small, but for some firms notable.

Table 3.6 Financial impact of impairment losses on nonfinancial firms

	Obs	Mean	Std.	Min	Median	Max
Impairment losses divided by net income	404	21.89	99.53	0.00	4.58	1773.86
Impairment losses divided by total assets	404	0.56	1.93	0.00	0.14	25.32
Impairment losses divided by owners' equity	404	1.13	3.55	−7.52	0.30	48.46

Implementation of FV disclosure requirements in practice

Apart from voluntary disclosure, the disclosure of FV information can be mandatory, partially mandatory, or conditionally mandatory. CEAS 8 (*Impairment of Assets*), CEAS 10 (*Enterprises Annuity Fund*), CEAS 11 (*Share-Based Payment*), CEAS 12 (*Debt Restructurings*), CEAS 30 (*Presentation of Financial Statements*), CEAS 31 (*Cash Flow Statements*), and CEAS 38 (*First-Time Adoption of Accounting Standards for Business Enterprises*) are mandatory in their requirement for an entity to disclose FV information in the notes. For example, CEAS 11 specifies that an enterprise should disclose the method of determining the FV of equity instruments in the notes. CEAS 12 stipulates that a debtor (creditor) should disclose, in the notes, information on the methods and bases of determining the FV of 1) noncash assets transferred (received), 2) capital converted from debt (equity interest received on conversion from debt receivable), and 3) the debt (receivable) after modification of other terms. FV information also is partially mandatorily required to be disclosed in the notes by CEAS 4, CEAS 20, CEAS 21, and CEAS 22. For instance, CEAS 20 stipulates that, for a business combination not involving enterprises under common control, the acquirer shall disclose, in the notes, information on the components of the cost of combination, their carrying amounts and FVs, and the methods of determining the FVs. Additionally, CEAS 3 (*Investment Property*) and CEAS 7 (*Exchange of Non-monetary Assets*) require enterprises to disclose FV information satisfying preconditions. For example, CEAS 3 specifies that an enterprise shall disclose the information on the bases and methods applied in determining the FV and the effect of FV changes on profit or loss if the enterprise chooses the FV model for the subsequent measurement of investment property.

Implementation of FV requirements relating to financial instruments

In order to fit to special Chinese circumstances and guide accounting practice well, the 2006 CEAS attempt to reduce the complexity transactions of financial instruments (FI) by dividing IFRS 39 (*Financial Instruments: Recognition and Measurement*) into three specific Chinese accounting standards, that is, CEAS 22 (*Recognition and Measurement of Financial Instruments*), CEAS 23 (*Transfer of Financial Assets*), and CEAS 24 (*Hedging*). Meanwhile, CEAS 37 (*Financial Instruments: Presentation and Disclosures*) further specifies the issues on information disclosure for FI. In these standards, FV is required for initial measurement and disclosure for all FI. Except for held-to-maturity investments and loans and receivables, firms are required to use FV for the subsequent measurement of FI as well. In addition, enterprises also should use FV to test the impairment of financial assets except for trading financial assets. It seems that FVA is largely applied to financial assets or liabilities in the 2006 CEAS, representing a major *de jure* convergence with IFRS. However, how do Chinese nonfinancial listed firms implement these standards in practice?

Table 3.7 first presents the industry distribution of nonfinancial firms with financial assets or liabilities. In this table, we represent manufacturing subindustries by second-level industry codes, and other industries by first-level industry codes. The results show that over half of the 600 nonfinancial firm-year observations (314 observations) held financial assets or liabilities. In particular, the two highest proportions of observations with financial assets or liabilities divided by total industry observations are found in the industries of electronic manufacture (C5) and wholesale and retail trade (H). Meanwhile, firms from extraction (B) and farming, forestry, animal husbandry, and fishery (A) held fewer financial assets or liabilities.

Table 3.8 reports the statistics on the implementation of FVA for financial assets or liabilities of sample nonfinancial firms. Trading financial assets include financial assets held for trading and those designated as at FV through profit or loss. The same classification is required for trading

Table 3.7 Industry distribution of sample nonfinancial firms with financial assets or liabilities

Categories	No. of obs. with financial assets or liabilities (% of industry obs.)
Farming, forestry, animal husbandry, and fishery (A)	0 (0)
Extraction (B)	7 (20.00)
Manufacture (C)	123 (45.56)
Including: Food and beverages (C0)	16 (35.56)
Textile, garment, leather, and feather (C1)	11 (73.33)
Petroleum, chemical, rubber, and plastics (C4)	13 (43.33)
Electronic (C5)	14 (93.33)
Metallic and nonmetal (C6)	18 (51.43)
Machinery, equipment, and instruments (C7)	35 (36.84)
Medicine and biological (C8)	16 (45.71)
Electric power, steam and hot water generation and supply (D)	26 (47.27)
Construction (E)	2 (40.00)
Transportation and warehousing (F)	27 (67.50)
Information technology (G)	25 (71.43)
Wholesale and retail trade (H)	29 (82.86)
Real estate (J)	54 (60.00)
Social services (K)	5 (50.00)
Media and culture services (L)	5 (100.0)
Conglomerates (M)	11 (73.33)
Total	314 (52.3)

Here financial assets or liabilities include trading financial assets or liabilities, available-for-sale financial assets, held-to-maturity investments, derivative financial assets or liabilities, financial assets purchased for resale, financial assets sold for repurchase, and hedging, but exclude loans and receivables because all sample firms held accounting receivables.

financial liabilities. As trading financial assets mainly consists of stocks, bonds, or funds that are purchased from secondary markets, the quoted prices of relevant assets or reliabilities are much easier to obtain from active markets. Table 3.8 shows that 163 out of the 600 observations held trading financial assets, involving 54 nonfinancial sample firms. Among these, 153 used the Level 1 FV measurement while 10 did not disclose relevant information. Also, few firms held trading financial liabilities. The results also reveal that 202 observations held available-for-sale financial assets, involving 54 sample firms, and most used Level 1 FV to recognize and measure the assets/liabilities. While FV is required to be used for initial and subsequent measurement of trading financial assets and available-for-sale financial assets, FV is only required for initial measurement of held-to-maturity investments. Table 3.8 shows that 11 nonfinancial firm-year observations (or 10 firms) involved the mandatory requirements of using FV in the initial measurement of held-to-maturity, including 10 firms. Among them, six used amortized cost instead of FV and the others did not disclose relevant information. Our data also show that all sample firms held loans and receivables. In addition, few sample firms held derivative financial assets or liabilities. In particular, nine sample firms held derivative financial assets, three held derivative financial liabilities, one held financial assets sold for repurchase, and four had hedging assets. Overall, Chinese listed nonfinancial firms mainly held trading financial assets and available-for-sale financial assets during 2007 to 2011, and they held few other financial assets or liabilities, particularly derivative financial instruments. Most firms complied well with the 2006 CEAS's requirements on the use of FV measurement and disclosed relevant information, though for a few firms information disclosure quality was low. Furthermore, Level 1 FV was the main input for recognizing the FV of financial assets or liabilities.

Table 3.8 Implementation of FVA for financial assets or liabilities by nonfinancial firms

	No. of obs. involving mandatory FV requirements (% of 600 Obs.)	Firms involved	Whether FV measurement was used or not			Implementation by the FV hierarchy			
			Yes	No	Undis closed	Level 1	Level 2	Level 3	Undis closed
Trading financial assets	163 (27.50)	54	153	0	10	153	—	—	10
Trading financial liabilities	27 (4.50)	11	22	0	5	17	—	5	5
Available-for-sale financial assets	202 (33.67)	54	189	2	11	184	—	5	11
Held-to-maturity investments	11 (1.83)	10	0	6	5	—	—	—	5
Loans and receivables	600 (100.00)	120	3	597	0	0	0	3	0
Derivative financial assets	26 (4.33)	9	22	—	4	18	—	4	4
Derivative financial liabilities	5 (0.83)	3	4	—	11	2	—	2	11
Financial assets purchased for resale	0 (00)	0	—	—	—	—	—	—	—
Financial assets sold for repurchase	3 (0.50)	1	—	—	—	—	—	—	—
Hedging	10 (1.67)	4	9	—	1	9	—	—	1

Table 3.9 reports the impact of gains or losses from FV changes in FI and from investing FI on sample nonfinancial firms' financial statements. We derive the percentages by dividing the amount of gains or losses from FV changes in FI or from investing FI by net income, total assets, and total owners' equity, respectively. Because a few firms had a negative net income, we dealt with them as absolute values. We also separately present the gains and losses as they have offsetting effects on earnings. Panel A of Table 3.9 shows that 75 out the 163 observations with gains or losses from FV changes in FI recognized gains, while 88 recognized losses. On average, the gains from FV changes in FI accounted for 15.72 percent of net income, 0.29 percent of total assets, and 0.78 percent of total owners' equity, respectively. However, based on the medians, the percentages became 0.71 percent, 0.03 percent, and 0.07 percent, respectively. The mean (median) losses from FV changes in FI accounted for 14.18 (0.80) percent of net income, 0.22 (0.03) percent of total assets, and 0.57 (0.10) percent of owners' equity, respectively. This suggests that the effect of FV application to financial instruments on accounting earnings was relatively small. However, the effect should be notable for a few firms because the gains and losses from FV changes in FI were quite volatile across the sample firms.

Similar results can be found for gains from investment in FI. Panel B of Table 3.9 shows that, among the 213 nonfinancial firm-year observations that recognized investment gains or losses in the sample period, more firms (accounting for 195 observations) recognized investment gains in FI, while few firms suffered investment losses. The mean (median) ratio of gains from investment in FI over net income was 23.94 (1.83) percent, with the standard deviation being 85.02. This indicates that the impact of gains from investing in FI on the income statements was significant, but was volatile across the sample firms. The mean ratio of gains from investment in FI was 0.63 percent of total assets and 1.25 percent of owners' equity, respectively, with the median percentages being 0.07 percent and 0.18 percent, respectively. This suggests that the impact of gains from investing in FI on the balance sheet was small. In addition, few firms (only 18 observations) recognized losses from investment in FI and the losses had less effect on financial performance than did gains.

Implementation of FVA by listed Chinese financial firms

Implementation of FVA for financial instruments

Consistent with nonfinancial firms, Chinese financial firms are also required by the 2006 CEAS to use FV for initial measurement of FI and to disclose related FV information.

Table 3.10 summarizes the implementation of FVA for FI in listed Chinese financial firms during 2007–2011. As financial firms often simultaneously held several financial products, such as stock, bonds, or funds, in an accounting period, and might use different levels of input in the FV hierarchy for financial assets or liabilities. Generally, financial firms held more financial assets and liabilities than nonfinancial firms did. Table 3.10 shows that all 27 sample financial firms (or 131 observations) held trading financial assets, and used FV as the measurement basis. The results also show that 120 observations with trading financial assets used Level 1 FV while 123 used Level 3 FV. This suggests that the quoted prices from active markets and appraisal values using valuation technologies were the two main inputs for measuring the FV of trading financial assets. Fifty-seven out of the 135 observations, representing 15 financial firms, held trading financial liabilities. Among them, 43 (47) observations used Level 1 FV (Level 3 FV), while 14 used Level 2 FV.

Table 3.9 The impact of the application of FVA to FI in the financial performance of nonfinancial firms

	Obs	Mean	Std.	Min	Median	Max
Panel A:Gains or losses from FV changes in FI						
Gains from FV changes in FI divided by net income	75	15.72	84.49	0.00	0.71	729.8
Gains from FV changes in FI divided by total assets	75	0.29	0.50	0.00	0.03	2.11
Gains from FV changes in FI divided by owners' equity	75	0.78	1.43	0.00	0.07	6.86
Losses from FV changes in FI divided by net income	88	14.18	62.64	0.00	0.80	521.97
Losses from FV changes in FI divided by total assets	88	0.22	0.45	0.00	0.03	3.17
Losses from FV changes in FI divided by owners' equity	88	0.57	1.32	0.00	0.10	10.37
Panel B: Gains or losses from investing in FI						
Gains from investing in FI divided by net income	195	23.94	85.02	0.00	1.83	740.42
Gains from investing in FI divided by total assets	195	0.63	1.67	0.00	0.07	14.99
Gains from investing in FI divided by owners' equity	195	1.25	3.19	0.00	0.18	30.74
Losses from investing in FI divided by net income	18	4.56	14.96	0.00	0.16	63.89
Losses from investing in FI divided by total assets	18	0.07	0.21	0.00	0.00	0.89
Losses from investing in FI divided by owners' equity	18	0.20	0.55	0.00	0.01	2.37

Table 3.10 also shows that 26 out of 27 sample firms, accounting for 127 observations, held available-for-sale financial assets. Similar to trading financial assets, the quoted prices from active markets (Level 1 FV) and appraisal values (Level 3 FV) were the main inputs for identifying the FV of available-for-sale financial assets. Only 39 observations with available-for-sale financial assets used Level 2 FV. The data also indicate that Chinese financial firms had relatively high quality of FV information disclosure on available-for-sale financial assets, and trading financial assets and liabilities. Nevertheless, these findings were not applicable to held-to-maturity investment. The results show that 68 out of the 135 observations engaged in the initial measurement of held-to-maturity investments, involving 19 financial firms. Further, bond investment was a dominant form of held-to-maturity investment. However, these firms only disclosed the objects of held-to-maturity investment, such as national bonds, local government bonds, corporate bonds, and short-term financing bonds, but did not disclose any information on how to initially measure and recognize them using FV. We find that 21 observations only disclosed that the measurement basis for held-to-maturity investments was FV, without other information. Forty-seven observations did not disclose any information. Additionally, Table 3.10 shows that, while all sample financial firms held loans and receivables, they did not use FV as the measurement basis. Few firms stated in the notes that the initial measurement of the amount of loans and receivables was based on the FV at the date of acquirement.

Table 3.10 Implementation of FVA for FI by listed financial firms

	No. of Obs. involving mandatory FV requirements (% of 135 obs.)	Firms involved	Whether FV measurement was used or not			Implementation by the FV hierarchy			
			Yes	No	Undis closed	Level 1	Level 2	Level 3	Undis closed
Trading financial assets	131 (97.04)	27	131	0	0	120	42	123	0
Trading financial liabilities	57 (42.22)	15	57	0	0	43	14	47	0
Available-for-sale financial assets	127 (94.07)	26	127	0	0	115	39	115	0
Held-to-maturity investments	68 (50.37)	19	21	0	47	0	0	0	21
Loans and receivables	135 (100)	27	0	135	0	0	0	0	0
Derivative financial assets	89 (65.93)	22	89	0	0	54	26	73	0
Derivative financial liabilities	83 (61.48)	19	83	0	0	52	26	73	0
Financial assets purchased for resale	108 (80)	25	—	—	—	—	—	—	—
Financial assets sold for repurchase	114 (84.44)	25	—	—	—	—	—	—	—
Hedging	5 (3.70)	3	4	0	1	4	0	0	1

Unlike nonfinancial firms, we found that financial firms held many derivative financial products. Table 3.10 shows that 22 sample financial firms (or 89 observations) held derivative financial assets and used FV as the measurement basis. Nineteen sample financial firms (amounting to 83 observations) held derivative financial liabilities and used FV measurement. Furthermore, 54 observations with derivative financial assets used Level 1 FV, 26 used Level 2 FV, and 73 used Level 3 FV measurement. Similar results were obtained for derivative financial liabilities. This suggests that the quoted prices from active markets and appraisal values were again the two main inputs for FV measurement of derivative financial assets and liabilities. Many financial firms also held financial assets purchased for resale and financial assets sold for repurchase, with 108 observations and 114 observations, respectively. However, few financial firms held assets for hedging.

Further, we summarize the impact of gains (losses) from FV changes in FI and from investing in FI on the sample financial firms' financial statements. Consistently, the amounts of gains (losses) from FV changes in FI and from investment in FI are scaled by net income, total assets, and owners' equity, respectively. The results reported in Table 3.11 show that 47 observations recognized gains from FV changes in FI, while 58 recognized losses. The mean (median) proportion of gains from FV changes in FI over net income is 5.49 (2.23) percent, suggesting that the implementation of FVA for FI resulted in considerable effect on financial firms' earnings. The biggest impact was as much as 33.06 percent of net income. The gains from FV changes in FI also on average accounted for 0.31 percent of total assets, and 1.32 percent of owners' equity. Nevertheless, FV changes in FI caused the sample financial firms to suffer more losses. Panel A of Table 3.11 indicates that the losses from FV changes in FI on average accounted for 32.66 percent of net income, 0.68 percent of total assets, and 2.40 percent of owners' equity, respectively. Meanwhile, the 142.5 standard deviation indicates that the impact of relevant losses on accounting earnings varied significantly across financial firms.

Panel B in Table 3.11 reports the impact of gains or losses from investing in FI on financial firms' financial statements. In general, more firms (105 observations) recognized gains from investing in FI. Panel B shows that the mean (median) proportion of gains from investing in FI over net income was 52.13 (23.87) percent, indicating that the gains related to investment in FI increase by nearly a quarter of accounting earnings for financial firms. On average, gains from investing in FI accounted for 1.56 percent of total assets and 6.88 percent of owners' equity. In contrast, losses from investing in FI had a small influence on financial statements of the sample financial firms.

Implementation of FVA for nonfinancial instruments

Use of FV for initial measurement of nonfinancial instruments

Table 3.12 summarizes the implementation of mandatory FV requirements for initial measurement in financial firms. The results show that 66 out of the 135 observations (or 48.89 percent) involved CEAS 10 (*Enterprises Annuity Fund*). However, the firms mentioned only that they established annuity fund schemes for employees but did not disclose detailed information on FV. This is consistent with the findings on listed nonfinancial firms, suggesting that Chinese listed firms generally had low quality of disclosures. Table 3.12 also shows that 32 out of the 135 observations involved CEAS 11 and most of them used the appraisal value (Level 3 FV) as the input of FVs of stock options or restricted stocks.

Table 3.13 reports the statistics on implementation of partially mandatory FV requirements for initial measurement in financial firms. We found that the sample financial firms did not

Table 3.11 The financial impact of FVA for FI on financial firms

	Obs	Mean	Std.	Min	Median	Max
Panel A: Gains or losses from FV changes in FI						
Gains from FV changes in FI divided by net income	47	5.49	7.27	0.07	2.23	33.06
Gains from FV changes in FI divided by total assets	47	0.31	0.70	0.00	0.03	4.01
Gains from FV changes in FI divided by owners' equity	47	1.32	2.55	0.01	0.30	14.80
Losses from FV changes in FI divided by net income	58	32.66	142.5	0.08	4.65	1080.61
Losses from FV changes in FI divided by total assets	58	0.68	1.77	0.00	0.07	10.88
Losses from FV changes in FI divided by owners' equity	58	2.40	5.50	0.01	0.44	27.54
Panel B: Gains or losses from investing in FI						
Gains from investing in FI divided by net income	105	52.13	119.9	0.00	23.87	1058.10
Gains from investing in FI divided by total assets	105	1.56	2.45	0.00	0.45	11.33
Gains from investing in FI divided by owners' equity	105	6.88	11.04	0.00	1.93	54.38
Losses from investing in FI divided by net income	25	0.63	2.33	0.00	0.01	11.43
Losses from investing in FI divided by total assets	25	1.90	6.00	0.00	0.19	28.93
Losses from investing in FI divided by owners' equity	25	8.86	20.03	0.00	1.22	74.40

Table 3.12 Implementation of mandatory FV requirements for initial measurement by financial firms

		CEAS 10 Enterprises Annuity Fund	CEAS 11 Share-Based Payment
No. of observations involving mandatory FV requirements for initial measurement (% of 132 observations)		66 (48.89)	32 (23.70)
Whether use FVA in initial measurement	Yes	—	32
	No	—	0
	Undisclosed	66	0
Implementation of FVA by levels of the FV hierarchy	Level 1	—	2
	Level 2	—	0
	Level 3	—	25
	Undisclosed	66	5

involve in FVA measurement in inventories, biological assets, revenues, government grants, and leases. In contrast, the implementation of partially mandatory FV requirements for initial measurement was more related to CEAS 20 (*Business Combinations*). The results show that 20 out of the 135 observations engaged in business combinations not under common control, and nearly three-quarters used FV for the initial measurement of related assets or liabilities. As indicated in the notes, the reason for using the carrying value instead of FV was that there was no significant difference between the carrying amounts of identifiable assets and liabilities and their FVs at the acquired data. Although 14 observations used FV, over half of them (eight observations) did not disclose information on how to identify the FV of related assets and liabilities. The 20 observations relating to business combinations not under common control were closely related to the implementation of FV requirements for the initial measurement of fixed assets and intangible assets. Table 3.13 shows that all 18 observations involving the partially mandatory FV requirements for the initial measurement of fixed assets were due to business combinations not under common control, but only 12 measured FV of related fixed assets, while six used carrying value. Ten out of the 11 observations involving the partially mandatory FV requirements for the initial measurement of intangible assets was because of business combinations not under common control. Among them, nine used FV of intangible assets, while two used carrying values. Moreover, few financial firms engaged in debt restructurings; if any firm did, its relevant information disclosure quality was low.

Finally, our data shows that only one out of the 600 observations had exchanges of nonmonetary assets. However, the firm argued in the notes that the exchange transaction had no commercial substance and thus did not use FV measurement.

Table 3.13 Implementation of partially mandatory FV requirements for initial measurement by financial firms

	CEAS 2 Long-term Equity Investments	CEAS 20 Business Combinations	CEAS 4 Fixed Assets	CEAS 6 Intangible Assets	CEAS12 Debt Restructurings
Panel A: Whether the standard was used					
No. of observations involving partially mandatory FV requirements for initial measurement (% of 135 observations)	2 (1.48)	20 (14.93)	18 (3.33)	11 (8.15)	7 (5.19)
Panel B: The way the asset was acquired					
Exchange of nonmonetary assets	—	—	—	1	—
Debt restructurings	2	—	—	—	—
Business combinations	—	—	18	10	—
Issuing equity securities	—	2	—	—	—
Cash	—	18	—	—	—
Panel C: Whether FV was used in initial measurement					
Yes	2	14	12	9	2
No	0	6	6	2	0
Undisclosed	2	0	0	0	5
Panel D: Implementation by the FV hierarchy					
Level 1	0	1	0	0	1
Level 2	0	0	0	0	0
Level 3	0	5	4	5	1
Undisclosed	2	8	8	4	0

Implementation of FVA in subsequent measurement of nonfinancial instruments

First, regarding the implementation of mandatory FV requirements for the subsequent measurement of nonfinancial instruments, some firms, despite having established annuity fund schemes and recognizing the annuity fund, did not provide relevant information in the notes. Twenty-seven observations (six financial firms) disclosed the methods for estimating the FV of equity instruments. Among them, five firms used valuation models such as the Black–Scholes option pricing model to estimate the FV of equity instruments, while one firm directly used the quoted prices from active markets. Furthermore, two firms disclosed detailed information on the assumptions, parameters, and inputs for valuation models.

Second, no sample financial firms were involved in the implementation of partially and conditionally mandatory FV requirements for subsequent measurement during 2007 to 2011.

Finally, the sample financial firms were more likely to engage in investment property and to choose the FV model for the subsequent measurement of investment property than nonfinancial firms. Our data show that 17 of the 27 financial firms (accounting for 77 observations) held investment property during 2007 to 2011. Among them, 12 firms used the cost model while five firms used the FV model as a subsequent measurement basis. We also found that one firm used Level 2 FV while the other four firms used the appraisal value as the FV of investment property. The firms also disclosed relatively adequate information on how to identify the FV of investment property.

Further, we summarized the effect of the *de facto* use of FV for measuring investment property on financial firms' financial statements. The unreported results show that the mean (median) proportion of investment property over total assets was 0.62 (0.07) percent, with the maximum being 12.35 percent, suggesting that the amount of investment property was considerably smaller than the total assets of financial firms. The mean (median) proportion of gains from FV changes in investment property over net income was 0.72 (0.22) percent, ranging from –6.66 percent to 9.65 percent. This indicates that the effect of FVA for investment property on accounting earnings of financial firms was relatively small, compare to nonfinancial firms.

Implementation of FVA in the impairment of assets

Table 3.14 reports that the statistics on impairment losses of relevant assets recognized by financial firms. In the process of impairment tests, FV was largely used to determine the recoverable amount of assets, and then to calculate the amount of impairment losses. In total, the sample financial firms were less likely to recognize impairment losses of assets, and predominately used the appraisal value as Level 3 FV to estimate the amount of losses. For example, the results reported in Table 3.14 show that 17 and 19 observations, accounting for 12.59 percent and 14.07 percent of the 135 financial firm observations, recognized the impairment losses of long-term equity investment and fixed assets, respectively. Fewer sample firms recognized the impairment loss of intangible assets owing to the greater difficulty in estimating their FV. One out of the 54 observations with investment property measured the assets using the cost model and recognized an impairment loss but the amount of loss was insignificant. Notably, over a quarter of the observations recognized impairment losses of available-for-sale financial assets. These firms were more likely to use quoted prices from active markets (Level 1 FV) or appraisal values derived by using valuation technologies (Level 3 FV) to identify the FV of available-for-sale financial assets at the balance sheet date. Additionally, 14 observations recognized impairment losses of held-to-maturity investments, accounting for 10.37 percent of the 135

Table 3.14 Implementation of FVA for impairment tests by financial firms

	No. of observations incurred impairment (% of 135 observations)	Implementation by the FV hierarchy			
		Level 1 FV	Level 2 FV	Level 3 FV	Undisclosed
Impairment of long-term equity investments	17 (12.59)	0	9	8	0
Impairment of fixed assets	19 (14.07)	0	0	19	0
Impairment of intangible assets	4 (2.96)	0	0	4	0
Impairment of investment property	1 (0.74)	0	0	0	1
Impairment of available-for-sale financial assets	35 (25.94)	29	6	34	0
Impairment of held-to-maturity investments	14 (10.37)	0	0	14	0

Table 3.15 The financial effect of FVA for asset impairment on financial firms

	Obs	Mean	Std.	Min	Median	Max
Impairment loss divided by net income	55	37.89	214.82	−0.80	0.89	1588.62
Impairment loss divided by total assets	55	0.22	0.57	−0.00	0.01	3.69
Impairment loss divided by owners' equity	55	1.55	5.44	−0.14	0.15	38.68

observations, and all used Level 3 FV. The high probability of recognizing impairment losses of financial assets was related to more financial assets held by financial firms.

Further, Table 3.15 summarizes the effect of FVA for impairment of assets on financial firms' financial statements. Similarly, we divided impairment losses involved in Table 3.14 by net income, total assets, and owners' equity, respectively. Overall, the effect of FVA for impairment of assets on income statements and balance sheets was small except for a few firms. In particular, the results show that the mean (median) proportion of impairment loss over net income was 37.89 (0.89) percent, ranging from -0.80 percent to 1588.62 percent. On average, the amount of impairment loss accounted for 0.22 percent of total assets and 1.55 percent of owners' equity, respectively.

Conclusions

This chapter reports the study to investigate the extent of adoption of FVA in the 2006 CEAS and the implementation in practice by listed financial and nonfinancial firms. On February 5, 2006, the MoF released one revised conceptual framework and 38 specific accounting standards, which are largely based on IFRSs, with effect for China's listed firms from January 1, 2007. As one of the most important changes and a key feature, FVA, which was previously abandoned in the Chinese enterprises accounting system stipulated by the MoF in 2000, was required or permitted for initial measurement, subsequent measurement and impairment recognition, and disclosures. We find that more than 23 standards of the 38 CEAS require or permit FVA, with four different forms of requirements ranging from mandatory, partially mandatory, and conditionally mandatory to voluntary.

Further, we empirically investigated the *de facto* implementation of FVA by China's listed firms by using the annual reports of 120 firms randomly drawn from all of China's listed firms, and 27 nonfinancial firms for the period between 2007 and 2011. Both sample financial and nonfinancial firms complied well with the mandatory or partially mandatory requirements concerning the use of FV to measure assets, liabilities, or transactions, but the quality of their FV information disclosure in the notes to financial statements was very low. Meanwhile, although mandatory, our sample firms were less likely to recognize impairment losses on goodwill and intangible assets than on fixed assets probably because it was more difficult to obtain and measure their FV. When firms were required to conditionally use FV to measure such assets, liabilities, or transactions (ALTs) as those involved in exchange of nonmonetary assets, few firms had reported such ALTs; if they had, they did not prefer FV measurement. Although firms were also allowed to opt to use the FV model for the subsequent measurement of investment property when reliable market prices and other relevant information of identical or similar assets could be continuously obtained, few sample firms (especially nonfinancial firms) preferred the FV model. And, if they did use the FV model, the adopters' information disclosure quality was also low.

The sample firms tended to use external asset appraisers to estimate the FV of nonfinancial assets or liabilities. Some even directly used carrying value as the FV of relevant assets or liabilities. In contrast, most firms determined the FV of financial assets or liabilities by using quoted prices of identical assets or liabilities in the active markets or appraisal values from asset appraisers. The firms also disclosed more FV information related to financial assets or liabilities. Finally, we find that the impact of FVA implementation in FI on financial statements was more significant for financial firms than that for nonfinancial firms during 2007 to 2011 in China.

Overall, these findings indicate that FVA was widely adopted not only in CEAS but also in practice in our sample period. However, the level of implementation of CFVA by Chinese listed firms was lower for nonfinancial assets or liabilities, but was relatively higher for financial assets or liabilities. This is consistent with the FVA implementation problems identified by several practitioner speakers at the ICAEW's 2011 Information for Better Markets conference, e.g., Harrington (2011), Harris (2011), and Wallace (2011).

Several Chinese institutional characteristics may have had a negative effect on the implementation of FVA. First, influenced by the former Soviet Union, China has a strong tradition of adopting uniform accounting systems (UAS) (Xiao *et al.*, 2004; Ezzamel *et al.*, 2007; Ezzamel and Xiao, 2015). This UAS tradition stresses uniform statutory control, rather than professional judgment, which is required for the effective implementation of FVA. Second, while improving rapidly, the Chinese accounting infrastructure is not well-developed owing to the suspension of higher education during the Cultural Revolution and of the accounting profession between the 1950s and the 1980s (Xiao *et al.*, 2000). This means that accountants, auditors, regulators, and users are not equipped with sufficient FVA knowledge and experience and the needed professionalism, and thus may affect the level of implementation of FVA in practice. Third, it is well-recognized that the implementation of FVA requires well-developed asset pricing markets (such as the capital market and property market) (Zeff, 2007). This is because the more developed the markets, the easier to obtain Level 1 FV, which is more reliable and relevant than Levels 2 and 3 FV (Song *et al.*, 2010). Although improving, the market conditions for applying FVA are less conducive in China and it is at present difficult to obtain

FV for many assets (Xiao *et al.*, 2004; MoF, 2008, 2009, 2010). Fourth, the weaker corporate governance mechanisms and legal enforcement in China may also have a negative effect on the implementation of FVA.

Overall, we believe that the results have several important policy implications for standards setters and market regulators. First, there is a need to improve FV accounting standards and provide more typical cases and greater operational guidance on the application of FVA. Since China has a strong uniform accounting system (UAS) tradition, which stresses uniformity and statutory control, it is less conducive to FVA implementation owing to the high complexity of estimating the FV (in particular at Level 3) of relevant assets or liabilities, the high need for significantly more professional judgment, and the lack of FV-related technical knowledge. This is one of the reasons for the low level of FVA implementation in China. Second, it is very important to improve the quality of FV information disclosure, given the extremely low amount and quality of FV information disclosed in the notes to financial statements by Chinese listed firms. Third, the need for separate standards for financial and nonfinancial firms, particularly for financial instruments standards, should be taken into serious consideration. We find that financial firms held significant more complex financial instruments than nonfinancial firms; importantly, the adoption of FVA for financial instruments had a significantly greater effect on financial statements of financial firms. Using the same accounting standards may reduce the quality of FVA implementation. Finally, there is a need to improve relevant regulatory measures relating to firms, asset appraisers, and external auditors. The results show that Chinese listed firms rely largely on the work of external asset appraisers because of the high complexity of FVA and the lack of FV-related knowledge. Therefore, the professionalism and independence of external asset appraisers and independent auditors are crucial to maintain the high quality of FV information.

Notes

1 This chapter is based on the project Fair Value Accounting in China, led by Jason Xiao and sponsored by the ICAEW Charitable Trusts (project number: 5-444). The authors, all of whom are members of the project team, would like to thank ICAEW Charitable Trusts for financial support. Guoqiang Hu and Jason Xiao also acknowledge financial support from the National Natural Science Foundation of China (71502122).
2 This does not include long-term equity investment due to business combinations not under common control, which is dealt with in CEAS 20 (*Business Combinations*).

References

Dai, B., Lu, Z. and Zhang, R. (2007) Write-downs: Conservatism or earnings management. *Accounting Research*, *12*, 36–42 (in Chinese).
Deloitte Touche Tohmatsu (2006) *China's New Accounting Standards*. Unpublished thesis.
Ezzamel, M. and Xiao, Z. (2015) The development of accounting regulations for foreign invested firms in China: The role of Chinese characteristics. *Accounting, Organizations and Society*, *44*(4), 60–84.
Ezzamel, M., Xiao, Z. and Pan, A. (2007) Political ideology and accounting regulation in China. *Accounting, Organizations and Society*, *32*(7/8), 669–700.
Feng, S. (2001) Overview of enterprise accounting system lectures. In Department of Accounting, MoF (Ed.), *Enterprise Accounting System Lectures*. Beijing: China Finance and Economic Press.
Feng, S. (2003) The internationalization of accounting under current circumstance in China. *Accounting Research*, *2*, 1–6 (in Chinese).
Harris, T. (2011) *Financial Instruments in Insurance Companies*. Paper presented at the ICAEW 2011 Information for Better Markets Conference on Accounting for Financial Instruments: Everybody's Problem? London, December 2011.

Harrington, R. (2011) *Financial Instruments in Non-financial Firms*. Paper presented at the ICAEW 2011 Information for Better Markets Conference on Accounting for Financial Instruments: Everybody's Problem? London, December 2011.

He, X., Wong, T.J. and Young, D. (2012) Challenges for implementation of fair value accounting in emerging markets: Evidence from China. *Contemporary Accounting Research*, *29*, 538–562.

Li, Jing and Li, B. (2010) The value-relevance of fair value measures for commercial banks: Evidences from the Chinese bank industries. *International Research Journal of Finance and Economics*, *60*, 86–93.

Ministry of Finance, China (2008) *A Report of an Analysis Accounting Standards Implementation by Listed Chinese Firms in 2007*. Retrieved from www.easc.gov.cn.

Ministry of Finance, China (2009) *A Report of an Analysis Accounting Standards Implementation by Listed Chinese Firms in 2008*. Retrieved from www.easc.gov.cn.

Ministry of Finance, China (2010) *A Report of an Analysis Accounting Standards Implementation by Listed Chinese Firms in* 2009. Retrieved from www.easc.gov.cn.

Peng, S. and Bewley, K. (2009) *Adaptability of Fair Value Accounting in China: Assessment of an Emerging Economy Converging with IFRS*. Unpublished thesis, York University.

Peng, S. and Bewley. K. (2010) Adaptability to fair value accounting in an emerging economy: A case study of China's IFRS convergence. *Accounting, Auditing & Accountability Journal*, *23*, 982–1011.

Peng, S., Graham, C. and Bewley, K. (2013) *Fair Value Accounting Reforms in China: Towards an Accounting Movement Theory*. Unpublished thesis, York University.

Qu, X. and Zhang, G. (2015) Value-relevance of earnings and book value over the institutional transition in China: The suitability of fair value accounting in this emerging market. *The International Journal of Accounting*, *50*, 195–223.

Song, C.J., Thomas, W. and Yi, H. (2010) Value relevance of FAS 157 fair value hierarchy information and the impact of corporate governance mechanisms. *The Accounting Review*, *85*, 1375–1410.

Wallace, P. (2011) *Accounting Standards Setting and Implementation Issues*. Paper presented at the ICAEW 2011 Information for Better Markets Conference on Accounting for Financial Instruments: Everybody's Problem? London, December 2011.

Wang, J. (2005) The research on environmental constraints to accounting internationalism, strategy selection, and its effectiveness: Empirical evidence from Non-Monetary Exchange standard. *Management World*, *3*, 15–22 (in Chinese).

Xiao, Z., Weetman, P. and Sun, M.L. (2004) Political influence and co-existence of a uniform accounting system and accounting standards in China. *Abacus*, *40*, 193–218.

Xiao, Z., Zhang, Y. and Xie, Z. (2000) The making of independent auditing standards in China. *Accounting Horizons*, *14*, 69–89.

Zeff, S. (2007) Some obstacles to global financial reporting comparability and convergence at a high level of quality. *The British Accounting Review*, *39*, 290–302.

Zhang, Y., Andrew, J. and Rudkin, K. (2012) Accounting as an instrument of neoliberalisation? Exploring the adoption of fair value accounting in China. *Accounting, Auditing & Accountability Journal*, *25*, 1266–1289.

4

Development of accounting and financial reporting practices in the Islamic Republic of Pakistan

Imtiaz Badshah[1] and Frode Mellemvik[2]

Introduction

Accounting in Pakistan needs to be studied because this field has not yet received sufficient attention from researchers. Earlier studies (such as Kennedy, 1987; Quddus, 1991a; Haider, 1979; Braibanti, 1965, 1968; Khan, 1987; Baloch, 2003) concerning Pakistan have discussed its political, administrative and judicial development. These researchers have mainly emphasized the role of bureaucracy in implementing various types of reform. They argued that resistance from bureaucracy was the sole impediment to the implementation of reforms. These studies were predominantly descriptive in nature and lacked a theoretical understanding, nor did they take into account a set of factors that may impede or facilitate accounting reforms. The notion of the policy objectives, the relevance of the cultural, economic and political conditions of the country, the institutional structure and the role of transnational organizations in the implementation of government accounting reforms have received little/or no attention. However, as some studies indicated (Bergevärn *et al.*, 1995; Tinker, 2004; Wickramasinghe and Hopper, 2005; Farazmand, 2002; Broadbent and Guthrie, 2008), these factors are crucial for understanding the development of accounting within societies. Therefore, this study is aimed at providing an understanding of the development of accounting in Pakistan.

Several studies have been made of the development of government accounting in various contexts. Among other countries, these have included studies on Nepal (Adhikari, 2005), Russia (Timoshenko, 2006), Norway (Gårseth-Nesbakk, 2007) and Sri Lanka (Kuruppu, 2010). These researchers have investigated accounting in non-Muslim countries. This study relates to a Muslim country. Pakistan, being a mainly Muslim country, differentiates the context of this research setting from that of earlier studies. Investigating the role of religion in the development of accounting is interesting because some historical studies (Carmona and Ezzamel, 2006; Baker, 2006; Ather and Ullah., 2009) have shown a relationship between religion and accounting.

Pakistan is unique for several reasons and differs from the countries mentioned above. Pakistan is a Muslim-majority country and Islam has been officially declared the state religion. First, the constitution of the country declares that no law can be made that is against Islam.

Therefore, this study incorporates religious and cultural perspectives and tries to investigate their role in the development of government accounting. Second, this means theoretically that government accounting may be influenced by religion, because religion plays a central role in determining the financial affairs of Muslims. Moreover, Islamic law describes the principles dealing with the financial matters of Muslims, which they are obliged to follow.

Several studies (Ryan *et al.*, 2007; Wickramasinghe and Hopper, 2005; Simpkins, 2006) indicate that politics play an important role in reforming government accounting and the process of accounting standards setting is not technical but rather a political decision. The history of Pakistan has witnessed both civil and military regimes. It is interesting to analyse the role of politics in initiating accounting reforms during various civilian and military regimes. Similarly, the government accounting reforms devised in developed countries are acknowledged as an international phenomenon (Guthrie *et al.*, 1999). Pakistan has opened up its economy and freed it from government control (The Government of Pakistan, 2011). The country has been of central importance at an international level since its independence in 1947. It played an important role in 1979 during the Soviet-Afghan war and in the war against terrorism after the 9/11 incident. It is important to study the global public-sector reforms in the context of Pakistan, which presents a unique context in its historical, cultural, political and religious aspects.

> The craft can now be talked about, discussed and analyzed in very different ways. Different linkages can be established between accounting and wider processes of organizational and social functioning and change. Accounting can now be intelligently interrogated and examined in the name of a number of different cultural, social and political agendas.
>
> *(Hopwood, 2005, p. 585)*

Previous research (Järvinen, 2006; Nobes, 2004; Ryan *et al.*, 2007) has concluded that accounting was the product of its context. This study raises questions connected to the development of accounting in the Pakistani context. This has been done by describing and analysing the development of accounting through the following research question: how has accounting developed in Pakistan?

A dialogue between the global wave of reforms vs public and private sector

The end of the last century witnessed profound reforms instigated to improve public-sector performance around the globe. Accounting is no exception to this general global trend (Timoshenko, 2006). This wave of reforms was called the 'new management era' by Hood (2000) as there was a paradigm shift from public administration to public management. However, the institutionalization of these reforms has varied greatly from one country to another (Olson *et al.*, 2001). As Ouda (2003) has pointed out, few countries have implemented these radical accounting reforms at different levels to enhance efficiency. Most countries still use the old management tools and accounting systems. He has pointed out that countries practising the old accounting system believe that modern management tools and informative accounting systems are most suitable for profit-oriented organizations, whereas public-sector organizations are aimed at serving the interests of the general public instead of just making profits (Ouda, 2003). Primarily, these public-sector reforms have come under the umbrella of New Public Management (NPM).

Hood (1995, p. 93) has argued that NPM movement was regarded as a 'global phenomenon', owing to its strong attachment to the financial management of the public sector. The

NPM-based reforms, specifically focusing on financial aspects, have been labelled 'New Public Financial Management' (NPFM) (Olson *et al.*, 1998). The transformation of public administration to public management has been the main focus of these reforms (Lapsley, 1999, p. 201), with the emphasis being put on result-based performance instead of cash spending. NPFM has particularly focused on accounting change (Ellwood and Wynne, 2005). The primary accounting change has included a shift towards full accrual accounting, with a significant emphasis on financial reporting and public accountability. Traditional cash-based accounting has been replaced by accrual accounting in many OECD countries, and financial performance has been evaluated on the basis of results, rather than cash spending.

Nevertheless, the global reforms have significantly changed the management of public-sector organizations (Olsen *et al.*, 1998; Broadbent and Guthrie, 2008; Barton, 2009). This happened because there was a growing need for fundamental change in the way that public organizations were structured and managed (Barzelay and Armajani, 1992; Osborne and Gaebler, 1992; Lapsley, 2009). Moreover, the private sector has grown rapidly and has operated in highly diversified areas, both effectively and profitably. The private sector now provides goods and services previously delivered by public-sector organizations. The emergence of an efficient private sector created a competitive environment in which both public- and private-sector organizations function. Inspired by the provision of better services provided by the private sector, people started to make comparisons between the private and public sectors, with the ultimate aim of receiving better services. This created pressure on the public sector and, consequently, successive governments all over the globe are under pressure to modernize their public sectors (English and Skærbæk, 2007). Pakistan is no exception to this trend.

In order to address the 'financial' aspects of the public sector, NPFM sparked a growing interest in financial reforms, government accounting and accountability. The idea is that the public sector can be managed like the private sector, resulting in better efficiency, effectiveness and accountability in delivering public services (Lapsley, 1999; Lapsley, 2009; Lapsley and Oldfield, 2001; Klumpes, 2001). According to Olson, Guthrie and Humphrey (1998, p. 17),

> the result has been the pursuit of policies of restraint on public spending, the selling of public assets, the adoption of market models and the promotion of performance measurement, auditing and business accounting system for a wide range of public sector organizations.

It seems that this global wave of reforms has helped to create liberal governments in developed societies with minimum intervention in the market; improvements in efficiency and effectiveness; and a greater customer focus through responsiveness and accountability at all levels of government.

This new liberal form of government emphasizes that market is 'self-regulated' and that buyers and sellers interact according to their cost-benefit analysis. However, there are differences between the private and the public sectors. The private sector performs efficiently and effectively because its core aim is profitability. The private sector operates within specific geographical areas and must bring profitable business for their owners. They do not invest in products, services and areas that are unprofitable for the owners or the managers. On the contrary, the public sector takes responsibility for the fundamental products and services that the private sector does not produce or produces at a cost level that is unaffordable for the mass public. This differentiates the public sector from the private sector, and therefore economists define public goods as those provided by the public sector. Nevertheless, the market, in which the public and private sectors interact, is very dynamic. It defines and redefines public goods. Therefore, the need to reform the public sector has continued for decades and the size of the government sector has continuously decreased.

The output of these reforms in diversified contexts shows that these reforms may have produced both positive and negative consequences. Public-sector organizations work in a 'cultural political economy' (Wickramasinghe and Hopper, 2005), providing 'public goods' at subsidized prices, especially in developing countries such as Pakistan, where GDP growth is relatively low and people have limited purchasing power owing to high unemployment. Therefore, the state arbitrates as well as controls the market in such economies. The role of the state seems to have become more important after the global financial crisis beginning in 2008, which the market seemed unable to control. This in turn stimulated the state to intervene and rescue economies by providing bailout packages using public taxation – even in advanced economies such as the US and Europe.

Although many countries have been moving in the same direction in a search for good governance in public service delivery, differences still prevail in the intensity of the aforementioned reforms (Guthrie et al., 1999, p. 210). There are substantial elements of diversity in the pace, nature and extent of accounting reforms across OECD countries. Variations in accounting systems may also exist because the needs of countries vary (Radebaugh et al., 2006; Nobes, 1998). Olson et al. (1998) hold the view that, although there are some similarities among the jargon in some national cases, 'actual practice' indicates significant differences in how concepts are applied in practice.

Pakistan has also followed these global waves of reforms initiated in developed countries and travelling across country borders. Although there is a long list of financial and public-sector reforms, recently the government approved the privatization of 57 public sector organizations,[3] and the restructuring of eight other public-sector institutions.[4]

Government accounting is an unexplored area in Pakistan and there are barely any empirical studies on it. This research attempts to fill out this academic gap in the accounting literature. Hopefully this can offer a valuable contribution for accounting researchers studying government accounting in various countries. This research also aims to provide theoretical contributions associated with the chosen perspectives integrating political, cultural and religious perspectives and their importance for the development of government accounting. Hopefully this research can contribute to the vacuum in accounting research concerning Islamic countries. As Meek and Thomas (2004) have pointed out, researchers have generally not paid much attention to accounting development research in Islamic nations.

Development of accounting and financial reporting in Pakistan (1947–2015)

Pakistan made significant efforts to institutionalise accounting and financial reporting since its independence from the British in 1947. The development of accounting and financial reporting practices in Pakistan can be understood through studying the historical development of accounting through following events.

Establishment of the auditor general of Pakistan

The main documents that regulated government accounting in Pakistan after independence included the 1935 Government of India Act, the 1936 Audit and Accounts Order and the Combined Set of Account Code, the first two of which were the genesis of accounting in

Table 4.1 Appointment, powers and functions of the auditor general of India

Article No.	Description
166	**Auditor-General of India** There shall be an Auditor-General of India, who shall be appointed by His Majesty and shall only be removed from office in like manner and on the like grounds as a judge of The Federal Court.
168	**Power of Auditor-General of India to give directions as to accounts** The accounts of the Federation shall be kept in such a form as the Auditor-General of India may, with the approval of the Governor-General, prescribe and, in so far as the Auditor-General of India may, with the like approval, give any directions with regard to the methods or principles in accordance with which any accounts of Provinces ought to be kept, it shall be the duty of every Provincial Government to cause accounts to be kept accordingly.
169	**Audit reports** The reports of the Auditor-General of India relating to the accounts of the Federation shall be submitted to the Governor-General, who shall cause them to be laid before the Federal Legislature, and the reports of the Auditor-General of India, or of the Auditor-General of the Province, as the case may be, relating to the accounts of a Province shall be submitted to the Governor of the Province, who shall cause them to be laid before the Provincial Legislature.

Source: Government of India Act 1935

Pakistan. By contrast, the Combined Set of Account Code outlined the detailed principles, methods and 'chart of classification'. The 'chart of classification' consisted of account codes for recording transactions. As had been the case under British rule, after independence the institution of the auditor general of Pakistan was established under the chapter (Audit and Accounts) of the 1935 Government of India Act. This Act included Articles 166, 168 and 169, which dealt with the appointment, powers and functions of the auditor general, as shown in Table 4.1.

Most of the informants for this study stated that Pakistan adopted its accounting system (procedures, policy and account codes) in 1924. The government accounting policy had been published in book form, namely the Combined Set of Account Code, presented in four volumes. Volume I outlined the general accounting principles, policies and methods of accounting related to the 'civil accounts' of government. The 'chart of classification' was added at the end of Volume I. Volume II dealt with the 'treasury accounts' of government, while Volume III outlined the accounting principles and methods dealing with 'departmental accounts' and Volume IV dealt with the closing of accounts.[5] This indicates that Pakistan inherited a well-developed system of government accounting in 1947 from the British as an integral part of its governance structure managed through a bureaucracy named the Indian Audit and Accounts Service.

The British had a well-developed bureaucratic service structure at a central level. This included, but was not limited to the police service, the agricultural service and the Indian audit and account service. The British government recognized the importance of the government accounting profession and established a government accounting system. A separate cadre of the Indian Audit and Accounts Service was instituted with responsibility for government accounting. The employees associated with government accounting were classified into two classes, Class I and Class II. The employees in Class I belonged to the executive level and were placed higher up in the hierarchy. They were given responsibility for formulating government accounting policies and methods. Operational-level employees were grouped into Class II. The Class II officers were named assistants in the Accounts and Audit Officers Service and held posts as operational-level accountants (Kennedy, 1987). The Class II posts were responsible for maintaining day-to-day accounting transactions. They were supposed to provide assistance to the top-level bureaucracy (Class I) in accounting policy formulation. As was the nature of the British bureaucratic structure, there existed an enormous power difference between these two classes because the employees in Class I were considered the elite of society, very different from the Class II employees (Hussain, 1976).

Kennedy (1987) and Quddus (1991b) argued that Pakistan, with some minor modifications, maintained the British government accounting system and adopted the bureaucratic service structure of the British. The Accounts Service remained centralized in Pakistan, as it had been under the British government, and comprised 1) the Pakistan Audit and Accounts Service (PAAS), 2) the Pakistan Military Accounts Service (PMAS) and 3) the Pakistan Railways Accounts Service (PRAS). The genesis of the Pakistan Audit and Accounts Service can be traced directly to the Accounts Department of the Government of India and the Indian Audit and Accounts Service. Military accounts were regulated separately by the Military Finance Department, at the time of partition under the direct control of the Secretary of State. This led to the formation of the Pakistan Military Accounts Service. The Pakistan Railways Accounts Service originated from the Railway Finance and Accounts Service of 1929. By the time of independence, these departments were grouped under the overall control of the Audit and Accounts Department. Moreover, separate branches and cadres were maintained for civil accounts, army accounts, railway accounts and postal accounts (Islam, 1989). The powers and responsibilities of the auditor general were defined in the Audit and Accounts Order 1936 as follows.

> The Auditor General shall be responsible for the keeping of the accounts of the Federation and of each province other than account of the Federation relating to defense or railways and accounts relating to transactions in the United Kingdom. . . . The Auditor General shall, from the accounts kept by him and by the other persons responsible for keeping public accounts, prepare in each year accounts (including, in the case of accounts kept by him, appropriation accounts) showing the annual receipts and disbursements for the purposes of the Federation and each Province distinguished under the respective heads thereof, and shall submit those accounts to the Federal Government, or as the case may be. . . . It shall be the duty of the Auditor General to prepare annually, in such form as he with the concurrence of the Governor General may determine, and to submit to the Governor General a General Financial Statement incorporating a summary of the accounts of the Federation and of all the Provinces for the last preceding year and particulars of their balances and outstanding liabilities

In 1948, postal accounts were merged with civil accounts, leading to three types of government accounting departments, which were the Pakistan Audit and Accounts Service (PAAS), the Pakistan Military Accounts Service (PMAS) and the Pakistan Railways Accounts Service (PRAS). However, their corresponding service structures remained intact. This division of accounts functions remained unchanged until the promulgation of the 1973 reforms (Kennedy, 1987, p. 38).

The higher-level employees performing government accounting jobs were integrated as part of the bureaucratic elite centrally managed under the accounts services. The bureaucracy could be characterized as overdeveloped because the structure of governance had depended on the bureaucracy since colonial times. This 'overdeveloped bureaucratic state' (Alvi, 1972 cited in Smith, 2003, p. 118) apparatus was customized according to the needs of the colonial period and was later transferred to Pakistan at the time of independence in 1947. The bureaucrats made up a very powerful elite of society and were described as a 'steel frame' (Khuhro, 1972). It was the strong Indian civil service that made it possible for the British to rule over one of the largest and ethnically, linguistically and religiously diversified colonies of the world. It had been argued that 'the Indian Civil Service (ICS) was the pivotal service around which the entire administrative edifice of British was organized' (Hakim, 1991, p. 6). Like other parts of the bureaucracy, the post of auditor general was also an integrated part of the inherited colonial bureaucracy and enjoyed the powers described above.

For the purpose of accountability, the auditor general was required to submit the annual accounts of the federal government to the governor-general (Government of India Act, 1935). These accounts included transactions that took place during the financial year running from 1 April to 31 March (Governemnt of Pakistan). It seems that the accounting cycle ran according to the natural economic cycle of the country, which mainly concerned agricultural products. This was described by informant #1 as follows.

> Pakistan is basically an agricultural country. The agricultural seasons started from 1st April and ending on 31st March. The British had developed this accounting cycle according to the agricultural products cycle.

The auditor general was required to submit annual financial statements, which combined the finance and revenue accounts of the federal government for the same financial year. This was a manually maintained accounting system and the accounting documents (such as cheques and vouchers) were sent from remote areas of the country by post or train to form part of the centralized government accounts. It seems that accounts sent from the remote areas could be delayed and financial statements could be prepared before all of the accounts had been received (by the end of the financial year) in the centralized system. This meant that there were risks of delays and losses of documents (information) owing to the old communication methods between the centre and the peripheries. In order to handle these situations, the auditor general introduced the Combined Set of Account Code (Government of Pakistan, p. 12):

> the government accounts of a year may be kept open for a certain period in the following year for completion of the various accounting processes inter alia in respect of the transactions of march, for the carrying out certain inter-departmental adjustments, and for the closing of the accounts of several Provident Funds and Suspense heads. Adjustments may also be made after the close of the year owing to mispostings and misclassifications coming to notice after the 31st March. An actual transaction taking place after 31st March should not, however, be treated as pertaining to the previous financial year even though the accounts for that year may be open for the purposes mentioned above.

Pakistani government accounting was criticized for lacking completeness by the close of the financial year. It took a long time to receive accounting information from the peripheries (8–22 months) and government accounts remained open after the end of the financial year. Moreover, a huge number of dubious transactions were recorded in the account codes, which were called 'suspense heads' because the exact transactions and their account codes were unknown. This was one of the critical aspects in manually recorded government accounting in Pakistan.

It was difficult to verify a transaction if a person who had made an entry (in a suspense head) had retired or been transferred and if the vouchers that might indicate the original transaction had been lost. This was illustrated by informant #4 as follows.

> Vouchers were paid all around Pakistan by The Post Office. These vouchers were sent to the Director Account of Pakistan's post office in Lahore. A huge number of vouchers and many heads of account (accounts code) were unknown. The reason is that the transactions were originated in periphery offices around the country and recorded at a centralized office at Lahore. For example, if a person recorded an accounting transaction, and he/she did not know whether the voucher was paid for purchase of a computer (account code#A09) or for repairing of a computer (account code#A13), then he would record it in suspense account (account code#A14). Afterwards, he would write a letter to the person who had originated the transaction and might get an answer to correct the transaction. But, in the majority of cases, answers were not received and there existed a huge number of entries in the suspense account, from my appointment till today, which were not adjusted.

The government accounts were maintained in Pakistani currency, Pakistani rupees, issued by the central bank of Pakistan. Initially, after independence, Pakistan used Indian currency notes and coins, simply overlaid with a 'government of Pakistan' stamp, until it issued its own new currency notes and coins in 1948. Accounting was maintained on a cash basis and transactions were recorded on actual cash receipts and payments. This showed that accounting was based on the 'recognition principle' of accounting, as evidenced in the documents (Government of Pakistan, p. 12):

> The transactions in Government accounts shall represent the actual cash receipts and disbursements during a financial year as distinguished from amounts due to or by Government during the same period.

Government accounts were organized into four divisions: revenue, capital, debt and remittances. The revenue account dealt with taxation and other receipts. The capital account dealt with expenditure, usually met from borrowed funds. The debt account comprised receipts and payments in respect of which the government had to repay the money received or the government had a claim to recover amounts paid to other organizations or governments. The remittance account is basically a control account for recording transactions between the various departments. The remittance account was used to record how much cash was withdrawn and deposited by the various departments (Government of Pakistan, p. 12). The transactions within each of these divisions were grouped into sections, which were further subdivided into a 'major classification'. Each major classification also had a 'minor classification'. For example, the Revenue Division was divided into three sections, namely tax revenue, non-tax revenue and capital receipts. Each of these transactions was further subdivided into a major classification and a minor classification. This inherited system was practised for a long time after independence and, compared to other administrative reforms, the government accounting reforms lagged behind. Moreover, government accounting was managed by the civil service and several reform commissions had been established in an attempt to reform the governance structure and higher bureaucracy. Some of the reform reports prepared during the formative stage included the Rowland Egger Report (1953), the Bernard L. Gladieux Report (1955) and the Paul L. Beckett Report (1957).

In 1956, after the introduction of the first constitution, the British-inherited governance structure was changed, which also changed the accounting cycle. The interim constitution was replaced by the 1956 constitution. The post of the auditor general was renamed the comptroller and auditor general in the 1956 constitution, which contained articles related to the appointment, functions and powers of the comptroller and auditor general. As opposed to the governor-general in the previous interim constitution, the president appointed the comptroller and auditor general, who had been given responsibilities for maintaining government accounting and auditing. However, accounting policies, methods and procedures were not changed. This meant that the 1936 Audit and Account Order 1936 and the 1924 Combined Set of Account Codes continued in force. The comptroller and auditor general was now required to submit annual financial accounts to the president, who in turn submitted such reports to the National Assembly. However, this system of governance was discontinued in 1958, when the military removed the civilian government, leading to the 'state-guided development era', lasting from 1958–1971.

The foundation of the Institute of Cost and Management Accountants of Pakistan (ICMAP)

In order to regulate and promote management accounting in Pakistan, the Institute of Cost and Management Accountants of Pakistan (ICMAP) was established in 1951. The ICMAP is chartered under the Cost and Management Accountants Act No. XIV of 1966 of the Parliament of Pakistan. Moreover, the activities of the Institute are governed under the Cost and Management Accountants Regulations of 1990. By law, the functions of the ICMAP extend to providing education, identifying internationally accepted certification and examining the competencies of individual professionals. The Institute awards designations of associate cost and management accountant (ACMA), and fellow cost and management accountant (FCMA) to its members on qualification and the completion of all prescribed requirements.

The Institute has around 5,000 members working at senior level position such as CEOs, CIAs, CFOs, financial analysts, management consultants and public practitioners, so the members of the ICMAP play a significant role in the economic and business development of the country.

The Institute is expanding substantially, with over 15,000 registered students, around 200 faculty members and more than 260 employees. The ICMAP has seven regional and six overseas branch councils, 11 campuses and 20 examination centres. The functions of the Institute include education, conducting examinations, carrying out research and publications, organizing CPD programmes and providing corporate training. Furthermore, the Institute is continuously providing support to governmental agencies including, but not limited to, the Planning Commission, the Ministry of Finance, the Securities and Exchange Commission of Pakistan, the Ministry of Commerce, the State Bank of Pakistan, the Accountant General of Pakistan Revenue, the Federal Board of Revenue and other ministries, policymaking organizations and regulators.

Formation of the Institute of Chartered Accountants of Pakistan (ICAP)

In order to regulate the accounting profession in the country, the government of Pakistan adopted the Companies Act of 1913 and the Auditors' Certificate Rules, 1932. The Auditors' Certificate Rules were reformed in the year 1950 to meet the needs of the country. Registered accountants established a private body named the Pakistan Institute of Accountants (PIA) to work for the interests of accountants through promoting the accounting profession in the country. The PIA worked for the establishment of an independent body, leading to the creation of a Department of Accountancy in 1959, with a controller of accountancy as its head. The advisory body of the PIA recommended the formation of the Institute of Chartered Accountants in Pakistan.

As a result, the government issued the Chartered Accountants Ordinance in 1961 (Government of Pakistan, 1961). This ordinance led to the formation of the ICAP, the accounting standard-setting organization in Pakistan, in 1961 as a statutory body to regulate the accounting profession. Public companies are required to audit their financial statements by 'chartered accountants' i.e., members of the ICAP (United Nations, 2007).[6] The members of the ICAP follow the professional guidelines of accounting, auditing and ethics. The ICAP has followed the accounting standards of the IFRS, issued by the International Accounting Standards Board (IASB). It adopted the auditing standards issued by International Standards on Auditing (ISA). Moreover, the ethics codes issued by the International Federation of Accountants (IFAC) have been adopted.

The ICAP has formulated various committees to technically review the IFRS. These committees also communicate their exposure drafts to the corporate sector, its registered members and other stakeholders. After the established due process of technical review and consultation, the ICAP recommend the adoption of particular standards to its council. The council is responsible for providing the strategic direction of the ICAP and for approving policies to secure the interests of the accounting profession and the public. The council is headed by the executive director, with the secretary and department directors as members. The council comprises 19 members in total. Fifteen out of 19 council members are elected from ICAP members for a term of four years, whereas the rest four council members are nominated by the government of Pakistan.[7]

The Council of the ICAP, after completion of due process, recommends a particular standard to the Securities and Exchange Commission of Pakistan (SECP) for adoption. The SECP, before notification of the adoption of standards to be followed by listed companies, follows its internal process of reviewing the recommended standards. It may be noted that Pakistan has been adopting IFRS standards without making any changes to them (United Nations, 2007). As a result, the Pakistan Generally Accepted Accounting Principles (GAAP) are based largely on the IAS.

The Council of the ICAP is working with the SECP and the State Bank of Pakistan to ensure that Pakistan GAAP comply fully with the IFRS by end of 2009 (United Nations, 2007). For this purpose, a committee has been formed by the Professional Standards and Technical Advisory Committee for gap analysis. The committee task is to identify inconsistencies between existing laws and the IFRS. The ICAP works closely with the SECP and the State Bank of Pakistan.

The Companies Ordinance, 1984

The Companies Ordinance, 1984, outlines the basics for accounting and financial reporting for companies operating in Pakistan. The ordinance requires all companies operating in Pakistan to prepare, present and publish their financial statements. Besides various provisions relating to financial reporting, the Fourth Schedule is called 'Requirements as to Balance Sheet and Profit and Loss Accounts of Listed Companies'. This describes the form, content and disclosure requirements for preparing financial statements for listed companies.

The Fifth Schedule of the Companies Ordinance, named 'Requirement as to Balance Sheet and Profit and Loss Accounts of Non-Listed Companies', dealing with the form, content and disclosure requirements of non-listed companies operating in Pakistan. In order to bring the ordinance into compliance with the IFRS, the Companies Ordinance, 1984, and its Fourth Schedule have been revised. Now it is mandatory for listed companies (with subsidiaries) operating in Pakistan to prepare consolidated financial statements in compliance with the IFRS as notified by the SECP.

Establishment of the Securities and Exchange Commission of Pakistan

The Corporate Law Authority (CLA), established in 1984, was the regulatory body of the corporate sector in Pakistan. The CLA worked under the Ministry of Finance and faced financial, independence and authority issues in carrying out its functions. In order to enhance its independence and bring more professionals, the Corporate Law Authority was restructured under the Capital Market Development Plan, initiated by the Asian Development Bank (ADB), in 1997. As a result of these reforms, the SECP was established by the Securities and Exchange Commission of Pakistan Act, 1997.

> This act institutionalized certain policy decisions relating to the constitution, structure, powers and functions of SECP, thereby giving it administrative authority and financial independence in carry out its regulatory and statutory responsibilities.
>
> *(UN, 2007, p. 9)*

The SECP started its work in January 1999. At the beginning, the task of the SECP was to regulate the corporate sector and the capital market. Lately, the scope of the SECP has been expanded through bringing the non-banking financial sector, insurance companies and private pensions under the supervision of the SECP. The SECP also examines the functions of various external companies providing services to the corporate and financial sector in Pakistan including, but not limited to, chartered accountants, brokers and corporate secretaries. The magnitude of the challenges of the SECP has increased with the growth of its responsibilities.

The SECP plays an important role in the development of accounting and financial reporting practices in Pakistan. The SECP notifies the IFRS and IAS, with the advice of the ICAP and the State Bank of Pakistan. SECP also ensure the compliance with the IFRS and IAS. Besides reducing a gap between international standards and local corporate financial reporting through adopting the IFRS, the SECP has developed a mechanism for their enforcement. This mechanism has led to a significant improvement in corporate financial reporting in Pakistan. SECP works closely with the ICAP and the State Bank of Pakistan in adopting the IFRS and IAS in Pakistan.

According to the Companies Ordinance, company directors are responsible for the timely preparation of annual financial statements and presenting these financial statements at the annual general meetings of shareholders (Companies Ordinance, 1984). The audited financial statements, along with the director's report, should be submitted to the Registrar of Companies within one month of the annual general meeting of shareholders. The failure to submit audited financial statements and director's report could lead to a fine, imprisonment or both.[8] All listed companies are required to prepare and file their quarterly financial statements with the SECP and the stock exchange. The failure to comply could lead to a fine of 100,000 Pakistani rupees for the responsible director, the chief executive officer (CEO) and the chief financial officer (CFO). Moreover, the SECP can demand additional accounts and reports if they are necessary to regulate the listed companies.[9]

SECP has an Enforcement and Monitoring Department. This department ensures the adoption of the IFRS by listed companies as listed companies are required to comply with SECP rules of corporate accounting and disclosure. The Enforcement and Monitoring Department uses a standard checklist format in order to ensure compliance with applicable accounting and reporting requirements. However, the SECP lacks capacity to monitor and enforce the IFRS, as discussed in a UN (2007) report:

> Strengthening SECP capacity would improve its monitoring and enforcement function.
>
> *(UN, 2007, p. 4).*

The Insurance Ordinance of 2000

The Insurance Ordinance was issued in 2000 to regulate the accounting and financial reporting of insurance companies in Pakistan. The Insurance Ordinance gives the SECP power to implement accounting, reporting and auditing laws relating to insurance companies. According to the Insurance Ordinance, certified charted accountants of the ICAP must audit the financial statements of the insurance companies. For this purpose, the SECP has issued a list of approved chartered accountants. The insurance companies are required to submit their audited financial statements to the SECP within four months of the financial year end.

State Bank of Pakistan

The State Bank of Pakistan (SBP) was established by the State Bank of Pakistan Order 1948 to function as the central bank of Pakistan. This order was changed on January 1, 1974 after the nationalization of banks as the functional area of the State Bank was increased. The Banking Companies Ordinance, issued in 1962, empowers the State Bank of Pakistan to regulate banks to comply with the accounting and auditing requirements as outlined in the ordinance. Additionally, the SBP also requires banks to follow the accounting and reporting rules of the Companies Ordinance of 1984, the SECP and the stock exchange. For the purpose of disclosure, banks in Pakistan are required to follow prescribed formats issued by the SBP for the preparation and disclosure of financial statements. The banking-sector accounting and financial reporting regime is not fully in compliance with the IFRS as financial institutions are granted an exemption from IFRS 39 and IFRS 40 (World Bank, 2005).

Banks and financial institutions are required to publish their audited financial reports and submit these reports to SBP within three months of the end of the accounting period. The financial statement needs to be audited by qualified and SBP-approved auditors. SBP-approved auditors are divided into three categories based on the size of the firm, its audit experience and ICAP-rated quality control. These categories are given below.

Current status of adoption of the IFRS

Besides reducing the gap between international standards and local corporate financial reporting by adopting the IFRS, Pakistan has also developed a mechanism for their enforcement. This mechanism led to a significant improvement in corporate financial reporting in Pakistan. According to the World Bank Reports on Observance of Standards and Codes 2005, Pakistan has adopted all IAS recommended by the ICAP and notified by the SECP for listed companies. The Word Bank has noted that IAS 29 (*Financial Reporting in Hyperinflationary Economies*), IAS 41 (*Agriculture*) and IFRS 1 to 6 have not been adopted. As a result of the report, the SECP

Table 4.2 Categories of SBP-approved auditors

Category	Description
A	Audit all banks and development financial institutions.
B	Audit banks and development financial institutions with total assets (net of contra items) up to 50 billion Pakistani rupees or with up to 99 branches.
C	Audit banks and development financial institutions with total assets (net of contra items) below five billion Pakistani rupees or with fewer than 10 branches.

Source: Report on the Observance of Standards and Codes (ROSC) Pakistan, International Monetary Fund (2005, p. 4)

approved IAS 41, IFRS 2, IFRS 3, IFRS 5 and IFRS 6, as recommended by the ICAP. The State Bank of Pakistan, on the recommendation of the ICAP and Pakistan Banks' Association, stopped the application of IAS 39 and IAS 40. However, they agreed to adopt these and other IFRS within the next two years. This will lead the banks' and financial institutions' financial reporting to comply fully with the IFRS.

Summary

Pakistan adopted accounting from Britain in 1947. Moreover, several institutions were established to strengthen the accounting profession in the country over a period of time. In this development process, various contextual factors played a crucial role. These factors include, but are not limited to, the role of the government and private-sector accounting organizations, the culture and institutional set-up of the country and the role of international organizations such as the IASB, the World Bank and the International Monetary Fund.

As a result, hybrid accounting developed in Pakistan over a period of time. This meant that country-specific accounting and reporting processes emerged. Such accounting change happened because the country's institutional set-up would not support the IFRS in their original shape. This showed that accounting rules coming from developed countries may not be applicable to developing countries in their exact form as developing countries may not have the necessary supporting institutional arrangements for their implementation. This could lead to a change in the process of accounting standards to meet local institutional requirements.

Notes

1 Imtiaz Badshah is an Assistant Professor at NUST Business School, National University of Sciences and Technology, Islamabad, and has a PhD in Accounting from Bodø Graduate School of Business, University of Nordland, Norway.
2 Frode Mellemvik is Professor at Bodø Graduate School of Business, Nord University, Norway.
3 Archives of Jang Group Newspapers. Retrieved from www.jang.com.pk/jang/mar2010-daily/05-03-2010/u23169.htm (accessed 10 March 2010).
4 Retrieved from www.jang.com.pk/jang/mar2010-daily/10-03-2010/u23694.htm (accessed 10 March 2010).
5 www.pifra.gov.pk/chart-of-accounts.html.
6 United Nations (2007), United Nations Conference on Trade and Development.
7 www.icap.org.pk/icap/council-president.
8 Section 236 of the Companies Ordinance.
9 Section 246 of the Companies Ordinance.

Bibliography

Adhikari, P. (2005) *Government Accounting in Nepal: Tracing the Past and the Present*. PhD thesis, Bodø University College.
Alavi, H. (1972) The state in post-colonial societies: Pakistan and Bangladesh. *New Left Review, 74*, 24–42.
Ali, S.B. (2012) *Corporate Governance and Accounting Practices in Pakistan*. MPRA Munich Personal RePEc Archive.
Ather, S.M. and Ullah, M.H. (2009) Islamic Accounting Systems and Practices. *The Cost and Management, 37*(6), 9–16.
Baker, R.C. (2006) Towards a genealogy of wealth through an analysis of biblical discourses. *Accounting History, 11*, 151.
Baloch, A. (2003) *Impact of Political and Constitutional Development on Administrative System: A Case Study of Civil Bureaucracy in Pakistan*. PhD thesis, University of Karachi.
Barton, A. (1999) Public and private sector accounting – the non-identical twins. *Australian Accounting Review, 9*, 22–31.

Barton, A. (2005) Professional accounting standards and the public sector – a mismatch. *Abacus*, *41*, 138–158.

Barton, A. (2009) The use and abuse of accounting in the public sector financial management reform program in Australia. *Abacus*, *45*, 221–248.

Barzelay, M. and Armajani, M. (1992) *Breaking Through Bureaucracy: A New Vision for Managing in Government*. Berkeley, CA: University of California Press.

Bergevärn, L.-E., Mellemvik, F. and Olson, O. (1995) Institutionalization of municipal accounting – a comparative study between Sweden and Norway. *Scandinavian Journal of Management*, *11*, 25–41.

Braibanti, R. (1965) Pakistan: Constitutional issues in 1964. *Asian Survey*, *5*, 79–87.

Braibanti, R. (1968) Comparative political analytics reconsidered. *The Journal of Politics*, *30*, 25–65.

Braibanti, R. (1987) Public bureaucracy and judiciary in Pakistan. In J.R. Khan (Ed.) *Evolution of Pakistan's Administrative System: The Collected Papers of Ralph Braibanti*. Islamabad: Pakistan Public Administration Research Center O & M Division.

Broadbent, J. and Guthrie, J. (2008) Public sector to public services: 20 years of 'contextual' accounting research. *Accounting, Auditing & Accountability Journal*, *21*, 129.

Carmona, S. and Ezzamel, M. (2006) Accounting and religion: a historical perspective. *Accounting History*, *11*, 117.

Ellwood, S. and Wynne, A. (2005) An accrual world? Questioning the universal validity of accrual accounting. In A. Bourmistrov, A. and Frode, M. (Eds) *International Trends and Experiences in Government Accounting*. Oslo: Cappelen Akademisk Forlag.

English, L. and Skærbæk, P. (2007) Performance auditing and the modernisation of the public sector. *Financial Accountability and Management*, *23*, 239–241.

Farazmand, A. (2002) *Administrative Reform in Developing Nations*. Westport, CT: Praeger.

Gårseth-Nesbakk, L. (2007) *Experimentation with Accrual Accounting at the Central Government Level in Norway*. PhD thesis, University of Nordland.

Government of India (1935) Government of India Act 1935.

Government of Pakistan (1956) Constitution of 1956. Retrieved from www.therepublicofrumi.com/archives/56_00.htm.

Government of Pakistan (1962) Constitution.

Government of Pakistan (1973) Contititution. Retrieved from www.pakistani.org/pakistan/constitution/part1.html.

Government of Pakistan (1980) Zakat and Ushr Ordinance, 1980.

Government of Pakistan (1981) The Departmentalization of Accounts Rules, 1981.

Government of Pakistan (1992) *Diagnostics Consultancy Project*. Pakistan Audit Department (PAD).

Government of Pakistan (1993) Pakistan Institute of Public Finance Accountants. Retrieved from www.pipfa.org.pk/aboutmembership.asp.

Government of Pakistan (1998) *Census Data*. Retrieved from www.census.gov.pk/religion.htm.

Government of Pakistan (2000a) *Accounting Policies and Procedures Manual*.

Government of Pakistan (2000b) *Civil Establishment Code Estacode*. Islamabad: Pakistan Public Administration Research Center: Management Services Wing.

Government of Pakistan (2000c) *Manual of Accounting Principles*.

Government of Pakistan (2000d) *Summary for the Chief Executive: Revision in the Form, Principles, and Methods of Accounts of the Federation and Provinces*.

Government of Pakistan (2001) Ordinance NO. XXIV of 2001.

Government of Pakistan (2003) *Report on Hudood Ordinances 1979*. Council of Islamic Ideology.

Government of Pakistan (2004) PC-I (Revised) Project Implementation of Financial Reporting and Auditing (PIFRA).

Government of Pakistan. (2005a) Fiscal Responsibility and Debt Limitation Act 2005.

Government of Pakistan (2005b) Project for Improvement of Financial Reporting and Auditing: PIFRA (Phase-II).

Government of Pakistan (2007) National Reconciliation Ordinance. Retrieved from www.pakistani.org/pakistan/legislation/2007/NationalReconciliationOrdinance.html.

Government of Pakistan (2008) *Report of the National Commission for Government Reforms on Reforming the Government in Pakistan*.

Government of Pakistan (2009) *Combined Set of Account Code*.

Government of Pakistan (2010) PIFRA (Phase II) Revised PC_I.

Government of Pakistan (2010a) *Chart of Accounts*. Retrieved from www.bbc.co.uk/urdu/india/2012/05/120525_india_billioneress_a.shtml.

Government of Pakistan (2010b) *Financial Statements of the Federal Government.*

Government of Pakistan (2011) Highlight: Pakistan Economic Survey 2011–12.

Guthrie, J., Olson, O. and Humphrey, C. (1999) Debating developments in new public financial management: The limits of global theorising and some new ways forward. *Financial Accountability & Management, 15*, 209–228.

Haider, M. (2011) All five-year plans of Pakistan were failures. *The News.*

Haider, S.M. (1979) *Public Service: The New Imperatives.* Lahore: Book House.

Hakim, M.A. (1991) Specialist-generalist relationship and the reform commissions of Bangladesh. *Asian Journal of Public Administration, 13*, 3–22.

Hamid, S., Graig, R. and Clarke, F. (1993) Religion: A confounding cultural element in the international harmonization of accounting? *Abacus, 29*, 131–148.

Hood, C. (1991) A public management for all seasons? *Public Administration, 69*, 3–19.

Hood, C. (1995) The 'new public management' in the 1980s: Variations on a theme. *Accounting, Organizations and Society, 20*, 93–109.

Hood, C. (2000) Paradoxes of public-sector managerialism, old public management and public service bargains. *International Public Management Journal, 3*, 1–22.

Hopwood, A.G. (2005) After 30 years. *Accounting, Organizations and Society, 30*, 585–586.

International Monetary Fund (2005) *Report on the Observance of Standards and Codes (ROSC) Pakistan: Accounting and Auditing*

Islam, N. (1989) Colonial legacy, administrative reforms and politics: Pakistan 1947–1987. *Public Administration and Development, 9*, 271.

Järvinen, J. (2006) Institutional pressures for adopting new cost accounting systems in Finnish hospitals: Two longitudinal case studies. *Financial Accountability & Management, 22*, 21–46.

Kennedy, C.H. (1987) *Bueaucracy in Pakistan.* New York, NY: Oxford University Press.

Kennedy, C.H. (2004) Pakistan's superior courts and the prohibition of ribai. In R.M. Hathaway and W. Lee (Eds), *Islamization and the Pakistan Economy.* Washington, DC: Woodrow Wilson International Center for Scholars.

Khan, J.R. (Ed.) (1987) *Evolution of Pakistan's Administrative System.* Islamabad: Pakistan Public Administration Research Centre O & M Division Islamabad.

Khan, M.H. (1997) Economic performance, structural reforms and government budgets in Pakistan. *Canadian Journal of Development Studies, 18*, 279–302.

Khan, M.H. (2002) *When Is Economic Growth Pro-Poor? Experiences in Malaysia and Pakistan.* Washington, DC: International Monetary Fund.

Khan, M.H. (2003) Zakah accounting and auditing: Principles, rules and experience in Pakistan. *Islamic Economic Studies, 10*, 31–43.

Khan, M.I. (2005) *Administrative Reforms in Pakistan: A Case Study of Administrative Tribunals.* PhD thesis, University of Karachi.

Khan, M.M. (2002b). Resistance to administrative reforms in South Asian civil bureaucracies. In A. Farazmand (Ed.) *Administrative Reform in Developing Nations.* Westport, CT: Greenwood.

Khan, S.R. (2004) *Pakistan under Musharraf, 1998–2002: Economic Reforms and Political Change.* Lahore: Vanguard.

Khuhro, H. (1972) The Ayub Khan era: Politics in Pakistan 1958–1969 by L. Ziring. *Modern Asian Studies, 6*, 248–255.

Klumpes, P. (2001) Generational accountability of public sector management: A case study of the State Authorities Superannuation Board of New South Wales. *Accounting, Auditing & Accountability Journal, 14*, 166–189.

Kouser, R., Makki, M.A.M. and Qureshi, M.U. (2012) Corporate financial reporting system and developments herein: An exploratory study from Pakistan. *Pakistan Journal of Commerce and Social Sciences, 6*(1), 12–26.

Kuruppu, G.C.J. (2010) *Development of Central Government Accounting in Sri Lanka: Three Perspectives on the Accounting Changes.* no. 25-2010, HHB.

Lapsley, I. (1999) Accounting and the new public management: Instruments of substantive efficiency or a rationalising modernity? *Financial Accountability and Management, 15*, 201–207.

Lapsley, I. (2008) The NPM agenda: Back to the future. *Financial Accountability & Management, 24*, 77–96.

Lapsley, I. (2009) New public management: The cruellest invention of the human spirit? *Abacus, 45*(1), 1–21.

Lapsley, I. and Oldfield, R. (2001) Transforming the public sector: Management consultants as agents of change. *European Accounting Review, 10*, 523–543.

Meek, G.K. and Saudagaran, S.M. (1990) Survey of research on financial reporting in a transnational context. *Journal of Accounting Literature*, *9*, 145.

Meek, G.K. and Thomas, W.B. (2004) A review of markets-based international accounting research. *Journal of International Accounting*, *3*, 21–41.

Nobes, C. (1998) Towards a general model of the reasons for international differences in financial reporting. *Abacus*, *34*, 162–187.

Nobes, C. (2004) On accounting classification and the international harmonisation debate. *Accounting, Organizations and Society*, *29*, 189–200.

Nobes, C.W. (1983) A judgemental international classification of financial reporting practices. *Journal of Business Finance & Accounting*, *10*, 1–19.

Oliver, C. (1991) Strategic responses to institutional processes. *The Academy of Management Review*, *16*, 145–179.

Olsen, J.P. (1997) Institutional design in democratic contexts. *Journal of Political Philosophy*, *5*, 203–229.

Olson, O., Guthrie, J. and Humphrey, C. (1998) *Global Warning: Debating International Developments in New Public Financial Management*. Oslo: Cappelen akademisk forl.

Olson, O., Humphrey, C. and Guthrie, J. (2001) Caught in an evaluatory trap: a dilemma for public services under NPFM. *European Accounting Review*, *10*, 505–522.

Osborne, D. and Gaebler, T. (1992) *Reinventing Government: How the Entrepreneurial Spirit Is Transforming the Public Sector*. New York, NY: Plume.

Ouda, H.A.G. (2003) Public sector accounting and budgeting reform: the main issues involved with special focus on the Arab world. United Nations Department of Economic and Social Affairs.

Quddus, S.A. (1991a) *Bueaucracy and Management in Pakistan*. Karachi: Royal Book Company.

Quddus, S.A. (1991b) The public servant and his accountability. In S.A. Quddus (Ed.), *Bureaucracy and Management in Pakistan*. Karachi: Royal Book Company.

Radebaugh, L.H., Gray, S.J. and Black, E.L. (2006) *International Accounting and Multinational Enterprises*. New York: Wiley.

Ryan, B., Scapens, R.W. and Theobald, M. (1992) *Research Method and Methodology in Finance and Accounting*. London: Academic Press.

Ryan, C., Guthrie, J. and Day, R. (2007) Politics of financial reporting and the consequences for the public sector. *Abacus*, *43*, 474–487.

Sahlin-Andersson, K. (2001) National, international and transnational constructions of new public management. In T. Christensen and P. Lægreid (Eds) *New Public Management: The Transformation of Ideas and Practice*. Aldershot: Ashgate.

Smith, B.C. (2003) *Understanding Third World Politics: Theories of Political Change and Development*. Basingstoke: Macmillian.

Timoshenko, K. (2006) *Russian Government Accounting: Changes at the Central Level and at a University*. PhD thesis, University of Nordland.

Tinker, A. (1984) Theories of the state and the state of accounting: Economic reductionism and political voluntarism in accounting regulation theory. *Journal of Accounting and Public Policy*, *3*, 55–74.

Tinker, T. (2004) The Enlightenment and its discontents: Antinomies of Christianity, Islam and the calculative sciences. *Accounting, Auditing & Accountability Journal*, *17*, 442.

United Nations (2007) *Review of Practical Implementation Issues of International Financial Reporting Standards: Case Study of Pakistan*.

Wickramasinghe, D. and Hopper, T. (2005) A cultural political economy of management accounting controls: A case study of a textile mill in a traditional Sinhalese village. *Critical Perspectives on Accounting*, *16*, 473–503.

World Bank. (2005) *Improvement to Financial Reporting and Auditing Project*. Retrieved from http://projects.worldbank.org/P036015/improvement-financial-reporting-auditing-project?lang=en.

Part II
Management accounting

The 'Industrial Revolution', started in the UK in the eighteenth century, greatly boosted industrial technology and expanded production scale, alongside the rise of modern management practices to boost production efficiency and effectiveness. In particular, Frederick W. Taylor, an American engineer and the 'Father of Scientific Management', used some traditional accounting recording and reporting techniques to experiment with quantitative management methods and practices, which led in the early twentieth century to the birth of 'management accounting', a new subsystem of accounting that focused on generating relevant information and data to assist business managers on the front line to make effective operating and strategic decisions.

Following the boom of business production and industrial restructuring after World War II, management accounting gained substantial growth, driven by the rising demands of scientific management and by incorporating interdisciplinary knowledge and technologies. Thus, various new management accounting techniques and tools were invented or experimented with in practice, including product costing, standard costing, budgeting and budgetary control (management by objectives), responsibility accounting, performance evaluation, variance analysis (management by exception), cost-volume-profit (CVP) analysis etc., resulting in management accounting becoming a very important and useful management tool. Furthermore, in pace with the advance of information technology and production automation and global business competition, many new and innovative techniques and practices were initiated or experimented with in leading business entities in developed countries (mainly the USA and Japan), such as activity-based costing (ABC), activity-based management (ABM), just-in-time management (JIT), cost for quality (COQ), balanced scorecard (BSC), lean production management and so on. The adoption and expansion of these new techniques and practices have upgraded management accounting to the strategy-oriented level and significantly enhanced the positive role of management accounting in strategic business management.

This section consists of introductions to management accounting developments in four Asian countries, Japan (Chapter 5), Indonesia (Chapter 6), Thailand (Chapter 7) and Sri Lanka (Chapter 8).

Japan is an industrialized country; Japanese companies and management are innovative in developing contemporary management practices and have played a leading role in the advancement of management accounting techniques and tools. Chapter 5 elaborates how management accounting started to grow in Japan after government regulation on cost accounting during the economic recovery after World War II. As explained in the chapter, many innovative management accounting techniques with unique Japanese characteristics, such as target costing, *kaizen* costing, backflush costing, flexible budgeting, *hushing kari* (policy development), JIT, materials requirement (MRP), value engineering, manufacturing resource planning (MRP II) and company-wide quality control (CWQC), as well as more recent techniques of business continuity management (BCM), global performance management (GPM) and electronic resource planning (ERP) have been invented and popularized in the context of changing business environment with advanced information technology and economic globalization. The authors of this chapter have also outlined the integration in recent years of management accounting systems with business internal control and corporate governance reforms. The Japanese experience in management accounting has not only contributed to the efficiency and effectiveness of business operations in Japan but also set an exemplary role in innovation and the promotion of management accounting in Asia and in the world.

Indonesia is a very important economy in Asia. Chapter 6 describes the evolution of management accounting following a brief introduction to the accounting profession in Indonesia. As described in Chapter 6, management accounting in Indonesia has gone through four stages of development. In the first stage (before 1950), management accounting was applied mainly for planning (budgeting), product cost determination and cost control. During the second stage (1951–1965), management accounting shifted to providing information to assist business managers in planning and resource allocation and the introduction of responsibility accounting. In the third stage (1965–1985), the emphasis was on how to use management accounting information to reduce waste and production inefficiency through the use of process analysis and cost management. In the fourth stage (1985–present), the application of management accounting by Indonesian companies has turned to strategic perspectives aiming at creating values for various stakeholders such as customers, shareholders, creditors and employees. In addition, this chapter systematically reviews the development of management accounting research and the findings of major studies on the application of management accounting in Indonesia.

Chapter 7 introduces the development of management accounting in Thailand. Tourist and service industries are the major pillar of the Thai economy, while the manufacturing industry is relatively less developed. However, the Thai government has adopted development policy to raise the productivity and competitiveness of Thai businesses. Therefore, over the last two decades many Thai firms have adopted or implemented some management accounting techniques or practices in order to keep the costs of business and operations low and to penetrate into global markets with more competitive and affordable prices. Therefore, there is a positive association between management accounting practices and firms' financial performance in the country in recent years. Nonetheless, at present, Thai businesses, either the invigorating Thai businesses (ITB), which obtain services and support from the government on technical, investment and management practice, or the non-ITB, mainly apply traditional management accounting techniques or practices such as normal costing, variable costing, standard costing, financial budgeting and transfer pricing, although some firms have tried out a few more advanced management accounting techniques including ABC, benchmarking analysis and balanced scorecards. The authors of this chapter also explain why Thai firms are inclined to use traditional management accounting practices since they maintain to keep 'cost minimization', instead of 'value creation', as the primary business strategy, thus the adoption of strategic management accounting techniques remains limited in Thailand. However, the authors explore the future direction of management accounting application in Thailand, particularly the possible development of environmental management accounting.

Chapter 8 examines the evolution of management accounting in Sri Lanka. Compared to other countries, Sri Lanka is an emerging economy in South Asia as it was a British colony for a long period. Therefore the accounting systems and practices in the country bore strong British influences. The manufacturing sector is relatively weak, relying mainly on the textile and clothing industry. Owing to government changes and political and social turmoil in the 1970s to the 1990s, economic growth was slow, as were the development and application of management accounting in Sri Lanka. However, professional accounting associations relating to management accounting, although depending mainly upon foreign professional bodies (such as ICWA (UK), ICMA (UK) and ICMA (Australia)), did play a role in training management accountants and promoting management accounting concepts and techniques. Sri Lanka commenced economic transformation at the end of the 1990s to encourage private-sector business development. Along with the speed-up in economic growth and the expansion of industrial scale, the demand for professional management accountants has also increased, which should prompt the development of management accounting in the country. In addition, this chapter briefs the formation of the national professional management accounting association (the ICMA(SL)) in 2009, as well as its disputes and settlement with the foreign professional management accounting bodies that have long been existent in the country.

In sum, management accounting has been adopted at varied extents in Asian countries. Obviously, the development and application of management accounting are subject to the progress of economic growth and business management practices in individual countries. It can however be expected that management accounting should play a greater role in business management and production efficiency, keeping pace with the rapid economic growth in Asian countries.

5

Management accounting
in Japan

Current Practices

Susumu Ueno, Paul Scarbrough and Shoichiro Hosomi

Introduction

Starting with the industrial modernization of the 1870s, Japanese society and businesses imported and digested many management systems and practices from other industrialized countries (Ueno, 2011; Someya, 1999), particularly from Britain, the USA, Germany and France. Management and accounting systems and practices used in large companies in Japan, similar to those in other industrial countries, have changed over time to accommodate the demands of their operation strategy and industrial or organizational culture.

Japanese companies learned many innovative Western management accounting practices such as present value analysis, value engineering, management by objectives (MBO), material requirements planning (MRP), manufacturing resource planning (MRPII), enterprise resource planning (ERP), manufacturing operations management (MOM), manufacturing execution system (MES) and activity-based costing/management (ABC/ABM). However, they also developed and disseminated innovative and original management accounting practices such as just-in-time (JIT), *kaizen* costing, *genka kikaku* (target costing), *hoshin kanri*, (policy deployment) and company-wide quality control (CWQC). Table 5.1 shows some differences in management accounting practices between those developed in the West (mainly in the USA) and Japan.

However, these differences are not deterministic, and often are overemphasized. There are a number of management techniques developed in the West that are very similar to Japanese techniques in the aspects of *analysis level, employee participation, communication level* and *information used*. For example, balanced scorecards, management by objectives, value engineering, and training within industry were all developed in the USA but are manifested in a different way in Japan. Table 5.1 only shows the characteristics of management accounting practices as they originated, and organizations all over the world have used these practices successfully to varied degrees.

Researchers have speculated on the cultural reasons for different application patterns, i.e. the underlying drivers for the creation and development of these practices. Some academics have relied too much on cultural perspectives in explaining the between-nation differences in

Table 5.1 Differences in management accounting practices between the West and Japan

	Japan	The West (mainly in the USA)
Management accounting practices	JIT, *kaizen* costing, *genka kikaku* (target costing), *hoshin kanri* (policy deployment), company-wide quality control	Time value of money methods, MRP, MRPII, ERP, MOM, MES, ABC/M
Analysis level	Granular	Abstract
Employee participation	All managers and workers	Manager experts only
Communication used	Very high	Very low
Information used	Actual physical data	Financial data (mainly)

management and accounting practices. It is clear that business organizations in all countries try to adopt different innovative practices and techniques to meet varied conditions and needs. Since none of the management accounting practices is fully culture- or location-specific, researchers who rely heavily on a specific cultural perspective have failed to describe the reality.

There is extensive literature that describes Japanese management accounting practices in English, some written by overseas researchers and other by Japanese scholars (e.g. Okano and Suzuki, 2006; Nishimura and Willet, 2005; Baydoun *et al.*, 1997; Ueno and Wu, 1993; Ueno and Sekaran, 1992). This chapter aims to provide an objective and comprehensive overview of current management accounting practices in Japan. We do not want to overemphasize the cultural aspect, as cultural variables such as 'individualism' and 'collectivism' are explanatory as residual in between-nation studies; instead, we will pay more attention to historical evolution in explaining current management accounting in Japan.

A large part of this chapter relies on previous literature written in Japanese and English. Using both domestic and international sources, so we can identify and avoid some biases and misinterpretations of Japanese management accounting practices. The next section (Section 2) explains the initial development of management accounting in Japan after World War II. Section 3 reviews the practices in planning, management control and performance measurements employed at leading Japanese companies. Section 4 reports front-line management accounting practices, while the practices adopted by small and medium-sized enterprises (SMEs) are reviewed in Section 5. The influence of disclosure regulations on Japanese management accounting practices are discussed in Section 6. The last section provides concluding remarks.

Initial development of Japanese management accounting

As early as in the planned economy during World War II, the Japanese government promulgated cost and management accounting rules and guidelines for manufacturing industries, including:

- Rules of Manufacturing Cost Accounting Standards (1937)
- Guidelines on Cost Accounting for Army Armaments Manufacturers (1939)
- Rules of Cost Accounting for Navy Armaments Manufacturers (1939)
- Guidelines on Standard Cost Accounting for Army Armaments Manufacturers (1941)
- Guidelines on Budgetary Control for Army Armaments Manufacturers (1941)
- Cost Accounting Standards (1942)
- Guidelines on Cost Accounting for Manufacturing Industry (1942) and
- Guidelines on Cost Accounting for Mining Industry (1943).

Each of these standards had a significant influence on cost and management accounting practices in Japan (Ueno, 2011; Okano and Suzuki, 2006, p. 1124; Kobe Daigaku, 2007).

Japan surrendered in August 1945, and this was followed by the US-led occupation until April 1952, when the San Francisco Peace Treaty came into effect and Japan's independence was fully restored. Over the occupation period, the Japanese people worked to democratize and restructure social, economic and legal systems with heavy influence from US philosophy and principles, including US approaches of accounting. The German influence of the managerial economics school (*Betriebswirtschaftslehre*), which had started in the 1920s (Kuroda 2011), faded dramatically, although some Japanese accounting professors continued to study the Continental (German and French) disciplines for many decades. The Japanese government, concentrating on economic recovery, had further introduced new regulations and protectionism to stimulate private-sector growth.

The Industrial Rationalization Council, formed by the Ministry of International Trade and Industry (MITI) in 1949, greatly influenced the development of Japanese management accounting practices. It issued several reports that reflected the influence of the new US-style management philosophy:

- Framework for Internal Control of Business Enterprises (Report No. 1 1951)
- Implementation Guidelines for Internal Control (Report No. 2 1953)
- Profit Planning for Executing Business Policy (Report No. 3 1956)
- Profit Management for Divisional Structure (Report No. 4 1960)
- Cost Management: New Concept and Methods for Cost Reduction (Report No. 5 1966)
- The Future of Financial Policy in Business Enterprises (Report No. 6 1972).

The General Headquarters of the Supreme Commander for the Allied Powers (GHQ/SCAP) was keen to democratize Japanese social and economic systems, and forced the Japanese government to make significant changes to the constitution and civil and business laws to follow the US approach. Japanese society took these forced changes as an opportunity and a turning point. Large companies at the time effectively digested the aforementioned reports, and the knowledge imported from the US became mingled with domestic conditions in several ways. However, even when Japanese companies appeared to adopt the management techniques without altering them, the way companies used them would often be different.

In later years, leading Japanese manufacturers gradually innovated or created several new and refined management operation systems, such as *kaizen* costing (continuous improvement), *genka kikaku* (target costing), just-in-time process management, *hoshin kanri* (policy deployment), company-wide quality control (CWQC) etc. Today, management accounting textbooks in Japan consider these management techniques to be part of management accounting practices. Japanese scholars all know these techniques are a part of management operations that originated in operations engineering; however, including them in management accounting ensured that they could spread throughout business management systems.

Strategic management techniques

Planning, budgeting and financial performance indicators

Profit planning and annual budgeting are pervasive management control practices in large Japanese companies. In fact, the government's timely disclosure rules for financial accounting (described in a later section) request that listed companies implement budgetary control systems.

Most large Japanese companies have set their own accounting manuals and guidelines. Staff members at corporate, divisional or departmental levels are required to follow these manuals strictly in the processes of financial statement preparation, profit planning and budgeting, cost accounting and internal control. For the most part, the applied techniques appear to be quite similar to those seen outside Japan, however there is considerable difference in implementation, which shows unique features of Japanese practices.

The process of planning and budgetary control involves setting a performance target, measuring performance, comparing performance against that target, computing the difference (variance) between measured performance and the target and taking action if necessary. Horii (2015) conducted a survey on the budgeting practices of Japanese listed manufacturing companies in 2011 and reported the highest ranked roles for budgetary control were: 'it functions as an operational goal', 'a control tool' and 'a measure for departmental performance'. It is interesting that the 'communication and coordination' function was not ranked as highly as the other three items (Horii, 2015, p. 99).

Many large Japanese companies implement budgetary control in a way that is called 'catch-ball'. Senior management sets budgets for the revenues and profit needed, while lower-level managers develop the cost (expense) budgets. These two budgets are never initially aligned, and they are 'tossed back and forth like a ball' between the top- and lower-level managers until either they reach consensus in matching the varied parts of the budgets or they acknowledge that a match is not possible and both groups agree to accept the lack of a match and work to close the gap during the budget period. When implemented in the ideal way, such two-way participation creates the feeling among managers that 'this is our budget, and our obligation'. However, some Japanese companies use a top-down approach for budgeting, and lower-level managers and employees sometimes share the feeling that 'this is the budget imposed on us by upper managers', thus reducing the incentive or motivation for budget implementation.

A change in the key performance indicators (KPIs) in concern may occur over time. Currently, the key metrics for the success of an organization's strategies and tactics in planning and budgeting are profits, sales and costs. From the 1960s to the 1980s, when Japan enjoyed high economic growth, sales growth and profits were the supreme goals, thus sales volume and market share metrics were most popular in measuring performance at either the company or the division level (Ueno, 1992, 1997). Many foreign researchers have recognized that this is a characteristic of Japanese business management; however, they do not take account of the changes that have taken place after the 1980s.

During the 1990s, Stern Stewart heavily promoted the idea of economic value added (EVA). EVA, also referred to as economic profit, is an internal management performance indicator based on residual value calculated by deducting the cost of capital from operating profit (adjusted for taxes on a cash basis). EVA is almost the same as residual income, which has been used at General Electric since the 1920s to evaluate its business segments. A number of Japanese listed companies, such as HOYA Corporation, ORIX Corporation, Krin Company Ltd, Asahi Breweries Limited, Asahi Kasei Corporation, Panasonic Corporation, Toto Ltd, Daikin Industries Ltd, Tohoku Electric Power Co., Inc. and TDK Corporation, installed EVA as a key performance measure in the 1990s and early 2000s (Ueno, 2008). However, according to the survey of companies listed on the Tokyo Stock Exchange conducted by Kawano (2014) between 2011–2012, only 13 companies (7 per cent of all respondents) had implemented EVA. EVA can help managers align decision-making with company preferences and provide a valuable measure of value creation; however, it is another form of remote control that forces managers to place undue emphasis on the short-term bottom line.

The Life Insurance Association of Japan has conducted a survey of listed companies and institutional investors on 'Actions for increasing shareholder value by listed companies' (*Kabunushi kachi kojo ni muketa torikumi ni tsuite*) every year since 1974. According the 2014 survey, KPIs frequently used by companies in their mid-term planning (N = 385) are profit and profit growth (69.6 per cent of companies surveyed), followed by sales and sales growth (63.6 per cent), profit over sales (50.1 per cent), return on equity (ROE) (39.7 per cent) and market share (33.0 per cent). On the other hand, institutional investors (N = 86) consider ROE the most important KPI (93.0 per cent of respondents), followed by dividend pay-out ratio (54.7 per cent), total pay-out ratio (43.0 per cent), profit and profit growth (38.4 per cent) and profit over sales (32.6 per cent).

Total pay-out ratio to shareholders is calculated by adding dividends and treasury stock acquisitions and dividing the sum by net income for the same period. The dividend pay-out ratio is the percentage of net income that a company pays out as dividends to common shareholders. It should be noted that companies that disclosed dividend pay-out ratio and total pay-out ratio to shareholders, which are thought to be fairly important KPIs by institutional investors, are as few as 24.9 per cent and 3.9 per cent of all companies, respectively. Institutional investors think that yearly distributions to shareholders are important.

Use of information and communication technology for performance management

The early use of information and communication technology (ICT) in Japan was the introduction of electronic data processing (EDP) and automatic data processing (ADP) in the 1950s. Accounting and payroll management were the main usage. In the 1960s, integrated data processing (IDP) systems were developed and used. The adoption of end user computing (EUC) techniques spread in the 1980s and the client server system (CSS) became the central idea of network computing in business management in the 1990s.

Large companies in Japan developed a variety of in-house software application (e.g. Lotus 1-2-3 and/or Excel-based templates for planning and budgeting, as well as for entire customer packages) and vendors provided applications for mainframes and office computers in the early period.

Recently, many large and medium-sized companies started to use budgeting modules for the planning, budgeting and forecasting of ERP. Examples of popular accounting applications include NEC EXPLANNER/Ai, FUJITSU Enterprise Application GLOVIA smart, Oracle Hyperion, IBM Cognos Planning, SAP Business Planning and Consolidation (BPC) and Microsoft SharePoint Server. TKC Corporation and OBIC Co. Ltd are the main domestic vendors of business intelligence software solutions. The use of cloud services for planning and budgeting is also increasing.

Although directed at corporate governance issues, the introduction of the J-SOX legislation (described in a later section) accelerated this trend owing to a significant increase in both record-keeping and reporting work required.

Determining how far to go in standardizing global management practices and adapting home country practices to local companies is a critical issue for any diversified multinational enterprise (MNE) (Ueno, 1996). The main issue is how to balance international standardization and local adaptation in global performance management (GPM). The process of installing and customizing globally uniform ERP solutions is a challenge to Japanese multinational enterprises (MNEs) that demands their enculturation activities.

Hoshin kanri and balanced scorecards

Hoshin kanri (policy deployment, *hoshin* planning, or simply *hoshin*) is a method of ensuring that the strategic goals drive progress and action at every level within that company. Taking a top-down approach, *hoshin kanri* deploys corporate annual *hoshin* (strategic policy) to divisions, departments, sections and employees.

The corporate annual *hoshin* (strategic policy) is a complex and sophisticated plan that includes the vision, direction, targets and plans of the company. It is not just a forecast financial statement. People at all job levels develop their own action plans based on the policy. Then, plan–do–check–act (PDCA) cycles iterate within the action plan of each unit (department). All employees and managers report to their superiors with a PDCA process that cascades up from the lowest levels to the highest levels on both weekly and monthly cycles. As a company-wide activity, *hoshin kanri* makes everyone in the company aware of their critical success factors (CSFs) and key performance indicators (KPIs) via these weekly and monthly face-to-face horizontal and vertical communication sessions (catch-ball). In manufacturing processes, all of these cycles occur daily.

Hoshin kanri contains two simultaneous alignments owing to the catch-ball, top-down bottom-up approach: employees attempt to align with the strategic policy provided by senior management (top-down), and at the same time senior management realigns their policy based on input from their employees through middle management (bottom-up). It is an extremely arduous process since middle management ideally does not 'give in' to the power of senior management; its role is to pursue its true and real view of the situation. The reality, of course, is different across organizations. This tension between top, middle and lower management also plays out in the 'catch-ball' budgeting process.

Manufacturing companies such as Bridgestone Corporation, Komatsu Ltd and Toyota Motor Corporation developed *hoshin kanri* in the 1970s. It was further articulated by Panasonic Corporation in the 1970s and by NEC Corporation in the 1980s. Some Japanese companies use management by objectives (MBO) within a *hoshin kanri* framework. Some people view *hoshin kanri* as an innovative, multi-level application of Shewhart's and Deming's plan–do–check–act (PDCA) cycle to management activity.

Balanced scorecards (BSC) is a framework for defining and communicating strategy, for translating strategy to operational targets and for measuring outputs of strategy implementation. It is a management system for planning the actions and controlling performance of business units and individuals. BSC, as conceptualized by Robert S. Kaplan and David P. Norton in the US, became very popular in strategic management in the 1990s. Some companies in Japan were active in studying or implementing it, such as the Bank of Tokyo-Mitsubishi UFJ and Kansai Electric Power, Co. Inc., as well as some large hospitals and municipal governments.

Although the idea of BSC arrived in Japan in the 1990s, and attracted significant attention, not many companies actually installed it. A few companies discontinued the use of *hoshin kanri* after adopting the balanced scorecard, and others used BSC along with *hoshin kanri*. Several surveys report that only around 10 per cent of Japanese listed companies use BSC (Kawano, 2014; Yokota and Senoo, 2011; Moriguchi, 2010; Ueno, 2007; Matsubara, 2003). There are many possible reasons. One is that, for large Japanese companies, being accustomed to effective traditional management control systems such as budgetary control along with *hoshin kanri* does not provide sufficient motivation for replacing their traditional systems with BSC. BSC is, in effect, a tool for senior managers with a narrow scope of experience. Most Japanese business managers have had extensive experience in different functional areas based on job rotations regularly conducted within their companies, and, as a result, the BSC approach does not add to their understanding as much as it does for narrowly experienced managers. Another possible reason is the naive and ineffective approach to BSC implementation, i.e. BSC designed through a top-down approach. If BSC is designed for managers at senior management level who were lacking sufficient knowledge of front-line operations, it may not make sense and can even confuse operational managers and employees.

To facilitate BSC implementation, some companies develop BSC software specifically for their own use, and others purchase and customize commercial packages. Examples of popular BSC software being used by Japanese companies are Oracle Balanced Scorecard, Microsoft Balanced Scorecard, SAP Balanced Scorecard, and QPR Scorecard (QPR Metrics).

Performance management of a diversified company

Diversified companies in Japan generally adopt a divisional organizational structure to run their businesses. The divisional structure serves companies that have distinct products, customers and/or locations. The performance management system of Panasonic Corporation is illustrated here as an example.

Founded in 1918, Panasonic (originally known as Matsushita) started using a divisional structure in 1933. As of 31 March 2015, the Group employs 254,084 workers and comprises 468 consolidated and affiliated companies. Currently, Panasonic runs its businesses as by grouping them into five domains: consumer electronics, housing, automotive, B2B solutions and devices. Each of these domains has distinct R&D, production and sales functions.

To evaluate performance of the company and its business units, Panasonic installed the capital cost management system (CCM) in 1999. CCM is a key performance indicator that is similar to residual income and/or EVA. The equation below shows the calculation of CCM metrics:

CCM = (operating income plus investment income) − (capital charge for use of assets)

The company calculates CCM for each unit (division) on a global consolidated basis. Managers compute CCM by multiplying a uniform cost of capital rate, 8.4 per cent, to the business unit's assets (Ueno, 2008). Panasonic intended to introduce new capital rates in the 2016 fiscal year that could properly reflect the risk of each unit. The CCM is part of the formula used to determine the annual compensation of Panasonic directors and executive officers.

Compensation for executives and employees

Employee pay in Japanese companies is generally composed of two parts, salary and bonus. Most companies pay employee bonuses twice a year, usually in early summer and December. Although the bonus has a guaranteed base determined by an employee's monthly salary (a multiple of his/her monthly salary), it is determined by reflecting the quarterly and yearly performance of both the company and the individual. Salaries are to a certain extent linked to company and individual performance, even though Japanese companies generally adopt seniority-based pay plans. In most salary systems, the primary basis for pay increases is the employee's tenure system (years in both the company and the position).

The seniority-based pay and lifetime employment is often called 'Japanese-style human resource management'. It was developed in the 1920s and intended to attract and retain high-quality talent by offering the terms of employment that were close to a government official at the time. However, it was not without friction in its development, nor was it universally implemented. In fact, such an employment pay system has actually only been used by the very largest companies, mainly for a portion of their managers and employees. The general advantages of this Japanese-style management are employees' high loyalty, commitment and retention. In large companies where the Japanese-style management has been practised, most company directors are 'promoted' employees. Because of this, many people believe that directors and employees share the same incentive structure. On the other hand, fixed salaries are the largest part of executive pay in those companies. In times of growth and high consumer demand, this system may be advantageous, however the cost is very high and in a mature market with low growth and low profits it appears to be unsustainable.

During the past few decades, Japanese companies have had great difficulty in maintaining these stereotypical traditional Japanese-style employment practices because of the rising and high costs. Thus, change from a seniority-based pay plan to a performance-based pay plan is pervasive in practice.

There is a consensus in academia that the interests of senior managers and directors should be aligned with those of shareholders and that a performance-based pay plan is effective in achieving this objective. In the US, executives' base salaries account for a relatively small part of total compensation because executives' compensation is believed to be a tool for achieving goal congruence. In Japanese listed companies, fixed salaries are the largest part of executive pay, although the proportion of performance-based executive pay has increased.

Panasonic Corporation's compensation plan for directors and executive officers has three parts: basic compensation, performance-based compensation and stock options.[1] The basic compensation is a fixed amount. Performance-based compensation is determined based on a single-year performance evaluation. Performance indicators used for this evaluation are net sales, operating profit, free cash flow and the CCM (similar to EVA) of the company as a whole and the specific business unit (division) that each executive controls. Stock options are granted so that executives share the same profitability awareness with shareholders and strive to boost corporate value from a long-term perspective.

Practices in front-line management

Japanese cost accounting and cost management practices are reviewed in this section. The impacts of JIT, business continuity management, quality management and specific tools such as *kaizen* costing, target costing (*genka kikaku*) and *backflush* costing are introduced.

Japanese Cost Accounting Standards

The Cost Accounting Standards have a significant impact on cost management and management accounting in Japan. As described earlier, during the war Japanese manufacturers had to follow the cost and management accounting standards issued by the government in the 1930s and early 1940s. The Rules of Manufacturing Cost Accounting Standards (1937), promulgated by the Ministry of Commerce and Industry in 1937, referred to the Grundplan der Selbstkostenrechnung (Basic Plan of Cost Accounting) (1930). German influence faded away markedly after the war. On 8 November 1962, the Accounting Deliberation Committee of the Ministry of Finance released the Cost Accounting Standards, which reflect a strong US influence, as do other regulations set after World War II. For example, the standard costing section of the Cost Accounting Standards was edited by referring to 'How Standard Costs Are Being Used Currently (1951)', released by the National Association of Accountants (NAA), which later became the Institute of Management Accountants in the US.

Based on the state of the art in 1962, the objectives of the Cost Accounting Standards were to provide true costs for financial statements and to provide cost data for pricing decisions, for cost management, for budgeting and budgetary control and for strategic planning. The standards require companies to use absorption costing for financial reporting and stipulate details of account definitions, supportive cost allocation procedures, costing methods, product cost valuation and variance accounting. The standards contain 47 articles and are an integral part of current Japanese GAAP.

Since cost accounting systems reflect specific production processes, they are not uniform. The standards aim to provide multiple frameworks for product costing used by companies in developing their own cost accounting procedures and systems. However, while strongly recommended, the use of the standards is not mandatory. In Japan, organizations and individuals usually follow government recommendations because of the great need for social legitimacy. The extreme conservatism of statutory auditors and independent auditors in attesting the compliance with GAAP amplifies this tendency. All Japanese listed companies are thus strongly motivated to comply with the prescribed costing *procedures* and *methods* for their financial disclosure purposes. The basic structure of the Cost Accounting Standards in Japan is shown in Table 5.2.

The standards, released in 1962, are a rules-based set of procedures, and a part of Japanese GAAP, that is, they prescribe the accepted costing *procedures* and *systems* for financial reporting purpose. The standards of 1962 have inhibited the development of Japanese processes and systems and made it expensive and complex to adopt new approaches such as the ABC or backflush costing. Cost accounting courses provided by Japanese universities, high schools and vocational schools devote many lessons to the interpretation and explanation of the standards, in a way that is similar to a legal education. Of course, it is important to differentiate cost accounting education, which is anchored to the past, from cost management education, which is very keen to develop and use new procedures and methods from a variety of fields such as engineering, management and industrial psychology.

The use of standard costing has a relatively long history in Japan, and it is especially popular among listed manufacturing companies, which focus on production cost management. According to Kawano (2014), in surveys conducted between 2011 and 2012, 68 per cent of responding manufacturing firms used standard costing. This proportion is higher than in prior similar surveys. An important tool of standard costing is variance analysis, which breaks down the variation between actual costs and standard costs into various components (material variance, labour variance, factory overhead variance, etc.). When asked about the main purpose of standard costing usage, 53 companies (56 per cent of respondents) answered 'cost control and cost reduction' and 16 companies (17 per cent) answered 'budgeting' (Kawano, 2014, pp. 61–62).

Table 5.2 Contents of the Cost Accounting Standards of Japan

Chapter 1 The purpose of cost accounting, and general standards of cost accounting (Articles 1–6)
Chapter 2 Calculation of actual costs (Articles 7–39)
    Section 1 The classification criteria for manufacturing cost elements
    Section 2 Manufacturing overhead costing
    Section 3 Departmental costing
    Section 4 Costing for products and cost units
    Section 5 Calculation of selling and administrative expenses
Chapter 3 Standard costing (Articles 40–43)
Chapter 4 The calculation and analyses of cost differences (Articles 44–46)
Chapter 5 Accounting for cost variances (Article 47)

Regarding the use of direct (variable) costing, the survey by Kawano (2014) reports that 37 per cent of responding companies used direct costing. Supporting profit planning, budgeting and cost management are the main reasons for their adoption. Since the Japanese Cost Accounting Standards require companies to use absorption costing for product costs to be disclosed in financial statements, product costs calculated by direct costing need to be adjusted to absorption costs prior to financial reporting. Because of this, Japanese companies use direct costing mainly as a 'special cost study tool' (analysis), but not within a regular costing system.

Activity-based costing (ABC) is not popular in Japan, although some companies tried it for special cost studies in the early 1990s. One reason of the low adoption is that ABC is not described in the 1962 Japanese Cost Accounting Standards. ABC requires different allocation bases for overhead costs and procedures that are different from those prescribed by the Standards. For instance, the Cost Accounting Standards actually define specific costing accounts and account titles, and how to connect and allocate those accounts to costing units (departments and products), but ABC ignores departments to focus on operating activities for allocating indirect costs. According to Kawano (2014), only 13 per cent of responding companies had used ABC as a special cost study tool in Japan.

A variety of IT vendors provide software for job order costing, however the availability of software for process costing is limited. Product costing is contingent upon production processes. The diversity and complexity of process-oriented production motivate companies to develop Excel templates and spreadsheets for in-house use for process costing. Recently, more ERP, business intelligence and data warehouse applications allow companies to combine existing templates and spreadsheets for the process costing method with these systems.

Just-in-time (JIT) production

The Just-in-time (JIT) method was developed in many Japanese companies in the 1950s and 1960s, and transferred to Western countries in the 1980s. There, in the 1990s, it led to a new term, 'lean production', which includes JIT as well as other Japanese innovations. JIT production (manufacturing) refers to the production of goods to meet customer demand exactly, in time, quality and quantity, whether the 'customer' is a final purchaser of the products or another processing unit further along the production line. In JIT production, product parts are produced to meet the demand, not in surplus or in advance of need to meet a budget. Applying JIT can effectively decrease cycle time, lower inventory, increase productivity and improve the utilization of facilities and equipment. A fundamental principle of JIT is demand-based flow manufacturing.

Recent progress in information and communication technologies (ICT) has changed the manufacturing environment, while promoting the automation of JIT environment (and supply chains) that spreads out globally. Today, the use of manufacturing operations management (MOM) and manufacturing execution system (MES) are increasing. MOM is a holistic solution that provides full visibility into manufacturing processes in order to steadily improve manufacturing operations. As the evolution of MES, a manufacturing operation management system can consolidate all production processes to improve quality management, planning and scheduling, manufacturing execution systems, R&D management etc.[2]

JIT production and business continuity management (BCM)

JIT manufacturing is very efficient under normal conditions but is vulnerable to natural and human disasters (accidents) because it progressively removes the buffers that provide resilience in favour of the cost savings that will result. Natural disasters such as the Great East Japan earthquake on March 11, 2011 and the flood in Thailand during October 2011 disrupted the global and domestic supply chains of manufacturers, causing a shortage of components for electronics, vehicles etc. and demonstrated the vulnerability of Japanese MNEs' supply chains. Many large companies are analysing how to reach a balance between the benefits of keeping low buffers throughout their JIT systems and the negative impact of unpredictable disasters.

In order to enhance the resilience of their global supply chain, companies must disperse risk. For example, the Toyota Group is preparing for future emergencies by establishing a business continuity plan (BCP) that aims at quick recovery with limited resources.[3] The ways that a company can improve risk management include dispersion of key plants, standardization of parts and materials, and diversification of suppliers.

Quality culture, QC circles and small circle activities

After World War II, the first priority of Japan was to rebuild its industries. The quality of Japanese products was very low through the 1950s, and improvement was imperative. In 1950, the Union of Japanese Scientists and Engineers (JUSE) invited W.E. Deming, an American expert in quality control, to provide lectures on the basics of statistical quality control and its role in management. Then QC circles with small groups consisting of front-line workers were advocated. These circles became a central force of the Japanese QC movement, which was promoted and coordinated by JUSE, so QC activities spread rapidly over Japanese industry. Reportedly, in 1978 there were one million quality circles involving about 10 million workers. US companies did not follow suit and almost lost the quality gains they developed during the war, in particular, by regressing to a view that quality was a concern only of management with specific expertise.

A distinctive characteristic of the Japanese approach to quality control is company-wide involvement (company-wide quality control, CWQC), which requests efforts by all levels of employee to install, and make permanent, a climate in which the company as a whole can continuously improve its ability to deliver high-quality products and services to customers. Quality-oriented thinking focuses holistically on culture, people, production processes and products. This differs from the typical traditional US approaches to quality control, which depend mainly on experts rather than on the widespread use of integrated QC tools. However, in the US and other Western countries there has been a move over the last few decades to a company-wide approach through the increased use of lean production.

Kaizen *costing, target costing and backflush costing*

In the 1950s and 1960s, leading Japanese manufacturing companies developed *kaizen* costing and target costing (*genka kikaku*). Outside Japan, not many organizations use *kaizen* costing; however, target costing (TC) is an extremely well known management accounting practice and in recent years has been one of the most widely attempted new product development methods.

Kaizen costing (continuous improvement) is an approach of constantly introducing incremental cost reductions for existing products. *Kaizen* involves supervisors and workers in reducing the cost of existing products by simplifying production processes and eliminating non-essential product features. The activities are grassroots practices conducted at individual production level, or through a small *kaizen* group or a quality circle in a factory.

Target costing occurs at the development, design and production preparation stages for a 'new' product by a cross-function team of engineers and designers, procurement and marketing staff, accountants, outside suppliers etc. Since production processes and flows, types of equipment and other aspects of production are determined at the product planning/ development and design stages, cost control implemented at the production stage can only have a limited effect on cost reduction. The largest cost reduction will come from target costing in the design stage. By implementing TC at the development and design stages of a new product, a cross-functional team can eliminate extra features and materials that customers do not require. Target costing pursues intense value engineering (VE) activities and close cooperation across production departments. Target costing is, however, not a uniform set of practices. For example, Toyota continues to transform the way it implements target costing with almost every iteration.

In a just-in-time inventory environment with extremely low defect rates (for example, 4–6 sigma) and low inventory levels, backflush costing (also called delayed costing or endpoint costing) is often recommended as a product costing system. Backflush costing delays the costing process until the production of a product is completed. Backflush costing method was proposed in the late 1980s with a description of its use at Eaton Corporation's plant in Lincoln, Illinois, USA (Horngren et al., 1997).

Some Japanese management accounting books (such as Ueno, 2004) introduced the backflush costing approach. However, it is difficult to find Japanese companies that actually use backflush costing. One probable reason is that the portion of the journal entry procedure that works backwards to apply manufacturing costs to work-in-process (WIP) (Horngren and Foster, 1991, p. 941) is not a method that appears in the Japanese Cost Accounting Standards. The prescribed methods do not allow delay and/or skipping of journal entries. Manufacturing costs must be transferred from account to account, using physical triggers sequentially during the production process. In this way, the Japanese Cost Accounting Standards prescribe both the detail allocation methods and forms of costing systems as well as the valuation methods, and do not accept a simplified costing system. Additionally, after so many years of implementing a mandated system, some Japanese companies may actually believe that the sequential tracing of production costs assists cost reduction and not be motivated to examine the alternative of backflush costing system.

Management accounting practices in small and medium-sized enterprises

In Japan, as in most countries, SMEs outnumber large companies by a wide margin, and provide more jobs to people. Although some SMEs are innovative and competitive, this does not mean that large companies and SMEs have utilized management accounting practices with similar quality and sophistication. Roughly speaking, the quality and sophistication of management accounting of a company are proportional to the number of its employees.

Accounting skills and ability to produce accurate financial statements within a reasonable period are essential to all companies regardless of their size. However, small companies generally lack capable accounting talents. To prepare daily, weekly or monthly accounting records and reports, management and business owners of such companies must depend on outside services provided by tax accountant firms and CPA firms. Management accounting in Japanese SMEs are subservient to financial accounting, i.e. SMEs do not normally have a management accounting unit.

Tobita (2011) examined the use of budgeting and cost accounting at manufacturing SMEs in Kumamoto Prefecture, Japan. Of 17 companies with less than 10 employees, only three companies (17 per cent) used budgeting, and seven companies (41 per cent) used cost accounting. On the other hand, among 14 companies with between 51 and 100 employees, six companies (43%) used budgeting, and 11 (79%) used cost accounting. According to this survey, actual costing is far more popular than standard costing in Japanese SMEs. Since the response rate is low and the sample size is small, the survey did not represent Japanese SMEs; however, the results may indicate that the degree of management accounting application is roughly proportional to a company size.

Of course, some companies are the exceptions for institutional reasons. SMEs that belong to a large company group (*keiretsu*) and supply parts and products to the group generally have better management control owing to their connection with the group, regardless of their firm size.

SMEs with their own accounting units prepare financial statements in-house for tax returns, financing, performance evaluation etc. These companies implement management accounting practices (MAPs) such as conventional budgeting, cost-volume-profit (CVP) analysis and ratio analysis. Regarding operational management, front-line managers and supervisors rely more on simple and easily collected non-financial and financial measures. Popular non-financial measures used by SMEs are on-time delivery, product defects, number of customer complaints and number of new customers.

Vendors of information and communication technologies (ICT) in Japan have over the past few decades provided equipment and service to SMEs at reasonable prices. In the early days, stand-alone business solutions for bookkeeping and financial accounting (transactions recording, reporting etc.), tax return filing, human resource management, inventory management and business process management were their main products. Today, vendors provide ERP packages to medium-sized companies, sometimes through cloud services. Although some SMEs adopt ICT effectively to support their management control, the degree or level of sophistication in ICT usage is contingent upon the owner's enthusiasm and whether there are talented and knowledgeable persons on the staff.

Influence of disclosure regulations on management accounting practices

Management accounting practices in Japan are influenced by the mandatory disclosure regulations. We now examine such influence in terms of international financial reporting standards (IFRS), timely disclosure rules, internal controls and corporate governance regulations.

Influence of the IFRS on management accounting practices

Since 2010, the Japanese Financial Services Agency (FSA) has permitted eligible listed companies in Japan to use the IFRS in their consolidated financial statements in lieu of the Japanese GAAP. Companies can choose one of four different accounting frameworks in financial reporting: the IFRS, the Japanese GAAP, the US GAAP and Japan's modified IFRS. Over the past few years, there has been a move in Japan to adopt the IFRS. As of 31 July 2016, 86 of the 3,522 Japanese listed companies disclosed their financial statements based on the IFRS.[4] The use of the IFRS improves international comparability and transparency of segment and subsidiary performance, and allows management to monitor worldwide operations effectively (Ueno, 2010). Such a contribution to improving internal control has motivated more Japanese MNEs to adapt to the IFRS.

Timely disclosure rules

In Japan, the Companies Act, the Financial Instruments and Exchange Act and other laws, as well as the Tokyo Stock Exchange's Securities Listing Regulations, constitute what are called the timely disclosure rules. The rules request that companies timely disclose annual/interim reports, sustainability/integrated reports, environmental reports and corporate governance reports. Japanese listed companies generally disclose these reports in the investor relations (IR) libraries on their websites. These disclosure requirements compel companies to maintain reliable internal control systems and articulated management accounting practices, in addition to behaving as good corporate citizens in a global society.

Timely disclosure rules also require that companies prepare a forward-looking statement (a forecast) for the annual/interim reports. A forward-looking statement provides information on sales, profits and financial ratios for the next fiscal year. The rules ask companies to disclose the differences in their estimates and actual earnings promptly as 'amendments to performance estimates'. To respond to this request, listed companies must maintain systems that enable them to disclose the information in a timely and reliable manner. In other words, companies must maintain effective planning and budgeting systems that can provide relevant information across business units on time.

Internal control report

In Japan, the main sources of rules on internal control are the Companies Act (promulgated on 26 July 2005 and entering into force on 1 May 2006) and the Financial Instruments and Exchange Act (FIEA, enacted on 30 September 2007).

The Companies Act requires 'large companies' (that is, companies with capital of JPY500 million or more or with total debts of JPY20 billion or more) with boards of directors to establish basic policies about internal control system. The internal control system is, in this case, a system designed to provide reasonable assurance regarding the achievement of the objectives relating to operations, reporting and compliance by an entity's board of directors. The Companies Act applies to both public and private companies.

FIEA requires listed companies to disclose issues relating to corporate governance when filing annual securities reports or quarterly reports. Companies must submit an internal control report once every fiscal year to the Financial Services Agency with an assessment of the internal procedures designed to ensure the credibility of their financial statements and information disclosure. The section of FIEA relating to internal control, along with its subordinate regulations, is commonly called the J-SOX Act because of the similarity of the underlying ideas to the provisions of the US Sarbanes–Oxley Act (SOX).

A good implementation exists when management accounting activities such as analysis of actual results versus operating goals or plans, periodic and regular operational reviews and key performance indicators are properly administered along with the required governance activities. Some companies overhauled their business processes and integrated them into enterprise-wide governance systems. They are also installing software that produces continuously up-to-date business process documentation. J-SOX, similarly to SOX, facilitate the development of global corporate databases and management accounting systems to support governance systems. Compliance with J-SOX is extremely costly if a company has a weak underlying database structure, so many Japanese companies contain the spiralling costs of complying with J-SOX by utilizing computer solutions such as StarOffice X Audit Manager (NEC), Microsoft Visio and QPR J-SOX (Innovative Technology Lab Co.) and/or improving global ERP platforms.

Corporate governance

Corporate governance broadly refers to the mechanisms, processes and relations by which a company is controlled and directed. The Tokyo Stock Exchange (TSE) and the Financial Services Agency (FSA) in Japan jointly released the Corporate Governance Code on March 5, 2015. Adopting a principles-based approach, this code offers fundamental principles for the effective corporate governance of the listed companies. It adopts a 'comply or explain' approach to implementation. TSE regulations require all listed companies to submit a corporate governance report that outlines the corporate governance system, the basic policies regarding internal control system, and the relationship of directors, statutory auditors and executive officers with the company.

The presence of a relatively high number of outside directors is not always effective in preventing accounting scandals, especially for abuses carried out by a company's chief executive officer (CEO). An example is the recent accounting scandal at Toshiba Corporation. Founded in 1875 in Tokyo, Toshiba Co. is a huge industrial group that makes everything from nuclear reactors to microchips and home appliances, and has been a leader in introducing formal corporate governance mechanisms to Japan. Even so, the company announced a retrospective reduction of JPY224.8 billion in its pre-tax income for the period from April 2008 to December 2014.

At Toshiba, for the past several years (since the economic turmoil triggered by the 2008 collapse of Lehman Brothers), its CEO placed extreme emphasis on having good financial results for each accounting period to protect the pride and reputation of the company. This put intense pressure on a wide range of business unit heads to achieve extremely high profit targets. In trying to respond to pressure from the CEO, unit heads had to overstate sales and profits, understate losses and delay the recording of operating expenses. The dubious accounting was on a broad and systematic scale. The recent business climate, with weak financial results at the company, did not allow lower-level managers to go against their bosses. Similarly to other Japanese companies, the Toshiba scandal reveals not only weaknesses in Toshiba's corporate governance structure but also the risks of failure when some aspects of Japanese corporate culture rooted in lifetime employment go too far.

Concluding remarks

We have presented an overview of the development of management accounting practices in Japan. Unique and domestically developed practices such as *hoshin kanri*, *kaizen* and target costing and CWQC, have a relatively long history and have been developed and modified over time. Budgeting with the worldwide model has also a long application history, although with the 'catch-ball' style unique to Japanese companies. *Hoshin kanri* also uses the 'catch-ball' approach for complex and sophisticated strategy implementation systems.

Japanese textbooks and seminars on management accounting recommended the use of 'new and novel' practices such as ABC/ABM and balanced scorecards; however, these practices have not penetrated much in Japan. Other new methods such as life cycle costing, throughput costing and material flow costing are also not popular in practice (Kawano, 2014). Japanese companies tend to use traditional practices subject to statutory requirements for financial reporting, although they normally modify innovative practices, integrating them with new technologies and concepts and then implementing them in distinctive ways. The hindrance to Japanese organizations' innovating with alternate costing systems owing to the 1962 Cost Accounting Standards is obvious, however the recent move to use alternative forms of GAAP indicates the possibility that innovation in management accounting in Japan may be easier in the future.

Although some people may feel that Japanese companies have a passive/negative attitude to 'new and novel' management practices such as ABC/ABM or BSC, this may be the reflection of a strength related to typical personnel management practices. In large Japanese companies, job rotation is the normal career path for managers and management candidates. Managers with no accounting expertise transfer to accounting departments as a part of their job rotation to all functional departments. They must study intensely to do adequate work in these departments. After spending many years in job rotation in accounting departments throughout their career, Japanese managers thus become experienced generalists and lifelong learners. This practice has prevented companies from developing accounting specialists; at the same time, it ensures that a sufficient level of accounting knowledge is present in all functional areas, which means that all managers have a good understanding of how strategically important decisions will impact the organization. The trade-off is the depth of knowledge versus global effectiveness. Although an average generalist manager should be able to make better strategic decisions, there will be times when the lack of depth in a functional area will be a weakness in some specific tactical decisions.

Over the past few decades, Japanese companies have transferred their ways of costing and process management to overseas subsidiaries. Due to the spill-over effects in those countries, the overseas subsidiaries disseminated significant amounts of Japanese production and cost management practices and knowledge to the world. This chapter is an additional dissemination path for current Japanese management accounting practices.

Notes

1 Source: Panasonic Corporate Governance Report, updated on 10 November 2015.
2 In 2015, the Japanese software vendors Hitachi and NEC released the 'Hitachi Total Supply Chain Management Solution/IoT' (www.hitachi.co.jp/New/cnews/month/2015/10/1023.html; www.hitachi insightgroup.com/en-us/lumada-by-hitachi.html) and the 'NEC Industrial IoT' (www.hitachi.co.jp/New/cnews/month/2015/10/1023.html; www.nec.com/en/global/techrep/journal/g15/n01/pdf/150104.pdf), respectively. In September 2016, NEC supplied the 'IFS Applications for MES' (http://jpn.nec.com/press/201606/20160614_01.html).
3 See: www.toyota-global.com/sustainability/csr/governance/risk_management.
4 See: www.jpx.co.jp/listing/others/ifrs/index.html (accessed August 2016).

References

Baydoun, N., Nishimura, A. and Willet, R. (Eds) (1997) *Accounting in the Asia-Pacific Region*. Singapore: John Wiley & Sons.
Horii, S. (2015) *Budgetary management for innovation and strategic change (Senriaku Keiei ni okeru yosan kanri)*. Tokyo: Chuo-keizaisha.
Horngren, C.T. and Foster, G. (1991) *Cost Accounting: A Managerial Emphasis* (7th ed.). Englehood Cliffs: Prentice-Hall.
Horngren, C.T., Foster, G. and Datar, S.M. (1997) *Cost Accounting: A Managerial Emphasis* (9th ed.). London: Prentice-Hall.
Kawano, K. (2014) The present situation and problems of the management accounting and the cost accounting of the Japanese companies (Nihon kigyo no kanri kaikei genka keisan no genjo to kadai). *Shogaku kenkyu*, 30, 55–86.
Kobe Daigaku kaikei-gaku kenkyu-shitsu (Kobe University) (2007) *Accounting Dictionary (Kaikei-gaku jiten)* (6th ed.). Tokyo: Doubunkan-Shuppan.
Kuroda, M. (2011) Accounting tradition in Japan: an essay (Nihon ni okeru kaikei-gaku no dento). *Kokusai Kaikei Nenpo*, 2011(2), 93–110.
Matsubara, K. (2003) Overview of installation of BSC among Japanese companies (Nihon Kigyo ni okeru BSC dounyu no gaikyo). *Kigyo Kaikei*, 55(5), 678–683.

Moriguchi, T. (2010) Management accounting: Introduction purposes and role expectations of balanced scorecards in Japanese companies: a survey of balanced scorecards (Wagakuni kigyo ni okeru balanced scorecards no dounyu mokuteki to yakuwari kitai). *Keiri kenkyu*, 53, 126–141.

Nishimura, A. and Willet, R. (Eds) (2005) *Management Accounting in Asia*. Singapore: Thomson Learning.

Okano, H. and Suzuki, T. (2006) A history of Japanese management accounting. In C.S. Chapman, A.G. Hopwood and M.D. Shields (Eds), *Handbook of Management Accounting Research* (Vol. 2). Oxford: Elsevier.

Someya, K. (1999) *Japanese Accounting: A Historical Approach*. Oxford: Clarendon.

The Life Insurance Association of Japan (2014) *Actions for Increasing Shareholder Value: 2014 Questionnaire Survey (Kabunushi kachi kojo ni muketa torikumi ni tsuite: 2014 enquête survey)*. Tokyo: The Life Insurance Association of Japan. Retrieved from www.seiho.or.jp/info/news/2014/pdf/20150323_2.pdf (accessed 21 January 2016).

Tobita, T. (2011) A survey for the practice of small and medium sized enterprise's management and accounting in Kumamoto-pref. (Kumamoto ken-nai chusyo-kigyo no keiei kanri kaikei jissen ni kansuru jittai chosa). *Sangyo keiei kenkyu*, 30, 29–42.

Ueno, S. (1996) Profit management systems in MNCs: Exploring a conceptual framework (Takokuseki kigyo no rieki kanri: gainen framework no tansaku). *Kaikei*, 150(4), 108–119.

Ueno, S. (1997) *Budget Control Practices among U.S. and Japanese Companies; Cross-Cultural Approach* (augmented ed.) *(Nichi-bei kigyo no yosan kanri: hikaku bunkaronteki approach)*. Tokyo: Moriyama-shoten.

Ueno, S. (ed.) (2007) *Management Accounting Practices among Japanese MNEs: Findings from a Mail Questionnaire Survey (Nihon no takokuseki kigyo no kanri ka-ikei jitsumu: yubin shitsumonhyo chosa karano chiken)*. Tokyo: Zeimu-keiri-kyokai.

Ueno, S. (2008, 2004) *Management Accounting: A Quest for Corporate Value (4th ed.) (Kanri kaikei: kachi soshutu o mezashite)*. Tokyo: Zeimu-keiri-kyokai.

Ueno, S. (2010) An influence of international convergence of accounting standards on management accounting: Firm performance measures (Kaikei kijun no kokusaiteki shuren no kanri kaikei eno eikyo). *Kaikei*, 177(2), 35–46.

Ueno, S. (2011) Management accounting research in Japan: Evolution, current status and way forward. In *Proceedings of the 7th Conference of Asia-Pacific Management Accounting Association*,. Retrieved from http://papers.ssrn.com/sol3/cf_dev/AbsByAuth.cfm?per_id=1031395 (accessed 21 January 2016).

Ueno, S. and Sekaran, U. (1992) The influence of culture on budget control practices in the U.S.A. and Japan: An empirical study. *Journal of International Business Studies*, 23(4), 659–674.

Ueno, S. and Wu, F. (1993) The comparative influence of culture on budget control practices in the United States and Japan. *The International Journal of Accounting Education and Research*, 28(1), 17–39.

Yokota, E. and Senoo, T. (2011) A survey of management control systems in Japanese companies (Nihon kigyo ni okeru management control system no Jittai: shitsumonhyo chousa no chousa kekka). *Mita Shogaku kenkyu*, 53(6), 55–79.

6

Development of management accounting practices in Indonesia

Johnny Jermias

Introduction

Indonesia is located along the equator in South East Asia, consisting of approximately 17,500 islands and a population of more than 252 million (Statistics Central Bureau, 2015), which places the country as the fourth most populous in the world. Indonesia became independent when the Republic of Indonesia was established on August 17, 1945. Prior to its sovereignty from the Dutch, Indonesia was colonized by the Portuguese (1512), the British (1685), and the Japanese (1942–1945). The Dutch occupied Indonesia for about 350 years (1595–1945) (Meyer *et al.*, 2009). During Dutch colonization, all important economic activities were managed by the Dutch and the role of the islands' original inhabitants was limited to small-scale, family-owned businesses. It is not surprising that, prior to its independence, there was no accounting profession or accounting standards or regulations in Indonesia.

In its early stages after independence, Indonesian accounting practices were largely swayed by Dutch influence (Diga and Yunus, 1997). However, Indonesian accounting practice started to change in the early 1960s, when the Anglo-American system was gradually introduced. During the early periods, the main purpose of financial reporting was to apply for loans from domestic and foreign banks and for tax purposes (Abdoelkadir and Yunus, 1994). In 1973, the Indonesian Institute of Accountants published its first codified Indonesian Accounting Principles, which are largely based on the US generally accepted accounting principles (Saudagaran and Diga, 2000). Although the first Indonesian capital market act was issued by the government of Indonesia in 1952, the capital market did not come into operation in the country until the early 1980s.

This chapter examines the management accounting profession and the development of management accounting practices in Indonesia. The Indonesian accounting education systems and research on Indonesian management accounting published in international accounting journals will also be analyzed.

The management accounting profession in Indonesia

At national independence in 1945, Professor Dr. Abutari was the only Indonesian citizen with an accounting designation in the country. He was followed by Professor Soemardjo

Tjitrosidojo, who obtained his accounting designation in 1956 in the Netherlands. In 1954, the Indonesian government enacted the Accounting Designation Act to regulate the use of accounting as a professional designation. Following this act, in 1957 several financial analysts established the Indonesian Institute of Accountants. Until 1959, there were only 13 registered members, but by 1965 there were 232 certified accountants in Indonesia (Sukoharsono, 2000). Prior to 2007, to be an accountant, one must have completed a bachelor's degree in accounting from one of the state-owned universities or received a Level 4 diploma in the field from the State School of Accountancy (STAN).[1] Students from privately owned universities had to undertake an additional professional examination administered by the Ministry of Education after earning their bachelor's degree in accounting in order to obtain their designation. From 2007, to become a certified accountant, one has to undertake an examination offered by the Indonesian Institute of Accountants (to become a CA), the Indonesian Institute of Certified Public Accountants (to become a CPA), or the Institute of Management Accountants of Indonesia (to become a CMA).

Besides accounting professional bodies and the Ministry of Education, two other government agencies have also played important roles in the development of the accounting profession in Indonesia: the Ministry of Finance (MoF) and the Indonesian Capital Market Supervisory Agency (BAPEPAM). The MoF supervises and oversees the public accounting profession, with the authority to register accountants who have satisfied the requirements to be licensed as certified public accountants, to issue policies related to public accounting practices, to investigate violation of required policies, to impose administrative sanctions, and to revoke public accountants' practicing licenses (Maradona and Chand, 2014). The Capital Market Supervisory Agency has the authority to issue practicing licenses to public accountants and their firms, authorizing them to provide assurance services for companies listed on the Indonesian Stock Exchange. This agency is also responsible for setting rules and regulations related to the listed companies.

From its inception until 2007, the Indonesian Institute of Accountants had four departments: public accountants, management accountants, academic accountants, and public-sector accountants. Despite these four fields, there was only one designation of "accountant." In 2007, the Indonesian Institute of Accountants underwent a major restructuring. On May 24, the department of public accountants separated from the Indonesian Institute of Accountants and established an independent corporation named the Indonesian Institute of Public Accountants. The department of management accountants formed a separate establishment, called the Indonesian Institute of Management Accountants. Similarly, in June of the same year, the Indonesian Institute of Accountants dissolved the department of public-sector associates and incorporated it as a separate institutional entity. However, on September 1, 2009, this entity was adjourned and reinstated as an institutional member of the Indonesian Institute of Accountants.[2]

By 2015, the Indonesian Institute of Accountants housed three departments: public-sector accountants, educational-sector accountants, and tax-sector accountants. The Institute is a member of the International Federation of Accountants (IFAC) and administers the chartered accountant (CA) education and examination program. In early 2016, beside the Indonesian Institute of Accountants, there were two other accounting bodies in Indonesia: the Indonesian Institute of Certified Public Accountants, which administers the education and examination of the certified public accountants (CPA) programme, and the Certified Management Accountants of Indonesia, which administers the education and examination of the certified management accountants (CMA) programme. The CMA Indonesia is affiliated with the Institute of Certified Management Accountants (ICMA) of Australia.

Management accounting education

Accounting in general, and management accounting (or cost accounting) in particular, are taught in both formal and nonformal programs. Until 2014, the formal programs were offered by the Ministry of Education and Culture. In 2015, the Ministry was divided into the Ministry of Education and Culture of Indonesia (MEC) and the Ministry of Research, Technology and Higher Education (MRTHE). The MEC manages the education system from elementary schools to high schools. The MRTHE administers the corresponding systems for postsecondary education, for both degree and nondegree programs. Figure 6.1 shows the formal accounting education systems offered in tertiary institutions in Indonesia. The degree programmes are offered by both public and private universities and consist of a bachelor's degree in accounting (four to five years), a master's degree in accounting (one and a half to four years), and a doctoral programme in accounting (at least three years). In recent years, some Indonesian universities have collaborated with foreign academies to offer joint degree accounting programmes.

In the bachelor programme, students take introductory (first-year), intermediate (second-year), and advanced (third- or fourth-year) management accounting courses. The topics covered in these courses include, but are not limited to, cost concepts, cost behavior, job order costing, process costing, cost allocation, cost-volume-profit analyses, pricing decisions, transfer pricing, activity-based costing, budgeting, balanced scorecards, inventory management, variance analyses, and performance measurement and evaluation. In the process of obtaining a master's degree in accounting, students learn about various advanced topics in management such as strategic management accounting, activity-based management, balanced scorecards, and executive compensation. In addition, students are exposed to research on the subjects through a management accounting seminar course. In a doctoral programme in management accounting, the focus is on conducting research in management accounting. Students learn various research methodologies such as empirical, experimental, analytic, survey, and case study. To obtain a doctor of philosophy in accounting degree, specializing in management accounting, students need to write a thesis (dissertation) on specific management accounting topics using economic or behavior theories. A limited number of universities allow their doctoral students to write their thesis using qualitative approaches.

According to the National Standard for Higher Education, issued by the Ministry of Research, Technology and Higher Education of Indonesia (2014), the bachelor's, master's and doctoral degrees in accounting require a minimum of 144, 72, and 72 study credits, respectively. In most universities, students need to write a thesis as part of the requirement to get their bachelor's, master's or doctoral degrees in accounting. For the doctoral degree, after completing all the required courses, a student needs to conduct the following seminars to present: a thesis proposal, the research results, the thesis in a closed examination, and finally the thesis in an open examination. All seminars are open to the public and attended by the doctoral examination committee members.

The nondegree programmes are offered by polytechnics and academies. They offer Levels 1 to 4 diploma programmes. Students can complete each diploma programme for one year. The nondegree programmes emphasize the vocational/technical aspects of accounting. In general, graduates from the nondegree programmes cannot continue their studies at the master's and doctoral levels.[4]

Figure 6.2 shows the accounting education system of the nonformal stream, which is offered by private institutions in the form of short courses for elementary accounting one and two (three to six months for each course), intermediate accounting (three to six months) and advanced accounting courses (six to 12 months). Students can take accounting subjects through the nonformal stream while in high school or after they have graduated from high school.

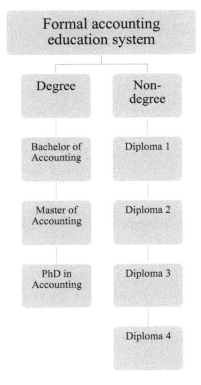

Figure 6.1   Formal system for *tertiary accounting* education in Indonesia[3]

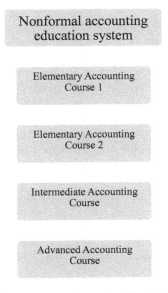

Figure 6.2   Nonformal system for postsecondary education in Indonesia

To obtain a management accounting designation, students need to take courses and pass the examinations administered by the Institute of Certified Management Accountants of Indonesia. CMA Indonesia was established on October 9, 2009. The professional body offers training, seminars, and other professional development activities to assist its members to obtain their designation, as well as to maintain their professional expertise. In addition, CMA Indonesia also offers industry-based certification for best practices in management information and control systems. The Institute has seven kinds of membership.[5] At the technical level, there are three types of membership: certified accountant technician (CAT), registered cost accountant (RCA), and registered business analyst (RBA). At the graduate level, there are two types of membership: graduate management accountant (GMA) and associate management accountant (AMA). At the postgraduate level, there is one type of membership: certified management accountant (CMA).

Evolution of management accounting in Indonesia

Management accounting is the process of identifying, measuring, analyzing, and reporting both financial and nonfinancial information to help managers make operating decisions to achieve the goals of an organization (Datar and Rajan, 2014). Traditionally, management accounting information was mainly financial in nature, with its primary focus on calculating product costs, adherence to standards, and feedback on budget variances (Horngren et al., 2016). More recently, however, management accounting information has expanded to include operational and nonfinancial information such as quality and process times, customer satisfaction, employee capabilities, internal business processes, and learning and growth (Kaplan and Norton, 1996).

Management accounting in Indonesia has evolved in accordance with the stages described by the International Federation of Accountants (IFAC). The IFAC (1998) identified four stages through which management accounting typically evolves. In Indonesia, the process went as follows. In the first stage (prior to 1950), the main function of management accounting was for planning (budgeting), product cost determination, and cost control. In this period, Indonesia was colonized by the Dutch for 350 years and then by the Japanese (1942–1945).

In the second stage (1951–1965), the role of management accounting shifted to the provision of information to assist managers in planning and allocating resources and the introduction of responsibility accounting. During the first two stages, management accounting was used mainly for recording cost information and for allocating resources through budgeting processes. Abdoelkadir and Yunus (1994) assert that management accounting as a tool for managerial effectiveness and efficiency was virtually nonexistent in Indonesia during this period. The main reason for this was that the Indonesian economy was dominated by state-owned enterprises (SOEs) with monopoly rights, accompanied by small to medium-sized enterprises owned by families. The SOEs were established for either strategic or fiscal reasons (Carmona, 2007). For example, the Indonesian government has monopoly rights in banking, agriculture, aviation, and even trading sectors. The capital market did not operate until the early 1980s.

In the third stage (1966–1985), management accounting information was used to reduce waste through the use of process analyses and cost management. At this time, companies in Indonesia started to experience more competition and, hence, the need to operate more efficiently and effectively. In 1977, the Indonesian government established the Jakarta Stock Exchange but the development was very slow. By 1988, there were only 24 companies listed on the exchange (Rosser, 1999). Kusuma (2005) argues that the unattractiveness of the capital market during this period is partly due to the complicated security listing procedures and the restriction on share price fluctuations.

In the fourth stage (1985–present), management accounting information is used to create value for important stakeholders such as customers, shareholders, creditors, and employees. This period is marked with intense competition among companies owing to the liberalization of the Indonesian economy. SOEs no longer enjoy monopoly rights and are restricted to limited sectors that affect the welfare of the public. By contrast, the private sector, particularly the capital market, has grown rapidly in this period. To promote capital market development, the Indonesian government simplified the listing procedures, abandoned the restriction on share price fluctuations, changed the investment tax on bank deposits, and allowed foreign investors to own shares. In 1989, the Indonesian government decided to open a second stock market, the Surabaya Stock Exchange, in Surabaya, the province of East Java. In 2007, the Jakarta Stock Exchange merged with the Surabaya Stock Exchange to collectively form the Indonesian Stock Exchange. By the end of 2015, there were 502 companies listed on the Indonesian Stock Exchange, with market capitalization of US$512.82 billion (Indonesia Investment, 2015).

Current management accounting practices

Lambert and Sponem (2012) assert that an effective management accounting system provides both financial and nonfinancial information to help managers to evaluate past decisions and enable them to improve strategic decisions to be made in the future. The following are some examples of decisions that benefit from management accounting information: allocation of limited resources, coordination across subunits, product costing, product pricing, preparation of operational and capital budgets, transfer pricing, measurement of business unit performance, and the evaluation and compensation of managers/employees. Unlike financial accounting, which focuses on reporting financial information to external users and must be prepared in accordance with the generally accepted accounting principles (GAAP), management accounting does not have to follow particular rules or principles. Rather, the information is provided if it is relevant for users to make decisions and the benefits of generating the information exceed the costs. Furthermore, Ittner *et al.* (2003) insist that, to be effective, management accounting information should include both financial and nonfinancial information useful for communicating a company's strategy to various stakeholders.

For many years, the main emphasis of management accounting in Indonesia had been to satisfy the needs of financial accounting in order to prepare financial statements for external users. Most companies use management accounting information mainly for inventory valuation and financial statement preparation rather than to provide information for internal managers. However, recent studies on management accounting practices in Indonesia suggest that it is at the fourth stage of its life cycle, i.e., Indonesian companies are now using management accounting systems to generate information that is used by managers to create value for important stakeholders such as customers, shareholders, creditors, and employees. Many companies use contemporary management accounting techniques such as balanced scorecards, activity-based costing, total quality management, target costing, employee productivity, and value-based management (e.g., Gani and Jermias, 2012; Lau and Sholihin, 2005; Sunarni, 2013; Jermias and Gani, 2005).

Research on management accounting in Indonesia

Indonesia is a member of the Group of Twenty (G20) and hence is considered one of the major economies of the world. Coupled with its large population, it is expected that researchers would be interested in examining various accounting issues in Indonesia. Unfortunately, research on management accounting in the country was almost nonexistent in the accounting literature, particularly before the year 2000. More recently, however, research on management accounting in Indonesia started to appear in international accounting journals. Many early scholars believed that this phenomenon is at least partly attributable to the change in performance evaluation for lecturers and professors in Indonesian universities.[6] During the New Order era (1965–1998), university educators were promoted based on their length of service at their universities and were tied to their job positions (ranks).[7] After the fall of the New Order Government in 1998, the Indonesian government issued Law no 43/1999 on Civil Service Administration to improve the quality of the civil service (Tjiptoherijanto, 2007). Following this law, in 2001 the Ministry of National Education[8] issued Ministry Regulation #36/D/O/2001, which contains the guidelines on the evaluation and promotion of university educators. Based on these guidelines, to be promoted to a senior lectureship or a professorship the candidate should have published at least one (for lectureship) or two (for professorship) papers in international journals named in the SCOPUS journal list.

Another plausible reason for increased number of publications on management accounting in Indonesia is that, starting in the late 1990s, more Indonesian students studied accounting in developed countries such as the United States of America, Canada, the United Kingdom, and Australia, where research and publications in high-quality international journals are crucial for career advancement. Furthermore, the role of international agencies such as the World Bank and the International Monetary Fund in promoting the development of the Indonesian accounting system cannot be ignored. For example, in the late 1990s, hundreds of students were funded by the World Bank through the Indonesian Accounting Development Programme to study accounting and related fields in developed countries. Many domestic universities also sent their lecturers abroad in the hope of improving their research profile and, in turn, their reputation. Their research profiles were also an important criterion for maintaining the university's accreditation by the Ministry of Research, Technology and Higher Education.

The following are some examples of studies on management accounting in Indonesia that have been published in international journals. Jermias and Armitage (2000) conducted a survey of management accounting practices on Indonesian companies listed in the Jakarta Stock Exchange. Questionnaires were sent to financial managers or equivalent. The main objectives of their study were to investigate the types of management accounting information used by Indonesian companies, the roles of management accountants in managerial decision-making, and the extent to which new initiatives in management accounting were being adopted by the companies. Their respondents were from the following sectors: manufacturing (49 percent), financial (15 percent), agriculture (11 percent), mining (10 percent) trading (10 percent), and others (5 percent). They found that the majority of companies in their survey used cash, revenue and expenditure budgets (97 percent), contribution margin analysis (92 percent), and break-even analyses (70 percent). Interestingly, fewer than 50 percent of the respondents used job or process costing systems. When evaluating capital budgeting projects, most companies used analytical tools of net present value, internal rate of return and payback period methods. For performance evaluations, most companies used net income combined with expenditure budgets to evaluate business unit performance. With respect to the role of management accountants, the results indicate that management accountants in the companies played crucial roles in helping value creation for their important stakeholders. For example, management accountants were involved in continuous improvement initiatives, assisting managers in achieving their key performance indicators, and engaging in activities to improve product quality, speed of production and delivery, and product prices to meet customer demands. Although their results suggest that the traditional view of management accountants as a function to provide routine schedules and reports are still being practiced, the respondents indicate that management accounting will play a more active role in the future, particularly due to an increase in market competition and customers that are more demanding.

The results of this study also reveals that management accountants in Indonesia are also involved in activities related to new initiatives in business management such as benchmarking, total quality management, standardization (through the International Organization for Standardization), flexible manufacturing, customer focus, team-based approached, activity-based accounting/management, social responsibility, employee empowerment, target costing, computer integrated manufacturing, just-in-time production, nonfinancial performance measurement, business process reengineering, value chain analyses, economic value added, and so on.

Jermias and Gani (2004) conducted a survey of companies listed on the Jakarta Stock Exchange in the consumer goods industry. One of the variables in their survey is related to the types of management accounting systems used by the companies and how important each system is. With respect to the types of management accounting system, two categories are set: systems that support cost leadership strategy (budgetary performance measures, variance analyses, improving existing process, activity-based costing, outsourcing, and cost advantages) and systems that support product differentiation strategy (customer satisfaction, on-time delivery, measurement of key activities such as cycle time and throughput time, quality, benchmarking, employee productivity, and strategic planning). Their study results indicate that the sampled companies had applied all the management accounting systems and practices, and most of them were used intensively. Moreover, managers perceived those systems as important in improving their companies' performance.

Lau and Sholihin (2005) conducted a study on the use of performance measures for performance evaluation by Indonesian companies listed on the Jakarta Stock Exchange. Based on the responses of 70 managers of companies in the manufacturing sector, they found that their sampled companies used both financial and nonfinancial information similar to those in a typical balanced scorecard, as proposed by Kaplan and Norton (1996). The results of their study also indicate that using both financial and nonfinancial measures in evaluating performance positively affected managers' job satisfaction through their perceptions of both the fairness of measurement and the interpersonal trust these measures promoted.

Jermias and Gani (2005) investigated the influence of contingent fit between strategy, management accounting, and control system on the relation between ownership structure and performance of privately owned and publicly owned companies in Indonesia. Their sampled companies manufactured and sold food and beverages, tobacco, pharmaceuticals, cosmetics, household items, textiles, and footwear. Based on responses from 281 business unit managers, this study revealed that both traditional and innovative management accounting techniques were used by the sampled companies. Furthermore, they found that publicly held companies performed better than their privately held counterparts, but the performance differential decreased with an increasing level of contingent fits between competitive strategy, management accounting system, and management control system.

Sunarni (2013) examined the types of management accounting used by manufacturing companies in Yogyakarta (a province in Indonesia) and the role of management accountants in managerial decision-making. This study assessed two types of management accounting issues: management accounting tasks and management accounting techniques. The study examined 12 tasks and 11 techniques. The specified tasks were: business performance evaluation, financial/cost control, profit improvements, budgeting, fixed assets management, tactical decision-making, productivity/efficiency improvement, generating customer value, product quality management, continuous improvement, managing customer/supplier relationships, and managing information technology. The 11 management accounting techniques were: budgeting, cost variance analysis, standard costing, activity-based costing, balance scorecards, total quality management, business forecasting, just-in-time, cost driver analyses, target costing, and value added analyses. Based on a survey conducted of 46 manufacturing companies in Yogyakarta, Sunarni found that companies considered budget preparation the most important management accounting task, followed by profit improvement and fixed asset management. With respect to the management accounting techniques, the results showed that budgeting is considered the most important, followed by cost variance analyses, standard costing and total quality management. Interestingly, this study revealed that most companies in her sample still relied heavily on traditional management accounting methods such as budgeting and standard cost analyses. More innovative management accounting procedures such as balanced scorecards and activity-based costing were not considered as important by these companies.

Jermias and Setiawan (2008) investigated the use of budgeting and management control systems in the public sector in Indonesia. They conducted a survey of government institutions in several cities, of which their respondents were government employees at the upper and lower levels of the hierarchy. Based on 204 valid responses, they reported that the government institutions in Indonesia used budgeting and budgetary control intensively. Budgets were used for both planning evaluation and control mechanisms. The results of their study indicated that participation in budget preparations, execution, and evaluation can improve organizational performance. They also find that government employees perform various management accounting tasks such developing long-term plans, formulating policies and procedures, coordinating interorganizational activities, developing performance evaluation criteria and procedure, and evaluating performance.

Gani and Jermias (2012) investigated the use of management accounting systems in the banking sector in Indonesia. They examined, among others, the use of performance evaluation and compensation systems to help banks improve in both financial and nonfinancial performance. The financial performance includes return on assets (ROA), return on equity (ROE), nonperforming loans (NPL) and net interest margin (NIM). The nonfinancial performance measures consisted of customer satisfaction and employee satisfaction. They reported that Indonesian banks used management accounting tools such as budgets, performance evaluation, compensation linked to budgets, and performance measurement systems for both financial and nonfinancial performance. Their results indicated that the fit between management accounting systems and a company's strategy can improve its financial and nonfinancial performance.

Conclusion

Management accounting practices in Indonesia have evolved from merely satisfying the requirements of financial accounting, assisting managers in planning, product costing, and resource allocation, to eventually focusing on creating value for important stakeholders. Recent empirical studies reveal that management accounting tools are being used by companies in various sectors including government agencies to improve organizational effectiveness. The Indonesian government plays a significant role in the development of accounting (including management accounting) systems. With the advancement of the capital market, the liberalization of the economy, and an increase of modernization in the field of accounting within education systems, organizations in Indonesia (privately held, publicly held, and governmental) will continue to utilize management accounting techniques commonly used by modern establishments. Furthermore, it is expected that these organizations in Indonesia will continue to adopt new initiatives in management accounting in order to thrive and succeed in addition to satisfying their stakeholders.

Notes

1 STAN is a government-funded school under the Ministry of Finance. Students at STAN have to work as assistant accountants after they graduate from the three-year Level 3 diploma program. After working for at least two years, they can take an entrance exam to continue their study in the Level 4 diploma program to become an accountant.
2 Prior to 2007, only individuals (not organizations/institutes) could be a member of the Indonesian Institute of Accountants.
3 Figure 6.1 and Figure 6.2 are both adapted from Sukoharsono (2000).
4 Some exemptions might be found in practice. For example, students who graduated from the State School of Accountancy (STAN), with Level 4 diploma can continue their studies with master's and doctoral degrees in accounting programs.
5 Detail explanations and requirement of the membership can be found in CMA Indonesia's website, www.cmaindonesia.org.
6 There are four ranks for university educators: expert assistant, lecturer, senior lecturer, and professor. The Ministry of Research, Technology, and Higher Education evaluates and promote all university educators (from both public and private universities).
7 There are four ranks and 17 grades. Ranks 1 to 3 have four grades each (a, b, c, and d) while Rank 4 has five grades (IVa to IVe). When university educators obtain their Rank IVe, they are promoted to professorship. No publications are required for promotion to full professor during this period.
8 In 2004, the Ministry of National Education changed its name to the Ministry of Education and Culture.

References

Abdoelkadir, K.K. and Yunus, H. (1994) Accounting education in developing countries: development in Indonesian accountancy. In J.O. Bruns and B.E. Needles, Jr. (Eds), *Accounting Education for the 21st Century: The Global Challenges*. Sarasota, FL: American Accounting Association.

Badan Pusat Statistik (Statistics Central Bureau) (2015) www.bps.go.id/linkTableDinamis/view/id/960 (accessed January 20, 2016).

Carmona, S. (2007) The history of management accounting in France, Italy, Portugal, and Spain, Chapman. In C.S. Chapman, A.G. Hopwood and M.D. Shields (Eds), *Handbook of Management Accounting Research*. London: Elsevier.

Certified Management Accountants of Indonesia (CMA Indonesia) (2016) www.cmaindonesia.org (accessed January 20, 2016).

Datar, S.M. and Rajan, M.V. (2014) *Managerial Accounting: Making Decisions and Motivating Performance*. Boston, MA: Pearson.

Diga, D. and Yunus, H. (1997) Accounting in Indonesia. In N. Baydoun, A. Nishimura and R. Willett (Eds), *Accounting in the Asia-Pacific Region*. Singapore: John Wiley & Sons.

Gani, L. and Jermias, J. (2012). The effects of strategy-management control system misfits on firm performance. *Accounting Perspectives*, *11*(3), 165–196.

Horngren, C.T., Datar, S.M., Rajan, M.V., Beaubien, L. and Graham, C. (2016) *Cost Management: A Managerial Emphasis* (7th Canadian Edition). Toronto: Pearson.

Indonesia Investment (2015) *Market Capitalization of Indonesia's Stock Exchange Grows Strong*. Retrieved from www.indonesia-investments.com/news/todays-headlines/market-capitalization-of-indonesias-stock-exchange-grows-strong/item745 (accessed January 20, 2016).

International Federation of Accountants Committee (IFAC) (1998) *Management Accounting Concepts*. New York, NY: IFAC.

Ittner, C.D., Larcker, D.F. and Randall, T. (2003) Performance implications of strategic performance measurement in financial services firms. *Accounting, Organizations & Society*, *28*(7/8), 715.

Jermias, J. and Armitage, H. (2000) Management accounting in Indonesia: Analysis of current system, potential for change, and forces behind innovation. *The International Journal of Accounting and Business Society*, *8*(1), 36–57.

Jermias, J. and Gani, L. (2004). Integrating business strategy, organizational configurations and management accounting systems with business unit effectiveness: A fitness landscape approach. *Management Accounting Research*, *15*(2), 179–200.

Jermias, J. and Gani, L. (2005) Ownership structure, contingent fit, and business unit performance: A research model and empirical evidence. *The International Journal of Accounting*, *40*, 65–85.

Jermias, J. and Setiawan, T. (2008). The moderating effects of hierarchy and control systems on the relationship between budgetary participation and performance. *The International Journal of Accounting*, *43*, 268–292.

Kaplan, R.S. and Norton, D.P. (1996) *The Balanced Scorecard: Translating Strategy into Action*. Boston, MA: Harvard Business School Press.

Kusuma, I. (2005) Indonesia. In S.M. Saudagaran (Ed.), *Asian Accounting Handbook: A User's Guide to the Accounting Environment in 16 Countries*. Singapore: Thomson Learning.

Lambert, C. and Sponem, S. (2012) Roles, authority and involvement of the management accounting function: A multiple case-study perspective. *European Accounting Review*, *21*(3), 565–589.

Lau, C.M. and Sholihin, M. (2005) Financial and non-financial performance measures: How do they affect job satisfaction. *The British Accounting Review*, *37*(4), 389–413.

Maradona, A.F. and Chand, P. (2014) *Development of Accounting Standards and the Process of Convergence with International Financial Reporting Standards (IFRS) in Indonesia*. Working Paper, Macquarie University, Sydney, Australia.

Meyer, J., Navichoque, T. and Riccardi, G. (2009) *Dutch Colonization in Indonesia*. Retrieved from http://weloveindonesia.tumblr.com/ (accessed January 20, 2016).

Ministry of Research, Technology and Higher Education of Indonesia (2014) *The National Standard for Higher Education Act*. Jakarta, Indonesia.

Rosser, A. (1999) *The Political Economy of Accounting Reform in Developing Countries: The Case of Indonesia*. Murdoch University Working Paper No. 93.

Saudagaran, S.M. and Diga, J.G. (2000) The institutional environment of financial reporting regulation in ASEAN. *The International Journal of Accounting*, *35*(1), 1–26.

Sukoharsono, E.G. (2000) Bookkeeping to professional accounting: a university power in Indonesia. *The International Journal of Accounting and Business Society*, *8*(1), 58–80.

Sunarni, C.W. (2013) Management accounting practices and the role of management accountant: Evidence from manufacturing companies throughout Yogyakarta, Indonesia. *Review of Integrative Business and Economics Research*, *2*(2), 616–626.

Tjiptoherijanto, P. (2007) Civil service reform in Indonesia. *International Public Management Review*, *8*(2), 31–44. Retrieved from www.ipmr.net (accessed January 20, 2016).

7

Evolution and development of management accounting practices in Thailand

Anbalagan Krishnan and Prem Lal Joshi

Introduction

Globalization has lead to increased competition among companies locally and internationally, however the focus of businesses in the twenty-first century is no longer on competitors but on customers and the quality of products, services provided to consumers, innovation, human capital development and other non-financial issues. In view of the competitiveness, complexity and dynamism of business operation, there is a need for new management accounting practices (MAP) that go beyond monitoring and controlling production costs. Johnson and Kaplan (1987) assert that, with the rapid changes in technology that have expanded information processing capabilities and vigorous global competition, traditional management accounting practices are unable to provide useful information in fulfilling organizational objectives, decision-making, planning and control. According to Said *et al.* (2003), competition has compelled firms to adopt a different management accounting approach, in particular performance measurement, to address the inadequacy of traditional financial measurement systems that have a limited short-term perspective.

For the last two decades, scholars from several disciplines have devoted significant effort into the development of new management accounting systems that reflect the fast-changing business environment (Kaplan and Norton, 2000; Neely *et al.*, 2000). Pressure from domestic and global competitors, demands for quality and reliable products from customers, high expectations from stakeholders and the use of new and advanced manufacturing technologies have contributed to a need to develop and implement a better management accounting system to improve organizational performance (Jusoh *et al.*, 2006).

This chapter provides an extensive review of the traditional versus new dimension of management accounting practices (MAP), followed by a detailed discussion of the evolution of MAP in the context of Thailand. Finally, the discussion focuses on the new management accounting techniques that Thai firms should adopt to be at par with their counterparts in the ASEAN nations.

Management accounting practices in Thailand

Thailand is an emerging economy located in the East Asia and Pacific region and it has been a key member of the ASEAN since 1967; its economic growth is comparable to neighbouring countries. According to the World Bank (2009a), Thailand is a regional centre of air travel within South East Asia. In recent times, Thai economic growth has been slow owing to weak private investments and the uncertainty of the political environment has drawn down the confidence of investors and consumers. Nevertheless, in recent years Thailand has evidenced economic recovery, which has placed it in a strong financial position (World Bank, 2009b). In order to boost economic recovery, the Thai government has set several initiatives to closely align the country's medium-term development framework and its longer-term goals under the Country Partnership Strategy Plan, sponsored by the Asian Development Bank (ADB, 2013). Thailand's key development challenges are productivity and competitiveness, regional equity and inclusive growth, environmentally sustainable development and regional cooperation and integration. The Thai government's new economic growth initiatives include three strategy pillars as follows:

1   knowledge advancement and innovation
2   support for private-sector development
3   facilitation of regional cooperation and integration.

The main aim of the strategic initiatives is to support private-sector development, and, therefore, it is crucial for the government to invest on human resource development. This is necessary to foster talented citizens to support the growth of the private sector and to contribute significantly to the changes in the way in which businesses operate and compete. On the whole, the uncertainty and financial crisis in the global economy have changed the business goal of profit maximization, and the adoption of strategic management accounting is seen as crucial for businesses' survival and growth.

According to Nimtrakoon and Tayles (2015), management accounting research in Thailand is limited. Based on a literature review of MAP in less developed countries, Hopper et al. (2008) revealed that only one study on management accounting research had been conducted in Thailand in the previous two decades. Nimtrakoon and Tayles (2015) identified a few researchers from Thailand with a number of papers published locally in English medium, including Rattanaporn et al. (2000) and Komaratat and Boonyanet (2008); Chongruksut (2009) found that MAP in Thailand was mainly focused on traditional practices, concentrating on full costing and financial reporting support.

One of the factors for Thailand's relatively rapid economic growth is the significant foreign direct investment. As a result, competition among businesses hass also intensified owing to increasingly competitive global markets. After the financial crisis in 1997, business management in Thailand had to look again at their MAP, in order to keep low business and operational costs and to penetrate into the global market with more competitive and affordable prices. Rodpetch (2003) noted that there were significant changes in the adoption of MAP, as well as in the perceived benefits derived from MAP in Thailand over the period 1996–2001. Thus there is a positive association between MAP and firms' financial performance. The main factor that this change is attributed to is the transfer of product and technology knowledge alongside intense competition.

Despite solid findings in some Thai research that changes in business trend influence the adoption of new MAP, the inclination towards using traditional management accounting practices in Thailand is still obvious. Traditional management accounting tools such as variables costing, absorption costing, standard costing, normal costing, actual costing, job order costing, process costing, segment reporting, transfer pricing, operational budget, financial budget, flexible budget and capital budget are popular in Thai business practices, while contemporary management accounting practices or advanced management accounting techniques, such as activity-based costing, value chain analysis, total life cycle costing, target costing, balanced scorecards and quality costing, remain in the early experimental stage in practice in the country.

The evolution and application of modern management accounting in Thailand

Management accounting is an important management system of organizational development. According to Tonitiset and Usshawanitchakit (2010), management accounting provides useful information for strategic decision-making, which is a sustainable advantage that helps a business entity to operate efficiently in a highly competitive environment. The concept of traditional and modern management accounting has been discussed extensively in Thailand. In theory there are two types of management accounting concepts: traditional management accounting, that is, with a financial orientation, and contemporary or advanced management accounting, focusing more on strategy formulation and implementation. Both types of management accounting techniques have been explored in Thailand.

For instance, a study was conducted to determine the adoption of MAP among small and medium-sized enterprises (SMEs) in Thailand by Rodpeth from Kasetsart University (2003). His study examined two type of SMEs: ITB and non-ITB. ITB are known as 'invigorating Thai businesses' since they obtain services or support from the government on technical, investment and management practices, while non-ITB have not applied for this kind of support from the government. Rodpeth's study provides interesting findings for ITB and non-ITB in terms of the perceptions (knowledge) and application of management accounting techniques as outlined in Table 7.1 below.

Rodpetch's study revealed that whether the traditional or advanced management accounting techniques are adopted in Thailand is influenced mainly by the business strategy or business characteristics of business entities. For instance, the combination of traditional and advanced management accounting techniques such as variables costing, absorption costing, normal costing, actual costing, activity-based costing, segment reporting and transfer pricing, operating budget, financial budget, flexible budget, capital budget, value chain analysis, total life cycle costing, target costing, environmental costing, benchmarking, balanced scorecards and cost for quality are highly influenced by business characteristics. Interestingly, the study also revealed a few management accounting techniques, both advanced and traditional, which are not associated with business characteristics, namely standard costing, job order costing, process costing and *kaizen* costing.

The notion of management accounting practices being associated with the characteristics of the business is also further supported by Grahovac and Devedzic (2010), who elaborated that cost management innovation is one of the new processes for contemporary management to achieve a competitive advantage in changing circumstances, thus it is crucial to successfully achieve the business goals. However, many different definitions of modern cost management innovation are proposed by different researchers (Namnai *et al.*, 2015), which can be summarized in Table 7.2.

117

Table 7.1 Management of accounting practices of SMEs in Thailand

Management accounting technique	Level of knowledge of management accounting	ITBs		Non-ITBs	
		Know	Use	Know	Use
Total life cycle costing, *kaizen* costing, environmental costing, value chain analysis	Advanced techniques	✗	✗	✗	✗
Benchmarking	Advanced techniques	✓	✗	✓	v
Absorption costing	Advanced techniques	✓	✓	✗	✗
Normal costing, variable costing, actual costing, standard costing, activity-based costing, job order costing, financial budgeting	Traditional or advanced techniques	✓	✗	✓	✗
Activity-based costing, transfer pricing, balanced scorecard, process costing, cost for quality	Advanced techniques	✗	✗	✓	✗
Job order costing	Traditional techniques	✓	✓	✓	✓
Variable costing, standard costing, financial budgeting, actual costing, target costing	Traditional techniques	✓	v	✓	v
Benchmarking and balanced scorecards	Advanced techniques	✓	v	✓	✓
Normal costing, flexible budget, capital budget	Traditional techniques	✓	v	✓	✓

✓: Yes; ✗: No; v: intended to use

Source: Adapted from Rodpetch (2006)

Table 7.2 Definitions of modern cost management innovation

Research	Definitions	Key focus of cost management
Choi, S. and Chan, A. (2004)	Achieving efficient management and operation in the industrial process	Innovation in all aspects, i.e. customer orientation, process and learning and growth. The main focus is cost reduction and efficiency in production.
Unger, K. (2011)	Focusing on new product development, emphasizing absorptive capacity and disruptive innovations.	
Abulrub, A.G., Attridge, A. and Williams, M.A. (2011)	Innovation is an important component of company's growth and advancement in the industry.	
Abulrub, A.G., Yin, Y. and Williams, M.A. (2012)	Embrace innovation to cut costs and time in product development.	
Fayard, D., Lee, S.L., Leitch, A.R. and Kettinger, J.W. (2012)	Strategy management to control cost in the supply chain.	

Source: Adapted from Namnai *et al.* (2015)

Namnai *et al.* (2015) developed a conceptual model based on this modern cost management innovation, Thor, and investigated its impact on firms' performance. In their study's conceptual framework, three underlying elements were identified, namely: 1) value chain cost focus, 2) strategic cost relationship concern, and 3) competition-based cost emphasis. All of these dimensions belong to contemporary management accounting, thus it can be argued that the ability to implement these cost management functions will enhance organizational performance, including cost minimization, operational effectiveness, business excellence, goal-matching decision-making and firm performance (Namnai *et al.*, 2015, p. 119).

- *Value chain analysis*: this is a form of analysis that looks at the value added from every activity or process within a company. It is a process by which a business entity adds value to its operating chain based on the available resources and capabilities (Dankbaar, 2007). In this value chain process, the costs of various activities should add value to production, distribution, sales and service.
- *Strategic cost relationship concern*: the strategic cost relationship concern is the creation of linkages between a firm and outside beneficiaries to achieve its strategic goals and increase its performance (Namnai *et al.*, 2015, p. 111). This modern cost management concept shifts the focus from a shareholder-oriented to a customer-shareholder integrated solution, which includes customer strategy, manufacturing strategy and quality strategy (Valancience and Gimzauskiene, 2007).
- *Competitive-based cost emphasis*: this emphasis is on re-evaluating operating processes and activities that do not provide benefits. Companies must find ways to cut costs and look to produce more cost-saving technology and facilities that would help achieve a cost advantage (Namnai *et al.*, 2015, p. 112). One such management accounting practice widely adopted to create a competitive-based cost emphasis is activity-based costing (ABC), which can facilitate the control of activity costs better and provide information for decision-making that will ultimately increase the competitive advantage of the firm. A similar management accounting technique is 'target costing'.

Another study was conducted by Nimtrakoon and Tayles (2015) to explore the use of contemporary and traditional management accounting practices that fit business strategies in Thailand. They examined 135 out of 451 companies listed on the Thai Stock Exchange (TSE), both manufacturing and non-manufacturing firms. Their findings indicated that management accounting gradually evolved over time from a narrow scope (traditional approach) to a broader scope (contemporary approach) in application.

According to Nimtrakoon and Tayles (2015), the adoption of contemporary (advanced) management accounting practices (CMAP) or traditional management accounting practices (TMAP) can be classified into three categories: high adoption, moderate adoption and low adoption. We find that, in regards to CMAP, the Thai firms listed on the TSE had to a large degree adopted the techniques of product profitability analysis and performance evaluation based on customer satisfaction surveys. The survey result indicates that Thai firms set priorities on satisfying customers and also sustaining their businesses in order to provide a good return. Although activity-based costing is identified as a tool to generate the highest benefits, its adoption rate is low owing to the lack of expertise and difficulty of practical usage in Thai firms. Alongside this, time involvement and financial commitment were also the main reasons for the low adoption.

On the other hand, the relatively rarely adopted CMAP in Thailand are balanced scorecards, economic value added, share value added, performance evaluation based on residual income, product life cycle analysis, target costing, throughput accounting, cost for quality, activity-based budgeting, activity-based management, performance evaluation based on employee attitudes, *kaizen* costing and value chain analysis. It is contended that the main reason for Thai firms' low adoption of CMAP is mainly cost, and as a result they are inclined to use TMAP. The widely adopted TMAP include budgeting systems for controlling costs, performance evaluation based on budget variance analysis, capital budgeting techniques, performance evaluation based on return (profit) on investment, budgeting systems for planning cash flows, cost-volume-profit analysis, standard costing and absorption costing. All these TMAP focus mainly on financial measures rather than non-financial ones such as customer service orientation, quality, employee development, innovation culture etc. In sum, the findings of Nimtrakoon and Tayles (2015) reveal the following:

- Firms pursuing differentiation/prospector/entrepreneurial strategies can obtain higher benefit from the use of CMAP than those pursuing cost leadership/defender/conservative/harvest strategies; and
- It is expected that the firms pursuing cost leadership/defender/conservative/harvest strategies can obtain higher benefits from TMAP than those pursuing differentiation/prospector/entrepreneurial strategies.

This study reveals an interesting finding that those Thai firms that adopted their strategy mission did not show any relationship with traditional budgeting. Furthermore, the Thai firms mainly pursued a 'cost leadership' strategy derived from TMAP rather than CMAP. Unsurprisingly, Thai firms put emphasis on TMAP. Overall, the Thai firms listed on the TSE perceived greater benefits of adopting the TMAP than adopting CMAP. This is mainly because the economic uncertainty in Thailand forced Thai listed firms to take precautionary steps to run their business operations mainly through traditional cost control techniques.

However, Shutibhinyo (2012) conducted a study to investigate the adoption and implementation of balanced scorecards by the firms listed on TSE and found positive evidence that many Thai firms had adopted this contemporary management accounting technique. The empirical findings revealed that, out of 81 surveyed firms, 73 firms had adopted the BSC while only eight firms had not. The main determinants of adopting the BSC are economic uncertainty and CFO recommendations. In addition, the positive attitude and strong support by senior management in adopting this strategic performance system with a multidimensional perspective containing both financial and non-financial measurements is a key driver. Although in his study surveyed firms were driven by key performance measures, cause and effect could not not be established (Shutibhinyo, 2012, p. 67) since the empirical evidence of such a causal relationship was still lacking.

Why Thai firms are inclined to use traditional management accounting practices

The empirical findings conclude that the majority of Thai firms, whether SMEs or firms listed on the Thai Stock Exchange, adopted mainly TMAP rather than CMAP. The management teams in these firms were more concerned about cost minimization, although they strove to be entrepreneurial firms. Consequently, great efforts were spent by Thai firms in providing financial information related to profitability, which is considered most important. Thus, Thai firms relied heavily on TMAP rather than the new management accounting techniques such as activity-based costing, balanced scorecards etc. Nevertheless, as indicated by recent studies, some firms have been inclined to adopt CMAP even though they would have been used to supplement TMAP to achieve the cost minimization strategy.

Various reasons were identified and indicated by Rodpetch in his study of *The Use of Management Accounting Techniques by Thai Small and Medium Enterprises* (2006) to explain the tendency of Thai firms to use TMAP as the unique business characteristics were the major influential factors. However, there are other barriers encountered by firms (both ITB and non-ITB) in Thailand, in the adoption of CMAP, which are listed in Table 7.3.

Adding to the barriers mentioned above, intense global competition has also put high pressure on Thai firms to be serious about the hidden environmental costs they are incurring in the changing business environment. This kind of hidden environmental cost is not reported in financial statements. According to the United Nations Division of Sustainable Development (UNDSD) (2001), the environmental costs cannot be completely presented and will result in a distortion in the analysis of improvement options. The International Federation of Accountants (IFAC) (2005) has also indicated that business managers pay little attention to minimizing their organizations' environmental impacts and controlling their environmental costs. Why is the environmental cost not easily measured in either the traditional or conventional costing systems? Some contributing factors are as follows.

- The economic costs or benefits are not easily visible till the end of production;
- The cause of treatment related to environmental impact is not visible, which has a lagged effect with long latency periods;
- Customers are more focused on quality and price than on environmental costs; and
- Business managers are not willing to take responsibility for actions to reduce the environmental cost.

Source: Chinander (2001); Tsui (2014)

Future trend of environmental management accounting practice

In the case of Thailand, the use of environmental management accounting to account for the environmental costs has so far been a low priority. This is attributed to a lack of knowledge as well as a lack of skills in adopting management accounting techniques beyond the traditional approach by Thai firms. Setthasakko (2010), when empirically exploring management accounting practices by the pulp and paper industry in Thailand, noted that the integration of environmental management issues or related costs to the existing management accounting practices is not visible, mainly because management accountants did not have sufficient environmental knowledge and experience. The Thai accountants did not consider themselves sufficiently expert to develop environmental management accounting (EMA) techniques within their organizations (Tsui, 2014, p. 14).

Table 7.3 List of difficulties for the adoption of CMAP by SMEs in Thailand

Type of SME[1]	Barriers encountered	Cause of problem
ITB	Delay and incomplete data received by the accounts department	Owing to the accounting system, use is not compatible with business expansion
	A lack of proper accounting system	
	Accountants having inadequate knowledge of new management accounting practices	A lack of funds for training and development owing to the low profitability of the company
Non-ITB	Lack of proper accounting systems	
	Accounting staff have insufficient knowledge on management accounting	
	Management lacks skill in adopting management accounting	

Source: Adapted from Rodpetch (2006)

Some researchers have suggested that accountants in Thailand should make efforts, at least, to report two aspects of EMA: *physical* and *monetary*, if a firm is deemed to have a social impact. The former covers information such as flows of energy, water, materials and waste, which allows access to and the reporting of physical environmental performance. The latter involves the costs that the firm spends for the consumption of natural resources (e.g. covering water and energy) and also includes other preventative costs that the firm incurs to reduce or avoid environmental damages such as clean up and waste treatments (Tsui, 2014). This environmental management accounting information could be presented either as financial or non-financial disclosure in the annual reports.

An initiative to provide a report on environmental issues using EMA will certainly also place Thailand on a par with other ASEAN nations in the global arena. As defined by the United Nations Division of Sustainable Development (UNDSD) (2001), this new management accounting practice of EMA is 'a combined approach which provides for the transition of data from financial accounting and cost accounting to increase material efficiency, reduce environmental impact and risk and reduce costs of environmental protection'. The International Federation of Accountants (IFAC) (2005) has also asserted that

> the management of environmental and economic performance through the development and implementation of appropriate environment-related accounting systems and practices. While this may include reporting and auditing in some companies, environmental management accounting typically involves life cycle costing, full-cost accounting, benefits assessment, and strategic planning for environmental management.

Firms in many countries have adopted EMA by incorporating environmental costs within the contemporary management accounting systems and it is no longer optional but necessary to do so in business operations. This is also an instrument to attract foreign investment, for which Thailand, among other ASEAN countries, is competing to stabilize its economy. The recent development of new MAP by incorporating environmental issues measured through EMA practice should add a new business edge to improve firms' financial positions. The use of the advanced CMAP can contribute to spur economic development by attracting foreign investors and improve firms' sustainable growth.

Member countries of ASEAN are seen to be potential emerging economic stars in the global economy. Therefore, an awareness of new developments in MAP is necessary to take advantage of greater financial investments. The integration of member countries to develop the ASEAN Economic Community will further strengthen economic growth in this region. Thus, Thailand, as a key member of the ASEAN, has good potential to grow as an economic hub among other ASEAN countries. However, the biggest hurdle is educating and changing the organization culture of Thai businesses in order to effectively adopt CMAP. Added value to business growth should be the priority of businesses in Thailand in the coming years. With the strategic objectives in place, management accounting in Thailand will play a more significant role, keeping pace with the growth of the Thai economy.

Note

1 This study classified SMEs in Thailand into ITB and non-ITB. ITB, abbreviated from 'invigorating Thai business', is related to a Thai government project that was aimed to provide technical and advisory support to SMEs from the public sector with respect to investment advice and the upgrading of management capability. Non-ITBs are SMEs that did not apply to the ITB Project (Rodpetch, 2006).

References

Abulrub, A.G., Attridge, A. and Williams, M.A. (2011) Virtual reality in engineering education: The future of creative learning. *International Journal of Emerging Technologies in Learning*, 4(6), 71–78.

Abulrub, A.G., Yin, Y. and Williams, M.A. (2012) Acceptance and management of innovations in SMEs: Immersive 3D visualization. *Social and Behavioural Sciences*, 41, 304–314.

Asian Development Bank (ADB) (2016) *ADB-Thailand Partnership Strategy*. Retrieved from www.adb.org/countries/thailand/strategy.

Chinander, K.R. (2001) Aligning accountability and awareness for environmental performance in operations. *Production and Operations Management*, 10(2), 276–291.

Choi, S. and Chan, A. (2004) A virtual prototyping system for rapid product development. *Computer-Aided Design*, 36(5), 401–412.

Chongruksut, W. (2009) Organizational culture and the use of management accounting innovations in Thailand. *Ramkhamhaeng University International Journal*, 3(1), 113–126.

Dankbaar, B. (2007) Global sourcing and innovation: The consequences of losing both organizational and geographical proximity. *European Planning Studies*, 15, 71–288.

Fayard, D., Lee, S.L., Leitch, A.R. and Kettinger, J.W. (2012) Effect of internal cost management, information systems integration, and absorptive capacity on inter-organizational cost management in supply chains. *Accounting, Organizations and Society*, 37(3), 168–187.

Grahovac, D. and Devedzic, V. (2010) COMEX: A cost management expert system. *Expert System with Application*, 37, 7684–7995.

Hopper, T., Tsamenyi, M., Uddin, S. and Wickramasinghe, D. (2008) Management accounting in less developed countries: What is known and needs knowing. *Accounting, Auditing & Accountability Journal*, 22(3), 469–514.

International Federation of Accountants (IFAC) (2005) *International Guidance Document: Enviromental Management Accounting*. Retrieved from www.ifac.org/sites/default/files/publications/files/international-guidance-docu-2.p.df.

Johnson, H. and Kaplan, R.S. (1987) *Relevance Lost – The Rise and Fall of Management Accounting*. Boston, MA: Harvard Business School Press.

Jusoh, R., Ibrahim, D.N. and Zainuddin, Y. (2006) Assessing the alignment between business strategy and use of multiple performance measures using interaction approach. *The Business Review*, 5(1), 51–60.

Kaplan, R.S. and Norton, D.P. (2000) Having trouble with your strategy? Then map it. *Harvard Business Review*, 78(5), 167–176.

Komaratat, D. and Boonyanet, W. (2008) Diversification of management accounting practices in the Thai listed companies. *Chulalongkorn Business Review*, 30(1), 116–134.

Namnai, K., Usshawanitchakit, P. and Janjarasjit, S. (2015) *Modern Cost Management Innovation and Performance: A Conceptual Model*. Paper presented at the Allied Academies International Conference, Academy of Accounting and Financial Studies.

Neely, A.D., Mills, J.F., Platts, K., Richards, H., Gregory, M.J., Bourne, M. and Kennerley, M.P. (2000) Performance measurement system design: Developing and testing a process based approach. *International Journal of Operations & Productions Management*, 20(10), 1119–1145.

Nimtrakoon, S. and Tayles, M. (2015) Explaining management accounting practices and strategy in Thailand. *Journal of Accounting in Emerging Economics*, 5(3), 269–298.

Rattanaporn, S., Komaratat, D., Cheniam, S. and Bailes, J.C. (2000) *Management Accounting Practices of Thai Manufacturing Companies*. Paper presented at the Proceedings of the 12th Asia-Pacific Conference on International Accounting Issues, Beijing, October.

Rodpetch, V. (2006) *The Use of Management Accounting Techniques by Thai Small and Medium Enterprises*. Department of Accounting, Faculty of Business Administration, Kasetsart University.

Rodpetch, V. (2003) Success factors of small and medium enterprises (SMEs) in Thailand: An investigation into management accounting practices. Business Research Project, University of Northumbria.

Said, A.A., HassabElnaby, H.R. and Wier, B. (2003) An empirical investigation of the performance consequences of nonfinancial measures. *Journal of Management Accounting Research*, 15, 193–223.

Setthasakko, W. (2010) Barriers to the development of environmental management accounting: An exploratory study of pulp and paper companies in Thailand. *EuroMed Journal of Business*, 5(3), 315–331.

Shutibhinyo, W. (2012) *Balanced Scorecard Practices and Determinants: An Empirical Study of Listed Companies in Thailand*. Paper presented at the Global Conference on Business and Finance.

Sulaiman., M.B., Ahmad., N.N. and Alwi., N. (2004) Management accounting practices in selected Asian countries – A review of the literature. *Managerial Auditing Journal*, *19*(4), 493–508.

Tonitiset, N. and Usshawanitchakit, P. (2010) Building successful cost accounting implementation of electronics manafucturing businesses in Thailand: How do its antecedents and consequences play a significant role? *Journal of Academy of Business and Economics*, *10*(3), 1–23.

Tsui, C.S.K. (2014) A literature review on environmental management accounting (EMA) adoption. *Web Journal of Chinese Management Review*, *17*(3), 1–19.

Unger, K. (2011) Modern innovation management theory and the evolving US lighting industry. *Journal of Management History*, *17*(1), 9–26.

United Nations Division for Sustainable Development (UNDSD) (2001) *Environmental Management Accounting: Procedures and Principles*. Retrieved from www.un.org/esa/sustdev/publications/procedure-sandprinciples.pdf.

Valancience, L. and Gimzauskiene, E. (2007) Does implementation of modern management accounting conceptions ensure corporate value creation? *Economics and Management*, *12*, 154–164.

World Bank (2009a) *Thailand data & statistics*. Retrieved from www.worldbank.org/en/country/thailand (accessed 28 November 2009).

World Bank (2009b) *Thailand economic monitor*. Retrieved from www.worldbank.org/en/country/thailand (accessed 28 November 2009).

8

Development of management accounting in Sri Lanka

Janek Ratnatunga, Kashi Balachandran and Michael Tse

Introduction

Management accountancy in its rudimentary form was practised even in ancient times, when great civilizations dawned and man was faced with the problems of allocating and managing resources and of keeping records. The earliest surviving examples are records of the incomes of temples in Mesopotamia dating back to 4000 BC, and wages paid in the form of grain to labourers in Samaria in 2000 BC.

The Venetian merchants in the sixteenth century created some bookkeeping techniques as they undertook trading ventures along various 'silk routes' – an ancient network of trade routes that were central to the cultural interaction through the regions of the Asian continent – connecting the West and East from China to the Mediterranean Sea. Although the silk routes (or silk roads) derive their name from the lucrative trade in Chinese silk carried out along their length, many other goods were also traded, and religions, philosophies and various technologies also travelled along the silk routes. Trade on these silk routes was a significant factor in the development of the civilizations of China, the Indian subcontinent, Persia, Europe, the Horn of Africa and Arabia, opening long-distance political and economic relations between the civilizations. Sri Lanka was one of the key hubs of the maritime silk route and benefited much from these international trading ventures.

At the beginning of the twentieth century, the Institute of Cost and Works Accountants (ICWA) was founded in England in 1919. The ICWA specialized in the development of accounting techniques for use in the internal control of manufacturing, especially in the blue-collar 'works areas' of factories. As such, its members were considered lesser versions of the chartered accountants in the United Kingdom (UK) and the Commonwealth, who usually worked in white-collar jobs in business and public services. It is for this reason that Sri Lanka (and most of the Commonwealth) did not benefit much from the advances made with regards to the professionalization of the cost accounting profession in the UK till much later in the twentieth century. However, once introduced, it quickly took root, and today some of the most senior white-collar positions in business, commerce and government are held by management accountants. This chapter traces the history of how management accounting has developed rapidly in Sri Lanka, from slow beginnings to becoming a very powerful profession in the country.

The beginnings of the accountancy profession in Sri Lanka

In Sri Lanka (then called Ceylon), the birth of the accountancy profession can be traced to two legislative enactments, the Income Tax Ordinance of 1932 and the Companies Ordinance of 1938, which had specific requirements in terms of the qualifications and registration of auditors. These two Acts created the need for tax consultants and accountants, and initially this need was satisfied by Indian graduates in commerce and about 25 British-qualified chartered accountants in the country (CA(SL), 2009b). Cost accounting as a legitimate branch of professional accountancy was not recognized in any legislative enactments, and neither was it given any recognition as a profession by business and society in general. At that time, in Sri Lanka, cost accountants were given the same professional status as bookkeepers.

The establishment in Ceylon in 1941 of the Accountancy Board, as a controlling body for the profession of accountants, was a landmark in the development of the accountancy profession in Sri Lanka. However, the authority of the board was limited to the approval and control of accountants (mainly qualified in the United Kingdom), merely to fulfil the requirements of the Companies Ordinance. Apart from this, any individual, qualified or otherwise, was free to offer his/her services to the public as an accountant (CA(SL), 2009b).

Soon after the Accountancy Board in Ceylon was set up, World War II escalated with the Japanese bombing of Pearl Harbor in December 1941. There was a significant Japanese threat to Ceylon, as the British Royal Navy was stationed in Trincomalee, a natural harbour on the eastern coast of Ceylon. This had two impacts on the accounting profession. It became difficult for Ceylonese to undertake accountancy studies in Britain owing to financial constraints, and several UK accountancy bodies that were conducting examinations in Ceylon ceased to do so. In that context, the Accountancy Board proposed to conduct examinations for registered accountants in Sri Lanka. Despite fierce opposition by UK accountants, who had a vested interest in maintaining their monopoly power, Accountancy Board examinations in Ceylon became a reality (CA(SL), 2009b). However, the examinations were only for registered auditors, since the cost accounting profession was not under the Accountancy Board's purview.

At this time, the accountancy profession was little known in Ceylon compared to the traditional professions like engineering, law and medicine. Training in these professions were available at universities, while few offered accounting programmes. In an attempt to counter this lack of social acceptance, an attempt was made to establish a professional body of qualified accountants in the country. This Ceylon Society of Accountants and Auditors was founded sometime after the establishment of the Accountancy Board. The society soon set standards, developed syllabi for preparatory courses and conducted examinations on behalf of the Board. Those successful candidates were denoted as 'registered accountants' and soon found employment in the commercial sector. But the public sector was slow in recognizing the qualifications of the Board in Ceylon (CA(SL), 2009b). However, these registered accountants were involved principally in account preparation, auditing and taxation. No registration was required to undertake cost accounting work.

In 1946, a commission was set up by the then minister of commerce and trade, Sir Claude Corea, to review the company law and to draft a suitable law for establishing an Institute of Chartered Accountants of Ceylon. The commission heard views for and against such an establishment. One argument 'against' was that the Ceylonese were incapable of setting up and ensuring the high-quality standards required for chartered accountants, and only the British were capable of doing so. Despite these views, the Companies Ordinance was modified in 1947 to recognize members of the Institute of Chartered Accountants of Ceylon.

Subsequently, the Institute of Chartered Accountants of Ceylon Act of Parliament No. 23 was passed in 1959, heralding the recognition of the accounting profession as being on par with the other more traditional professions in the country. The institute was renamed the Institute of Chartered Accountants of Sri Lanka (CA(SL)) when Ceylon changed its name to Sri Lanka in 1972. It is the sole organization with the right to award the chartered accountant designation and it is responsible for setting accounting and auditing standards in Sri Lanka. Today, the CA(SL) is a member of the International Federation of Accountants, the Confederation of Asia Pacific Accountants and a founder member of the South Asian Federation of Accountants.

The beginning of management accountancy in Sri Lanka

After the end of World War II in 1945, the need for more individuals with professional qualifications, especially financial qualifications, emerged to expedite the recovery of devastated economies around the world. The ICWA(UK) founder, Lord Leverhulme, said at the time that he needed a separate discipline of accountants to tell him not what has happened but what should be done in the future (Perera, 2015). Despite this recognized need, management accounting remained subservient to financial accounting and auditing, even in the UK and certainly in Ceylon.

In 1965, about five years after the setting up of the Institute of Chartered Accountants of Ceylon, Frank Hayhurst,[1] a British national who was the deputy general manager of Walker Sons and Co. Ltd. (a company still operating in Sri Lanka), and M.T.A. Furkhan,[2] the chief accountant of that company, were invited to a top-level business luncheon meeting organized by the Ceylon Chamber of Commerce. As recalled by Mr Furkhan, L.A. Weerasinghe, the first president of the newly formed institute, said something to the effect that:

> All important challenges of the Accountancy profession in Ceylon would in future have to be handled by the members of the Institute of Chartered Accountants of Ceylon leaving lower levels of accountancy functions to be handled by people such as book-keepers, cost accountants and others.
>
> *(Furkhan, 2015)*

It could be said that management accounting as a profession started that evening, when Mr Hayhurst and Mr Furkhan met at Mr Hayhurst's office and decided to organize a meeting of all members of the ICWA(UK) who were resident in Ceylon. They got in touch with cost accountants residing in the country at that time and summoned a meeting, to be held at the GOH Hotel in late 1965.

As scheduled, on 1 October 1965, all 21 qualified members of the ICWA(UK) resident in Ceylon convened a meeting that led to the formation of the Association of Cost and Works Accountants of Ceylon. All who attended the inaugural meeting signed the scroll, and those who were unable to be present placed their signatures later.[3] With the blessing of the ICWA(UK), office bearers were elected and continued to function even though the parent body did not have any provision to recognize the newly formed association.

Soon after the formation of the association, an executive committee was appointed that initiated lectures for the ICWA(UK) examination. The number of students for this qualification gradually increased such that the association had to set up a secretariat of their own (CIMA, 2015). The formation of this cost accounting association in Ceylon also had an impact on the education and training of chartered accountants, as the CA(SL) introduced a 'cost and management accounting' paper into its syllabus soon after.

In the early 1970s, Sri Lanka was ruled by a socialist government, which nationalized many large private-sector enterprises. The period from 1970 to 1977 saw further government intervention in the economy under the guise of creating a 'socialist society'. Significant and ever-increasing segments of trade, industry, agriculture and banking were owned and managed by state-owned enterprises (SOEs). The government expanded and consolidated the role of the state in the economy (and consequently marginalized the private commercial sector). By the mid-1970s the Sri Lanka economy was one of the most inward-oriented and regulated economies outside the Communist bloc, characterized by stringent trade and foreign exchange controls and pervasive state interventions in all areas of economic activity (Athukorala and Jayasuriya, 2004). Jobs for qualified accountants in the commercial sector were increasingly sparse.

In the early 1970s, education was free to all Ceylonese, from primary school to high school to university. While entry into university remained the primary focus of individuals seeking higher education, this free education had resulted in thousands of arts graduates without jobs. Many of these arts graduates spoke only the native language, Sinhalese, while much of the work in the commercial sector was still conducted in English. Many of these unemployed college graduates had joined a Marxist-oriented youth party referred to as the JVP, and had carried out an (unsuccessful) armed revolt in 1971 against the government of Ceylon. In this turbulent economic and social environment, a job paying a low salary was still seen as better than no job at all, and accountancy was seen as a worthy profession to get into as a job was virtually guaranteed on completion. As a result, the numbers wanting to study accountancy increased significantly.

In 1972, Ceylon changed its name to Sri Lanka, and the ICWA(UK) changed its name to the Institute of Cost and Management Accountants (ICMA(UK)). In 1973, the local Association of Cost and Works Accountants was elevated as an official branch of the UK body. At this time, the education for both chartered accountants (via the CA(SL)) and management accountants (via ICMA(UK)) was only in English. Also, there were costs involved that (while not exorbitant in an absolute sense) were still beyond the less-affluent majority of Sri Lankans. The result was that those opting to pursue chartered accountancy and management accountancy careers were mostly English-speaking youth from a relatively more affluent minority of families in Colombo, Kandy and Jaffna (a city in the north of Sri Lanka). Chartered accountants still held dominant positions in terms of social status and job opportunities, with many chartered accountancy students also opting to take the ICMA(UK) examinations simultaneously to keep open an escape route overseas if the domestic economy should further deteriorate from socialism into communism. The happenings in Vietnam and the atrocities committed by Pol Pot in Cambodia during that time had demonstrated how quickly a situation could deteriorate into chaos. This view was to prove prophetic given the events that transpired later in Sri Lanka.

Throughout the 1970s, the CA(SL) maintained the high salaries demanded for chartered accountants by restricting the output of freshly minted CA professionals. For example, in 1975, 4,000 individuals applied to undertake chartered accountancy studies. After a five-minute interview to ascertain an applicant's command of the English language and general knowledge, this number was cut down to 400. These 400 hopefuls were given a month's training in basic bookkeeping and auditing and then examined on the knowledge acquired. Only 120 passed the examinations to be given a four-year 'apprenticeship' in a chartered accounting firm and paid low wages while undertaking their training and education. At the end of the four years, only 19 of this batch of 120 passed all of the examinations at their first sitting and were granted the qualification of 'chartered accountant'.

Since there was no 'apprenticeship' under the ICMA(UK) system, those who could not get into chartered accountancy examinations for the ICMA(UK) had to take studies in private (unregulated) tutorials and via self-study. Thus, in the 1970s there were many more students studying management accountancy than chartered accountancy. Two events that happened in the mid-1970s gave a significant boost to the management accounting profession in Sri Lanka. First, in 1973 the CA(SL) Council, under pressure from the socialist government, opened up the training and education of chartered accountancy to students speaking predominantly Sinhalese and Tamil, allowing them from 1974 to sit for examinations in these languages (in addition to English). Many chartered accountants who graduated four years later were not conversant in English, which was still the language of the commercial sector. This became less important when more and more companies were being nationalized and Sinhalese was the language spoken in such SOEs. However, the socialist government was defeated in a general election by a more capitalistic government in 1977, which resulted in a complete turnaround in the economic policies of the country. This was the second event that gave a boost to the management accounting profession in Sri Lanka. The heavily state-controlled economy was opened to market forces, which resulted in significant economic growth. More liberal economic policies were introduced to emphasize private sector-led development. The commercial sector demanded more English-speaking accountants to fill the supply gap created by the CA(SL) (as a result of the deteriorating English language skills and low completion rates of CAs in Sri Lanka). This gap was filled by ICMA(UK) accountants despite the fact that these accountants had to study UK company law and commercial and taxation laws (which were very different from Sri Lankan laws). Further, most of these ICMA(UK) professionals were being hired for financial accounting and reporting roles in the commercial sector, and not for practising cost and management accounting.

In 1986, ICMA(UK) was renamed the Chartered Institute of Management Accountants (CIMA) after it was granted a royal charter. In 1988, CIMA's Sri Lanka branch was elevated to the highest rank of a division of the UK body. Thereafter, a CIMA divisional secretariat was established in Colombo.

At the beginning of the 1990s, 'accountancy' studies were provided in Sri Lanka mainly by professional organizations and technical colleges, despite university degrees in accounting having been started many decades before overseas, especially in the USA, and some professional organizations (e.g. Australian Chartered Accountants) only admitted members who had university degrees. Therefore, in November 1991, when the University of Sri Jayewardenepura (USJ) set up the first Department of Accountancy and Financial Management, with the objective of offering a special degree programme in accountancy, it was the start of accountancy being legitimized as an area worthy of university education in Sri Lanka. Although the concept of a 'degree in accounting' was finally recognized in Sri Lanka, professional accountants were still preferred over accounting degree holders in the job market, especially in the private sector. This was because the system of management education in universities at the time was aimed mainly at producing graduates with paper qualifications without producing the employable graduates and business leaders needed for future economic development. Another reason was that most of the graduates had studied in Sinhalese, but the private commercial sector used English as its medium of communication.

As a result, the Department of Accounting at USJ designed its undergraduate accountancy degree to suit the demands of the employment market by including a two-year practical training component, training in the latest computer packages and a curriculum to suit the latest developments in accounting. Most importantly, this programme was taught in English. Hence, by incorporating the requirements of the job market as its salient features, the new undergraduate accounting degree programme brought about significant changes to the traditional obsession for producing graduates who could not satisfy the needs of the customers (business organizations). This new approach acted as a catalyst for other management and commerce studies at USJ and in the country, to change their programmes by incorporating an applied approach to university education.

The introduction of strategic management accounting concepts in Sri Lanka

By the end of the 1990s, the Sri Lankan economy was at a crossroads. In 1983, the group of individuals from the Tamil-speaking community called the LTTE demanded through violent means a separate state in the north of Sri Lanka. This violence soon escalated and, until the 1990s, Sri Lanka experienced ongoing violent terrorist activities, which significantly slowed down economic growth. Aside from the riots in the north, a violent JVP uprising by the Marxist-oriented Sinhalese-speaking youth broke out in the south of Sri Lanka in 1987 and 1989. Although both revolts were ultimately unsuccessful, they caused extensive upheavals in the economic climate of Sri Lanka. The economy stagnated in the face of a multitude of global and domestic economic and political challenges. Overall, the country's average annual GDP growth rate was only 5.2 per cent in the 1991–2000 period.

During this decade, the CA(SL) updated its syllabus (adding more cost and management accounting subjects) and opened its doors to those seeking its CA qualification (which was similar to the CIMA's). The system of having to serve an 'apprenticeship', and to do so only in a CA firm, was replaced with the ability to gain accounting experience in a designated large business (in a similar way to CIMA). The CA training, which was previously done exclusively by the CA(SL), was now outsourced to a number of training organizations in the private sector that were 'accredited' by the CA(SL) (again, similarly to the CIMA). This resulted in a very significant increase in the supply of qualified CAs, though with much variability in the quality of their education and training, and in their command of the English language. While the education, training and experience requirements of CAs were now similar to those required by the CIMA in the UK, two cultural differences remained. The first was that, as the fees for CIMA education, training, examination and annual membership[4] had to be paid in foreign currency and could only be afforded by those from relatively rich families, it cost significantly more to educate domestic CAs. The second was that the command of English by CIMA-qualified professionals was much stronger in general than that of their CA counterparts as CIMA candidates were from richer families. These factors resulted in CIMA qualifications becoming in greater demand by the commercial sector and the societal status of CIMAs surpassed that of CAs in Sri Lanka, which forced the CA(SL) to take action to reverse the cultural gap with the CIMA that had developed in the 1990s.

The initial move to reverse the situation was made by the CA(SL) in 1999 via its Management Development Centre, chaired by Ranel Wijesinha.[5] The CA(SL) Council signed a memorandum of understanding (MoU) with the Institute of Certified Management Accountants in Australia (ICMA(Aust)) to provide technical collaboration to conduct a course in the new area of strategic management accounting for CA(SL) members as well as members of other professional accounting bodies. The first course was conducted in July 1999 at the CA(SL) headquarters in Colombo by two senior professors from the ICMA(Aust).[6] The course was attended by over 40 senior management accountants in the country (CA(SL), 2009a). This was the first initiative that the CA(SL) took to reverse the strides made by the CIMA in the management accounting profession in Sri Lanka, and the first time that advanced-level management accounting courses were introduced in the country.

The ICMA(Aust) is a professional association incorporated in Australia in 1996; it offers a number of seminars, training programmes and other development activities worldwide and has programmes that offer industry-based certification for best practice in decision information and control systems. ICMA(Aust) members are required to pass examinations and other assessments and have five years of relevant work experience before being qualified as certified management accountants (CMAs). Business organizations worldwide are also accredited by the ICMA(Aust) as providing suitable training and experience programmes for prospective members to fulfil their experience requirements for membership. Therefore, after completing the strategic management accounting programme organized by the CA(SL) in 1999, participants interested in ICMA(Aust) membership were required to pass two examinations: advanced management accounting and advanced strategic management accounting. Twelve of the candidates who undertook the examinations were successful. The introduction of this programme opened an avenue for CA(SL) members to enhance their expertise in strategic management accounting and gave an impetus to those seeking overseas employment (CA(SL), 2009a).

The introduction of contemporary strategic management accounting techniques such as activity-based costing, lean accounting, benchmarking, activity-based management, strategic pricing, supply chain management, risk management and balanced scorecards had a profound impact on the manufacturing sector in the country. The courses delivered by ICMA (Aust) instructors at CA(SL) headquarters were scheduled twice a year, and a large number of senior managers from manufacturing companies, especially the clothing industry, attended. The courses were very applied in nature and could be immediately implemented in practice.

By 2002, the private-sector manufacturing industry was gaining momentum in Sri Lanka. The textile and clothing sector accounted for 6 per cent of GDP, 30 per cent of industrial production, 33 per cent of manufacturing employment, 52 per cent of total exports and 67 per cent of industrial exports. The CA(SL) Council realized that it was time that it should put an increased emphasis on the subject of strategic management accounting and made a decision to establish a Strategic Management Accounting Faculty in 2002. The faculty was chaired by Manilka Fernando, a prominent and highly respected chartered accountant and management consultant. The objectives of the faculty were: 1) to provide an avenue for members' interests in strategic management accounting; 2) to create a technical centre for strategic management accounting development and research; and 3) to set up a facility for the continuing professional education (CPE) of its members (CA(SL), 2009a). In addition to continuing the highly successful courses delivered by ICMA(Aust) trainers, a number of training symposiums were organized, many of which attracted over 200 participants.

Competition and shadow branding in the management accounting profession

In 2000, Lakshman Watawala,[7] a former president of the Association of Accounting Technicians in Sri Lanka (AAT) formed an association called the Society of Certified Management Accountants of Sri Lanka (SCMA) and became its first president. Mr Watawala approached the ICMA(Aust) to provide the SCMA with technical assistance, but this was declined owing to the restriction of ICMA(Aust)'s MoU with the CA(SL). Mr Watawala then obtained funds from the Canadian International Development Agency (CIDA) to get some initial technical assistance from the CMA(Canada). In its early years, the SCMA promoted itself as running the CMA(Canada) programme, much to the annoyance and protestation of the Canadian body.

The professional qualifications of the SCMA at associate (ASCMA) and fellow (FSCMA) membership levels were somewhat different from those of the CIMA (ACMA and FCMA) and ICMA(Aust) (AMA and CMA) memberships. Therefore, the main professional bodies in Sri Lanka at the time, the CA(SL), the CIMA and the CMA(Aust), hardly took any notice of the SCMA, dismissing Mr Watawala's tenacity and influence with the governing bodies of Sri Lanka.

Later, Mr Watawala convinced the then minister of trade, commerce, consumer affairs and marketing development, the Hon. Bandula Gunawardena, to table in Parliament on 18 March 2009 the Bill for the Incorporation of the Institute of Certified Management Accountants of Sri Lanka (ICMA(SL)). The legislation process was usually very slow in Sri Lanka. However, in the case of this new professional body, interested parties such as the CA(SL) and the CIMA were given just 48 hours' notice to submit their views on the new Act (Shauketaly, 2009a), and the CMA(Aust) was not even consulted.

The main rationale for the formation of the new institute was to provide opportunities for students throughout Sri Lanka to undertake a professional course in management accountancy at affordable rates. The CA(SL) opposed this argument and was of the strong view that the country did not require a professional body in management accounting as it had covered relevant areas in its CA programme, which was also available throughout the country (*Financial Times*, 2009).

The Act stated that the use of the terms ACMA and FCMA and CMA would be the exclusive right of the ICMA(SL). As such, the CIMA(UK), which had been using the ACMA and FCMA membership designations for over 40 years in Sri Lanka voiced the view that the formation of the new institute might cause confusion about where the qualification originated from – that is, whether it was from the United Kingdom or Sri Lanka (Shauketaly, 2009a). The ICMA(Aust) representative in Sri Lanka was not invited to give any input into the drafting of the Act, despite the name of the new institute being a direct copy of the Australian institute.

These concerns were ignored, and the bill was approved by parliament; the Institute of Certified Management Accountants Act No. 23 was passed on 20 April 2009. Almost immediately, the new institute placed notices of 'cease and desist' in most major newspapers in the country that 'as per the Act no person shall take or use the title Certified Management Accountant, CMA or use the additions ACMA or FCMA unless they are Members of ICMA(SL) or has been authorized by its Council'.

This started a furious debate in the newspapers. The CIMA described such notices as 'unfair trade practice' and 'creat[ing] confusion as these acronyms have been registered by them under intellectual property laws'. The ICMA(SL) counter-argued that national bodies must be given preference in how they describe themselves.

Many accounting professionals viewed the placing of these 'cease and desist' notices as wholly 'unethical practices' and considered that the recognition of Sri Lanka's quality accountants were at stake, as by that time Sri Lanka had established for itself a worldwide recognition for its accounting skills. The ICMA(SL) was labelled a 'copycat' body, attempting to 'shadow brand' by copying the established name of CIMA(UK), and that this was tantamount in law to 'passing off' (Shauketaly, 2009a). However, Mr Watawala responded to the above accusations by writing a letter to one of the newspapers claiming that

> the Bill in Parliament was discussed at many meetings of the Consultative Committee of Parliament consisting of members of parliament from both the opposition and government and also the other accounting bodies. Chartered and CIMA were also invited for these meetings and many changes were made as per their requests.
>
> (*Watawala, 2009*)

One author of this chapter had many discussions with senior members of both the CA(SL) and the CIMA, and this claim of consultation was vehemently denied and stated to be false. A CIMA fellow held the view that the Act had come into effect without taking into consideration all the facts, such as the CIMA's registration of the 'nominal stamp' (Gunaratne, 2009).

The allegations against the ICMA(SL) spread widely as the other professional bodies and business executives criticized Mr Watawala and his actions in dominating the use of the CMA designation in Sri Lanka. The legal battles between the ICMA(SL) and the CIMA and between the ICMA(SL) and the ICMA(Aust) were separately fought, and it took two years to settle out of court, with all parties dropping their legal claims. Thus, the issue as to which organization has legal ownership of the use of designatory letters remains untested in a court of law. The main reason for this 'settlement' was that the members of the ICMA(Aust) and the CIMA(UK) started using the country where their qualifications originated in brackets to differentiate themselves from local ACMAs, FCMAs and CMAs, who were deemed substandard professionals. Therefore, in a convoluted way, ICMA(SL) members have to use their professional designation without stating that Sri Lanka is their country of origin.

Summary

While the origins of management accounting can be traced to the land and maritime silk routes, 'modern' cost accounting, which originated in the eighteenth century in the UK, was brought to the country by 21 members of (a precedent organization of) the UK-based Chartered Institute of Management Accountants (CIMA) who resided in Sri Lanka in 1965. The CIMA grew unchallenged in the field of management accounting until, in 1999, the Institute of Chartered Accountants of Sri Lanka (CA(SL)) and the Australian Institute of Certified Management Accountants (ICMA(Aust)) took an active role in introducing and applying the concepts and techniques of strategic management accounting to the manufacturing and service industries of an expanding economy in the country. The three professional bodies have since played a significant role in the development of the profession and practice of management accounting in Sri Lanka. In the 1990s, 'accounting' was also accepted as a legitimate field of university study, and the University of Sri Jayewardenepura introduced the first degree programme in accounting in Sri Lanka.

By the early 2000s, management accounting as a profession was in its prime in Sri Lanka. Many senior positions in business were held by those with a management accounting qualification. The social status of management accountants was on a par with (and sometimes higher than) that of more traditional professions like medicine and engineering. In 2009, there was a period of disruption in the profession, when a hastily drafted Act of Parliament established the Institute of Certified Management Accountants of Sri Lanka (ICMA(SL)), which then proceeded to shadow brand its membership designations by mimicking those of the more established professional bodies. Legal battles followed but were settled out of court when members of the overseas management accounting bodies took action to differentiate themselves from what they perceived as a lower-quality local body by adding the country where their foreign qualifications originated in brackets next to their membership designations.

In 2015, the CIMA celebrated its fiftieth anniversary in Sri Lanka, and could be proud of its many achievements and long existence in the country. Starting with a handful of students, the CIMA now has a growing student base of over 14,000, along with a strong membership fraternity of about 4,000 residing in the country; about 3,000 members who qualified in Sri Lanka are now living abroad.

The Australian Institute of Certified Management Accountants (ICMA(Aust)) has grown significantly in Sri Lanka over the last 20 years, although it is very specific in underlining that the 'exclusivity' of membership is its objective, and not membership growth per se. Its education programmes have been embedded in many master's degree programmes of Australian and overseas universities, and receiving a master's degree in such accredited universities provides an alternative path to satisfying the education requirement of CMA membership. The ICMA(Aust) took a different route to the continuing professional development of its members by sponsoring the establishment of Calwest University in the USA and giving members an opportunity to obtain Master of Business Administration (MBA) and Doctor of Business Administration (DBA) degrees through blended learning. The success of these intensive training programmes and the integration of the CMA courses within master's degrees are evidenced by the fact that that its competitor, the CIMA, has followed suit by having similar intensive programmes and university-embedded courses for its recently launched CGMA designation. A local professional body, the ICMA(SL), was established in 2009 under a new Act, although its legitimacy and social recognition remain debatable.

Today, universities and professional bodies cannot survive merely as education and training institutions. They also have to invest heavily in research. University research has found its way into best practice management accounting, with techniques such as activity-based costing and balanced scorecards first originating as university research publications. The accounting profession and universities in Sri Lanka are making concrete efforts to attract students to undertake management accounting studies. The management accounting profession in Sri Lanka will grow in step with the economic development of the country.

Notes

1 After his stint in Sri Lanka, Mr Hayhurst returned to England and was elected president of the Institute of Cost and Management Accountants (UK) in the 1979–80 period.
2 M.T.A. Furkhan went on to hold many business and academic positions, including professor of management accounting of the University of Sri Jayewardenepura, Sri Lanka. In recognition of the services rendered to education and generally to the country, in 2005 the president of Sri Lanka awarded Professor Furkhan the title of Desamanya, a Sri Lankan award equivalent to a British knighthood.
3 The 21 pioneers who signed the scroll were: F.V. Hayhurst, M.T.A. Furkhan, H. Dhanapala, O. Gunawardena, K.S. Venkataraman, M.V. Theagarajah, V.B.V. de Costa, M.T.M. Hamza, M.S.M. Thawfeek, P. Sivapalan, K.V. Kandarajah, P. Ramasamy, P.N. Wickramasuriya, S. Thillarajah, P.S. Mahawatte, E. de S. Wickramaratne, I.R. Peries, S.W. Nelson, G. de Alwis, M.J. Alles, and A.W.P. Samarasinghe (Furkhan, 2015).
4 The membership qualifications of ICMA(UK) professionals at that time were associate chartered management accountant (ACMA) and fellow chartered management accountant (FCMA).
5 Mr Wijesinha is a former president of both the CA(SL) and the Confederation of Asian and Pacific Accountants (CAPA).
6 They are Professor Janek Ratnatunga, the head of accounting at Monash University in Australia, and Leon Duval, the president of the ICMA(Aust).
7 Mr Watawala's professorial claims have been questioned in the newspapers (Shauketaly, 2009b). He has not responded to the accusations that, although he calls himself 'professor', he has no academic qualifications and has held no academic position in any university.

References

Athukorala, P. and Jayasuriya, S. (2004) *Complementarity of Trade and FDI Liberalization in Industrial Growth: Lessons from Sri Lanka.* ASARC Working Paper 2004–10, The Australian National University, Canberra Australia, 27 and 28 April, pp. 1–28. Retrieved from https://crawford.anu.edu.au/acde/asarc/pdf/papers/2004/WP200410.pdf (accessed 20 March 2016).

CA(SL) (2009a) Global networking. In *Saga of an Enduring Journey* (pp. 170–201). The Institute of Chartered Accountants of Sri Lanka, Part A.

CA(SL) (2009b) The changing role of the accountancy profession in the historical perspective. In *Saga of an Enduring Journey* (pp. 14–28). The Institute of Chartered Accountants of Sri Lanka, Part A.

CIMA (2015) History of CIMA in Sri Lanka, CIMA- 50 Years in Sri Lanka. *Daily Mirror*, 24 September, p. 2.

Financial Times (2009) Clash of the Accountants. *Sunday Times*, 16 August. Retrieved from www.sundaytimes.lk/090816/FinancialTimes/ft06.html (accessed 24 March 2016).

Furkhan, M.T.A. (2015) Message from Desamanya MTA Furkhan, CIMA – 50 Years in Sri Lanka. *Daily Mirror*, 24 September, p. 6.

Gunaratne, N. (2009) CIMA and ICMA in copycat drama. *Sunday Times*, 16 August. Retrieved from www.sundaytimes.lk/090816/FinancialTimes/ft26.html (accessed 24 March 2016).

Perera, S. (2015) CIMA's reputation as a professional and regulatory body has never been stronger. *The Island*, 24 January. Retrieved from www.island.lk/index.php?page_cat=article-details&page=article-details&code_title=118254 (accessed 20 March 2016).

Shauketaly, F. (2009a) Copycat qualification in trouble. *Sunday Leader*, 19 July. Retrieved from www.thesundayleader.lk/archive/20090823/issues.htm (accessed 21 March 2016).

Shauketaly, F. (2009b) Is Lakshman Watawala a professor or is he not? *Sunday Leader*, 23 August. Retrieved from www.thesundayleader.lk/archive/20090823/issues.htm (accessed 21 March 2016).

Watawala, L.R. (2009) CMA on confusion. *Sunday Leader*, 26 July. Retrieved from www.thesundayleader.lk/archive/20090726/issues.htm (accessed 21 March 2016).

Part III
Accounting and auditing professionalization

To maintain the comparability and reliability of the financial statements provided by economic entities to external users, attesting by independent professionals is a necessary mechanism. The attestation service is referred to as 'auditing' or 'assurance' and is performed by qualified and competent professional accountants (auditors) or certified public accountants (CPAs). To ensure the quality of auditing or attestation services, the professional accountants must be equipped with professional qualifications and practising capability, so they should be regulated and monitored by authoritative professional associations and the relevant market regulators. Therefore, the professional accounting association in every country, mandated by relevant laws and regulations, should set stringent requirements regarding professional qualifications, auditing standards and professional ethics, as well as the discipline of individual public accountants or auditors, and will directly exercise professional monitoring or supervision over auditing and attestation services. The quality of the accounting profession has a direct and significant impact on the reliability and usefulness of financial statements provided by business entities and on the effectiveness of the operation of the capital market.

Accompanying the global integration of capital markets in recent years, there is also a trend towards the internationalization of the auditing and accounting profession. The international organization of professional accountants, the International Federation of Accountants (IFAC), has made substantial effort to establish international standards on professional accountants' educations and qualifications, practising standards and professional ethics over the years, which are intended to be adopted or implemented through its members (i.e., the national professional accountants' associations) and some international organizations such as IOSCO, the World Bank and the IMF. Adoption of these international standards has influenced the development of accounting professionalization in individual countries around the world.

This section focuses on the development of accounting professionalization and auditing standards and practices in a few Asian countries or region, including China (Chapter 9), Cambodia (Chapter 10) and Taiwan (Chapter 11).

As mentioned in an earlier section, China has successfully transformed into a market-oriented economy following significant economic reforms over the last three decades. Chinese capital markets are in full operation and the group that uses the financial statements of economic entities has expanded to include external investors, creditors and other capital market participants besides government agencies. Thus, independent financial statement audits are crucial to warrant the reliability and usefulness of accounting information and financial disclosure. As a result, the Chinese accounting profession and auditing practices have undergone rapid changes in recent years. Chapter 9 provides a summary of the development of auditing standards and practices in China in the last two decades from the perspective of reviewing the recent empirical studies in the literature. In particular, the authors analyse how the major reforms introduced by the Chinese government in recent years (which have changed the institutional auditing environment) have affected external auditing quality and whether the auditing reform measures have prompted the improvement of auditing services in China. Empirical evidence is provided to demonstrate that both auditor independence and audit quality have been enhanced by the improvement in institutional environment (i.e., reducing government ownership and increasing foreign ownership), the implementation of new auditing standards adopted from the international auditing standards in the late 1990s and in 2006, the disaffiliation programme to delink auditing firms from the government-backed sponsorship in the late 1990s, the merging of accounting/auditing firms in 1999–2006 (especially in the case of multi-licence mergers), the 2002 requirement for listed companies to set up audit committee functions, the 2003 mandatory audit partners rotation policy and the 2005 engagement of CPA firms rotation, the 2004 regulation on auditor choice and auditor tenure, the change of organizational form of accounting/auditing firms to limited liability partnership in 2010 and onward, and so on. The demands for and the quality of independent auditing services have in the meantime been significantly reshaped by the specific institutional environment and policy changes in the accounting profession in China.

Chapter 10 introduces the development of accounting profession in Cambodia, which is also a transitional economy in Asia. As stated in the chapter, after inheriting the French influence, having being a French protectorate for about 90 years, Cambodia has opened to the world and been building up necessary financial infrastructure (e.g., capital markets) to attract international aid and foreign investments. The Cambodian government has realized the importance of accounting in economic growth and has promulgated laws and regulations to support accounting professionalization. Following the Accounting Law of 2003, the Kampuchea Institute of Certified Public Accountants and Auditors (KICPAA) was formed under the Ministry of Finance and Economy to regulate the profession, although the KICPAA's daily operation is still directly influenced by the government. The KICPAA has since then devoted great effort to the training and qualification of professional accountants in Cambodia, following the international norms as requested by international aid organizations and donors (such as the World Bank and the Asian Development Bank), in order to ensure the adequate function of statutory reporting and auditing. Nonetheless, many challenges remain to be solved for an effective functioning of financial market and audit services in the country.

Chapter 11 illustrates accounting professionalization in Taiwan. Following the institutional set-ups brought over from the Mainland before 1949 and the governmental development initiatives, Taiwan experienced rapid economic growth in the 1960s and 1970s and its capital market has become prosperous in the last 60 years, making professional accounting services more important. The Taiwanese government has taken a series of actions to regulate accounting profession, including the government-run CPA examination and qualification (screening) systems, the establishment of the Securities and Futures Commission (SFC) in 1997 and the Financial Supervision Commission (FSC) in 2004 to strengthen the regulation of the financial sector, including the accounting profession. Statutory auditing has been required in Taiwan since the 1960s and the Taiwanese regulatory authorities have mandated that a public company's financial statements be jointly audited by two or more practising CPAs (a dual attestation system) in response to a few significant accounting scandals in the securities market in recent years, aiming to enhance audit quality by continuing CPA review of audit works to reduce audit risks. In particular, since the 2009 Taiwanese auditing standards, CPA firms in Taiwan are required to perform dual attestation, i.e., to have at least three CPAs to participate in every listed client audit engagement, two as signing CPAs and one as a quality control reviewer, a unique practice in public accounting. This chapter also elaborates the recent progress of internationalization of the accounting profession in Taiwan.

9

Auditing standards and practice in China

An overview of the development in the past two decades

Guiru Hua and Haiyan Zhou

Introduction

The market for independent auditing was not resumed in China until the country started to transform its state-controlled economy and solicit foreign investments in the early 1980s. Along with the economic reforms and the reopening of stock markets, the auditing profession has undergone rapid development. At present, there are more than 7,400 accounting firms, over 8.5 million certified public accountants (CPAs) and nearly 30 million accounting and auditing employees in China (Wang and Dou, 2015). Meanwhile, in order to improve auditing quality and increase the credibility of the financial statements, the Chinese government has gradually adopted and implemented a series of auditing reforms that have greatly promoted the development of independent auditing in the country.

However, the capital market in the emerging markets of China has been criticized for the weak institutional environment (Sami and Zhou, 2004) that for a long time featured alongside dominant government ownership (Choi *et al.*, 2010), which significantly affects the landscape of independent auditing. For instance, there was no effective and complete framework for the legal responsibilities of CPA, and the litigation risk confronted by Chinese auditors was relatively low. In addition, the unique characteristics of business ownership structure, in which the government takes up an extremely high percentage of equity shareholding, also affect the demand for independent auditing.

From the perspective of institutional environment and auditing reforms, this chapter reviews the development of auditing standards and practices in China during the last two decades and addresses two main questions: how does institutional environment, dominant government control and some foreign ownership affect external auditing in China and how do auditing reforms promote the development of audit services in China?

A weak institutional environment results in a lower supply and demand of quality audits, while institutional reforms and improvements can help change the demand and supply in the auditing markets. The emerging market in China provides unique settings to investigate the impact of institutional reforms such as the implantation of accounting and auditing standards in the audit markets. Chinese stock markets also provide unique settings to observe the role of government ownership and foreign ownership in the demand for high audit quality. A few studies find that high levels of government ownership create little demand for high-quality audits, but auditing quality has enhanced following the increase of foreign ownership (e.g., Wang *et al.*, 2008; He *et al.*, 2014). In addition, prior studies also document how the Chinese government has gradually adopted and implemented a series of regulations and reforms that have greatly improved auditing quality (e.g., Gul *et al.*, 2009; Zhou, 2007).

From the agency theory perspective, Watts and Zimmerman (1983) investigate the bonding and auditing practices in the UK and the US and conclude that voluntary auditing practice is useful in reducing agency costs and that independent audits are not a direct result of government intervention. Contributing to the auditing literature, studies on auditing issues in the emerging Chinese markets provide evidence that institutional and regulatory changes have been shaping the development of external auditing. The Chinese experience can have implications for policymakers and regulators in other countries, especially for those in emerging economies. It is generally recognized that high-quality accounting standards 'result in greater investor confidence, which improves liquidity, reduces capital cost, and makes informative market prices possible' (Levitt 1998, p. 81). Thus, good effort in accounting/auditing policymaking and regulation will assist the emerging economies in improving the information environment and market liquidity and efficiency. The auditing development in China provides vivid evidence in this regard.

The remainder of this chapter is organized as follows. The next section discusses the related literature on the effects of institutional environment and ownership structure on external auditing in China. The third section describes studies on government-driven auditing reforms and their effectiveness, and the final section concludes.

Effect of institutional environment and ownership structure on external auditing

As mentioned earlier, the capital market in China has been criticized for its weak institutional environment (Sami and Zhou, 2004), and has for a long time featured dominant government ownership (Choi *et al.*, 2010). These markets in China generate unique settings for investigating the impact of institutional reforms, such as the implantation of new accounting and auditing standards in audit markets, and observing the role of government ownership and foreign ownership in the demand for high audit quality. In general, both country-level and firm-level factors (e.g. unique government ownership and foreign shareholding) influence external auditing. A few recent studies on institutional environment, ownership structures and external auditing in China are summarized in Table 9.1.

Table 9.1 Summary of studies about the impacts of institutional environment and ownership structure on external auditing

Institutional environment (country level)		Ownership structure (firm level)	
Weak institutional environment	Institutional improvements	Government ownership	Foreign shareholding
Ke *et al.* (2015)	Chen *et al.* (2010)	Lin *et al.* (2009, 2010)	He *et al.* (2014)
		Chen *et al.* (2010)	Gul *et al.* (2009)
	Wang *et al.* (2008)		

Institutional environment and external auditing

Institutional environment in China's stock market

Accounting and auditing practices in China have experienced dramatic changes over the past two decades. These were driven mainly by the establishment of the two major Chinese security exchanges – the Shanghai Stock Exchange (SHSE) and the Shenzhen Stock Exchange (SZSE) – owing to investors' demand for reliable information to make their investment decisions (Sami and Zhou, 2004). The Chinese stock market has developed rapidly, with listed companies on the main boards rising from 14 in 1991 to 1,059 in 2000, and increasing to over 2,000 in 2015. Annual trading volume rose from 300 million shares in 1991 to 455.6 billion US dollars in 2000 and skyrocketing to about 43 trillion US dollars in 2015. In addition, as of 31 December 2015, over 1,200 companies were listed on the SME and ChiNext Boards, with a combined market value of 2.5 trillion US dollars. To meet the market's demand for high-quality financial information, the Chinese government has taken a series of measures to improve the institutional environment, such as the first set of accounting standards, copied from the International Auditing Standards, adopted in 1996, the disaffiliation programme to separate CPA firms from their sponsoring bodies (most were government agencies) in 1997–1998, and the reform of CPA firms' organizational form in 2010 following the promulgation of the Interim Provisions on Auditors' Organizational Transformation. Consequently, such a series of important changes in auditing practice has transformed Chinese auditors' roles in accounting and financial reporting practice from government agencies to regulated accounting and auditing practices to independent assurance provided on accounting information over the last two decades (Gul *et al.*, 2009).

There have also been a series of reforms in the judicial system in China during this period. For instance, the CPA Act was enacted and implemented in 1994, indicating for the first time that Chinese auditors are liable to clients and other parties who may suffer loss due to audit failures. Such liability was further emphasized by the Chinese High Court in Document No. 56, issued in 1996 (Gul *et al.*, 2009). Starting from the first case, in 1996, litigation against auditors increased to about 400 cases in 1998, according to the CPA *Newsletter* (1998, quoted by Yang *et al.*, 2001). However, criminal charges against auditors in China are rare (Lisic *et al.*, 2015). According to China Securities Regulatory Commission (CSRC) enforcement releases quoted by Liu and Wang (2015), only two CPAs were transferred to a judicial body for an investigation of criminal responsibility in 1993–2015.

The two stock exchanges, the CSRC and the Chinese Institute of Certified Public Accountants (CICPA) have also enhanced their surveillance of CPAs and audit practices. To enforce the new auditing standards, Chinese CPAs are subject to warnings, fines, suspensions of operation and withdrawal of licences if found in violation of their professional standards (Gul *et al.*, 2003). According to the *CPA Newsletter* (1998, quoted by Yang *et al.*, 2001), such cases increased from about 100 in 1994 to around 500 in 1997. According to the CSRC enforcement releases quoted by Liu and Wang (2015), cases of warnings, fines, revocations of certificate and other sanctions from the CSRC against auditors increased dramatically, from 27 in 1993–1997 to 322 in 1998–2015.

These reforms represent significant milestones in the development of the legal liability of CPAs or auditors in China, although the legal systems there have been criticized owing to a lack of sufficient independence and inexperienced or poorly trained judges and lawyers (Chen, 2003). In particular, there was no effective and complete legal framework for the civil liability of CPAs before the judicial reforms. The Civil Law, which did not give consistent definitions on auditor liability, was ambiguous in compensation procedures and explicitly forbade class action litigation (Li and He, 2000). In addition, the penalties for auditors' violation of the audit regulations remained mostly at the administrative level, taking the form of public reprimands, warnings, fines and suspensions of licences (Chen et al., 2010). The number of CPA firms brought to court for civil or criminal liability was negligible (Pistor and Xu, 2005). Consequently, unlike those in developed markets such as the US, the litigation risk faced by Chinese auditors was relatively low in the 1990s and early 2000s.

The effect of weak institutional environment on external auditing

Corporate governance theory, such as that of La Porta et al. (2000), argues that institutional environment is one of the most important determinants of financial and accounting behaviour. Consistent with this theory, empirical studies explain why institutional environment affects the supply of quality audits. Using a sample of 39 countries, Choi and Wong (2007) found that high-quality auditors are more likely to decline risky engagements and charge high audit fees to reduce potential legal costs in high legal risk environments, where auditors' legal liabilities are clearly defined and litigation risk is high. Thus, an interesting question is whether a weak institutional environment, such as exists in emerging Chinese markets, can result in auditing firms providing lower-quality audits.

To address such a question, Ke et al. (2015) explore the unique features of the A-share and H-share companies in China, which are required to prepare two sets of audited financial statements (Chinese accounting standards are adopted for A-share companies, while International Accounting Standards applying to the financial statements for listing requirements on stock markets abroad, such as H-shares, listed on the Hong Kong Stock Exchange). Compared with companies cross-listed in Hong Kong, the Big Four international CPA firms are more likely to assign less experienced partners, issue unqualified audit reports and charge lower audit fees for clients that are listed only in domestic markets in China. Furthermore, companies listed only in domestic markets have larger abnormal accruals than companies cross-listed in Hong Kong. These findings suggest that China's weak institutional environment will result in the lower supply of quality audits.

The effect of institutional improvements on external auditing

Theoretical studies, such as that of Jensen and Meckling (1976), argue that, in order to relieve agency problems, firms must have incentives to employ independent auditors. An important question is whether institutional improvement affects a firm's demand for independent auditors in the Chinese capital market. Using a sample of all listed companies in China from 1993–2003, Wang et al. (2008) find that, in regions with less developed institutions, the state-owned enterprises (SOEs) controlled by central government are more likely to employ small auditors. However, the tendency in the sample of local and central SOEs is attenuated with institutional developments. Thus, their evidence supports the notion that institutional improvement results in the increase of a firm's demand for high-quality audits in China.

Another important issue is whether the institutional improvements in China increase the supply of external auditing and improve audit quality. Prior studies, based on individual- and office-level auditor analyses, find that the propensity to issue modified audit opinions (MAOs) is negatively correlated with client importance over the 1995 to 2000 period, when the legal and regulatory environment was weak; in contrast, between 2001 and 2004, when the institutional environment was improved, auditors' propensity to issue MAOs is positively associated with client importance (e.g., Chen *et al.*, 2010). These empirical results indicate that the institutional improvements help increase the supply of high-quality audits in China.

Unique ownership structure and external auditing

Characteristics of business ownership structure in China

In order to reorient its centrally planned economy towards a market-based economy, since 1979 the Chinese government has launched a series of economic reforms. Among these, the most important reform has been to privatize SOEs that performed poorly. This normally involves IPOs to transfer a portion of the companies' shares from the government to individual investors, who can trade their shares freely on the stock exchanges, while the majority ownership of these newly listed companies is still controlled by their parent firms – namely, the SOEs or government agencies. By the end of 2005, over 1,000 medium-sized and large SOEs had been privatized, representing about 93 per cent of all publicly listed firms in Mainland China.

Thus, the overwhelming majority of listed firms are state-owned enterprises in China; the government maintains the role of a major shareholder and retains two key control rights: the ultimate decision right concerning disposal of assets and mergers and acquisitions, and the appointment of chief executive officers (Chen *et al.*, 2011). Although China's stock market has changed dramatically since the non-tradable share reform in 2006, it has kept the unique characteristic of ownership structure with high levels of government ownership, unlike Western countries.

The effect of government ownership on the demand for external auditing

Agency theorists argue that firms have incentives to hire external auditors to mitigate their agency conflicts (Jensen and Meckling, 1976) and a firm's ownership structure affects its demand for independent audits (Chow, 1982). However, it remains an empirical question whether the high levels of government ownership in Chinese public firms affect the demand for independent auditing. From the perspective of political and economic institutions, Wang *et al.* (2008) and Chan *et al.* (2007) find that high levels of government ownership create little demand for high-quality audits in Chinese stock markets.

In their study, Wang *et al.* (2008) report that, compared with non-state-owned firms, SOEs controlled by local governments are more likely to hire small auditors. SOEs controlled by central government also have this tendency in regions where the institutional environment is weak, which indicates that SOEs do not demand high-quality audits owing to preferential treatment from the government and state banks.

Over the past few years, the Chinese government has gradually taken measures to reduce its equity holdings in listed companies through ownership reforms. Chan *et al.* (2007) examined how changes in ownership structure affect auditor choices. Based on 130 voluntary auditor switches from 1997–2005, they found that a decrease in government ownership and a corresponding increase in institutional ownership resulted in an increase in the demand for high-quality audits in China.

The effect of foreign shareholding on the demand for external auditing

Since the economic reforms of 1978, many foreign investors have begun to show interest in the Chinese market and foreign capital has become an increasingly important source of financing to Chinese firms. Foreign investors are at an informational disadvantage relative to domestic investors because of higher information acquisition and processing costs (see e.g. Kang and Stulz, 1997). Thus, there are two important empirical research questions: 1) do foreign investors have a demand for high-quality auditing in the Chinese capital market? and 2) are auditors more conservative in auditing clients with more foreign ownership?

To address the first question, Wei *et al.* (2008) examine whether there was any significant change in the relationship between audit opinions and default probability following the entry of qualified foreign institutional investors (QFIIs) in the Chinese stock market in 2002. They found that audit opinions began to provide signals of potential default risk only after QFIIs entered the market, suggesting that auditors became more conservative when foreign institutional investors began to play a monitoring role.

Foreign investors are more likely to demand high-quality financial reporting and have a stronger demand for high-quality auditors (He *et al.*, 2014). They are also more likely to serve a governance role in monitoring senior management and preventing controlling shareholders from extracting private benefits from the public firms. Based on the unique institutional background of the B-share stock market in China, He et al. (2014) found that the percentage of B-share firms audited by Big Four auditors had decreased since the originally segmented B-share market was opened to domestic investors in 2001, indicating a decrease of foreign ownership in the listed firms and hence reducing the overall demand for high-quality auditors in China.

Government-driven auditing reforms and relevant effectiveness

Over the past few years, to improve audit quality and increase the credibility of financial disclosures, the Chinese government has gradually adopted a series of auditing reforms. These reforms and the relevant studies are summarized in Table 9.2.

Adoption of the International Auditing Standards in 1996

From December 1995 to January 1997, in an attempt to increase the credibility of its capital markets, the Chinese Ministry of Finance issued a series of new auditing standards, which were closely modelled on the International Auditing Standards. The new auditing standards consisted of three major parts: five general auditing standards, 15 specific auditing standards and four practice pronouncements. In order to implement the new auditing standards, the CSRC and the CICPA strengthened the enforcement of auditing regulations and imposed penalties on auditors who failed to comply. Two relevant empirical questions are: 1) has the accounting disclosure and information environment of the public companies improved since the adoption of the new auditing standards? and 2) have the new auditing standards increased auditor independence and affected audit market concentration?

Using a sample of firms listed on either the Shanghai Stock Exchange or the Shenzhen Stock Exchange between January 1995 and June 2001, Zhou (2007) found that the implementation of new auditing standards reduced information asymmetry, as reflected in the bid–ask spread, suggesting that there was an improvement in the information environment of public companies in China. Sami and Zhou (2008) found that, from the market perspective, since the implementation of the new auditing standards Chinese listed firms had experienced an increase in trading volume and price volatility and a decrease in the synchronicity of stock prices. They also document that, from the accounting perspective, earnings management had decreased and the quality of earnings had improved since the implementation of the standards. These results suggest that implementing the new auditing standards helped improve audit quality, and hence

Table 9.2 Summary of studies on government-driven auditing reforms and relevant effectiveness

Year	Reforms	Effectiveness	Papers
1996	The first set of auditing standards modeled after the International Auditing Standards	Improved accounting disclosure and information environment; improved auditor independence; decreased audit market concentration	Sami and Zhou (2008) Zhou (2007) DeFond *et al.* (2000)
1997–1998	The disaffiliation program	Improved auditor independence	Yang *et al.* (2001) Gul *et al.* (2009)
1999–2006	Audit firm mergers induced by Chinese government	Improved audit independence	Hung and Wu (2011)
2002	The establishment of an audit committee	Faced issues with regard to coordination with the supervisory board	Wang & Ren (2011) (in Chinese) Tang (2008) (in Chinese) Lee (2015)
2003	Mandatory audit partner rotation	Resulted in higher quality audits; mandatory rotation may play a more important role	Lennox *et al.* (2014) Firth *et al.* (2012)
2004	Regulations on auditor appointment and tenure	Improved audit quality	Chi *et al.* (2013)
2006	The new risk-oriented auditing standards	Increase in accounting firms' sensitivity to clients' risk in small accounting firm	Li *et al.* (2015) (in Chinese)
1997–2010	Transformation of accounting firms' organizational form	Improved audit quality	Firth *et al.* (2012) Wang *et al.* (2014)

helped improve accounting disclosure quality and the information environment of the public companies in China.

DeFond *et al.* (2000) investigated the effect of the new auditing standards on auditor independence and audit market concentration and found that the adoption of the new auditing standards improved auditor independence, which is measured by the frequency of modified auditor opinions, but reduced the audit market share among large auditors.

The disaffiliation programme in 1997–1998

Auditing practice resumed in China in the 1980s as a result of the privatization of SOEs and the separation of the government from enterprises (Xiang, 1998). Auditing firms were initially established and owned by government agencies. Before 1996, almost all Chinese audit firms were affiliated with government agencies or government-sponsored entities (e.g. universities and research institutions). This government sponsorship has caused many criticisms of auditor independence in China. As the demands for independent auditing services have grown with the continuing development of capital markets, such as the arrival of foreign capital and the privatization of the SOEs, a programme to disaffiliate CPA firms from their sponsoring bodies was launched by the Chinese government in 1997–1998. All accounting firms were required to independently bear legal liabilities and face audit risk, taking the form of either a limited liability company or a limited liability partnership.

Did the disaffiliation programme introduced by the Chinese government improve auditor independence? Yang *et al.* (2001) found that auditor independence, which is measured by the number and percentage of non-standard audit opinions, had improved since the introduction of the disaffiliation programme. In comparison to affiliated accounting firms, disaffiliated accounting firms face a higher degree of market risk and therefore act more independently. Using the sample listed on the Shanghai and Shenzhen exchanges from 1995–2000, Gul *et al.* (2009) found that auditor independence, measured by the likelihood of receiving qualified audit opinions, had increased significantly, and earnings management, measured by non-core operating earnings, had decreased significantly since the introduction of the disaffiliation programme. In addition, they found that the relationship between the disaffiliation program and auditor independence is stronger for small auditors than for large auditors, indicating the initial lower audit quality of small auditors.

Mergers of accounting firms in 1999–2006

Accounting firms in China have experienced a rapid development since the 1980s. However, most domestic accounting firms remain small in scale, with very low market concentration. Following China's entry to the WTO in the early 2000s and the growth of the Chinese economy, the government has gradually allowed large international accounting firms to operate in China. As a result, competition among accounting firms has intensified further. The Chinese government and the auditing profession are concerned about whether domestic CPA firms would be able to compete with large, international firms. In order to strengthen the competitive ability of domestic auditors, the merger of accounting firms in two forms was induced by the government in 1996–2006: multi-licence mergers and single-licence mergers. In multi-licence mergers, two (or more) accounting firms that are licenced to audit publicly listed companies merge, while in single-licence mergers a licensed accounting firm merges with a firm that does not have a licence to practice. The first merger occurred in 1999, when Zhong Rui CPAs merged with Hua Xia CPAs Ltd. During the period from 1999 to 2006, there were a total of 68 mergers that involved accounting firms who had licences to audit publicly listed firms in China (Chan and Wu, 2011).

Did CPA firm mergers induced by the Chinese government improve audit independence? Using a sample of accounting firm mergers in China from 1999 to 2006, Chan and Wu (2011) investigated the effect of such mergers on auditor independence, measured by auditors' propensity to issue modified auditor opinions. They found that auditor independence improved in multi-licence mergers but not in single-licence mergers, indicating that aggregate quasi rents are more evident in multi-licence mergers.

Audit committees in listed firms

Unlike those in developed markets such as the US and the UK, the establishment of audit committees has since 2002 been optional rather than mandatory in China. However, in practice, the willingness among listed companies to establish audit committees has increased from 1 per cent in 2000 to 99.86 per cent in 2010 (Lee, 2015). Who prefers to set audit committees in China? Does the establishment of an audit committee improve audit quality? Wang and Ren (2011) found that government-controlled firms had stronger motivations than private-controlled firms. Using a sample of Chinese firms during 2002–2005, Tang (2008) found that the independence and diligence of audit committees played a more significant role in auditing judgements and audit opinions of external auditors than the simple existence of an audit committee.

Mandatory audit partner rotation policy in 2003 and mandatory CPA firm rotation policy in 2005

On 8 October 2003, the CSRC and the Ministry of Finance (MOF) of China jointly issued a policy on mandatory audit partner rotation to enhance auditor independence, which took effect in the 2003 annual audits. The policy required the engaging partners to be rotated off after five consecutive years of audit service, and also required a two-year time-out period before a partner may return to a particular audit engagement. Further, in 2005, the Supervision and Administration Commission for State-owned Assets of the State Council (SACSA) required each SOE to rotate its auditing firm after five consecutive years of audit engagement. The new practice raises two important empirical questions: 1) does the mandatory rotation of audit partners and accounting firms improve audit quality in China? and 2) how do varied types of auditor rotation affect audit quality?

Using a sample of Chinese listed firms during the period of 2006–2010, Lennox et al. (2014) found that mandatory partner rotation in China improved audit quality, measured by audit adjustments. They also found improvement in audit quality during the departing partner's final year of tenure prior to the mandatory rotation and during the incoming partner's first year of tenure following the mandatory rotation. Compared with the mandatory rotation of a review partner, the mandatory rotation of engaging partners resulted in higher-quality audits in the years immediately surrounding the rotations. In addition, Bandyopadhyay et al. (2014) found that audit quality improved following mandatory audit partner rotations during the period 2004–2011. They also showed that the improvement was more pronounced in those provinces with both lower levels of audit market concentration and lower levels of legal development.

However, using auditors' propensity to issue a modified auditor opinion (MAO) as a proxy for audit quality, Firth et al. (2012) found that, while mandatory audit partner rotations improved audit quality, mandatory audit firm rotations and voluntary audit partner rotations had no effect on audit quality. Nevertheless, Lin et al. (2009) found that client firms switching to larger auditors may signal high-quality earnings, as reflected in the increases in earnings response coefficients (ERCs) in the Chinese capital market.

Regulations on auditor choice and auditor tenure in 2004

Senior business management used to play a crucial role in choosing auditors in China, resulting in many concerns over auditor independence and audit quality. In order to improve audit quality and auditor independence in the audits of SOEs ultimately controlled by the central government, the SACSA issued two policies: SACSA Order No. 5, which terminates management's authority to appoint auditors to audit engagements of SOEs and mandates that the SACSA assign auditors for SOEs under its supervision, and SACSA Rule No. 173, which further specifies the tenure of auditors and mandates that management retain these auditors for at least two years and at most five years.

The two polices significantly restrain the management discretion of auditor appointment and termination. An important question is whether the regulations limit management's influence over auditor choices and hence improve audit quality. Using the difference-in-difference approach and a sample of Chinese listed firms in 2001–2009, Chi *et al.* (2013) found that, relative to non-SOEs, the implementation of the regulations improved audit quality, as measured by abnormal accruals, in the audits of SOEs.

The implementation of the risk-oriented auditing standards in 2006

To introduce the risk-oriented auditing concept, the Chinese Ministry of Finance issued a new set of auditing standards – the Auditing Standards for Chinese Certified Public Accountants – in 2006. Does the implementation of the risk-oriented auditing standards improve auditors' sensitivity to client risks? Li *et al.* (2015) examined the changes in auditors' sensitivity to client risks before and after the implementation of the new risk-oriented auditing standards and found that auditors were more likely to issue modified and qualified audit opinions to clients with earnings management risks after the implementation of the new auditing standards, suggesting that new auditing standards improve auditor's sensitivity to client risks. However, there is no significant change in auditors' sensitivity to clients' bankruptcy risks and governance risks.

Organizational form of accounting firms and its transformation during 1997–2010

Changes in organizational form of accounting firms in 1997–1998

As mentioned earlier, before the implementation of the disaffiliation programme, most accounting firms in China were affiliated to government agencies or government-sponsored entities (DeFond *et al.*, 2000; Gul *et al.*, 2009). After the disaffiliation programme came into effect in 1997–1998, all accounting firms were separated from their sponsoring governmental bodies. Disaffiliated accounting firms could be registered in the form of a limited liability partnership or a limited liability company subject to the approval of local regulatory authorities from 1997 to 2010.

The unique setting provides a chance to investigate empirically how the change of the organizational form of accounting firms affected auditors' behaviour and audit quality in China. Using observations of public firms during 2000–2004, Firth *et al.* (2012) found that the organizational form of accounting firms could affect auditors' reporting conservatism, which is measured by an auditor's propensity to issue a modified auditor opinion, owing to the different legal liabilities embedded in the organizational form. Compared with their limited liability peers, accounting firms in partnership form were more likely to issue modified audit reports, providing higher-quality audit services.

The transformation from limited liability company to limited liability partnership in 2010

To further improve audit quality, the State Council and the Ministry of Finance issued Several Opinions on Accelerating the Development of Chinese CPA Industry in 2010. At the same time, the Ministry of Finance and the General Administration for Industry and Commerce jointly issued The Regulation on Promoting Large and Medium Accounting Firms to Transform to Limited Liability Partnerships. Large accounting firms were among the first batch to restructure from limited liability companies to limited liability partnerships (Wang and Dou, 2015).

The transformation was expected to increase practising partners' legal liabilities and improve audit quality.

Does the transformation of organizational form of accounting firms improve audit quality in China? Using a sample of A-share companies during 2007–2012, Wang and Dou (2015) examined the impact of the transformation on audit quality. They found that the restructured accounting firms had a significant and negative effect on the absolute value of discretionary accruals reported by their client firms. The results also showed that the transformation significantly decreased the level of positive discretionary accruals, but had no significant effect on negative discretionary accruals. However, the positive effect of such reform on audit quality only lasted for one year.

Summary and conclusions

This chapter has reviewed the development of auditing standards and practices in China from 1995–2015. From the perspective of an institutional environment and its improvements, it is documented that China's weak institutional environment led to lower supply of, and demand for, quality audits, while institutional improvements have resulted in improving the condition. From the perspective of change in government ownership and foreign ownership, it is documented that high-level government ownership created low demand for high-quality audits in the Chinese stock markets. However, auditors' decisions in China become more conservative following the increase of foreign ownership in business enterprises. To improve audit quality and increase the credibility of financial disclosures, the Chinese government has gradually adopted and implemented a series of auditing reforms, which have relatively improved audit quality over the last two decades.

Based on the findings in the literature, it is concluded that institutional and regulatory changes have been shaping the development of external auditing, and have spawned a stream of auditing research using the unique setting of the emerging capital market in China. However, as the economic reforms continue and the participation of foreign investors in the Chinese capital market increases, business firms grow, with more diverse ownership and increasingly complicated business transactions. The demand for quality accounting disclosures and quality audit services will continue to grow. Studies on accounting and auditing issues in the emerging Chinese market will continue to provide evidence regarding the impacts of institutional and regulatory changes on the development of external auditing. The Chinese experience can have significant implications for policymakers and regulators in other countries, especially for those in emerging economies.

References

Bandyopadhyay, S.P., Chen, C. and Yu, Y. (2014) Mandatory audit partner rotation, audit market concentration, and audit quality: Evidence from China. *Advances in Accounting, 30*(1), 18–31.

Chan, K.H. and Wu, D. (2011) Aggregate quasi rents and auditor independence: evidence from audit firm mergers in China. *Contemporary Accounting Research, 28*(1), 175–213.

Chan, K.H., Lin, K.Z. and Zhang, F. (2007). On the association between changes in corporate ownership and changes in auditor quality in a transitional economy. *Journal of International Accounting Research, 6*(1), 19–36.

Chen, H., Chen, J.Z., Lobo, G.J. and Wang, Y. (2011) Effects of audit quality on earnings management and cost of equity capital: Evidence from China. *Contemporary Accounting Research, 28*(3), 892–925.

Chen, S., Sun, S.Y.J. and Wu, D. (2010) Client importance, institutional improvements, and audit quality in China: An office and individual auditor level analysis. *Accounting Review, 85*(1), 127–158.

Chen, Z. (2003). Capital markets and legal development: The China case. *China Economic Review, 14*(4), 451–472.

Chi, W., Lisic, L.L., Long, X. and Wang, K. (2013) Do regulations limiting management influence over auditors improve audit quality? Evidence from China. *Journal of Accounting & Public Policy, 32*(2), 176–187.

Choi, J. and Wong, T.J. (2007) Auditors' governance functions and legal environments: An international investigation. *Contemporary Accounting Research, 24*(1), 13–46.

Choi, J., Sami, H. and Zhou, H. (2010) The impacts of state ownership on information asymmetry: Evidence from an emerging market. *China Journal of Accounting Research, 3*(1), 13–50.

Chow, C.W. (1982) The demand for external auditing: size, debt and ownership influence. *The Accounting Review, 57*(2), 272–291.

DeFond, M.L., Wong, T.J. and Li, S. (2000) The impact of improved auditor independence on audit market concentration in China. *Journal of Accounting & Economics, 28*(3), 269–305.

Firth, M., Mo, P.L.L. and Wong, L.L. (2012) Auditors' organizational form, legal liability, and reporting conservatism: Evidence from China. *Contemporary Accounting Research, 29*(1), 57–93.

Firth, M., Rui, O.M. and Wu, X. (2012) How do various forms of auditor rotation affect audit quality? Evidence from China. *International Journal of Accounting, 47*(1), 109–138.

Gul, F., Sami, H. and Zhou, H. (2009) Auditor disaffiliation program in China and auditor independence. *Auditing: A Journal of Practice & Theory, 28*(1), 29–51.

He, X., Rui, O., Zheng, L. and Zhu, H. (2014) Foreign ownership and auditor choice. *Journal of Accounting and Public Policy, 33*(4), 401–418.

Jensen, M.C. and Meckling, W.H. (1976) Theory of the firm: Managerial behavior, agency costs and ownership structure. *Journal of Financial Economics, 3*, 305–360.

Kang, J.K. and Stulz, R. (1997) Why is there a home bias? An analysis of foreign portfolio equity ownership in Japan. *Journal of Financial Economics, 46*(1), 3–28.

Ke, B., Lennox, C.S. and Xin, Q. (2015) The effect of China's weak institutional environment on the quality of Big 4 audits. *The Accounting Review, 90*(4), 1591–1619.

La Porta, R., Lopez-de-Silanes, F., Shleifer, A. and Vishny, R. (2000) Investor protection and corporate governance. *Journal of Financial Economics, 58*, 3–27.

Lee, P. (2015) Problems of implementing audit committee and supervisory board simultaneously in China. *Journal of Accounting, Auditing & Finance, 30*(4), 509–528.

Lennox, C.S., Wu, X. and Zhang, T. (2014) Does mandatory rotation of audit partners improve audit quality? *The Accounting Review, 89*(5), 1775–1803.

Levitt, A. (1998) The importance of high quality accounting standards. *Accounting Horizons, 12*, 79–82.

Li, M., Zhou, H. and Xia, L. (2015) Do risk-oriented auditing standards improve accounting firms' sensitivity to clients' risk? *Financial Studies, 9*, 96–107 (in Chinese).

Li, R. and He, H. (2000) An analysis of the development and current situation of the civil legal liabilities of CPAs in China. *China Accounting and Finance Review, 2*(1), 104–120.

Lin, Z.J., Liu, M. and Wang, Z. (2009) Market implications of the audit quality and auditor switches: Evidence from China. *Journal of International Financial Management & Accounting, 20*(1), 35–78.

Lisic, L.L., Silveri, S., Song, Y. and Wang, K. (2015) Accounting fraud, auditing, and the role of government sanctions in China. *Journal of Business Research, 68*(6), 1186–1195.

Liu, M.H. and Wang,Y.L. (2015) Regulation, supervision and development of China's auditing market. *Research on Financial and Economic Issues, 2*, 86–94 (in Chinese).

Pistor, K. and Xu, C. (2005) Governing stock markets in transitional economies: Lessons from China. *American Law and Economics Review, 7*(1), 184–210.

Sami, H. and Zhou, H. (2004) A comparison of value relevance of accounting information in different segments of the Chinese stock market. *International Journal of Accounting*, 403–427.

Sami, H. and Zhou, H. (2008) Do auditing standards improve the accounting disclosure and information environment of public companies? Evidence from the emerging markets in China. The International *Journal of Accounting, 43*(2), 139–169.

Tang, Y. (2008) Audit committee and audit opinions. *Financial Studies, 1*, 148–162 (in Chinese).

Wang, C. and Dou, H. (2015) Does the transformation of accounting firms' organizational form improve audit quality? Evidence from China. *China Journal of Accounting Research, 6*(1), 34–48.

Wang, Q, Wong, T.J. and Xia, L.J. (2008) State ownership, institutional environment and auditor choice: Evidence from China. *Journal of Accounting and Economics, 46*(1), 112–134.

Wang, Y. and Ren, F. (2011) Who prefer to set audit committee? Research on motivation for setting audit committee. *Accounting Research, 6*, 86–96 (in Chinese).

Watts, R.L. and Zimmerman, J.L. (1983) Agency problems, auditing, and the theory of the firm: Some evidence. *The Journal of Law & Economics, 26*(3), 613–633.

Wei, T., Yen, S.H. and Chiu, C.L. (2008) The influence of qualified foreign institutional investors on the association between default risk and audit opinions: Evidence from the Chinese stock market. *Corporate Governance: An International Review, 16*(5), 400–415.

Xiang, B. 1998. Institutional factors influencing China's accounting reforms and standards. Accounting Horizons 12 (2): 105-119.

Yang, L., Tang, Q., Kilgore, A. and Jiang, Y. (2001) Auditor-government associations and auditor independence in China. *The British Accounting Review, 33*(2), 175–189.

Zhou, H. (2007) Auditing standards, increased accounting disclosure, and information asymmetry: Evidence from an emerging market. *Journal of Accounting and Public Policy, 26*(5), 584–620.

10

Development of the accounting profession in Cambodia[1]

Juliet Cadungog-Uy

Introduction

Most historical records show that Cambodia took its economic management system from the French during its colonial period and still continued to follow the same system even after gaining independence in 1953. Yapa and Jacobs (n.d., p. 8) noted that:

> The first Western accounting system was imported into Cambodia in 19th century by the French to support the colonial rule and the country's legal and accounting system developed along the lines of those in France. In particular, the French system of accounting was partly introduced to state agencies during the colonial rule. However, in the economic performance management of the economy, the French did not introduce a proper accounting system in Cambodia.

Cambodia was under French protection for 90 years; since then, it has gone through harsh years of conflict and civil war and the "Year Zero" adversity. Today, Cambodia has proven to the world that its painful past has purged and shaped the country to be a resilient, strong-willed nation that slowly but continuously strives to heave itself from severe economic paucity. Cambodia has been making remarkable strides and demonstrated optimism, placing itself as the "sixth fastest growing country in the world over the last two decades." It was counted among the "Olympians of growth," with fast and resilient economic growth (WB, 2014); placed eleventh in the world in terms of GDP growth over the last decade, as reported by Cambodia Business Review (2015, p. 22); and its capital city, Phnom Penh, is "one of the fastest-growing cities in Southeast Asia" (Phorn, 2015).

The president of the Asian Development Bank (ADB) has also claimed that "Cambodia is among the world's fastest-growing economies. It has rapidly reduced poverty from nearly 50 percent of the population in 2007 to just 19 percent in 2012." With the country's rapid economic growth, Cambodia is close to elevating its status "from a low-income to a middle-income country" (ADB News Release, 2015). By the time of the 2016 census, Cambodia's population had risen to 15,626,444 (Cambodia Health Management Information System, 2016), with 59.4 percent of the population aged under 30 (Cambodia Demographic and Health Survey, 2015).

Cambodia has opened to the world and in 1999 became a member of the Association of Southeast Asian Nations (ASEAN), in October 2004 the second least-developed country to join the World Trade Organization (WTO), and in February 2016 the eighth least-developed country to have ratified the Trade Facilitation Agreement (TFA) (WTO, 2016). It has taken notable steps in changing its economic tone by embarking on numerous economic reforms and gradually adopting more liberal trade policies to raise its trade competitiveness and enhance its investment landscape. In the regional economic sphere, as the 10 ASEAN member states move toward economic integration and the establishment of ASEAN Economic Community (AEC), Cambodia has stepped up the improvement of its accounting standards along with its market and financial reporting quality to be on par with its more developed neighboring countries and to attract more foreign investors into its fertile territory.

An article from *The Southeast Asia Weekly* (2011, as cited by Open Development Cambodia (n.d.)) quoted Deputy Prime Minister Keat Chhon and the Ministry of Economy and Finance as having said that "accountancy is a very important issue in both the public and private sectors that we should not overlook the current context of national and global economic arenas."

Regulatory agencies and the professional accounting body in Cambodia

Yapa and Jacobs (n.d.) point out that

> there was no professional accounting body in Cambodia until 2002 when the promulgation of the *Law on Corporate Accounts, Their Audit and the Accounting Profession 2002* resulted in the creation of two accounting institutions: the National Accounting Council (NAC) and the Kampuchea Institute of Certified Public Accountants and Auditors (KICPAA).

The Law on Accounting was promulgated by Royal Kram No. NS/RKM/0702/011 on July 8, 2002, mandating the "organization, management, and function of accounting system based on international accounting standards for enterprises either natural persons or legal entities to have an independent profession in the Kingdom of Cambodia." Article 6 of this Law authorized the establishment of the National Accounting Council under the auspices of the Ministry of Economy and Finance and Article 14 requires the formation of the Institute of Khmer Certified Public Accountants and Auditors (KICPAA) among accountancy professionals. It further provides that KICPAA shall operate "under the auspices of the Ministry of Economy and Finance." A subdecree was later issued to determine the organization and functioning of the institute, and the formulation of professional regulations for certified public accountants and auditors in the country.

The Ministry of Economy and Finance

The Ministry of Economy and Finance (MEF) of Cambodia was established pursuant to Royal Kram No. NS/RKM/0196/18 dated January 24, 1996. The composition, mission, and functions of the Ministry of Economy and Finance were determined by Subdecree No. 04/ANKr/BK, dated January 20, 2000. Article 2 of the subdecree states:

> The Ministry of Economy and Finance is delegated by the Royal Government to perform the mission of guidance and administration of the economy and finance of the Kingdom of Cambodia in order to support economic development and to improve the living standards of Cambodian people based on the principles of a free market economy and social equality.

The National Accounting Council

The National Accounting Council (NAC) of Cambodia was established under the Law on Accounting in July 2002 and its composition and functions were stipulated by Subdecree No. 08/ANKr/BK dated March 30, 2003. The NAC, as a policy overseer in the field of accounting, sets and regulates accounting and auditing standards as well as the financial reporting requirements of local businesses. The NAC's mission is to develop and promote high-quality accounting, auditing, and reporting standards that are consistent with international standards for the benefits of users, preparers, auditors, and the public in Cambodia (NAC 2013).

Yapa and Jacobs (n.d.) describe that the NAC is a regulatory body under the Ministry of Economy and Finance (MEF) and has four functions: 1) to review and give its opinion on all accounting-related draft laws and regulations, including accounting provisions for whatever status of enterprises concerned, or their sector of activity; 2) to develop the conceptual framework and accounting standards; 3) to come up with proposals aimed at improving accounting; and 4) to represent Cambodia in international organizations and forums dealing with accounting.

The Kampuchea Institute of Certified Public Accountants and Auditors

The Kampuchea Institute of Certified Public Accountants and Auditors (KICPAA) was established by the Accounting Law in 2003, and Subdecree No. 18/ANKr/BK dated March 19, 2003, described its composition and functions. The Accounting Law mandates the KICPAA to regulate the accountancy profession under the Ministry of Finance and Economy supervision (World Bank, 2007). KICPAA's day-to-day functions are still directly influenced by the state. "This is the national accounting body having responsibility in representing its members, promoting and defending the status and the interests of the profession and to participate in the work of the National Accounting Council" (Yapa and Jacobs, n.d.).

The fundamental objective of the KICPAA is to act as a body for determining and maintaining adequate professional standards for its members and awarding licenses for its members to engage in public accounting practices. KICPAA operates through its governing council, which comprises nine elected members. The major statutory functions of the KICPAA Council include designing and implementing policies regarding membership admission, administering programs for members' professional development, ensuring adherence to professional ethics and standards, and taking disciplinary action against violating members.

The World Bank (2007, p. 10) reported that

> the public accountancy profession in Cambodia is at an early stage of development. KICPAA is unable to move the profession forward or project its image as an effective regulator of the public accountancy profession in Cambodia due to its lack of technical capabilities and scarce governance structure.

The same report stated that "all KICPAA members hold foreign accountancy qualifications. KICPAA recognizes foreign professional accountancy qualifications for membership without requiring further examination. A majority of its members are qualified under the Association of Chartered Certified Accountants (ACCA) of the United Kingdom."

In addition, the World Bank (2007) noted that the National Accounting Council has issued Cambodian Standards on Auditing. There is no legislation on which auditing standards are to be applied for statutory audits. Auditors in Cambodia should comply with the Cambodian Standards on Auditing. KICPAA members with three years of practical training in the field of accounting and auditing are eligible to undertake audit services. In 2007, most KICPAA members were foreigners. All current members can perform audit services regardless of their nationality. However, by a legislative order beginning January 1, 2010, the Ministry of Economy and Finance mandated that only qualified members of the KICPAA who are Cambodian citizens can provide auditing services in the country (ibid.).

The World Bank recommended in 2007 that

> Gaining IFAC membership would help KICPAA to obtain exposure to international developments and capitalize on other allied membership benefits. This will also enhance the KICPAA image as a professional body. Furthermore, such membership would facilitate creating a better enforcement and compliance culture with regard to accounting and auditing practices in Cambodia.
>
> *(World Bank, 2007, p. 32)*

KICPAA joined the ASEAN Federation of Accountants (AFA) on January 11, 2003. It is a primary member of the AFA but has not until now been a member of the International Federation of Accountants (IFAC).

KICPAA Code of Ethics

The World Bank Group (2014) states that the Accounting Law basically indicates the duties of KICPAA as representing and promoting the professional interests of its members and does not specifically include serving the public interest. It recommends that

> the mandate of a professional auditors' association should be as much to defend the public's interests as their own and make it as an expected duty of KICPAA to serve the public who rely on the objectivity and integrity of auditors.

The World Bank outlines that

> high standards of professional ethics are just as important as having high quality accounting and auditing standards. None of the ASEAN countries have adopted IFAC's Code of Ethics in full and there are some wide variations across ASEAN countries in some areas.

Cambodia has adopted the Code of Ethics for Professional Accountants and Auditors pursuant to Subdecree No. 83 (ANKR.BK), dated June 17, 2005, signed by the country's prime minister. The development of this KICPAA Code of Ethics was based on the IFAC's International Code of Ethics for Professional Accountants. The code adopts the IFAC's fundamental principles of integrity, objectivity, professional competence and due care, confidentiality, and professional behavior. Article 3 of this code states that "a distinguishing mark of the accountancy profession is its acceptance of the responsibility to act in the public interest. Therefore, a professional accountant's responsibility is not exclusively to satisfy the needs of an individual client or employer." This provision was taken verbatim from the IFAC's Code of Ethics. Hence, the responsibility of auditors to defend public interest is embodied in the KICPAA Code of Ethics and not in the Accounting Law.

KICPAA membership

Under the KICPAA's constitution, "no person shall exercise the profession of certified public accountant unless that person is registered as a member of KICPAA" (Article 13).

The KICPAA constitution also classifies its membership into three categories: 1) affiliated member, 2) active member, and 3) trainee member (Article 10). The KICPAA By-Laws of 2004 defined the three classifications of membership as follows:

1   An *affiliated member* is any person holding university qualification in accounting, business, or finance of a standard recognized by and acceptable to the registration committee of certified public accountants and auditors. But an affiliated member cannot act as a public accountant and auditor independently;

2   An *active member* is any affiliated member meeting the requirements to be registered on the list provided in Article 9 of the Anukret referred to in Section 2 of the By-Laws, satisfying the requirements for competency, diploma, and aptitude in practicing the profession; and

3   A *trainee member* is any person having accounting and financial knowledge deemed sufficient by the registration committee to follow a professional training period or carry out studies leading to the qualification of certified public accountant and/or auditor.

For the first time, the KICPAA issued license certificates to members who were practicing their professional career in Cambodia in 2006. KICPAA had a total of 83 members, composed of 11 firms and 72 individual members in 2006. Of the 72 individual members, 37 were active members, three were affiliates, and 32 were trainees. In 2010, the membership rose to 236. Firm membership increased by more than 200 percent, while individual membership grew by 180 percent. In 2015, the total membership increased to 277, as shown in Table 10.1.[2]

The Professional Qualification Programme

The World Bank in its *Report on the Observance of Standards and Codes* (2007) made several recommendations to improve the accounting and auditing profession in Cambodia. One recommendation is related to developing professional examination for Cambodian accounting practitioners, thus KICPAA should develop effective ways of monitoring and enforcing the continuing professional development of its members. KICPAA should also take action to develop its own curriculum and examination system for prospective accountants, the professional examination for practicing accountants, and link with professional bodies in the region.

Efforts have been made by the KICPAA to develop the national CPA qualification program. The strategic plan has been discussed by its governing council members and the secretariat,

Table 10.1 KICPAA membership 2006–2015

Membership	2006	2010	2015
Firms	11	34	52
Individuals:			
Active	37	133	161
Affiliates	3	13	19
Trainees	32	56	45
Total	83	236	277

Source: KICPAA, January 28, 2016.

however a lack of financial support for the development and execution of this program is a major constraint. The KICPAA is searching for potential donors to support the institute to implement the project:

> The primary purpose of the Professional Qualification Programme is to produce a standardized professional accountancy programme that would contribute positively to the profession, economy and society in general; KICPAA's ultimate goal in this regard is to produce sufficient qualified Cambodian accountants who could serve the public interest and to ensure transparency of financial reporting.
>
> *(AFA, 2014, p. 21)*

The KICPAA and the National Accounting Council (NAC) of the Ministry of Economy and Finance have signed a joint examination scheme agreement with the UK-based Association of Chartered Certified Accountants (ACCA), which will run until January 2019 (ibid., p. 20). This agreement was first signed in 2004 and it was then renewed in 2008 and 2014 (Chen, 2016).

Currently, there is only one ACCA-accredited training provider in Cambodia, the CamEd Business School, which provides an ACCA qualification program in Cambodia that offers an international professional accounting and auditing qualification (ACCA and CAT) and a diploma in Cambodian tax. The ACCA qualification allows an accountant to legally engage in private or public practice and leads to membership in the KICPAA.[3] At present, there are a number of schools and universities in Cambodia offering accounting courses and producing accounting graduates every year. Most of these schools and universities are located in Phnom Penh and in other major cities of Cambodia, including schools in Phnom Penh at FTMS Global Academy (Cambodia), an ACCA and FIA/CAT and CFA professional training school; the Vanda Institute, specializing in accounting, auditing, and taxation; Limkokwing *University*, a private Malaysian university, offering Bachelor of Business in Accounting degrees; Pannasastra University of Cambodia, offering Bachelor of Arts degrees with a major in accounting; and Norton University, offering Bachelor of Business Administration degrees with a major in accounting. These schools and universities, together with other learning institutions, will eventually boost the reservoir of KICPAA membership.

Continuing professional development

Improving the accounting and auditing profession in Cambodia through continuing professional education was also recommended by the World Bank (2007). It stressed KICPAA's role to undertake "high-quality training programmes on practical implementation aspects of accounting and auditing standards and the code of ethics for professional accountants." The KICPAA's efforts to provide capacity building opportunities to improve the professional competence of accountants in the country is evident in the series of continuing professional development programs published on its website.

1 In 2014, it conducted several workshops on the IFRS for regulators, the IPSAS for government officials, the IFRS for the microfinance and banking sectors, the IFRS in depth for professional accountants, the development of a standardized accounting syllabus for local universities, and capacity building training (AFA, 2014, pp. 19–20).
2 In 2015, the KICPAA conducted several workshops, such as on International Financial Reporting Standards, which focused on accounting for financial instruments; valuing a business; corporate fraud and forensic accounting; IFRS 15 (*Revenue from Contracts with*

Customers); and Cambodian corporate income tax (KICPAA, 2016). The KICPAA planned more workshops in the coming months, to demonstrate its commitment to continuously updating and upgrading the professional skills and knowledge of accountants in the country.

Development of accounting standards in Cambodia

Cambodian accounting standard setter

The Ministry of Economy and Finance of Cambodia issued Prakas No. 221 MEF/BK on March 25, 2008, on the promulgation of the Cambodian Accounting Standards and Cambodian Financial Reporting Standards, which authorized the implementation of 18 Cambodian Accounting Standards (CAS) and the two Cambodian Financial Accounting Reporting Standards (CFRSs) for state-owned entities and private companies as a basis for producing their accounting records and annual financial reports (Article 1). Large and medium-sized entities are bound by this Prakas. Other entities can adopt the CAS and CFRS whenever they judge it necessary to improve the presentation of their financial statements (Article 2). "Entities that are bound by this requirement must present their annual reports in compliance with CASs and CFRSs for accounting period 2008 onward" (Article 3). All regulations stated in this Prakas, however, have been "repealed and superseded" by Prakas No. 068 MEF/BK on January 8, 2009 (Article 5), which mandates the promulgation of Cambodian Financial Reporting Standards by the deputy prime minister and the minister of the Ministry of Economy and Finance of Cambodia. Accordingly, on August 28, 2009, the Ministry of Economy and Finance and National Accounting Council of Cambodia made an announcement (No. 097/09 MF-NAC) on the introduction of the Cambodian International Financial Reporting Standards (CIFRS) and the Cambodian International Financial Reporting Standards for Small and Medium Entities (CIFRS for SME).

With this announcement, the National Accounting Council started to adopt the IFRS issued by the International Accounting Standards Board without modifications and renamed them as the Cambodian International Financial Reporting Standards (CIFRS). These were to be applied for financial statements for periods on or after January 1, 2012. The IFRS for SMEs, which was named the Cambodia International Financial Reporting Standards for Small and Medium Entities was to be applied for periods on or after January 1, 2010 (Prakas No. 068 MEF/BK. January 8, 2009). The mandatory implementation of the CIFRS for banking and financial institutions was delayed until January 1, 2016, as approved by Prakas No. 086 SHV. KChK issued on July 30, 2012. NAC issued again a second notification (No. 058 MEF-NAC) on March 24, 2016, to delay the implementation of the CIFRS for banking, financial institutions, and insurance companies until 2019. To ensure its successful implementation, the NAC will set up a technical working group to support this project (Chen, 2016).

Article 3 of Prakas No. 068 MEF/BK also states that "the National Accounting Council shall translate every accounting and reporting standard, every interpretation, and any modification of the standards into Khmer language." Thus, the IFRS for SMEs has been translated into Khmer and has been published. The full set of the IFRS has also been translated into Khmer, but this has not yet been published (IFRS, 2013).[4] According to *The Southeast Asia Weekly* (2011, as cited by Open Development Cambodia (n.d.)), the NAC, the KICPAA, and the ACCA have recently co-organized a national conference on "Accountancy in Cambodia – Towards Global Standards" in Phnom Penh to reflect what is being implemented in Cambodia toward the international convergence of accounting and financial reporting, as well as what is being done by many countries in the region and the world.

The World Bank (2014) reported that, although all ASEAN countries have aligned their financial reporting standards with IFRS, to some extent, its full implementation in "less-developed" counties is limited because of "language constraint and capacity of professional accountancy organizations and regulators; these countries will struggle to achieve full implementation and compliance with the standards adopted without significant capacity development and support over the medium term."

IFRS application

All domestic companies and foreign companies whose securities are traded on the public market in Cambodia are required to use the IFRS in their consolidated financial statements. Companies whose securities are not traded on the public market may use the IFRS or the IFRS for SMEs (IFRS, 2013).

PwC (2015) explains that

> from the financial period beginning on or after 1 January, 2010, the entities that are required to submit their financial statements for audit but do not have public accountability, shall apply the CIFRS for SMEs which is equivalent to IFRS for SMEs. However, they have an option to use the full CIFRS. Non-public enterprises not required to submit their financial statements for audit can also select, on a voluntary base, to implement CIFRS for SMEs.

Further, in relation to any plan for IFRS statutory accounts as a basis for tax reporting,

> The local tax authorities have not announced any adoption or convergence plans of tax reporting to IFRS or IFRS for SMEs. The statutory financial statements (prepared under IFRS or IFRS for SMEs) are currently not required to be submitted to the Tax Authorities. Nonetheless, the audited financial statements are always requested by the General Department of Taxation during their audit.

Ganschow *et al.* (2009) explained that three potential ways can be used to measure a company's taxable profits: *independent*, *dependent*, and *quasi-dependent* approaches:

> In an *independent approach*, taxable income is determined in accordance with a specified set of tax rules and thus, there is generally no reliance on the statutory accounts of the company. Under this scenario, a conversion to IFRS is expected to have very little impact, if any, on the cash tax liability in the jurisdiction; however, deferred taxes and the effective tax rate disclosed in the financial statements may be impacted significantly.
>
> A *dependent approach* utilizes the statutory accounts to determine taxable income, in which case, an IFRS conversion is likely to impact cash taxes paid. An impact to deferred taxes is less likely; however, it could arise, for example, as a result of converting to new or changing tax accounting standards under IFRS. [In the *quasi-dependent* approach,] statutory accounts are used as a starting point for taxable income calculation, with specific departures allowed under tax law.

In this approach, a company's taxable profit is computed mainly in accordance with its financial accounts, thus it can impact both cash taxes and deferred tax balances (Ganschow *et al.*, 2009). At present, Cambodia adopts the quasi-dependent approach to measure the taxable profits of companies, where taxable profit is mainly "based on the legal entity statutory accounts, with a number of adjustments provided in the tax law" (PwC, 2015).

Mandates on statutory reporting

All enterprises in Cambodia, whether a natural person or a legal entity, are required to keep books and accounts and prepare financial statements on a yearly basis under the Accounting Law of 2002. The law also provides that the financial statements include a balance sheet, an income statement, a cash flow statement, and explanatory notes. Article 12 of the Accounting Law states that "all enterprises must keep their financial statements and the corresponding ledgers and documentary evidence for at least ten years. Such ledgers include a general journal, accounting ledger and inventory book." These accounting records must be prepared in the Khmer language and expressed in riels. The riel is Cambodia's official national currency but US dollars are commonly used in business transactions. Enterprises carrying out business with foreign countries or who are subsidiaries of foreign companies may be authorized to prepare accounting records in English and/or in a currency other than riels, alongside accounting records in Khmer and riels in compliance with the conditions set out by the Ministry of Economy and Finance. However, the financial statements prepared on a calendar basis must be prepared in Khmer and riels (Article 4).

The World Bank (2007) noted that "there is little awareness of the importance of quality financial information in Cambodia. Financial reporting is driven primarily by complying with the requirements of shareholders, obtaining bank loans, and satisfying the taxation regime." It further described that small and medium-sized enterprises (SMEs) dominate the private sector and, generally, businesses in Cambodia are owned by families and hence there is no separation between ownership and management. Thus "some banks and companies in Cambodia prepare separate sets of financial statements under IFRS and Cambodian Accounting Standards to satisfy the needs of shareholders or lenders." Companies that have foreign shareholders or have borrowed from international creditors, including multilateral or bilateral donors, usually "keep two different sets of financial statements, one for statutory purposes and the other for investors and lenders."

A survey by the International Finance Corporation in 2010, as cited by Tayi (2016), revealed that of the 59 percent of surveyed enterprises that had provided financial records, 84 percent of them recorded only profits and losses. To them, "keeping more detailed accounting records is too complicated and they don't consider it necessary." However, this lack of financial records prevents them from obtaining loans from financial institutions.

KPMG (2012) reported that the NAC of the Ministry of Economy and Finance has issued a notification (No. 113 Moe-NAC) to reiterate the provisions of the Accounting Law 2002, which mandates that:

- "All enterprises, whether natural person or legal entities, are required to keep books and accounts and have them audited in accordance with the terms and conditions provided for under this Law" (Article 3).
- "Enterprises shall prepare financial statements on a yearly basis that are in compliance with both the conceptual framework and Cambodian Accounting Standards (CAS), the principles set out by the Prakas proclaimed by the Minister of the MoEF and in line with the International Accounting Standards (IAS)" (Article 4).
- From the end of financial period 2012, all for-profit enterprises, nonprofit entities, and other obliged entities, as well as SMEs, must follow the Cambodian International Financial Reporting Standards (the CIFRS) and the Cambodian International Financial Reporting Standards for Small and Medium-sized Entities (the CIFRSs for SMEs) in the preparation of their financial statements.

- Meanwhile, banks and financial institutions shall follow Notification No. 086 (MeF-NAC, dated July 30, 2012), on postponing the implementation of the CIFRS for banks and financial institutions that the NAC has already sent directly to all banks and financial institutions.
- Any noncompliant enterprises or entities shall be fined, as stated in Section 7 of the Accounting Law.

In addition, it highlights that all enterprises that meet two of the three criteria set by Prakas No. 643 (dated July 26, 2007) of the MoEF—that is, 1) annual turnover above 3,000,000,000 riels (approximately USD750,000); 2) total assets above 2,000,000,000 riels (approximately USD500,000); and 3) more than 100 employees—shall submit their annual financial statements to be audited by an independent auditor registered with KICPAA.

Noncompliance is subject to fines as set out in Section 7 of the Accounting Law, which includes sanctions for violating the provisions in Articles 3, 4, and 5. It provides that all natural persons and directors of legally incorporated entities violating these provisions shall be "subjected to a fine between five and ten million *Riels*, and/or may serve a prison term from one to two years" (Article 18). Moreover,

> All natural persons and directors of legally incorporated entities who fail to prepare or file proper financial statements in compliance with the provisions stipulated in this Law, shall be subjected to a fine of between five and ten million *Riels* and/or may serve a prison term from three to six months.
>
> *(Article 18)*

However, according to one of the advisers to the NAC, Sam Ghanty, as cited by *Cambodia Daily* on August 30, 2012, the Ministry of Economy and Finance passed a series of proclamations requiring businesses to submit financial reports in 2007, "but many businesses still do not comply with the law" (Heijmans, 2012). The implementation of the Accounting Law remains to be improved in Cambodia.

Conclusion

Accounting and auditing are considered an important component of Cambodia's economic growth. The Ministry of Economy and Finance and the National Accounting Council of Cambodia are key players in regulating the accounting profession and financial reporting practices in Cambodia. Their efforts are laudable in establishing the necessary legislation. With all the accounting-related laws and regulations in place, creating an environment that can ensure compliance with the regulations remains a challenge as the country is in the transition toward developing a market economy and fully adopting international accounting and auditing standards.

Notes

1 I wish to acknowledge the following people who have provided me with information for this paper: H.E. Dr. Ngy Tayi, secretary of state of the Ministry of Economy and Finance of Cambodia, and chairman of the National Accounting Council (NAC); Chen Phat, chief of the Regulation and Control Office of the NAC; Savuth Daly, corporate services manager of the KICPAA; and Sam Sokuntheary, general manager of CamEd Business School.
2 The data were obtained via email on January 28, 2016, with Ms. Savuth, the corporate services manager of the KICPAA.

3 Based on the information from the general manager of CamEd, the school started in 2003 and by December 2015 had produced a total of 225 CAT and 99 ACCA graduates (CamEd website, 2016).
4 This was confirmed by the information obtained from the KICPAA office on December 29, 2015, that the CIFRS has not yet been published but it has already been translated into Khmer.

References

Primary sources

Email, January 28, 2016, Ms. Savuth Daly, corporate services manager of the KICPAA.
Email, March 1, 2016, Mrs. Sam Sokuntheary, general manager of CamEd Business School.
Email, March 31, 2016, Mr. Chen Phat, chief of the Regulation and Control Office of the National Accounting Council of Cambodia.
Opening Remarks of H.E. Dr. Ngy Tayi, the secretary of state of the Ministry of Economy and Finance of Cambodia and chairman of the National Accounting Council, during the Workshop on Cambodian International Financial Reporting Standards – CIFRS, Issues of the implementation of the CIFRS for SMEs in Cambodia. Phnom Penh, March 31, 2016.

Secondary sources

ASEAN Federation of Accountants (2014) *KICPAA Activities Throughout 2014 AFA Annual Report*. Retrieved from www.aseanaccountants.org/files/AFA_Annual_Report_2014.pdf (accessed March 10, 2016).
Asian Development Bank (2015) *ADB President Highlights Cambodia's Strong Growth, Remaining Challenges*. News Release, March 10. Retrieved from www.adb.org/news/adb-president-highlights-cambodia-s-strong-growth-remaining-challenges (accessed March 15, 2016).
Cambodia Business Review (2015) British businesses find Cambodia a fertilizing land (interview with chairman of BritCham and country manager for Hongkong Land by Tim Vutha on August 2015). Retrieved from www.britchamcambodia.org/press-releases (accessed March 10, 2016).
Cambodia Demographic and Health Survey 2014 (2015) Ministry of Health, Cambodia. ICF International, Rockville, Maryland, USA.
Cambodia Health Management Information System (2016), Ministry of Health, Cambodia.
CamEd Business School website (2016). Retrieved from http://cam-ed.com (accessed March 1, 2016).
Council for the Development of Cambodia (2002) *Law on Accounting (Law on Corporate Accounts, their Audit and the Accounting Profession)* (Unofficial English translation). Retrieved from www.cambodiainvestment.gov.kh/law-on-accounting-law-on-corporate-accounts-their-audit-and-the-accounting-profession_020708.html (accessed January 15, 2016).
Ganschow, C., Ciolek, R., Cresap, J. and Lickey, J. (2009) *Tax Implications of an IFRS Conversion on Debt Arrangements*. Retrieved from www.pwc.com/us/en/ifrs-tax-issues/assets/ifrs_conversion_debt_arrangements.pdf (accessed January 14, 2016).
Heijmans, P. (2012) Firms need to improve accounting standards. *The Cambodia Daily*, August 30, p. 19. Retrieved from www.opendevelopmentcambodia.net/news/firms-need-to-improve-accounting-standards (accessed January 15, 2016).
IFRS (2013) *IFRS Application Around the World Jurisdictional Profile: Cambodia*. Retrieved from www.ifrs.org/Use-around-the-world/Documents/Jurisdiction-profiles/Cambodia-IFRS-Profile.pdf (accessed March 16, 2016).
KPMG (2012) *Client Alert October 2012: Notification Regarding Requirement for Enterprises' Accounting*. Retrieved from www.kpmg.com/Global/en/IssuesAndInsights/ArticlesPublications/taxnewsflash/Documents/cambodia-nov2-2012.pdf (accessed February 15, 2016).
National Accounting Council (July 29, 2006) *Prakas (No. 1245 MEF/BK) on Establishment of Secretariat of the National Accounting Council* (Unofficial English translation). Retrieved from www.naccambodia.gov.kh/?page=&lg=en (accessed January 15, 2016).
National Accounting Council (January 28, 2009) *Prakas (No. 068 MEF/BK) on Promulgation of Cambodian Financial Reporting Standards* (Unofficial English translation). Retrieved from www.naccambodia.gov.kh/?page=&lg=en (accessed January 14, 2016).

National Accounting Council (August 28, 2009) *Announcement (No. 097/09 MF-NAC) on the Introduction of Cambodia International Financial Reporting Standards (CIFRS) and Cambodian International Financial Reporting Standards for Small and Medium Entities (CIFRS for SME)* (Unofficial English translation). Retrieved from www.naccambodia.gov.kh/?page=&lg=en (accessed January 14, 2016).

National Accounting Council (2013) Anukret on the Composition and Functioning of the National Accounting Council. Retrieved from www.naccambodia.gov.kh/?page=&lg=en (accessed February 15, 2016).

Open Development Cambodia (2016) Cambodia accountancy towards global standard. *The Southeast Asia Weekly* (August 25, 2011). Retrieved from www.opendevelopmentcambodia.net/news/cambodia-accountancy-toward-global-standard/#more-2901 (accessed 16 February 2016).

Phorn, B. (2015) Growing pains, as capital keeps expanding. *Voice of America-Khmer*, March 23. Retrieved from www.voacambodia.com/content/growing-pains-as-capital-keeps-expanding/2630483.html (accessed March 15, 2016).

Prakas on the Implementation of Cambodian Accounting Standards (CASs) and Cambodian Financial Reporting Standards (CFRSs) (2008). Retrieved from www.cambodiainvestment.gov.kh/content/uploads/2011/09/Prakas-221-on-the-Implementation-of-Cambodia-Accounting-Standards-and-Cambodian-Financial-Reporting-Standards_080325.pdf (accessed February 15, 2016).

PwC (2008) *IFRS: The Right Move toward Convergence.* Retrieved from www.financialexecutives.org/eweb/upload/FEI/IFRSTaxExecutivesPwC.pdf (accessed January 15, 2016).

PwC (2015) *IFRS Adoption by Country December 2015.* Retrieved from www.pwc.com/us/en/issues/ifrs-reporting/publications/ifrs-status-country.html (accessed January 14, 2016).

Senarath Yapa, P.W. and Jacobs, K. (n.d.) *Accounting in Transitional Economy: The Case of Cambodia.* Retrieved from: http://www.victoria.ac.nz/sacl/about/events/past-events2/past-conferences/6ahic/publications/6AHIC-113_FINAL_Paper.pdf.

Senarath Yapa, P.W., Jacobs, K. and Chan, B.H. (2010) *Revolution and the Accountant: The Practice and Profession of Accounting in Cambodia.* Retrieved from: http://apira2010.econ.usyd.edu.au/conference_proceedings/APIRA-2010-197-Yapa Rebuilding-accounting-in-Cambodia-following-the-Khmer-Rouge.pdf (accessed January 16, 2016).

World Bank (2007) *Report on the Observance of Standards and Codes (ROSC) Cambodia Accounting and Auditing.* Retrieved from www.worldbank.org/ifa/Cambodia_aa.pdf (accessed January 15, 2016).

World Bank (2014) *Cambodia Economic Updated.* Retrieved from www.worldbank.org/en/country/cambodia/publication/cambodia-economic-update-october-2014 (accessed March 10, 2016).

World Bank (2014) *Current Status of the Accounting and Auditing Profession in Asean Countries.* Retrieved from www.aseanaccountants.org/files/afa_report-printed_version.pdf (accessed February 15, 2016).

World Trade Organization (2016) *Cambodia Ratifies Trade Facilitation Agreement.* Retrieved from www.wto.org/english/news_e/news16_e/fac_12feb16_e.htm (accessed March 10, 2016).

11

The development of accounting professionalization in Taiwan

Wen-Ching Chang

Introduction

This chapter introduces the development of the accounting profession in Taiwan after World War II. The first section introduces the licence requirements for certified public accountants (CPAs), CPA firms and CPA associations in Taiwan. The second section describes Taiwan's standards setting, including accounting standards, auditing standards, code of professional ethics and auditor independence rules. The third section presents auditor supervision and disciplinary mechanisms in Taiwan, including peer reviews, inspections by the competent authority of CPAs, auditor sanctions and legal liability. The final section summarizes and concludes.

CPAs and the accounting profession in Taiwan

Obtaining CPA examination certificates in Taiwan

Currently, the regulations on certified public accountants (CPAs) around the world include three parts: 1) the qualification requirements, 2) professional standards and 3) supervision and disciplinary mechanisms. In Taiwan, the Department of Professional and Technical Exams of the Ministry of Examination (MOE) is responsible for CPA examinations. There are two ways to obtain a CPA examination certificate in Taiwan: pass the CPA examination or pass the CPA qualification screening examination. As time went by, there has become quite a difference in difficulty between the two types of examination. Before 1942, there was no CPA examination; instead, the MOE issued certificates to those who qualified in the screening process. In 1942, the Professionals and Technical Specialists Examinations Act was promulgated and the Commission of Examination (now the MOE) held qualification screening examinations frequently. In fact, examinations for professional and technical personnel were held at the same time as civil servant examinations. After 1947, the examinations for professional and technical personnel, as well as for civil servants, were combined for legislation purposes. Applicants who passed one examination received two types of qualification: civil servant and professional. However, the nature and functions of civil servants are fundamentally different from those of professionals and technical specialists; thus, in 1983, these two kinds of examination were separated, and the Professionals and Technical Specialists Examinations Act was promulgated in 1986 with a new mandate to administer the examinations for professional and technical personnel in three categories: the senior and junior qualification examination, the special qualification examination and the qualification screening examination. The current CPA examination is categorized as a senior qualification examination.

Historically, the only criterion for siting the CPA examination was that candidates should have a grade point average of at least 60 points out of 100. In 1990, the MOE adopted the criterion of the T-standard score of educational measurement and statistics. The maximum number of people who could pass the CPA examination was 16 percent of the total number of examinees. In addition, they needed at least 50 points out of 100 to pass. At the end of 1999, the Professionals and Technical Specialists Examinations Act was amended and from 1 January 2001 CPA applicants needed to score 60 points on each subject test to pass the examination. Their scores were valid for three years after taking the examination.

Panel A of Table 11.1 shows the number of participants who took the CPA examination, as well as the number who passed, in Taiwan from 1950 to 2015. Before 1983, few candidates passed the CPA examination (on average, less than 10 per year). By contrast, 145 persons passed the CPA examination in 1983. In 1988, the MOE relaxed the threshold of admission and the number increased to more than 200 persons.

The Qualification Screening Regulations for CPAs was promulgated in 1946. The CPA Qualification Review Committee of the MOE reviewed each applicant's education and work experience. An applicant who met the standards for examination exemption was granted an examination pass certificate, while other applicants had to take a written or oral test.

Accountants were greatly in demand after the government led by Chiang Kai-Shek moved to Taiwan. The Executive Council and the Council for US Aid held accountant training

Table 11.1 Statistics of qualified CPA examinees in Taiwan

Year	Panel A: Senior qualification exam			Panel B: Qualification screening exam			Total
	# of people passing the exam (A)	# of people taking the exam (B)	Passing rate (C=A/B)	# of people being exempt from the exam (D)	# of people passing the exam by written or oral tests (E)	Subtotal (F=D+E)	(G=A+F)
1950–1967	63	593	10.62	488	0	488	551
1968–1982	171	7,018	2.44	103	148	251	422
1983	145	825	17.58	16	18	34	179
1984–1987	268	4,294	6.24	55	91	146	414
1988	220	1,229	17.90	1	9	10	230
1989	283	1,422	19.90	2	22	24	307
1990	339	2,056	16.49	1	27	28	367
1991–2000	2,780	27,467	10.12	0	354	354	3,134
2001–2005	875	10,421	8.40	0	14	14	889
2006–2015	5,309	27,469	19.33	NA	NA	NA	5,309
Total	10,453	82,794	12.63	666	683	1,349	11,802

NA = abolished.

Sources: The statistics before 1990 were sourced from Yeh (1991). Those after 1990 were taken from the website of the Ministry of Examination: http://wwwc.moex.gov.tw/main/ExamReport/wFrmExamStatistics.aspx?menu_id=158.

classes in three separate periods between 1952 and 1956. These trained personnel went on to serve in public offices or the military or to teach accounting at universities. In response to the demand for accountants at the time, these trained personnel were granted CPA designation by customizing the qualification screening standards to them (Wan 1983). As a result, those getting the CPA designation via the qualification screening examination were mostly former government accountants, accounting professors and former military comptrollers.

The standards of the qualification screening examination have been raised continuously. Initially, the CPA qualification was dominated by examination exemptions, and later shifted to requiring that each applicant take a written or oral test. The qualification screening examination system was abolished by the amended Professionals and Technical Specialists Examinations Act of 1999. Those who had already applied for the qualification screening examination before the amendment were allowed to take the examination within five years of their application date. The Qualification Screening Regulations for CPAs were abolished in 2006.

Panel B of Table 11.1 shows the number of persons who passed the CPA qualification screening examination between 1950 and 2005. Before 1968, all CPA qualification screening examinations involved an examination exemption. Oral tests began in 1968 and ended in 1986. After 1990, no one has been able to be exempt from the examination. As shown in Table 11.1, the CPA qualification screening examination was the main method of obtaining a CPA certificate before 1983. In contrast, after 1983 the CPA examination became the main channel.

Licensing and continuing professional education of CPAs in Taiwan

Practising CPAs in Taiwan are regulated by the government under the Certified Public Accountant Act of 1945 (as greatly amended in 2007). After the government led by Chiang Kai-Shek migrated to Taiwan in 1949, the first regulatory authority of CPAs was the Taiwanese Securities and Exchange Commission (TSEC), established in 1960. In 1997, the TSEC was renamed the Securities and Futures Commission (SFC) owing to its involvement with futures trading. To cater to the international trend of unified financial supervision, the Financial Supervisory Commission (FSC) was set up in 2004 and the SFC was restructured as one of the bureaus of the FSC (the competent authority of CPAs is referred to in this chapter as 'FSC').

Those who received a CPA examination certificate from the MOE could apply for a CPA certificate from the FSC of the Executive Council. After being certified and gaining two years of work experience in accounting or auditing, those who planned to practise as CPAs had to register with the FSC and join a CPA association. The CPA Act, amended in 2007, allowed two-year pre-professional training instead of the work experience. CPA pre-professional training included course training and practical training. The course training, organized by the National Federation of Certified Public Accountants Associations (NFCPAA), included a minimum of 160 hours with no less than 120 hours of required coursework. As for the practical training, candidates must have one year of auditing experience in a CPA firm or an equivalent amount of experience (e.g. one year of accounting or internal audit experience in a public company).

Regarding continuing professional education (CPE), the NFCPAA issued *CPAs Continuing Professional Education* in 1981 to encourage and award CPAs for engaging in continuing education instead of penalizing violations (Wan, 1983). In 1985, the NFCPAA published the *Methods for CPA Continuing Professional Education*, which required that CPAs with public audit clients take CPE courses. In 1993, NFCPAA expanded this scope to all practising CPAs. The CPE hours that CPAs with public audit clients had to complete were at least 90 hours for three years in a row (a minimum of 15 hours per year). For CPAs who did not perform attestation services to public companies, the minimum CPE hours were half this number.

The FSC had the power to sanction violators, barring them from practising or revoking their CPA certificates. A licence could only be reinstated once the violators completed the required number of CPE hours.

The 2007 amended CPA Act required that CPAs should pursue continuing professional education. Therefore, in 2008 the FSC promulgated the *Regulations Governing CPA Pre-Professional Training and Continuing Professional Education*, stipulating that CPAs who performed attestation services to public companies should have at least 100 CPE hours for three years in a row, with no less than 24 hours per year. For CPAs who did not perform financial attestation for public companies, the minimum CPE hours were half of this number. In 2013, the FSC promulgated an amendment related to the number of CPE hours requirements, raising them to not be less than 40 hours per year for CPAs with public audit clients and 20 hours per year for CPAs without public audit clients.

Development of the attestation business in Taiwan

Through tax relief and facilitating the acquisition of industrial land and other preferential measures, the Statute for the Encouragement of Investment of 1960 stimulated investments and extended CPAs' attestation business. The Taiwanese Securities and Exchange Act of 1968 stipulated that the financial statements of a public company must be attested by CPAs, further expanding CPAs' attestation business. In 1970, the Income Tax Act was amended and it mandated that profit-seeking enterprises with capital or revenues exceeding a certain threshold should engage CPAs to certify and duly file their annual income tax returns. Furthermore, the Ministry of Finance amended the Directions for CPAs Attesting Financial Statements for Loans in 1980, stipulating that, if a company applied to a bank for a loan of more than NTD50 million (NTD30 million since 1981), it had to provide financial statements audited by a CPA. Finally, starting from 1981 under the Taiwanese Company Act, a company with capital of more than NTD30 million had to submit financial statements audited by a CPA to the Ministry of Economic Affairs. CPAs' attestation business has boomed thanks to these legal provisions.

From 1982 to 1983, several financial scandals involving Taiwanese listed companies occurred in quick succession. For instance, Choung Hsim and Wanyi prepared fraudulent financial statements that severely damaged investors' confidence in the Taiwanese capital market and economic development. To regain investors' confidence, TSEC enacted the Regulations Governing the Approval of Certified Public Accountants to Audit and Attest to the Financial Reports of Public Companies (hereafter, the Approval Regulations) in 1983. The Approval Regulations mandated that any public company's financial statements must be jointly audited by two or more practising CPAs from a joint CPA firm (this is also known as a dual attestation system). In addition, such a joint CPA firm had to comprise three or more CPAs and have no fewer than nine audit assistants. Before the Approval Regulations went into effect, there were 114 companies listed on the Taiwan Stock Exchange (TWSE) in 1982. Their financial statements were audited by 43 CPA firms, and half of the CPA firms were single-person organizations. In 1984, 50 joint CPA firms registered under the TSEC to perform financial statements for public companies (Chen, 1986).

A statutory purpose of the dual attestation system is to enhance audit quality by concurring CPAs reviews of audit work to reduce audit risks. Taiwan Statement of Auditing Standards (TSAS) No. 46 (ARDF, 2008) mandated that audits of listed companies must include quality control reviews. As a result, CPA firms were required to have at least three CPAs to participate in every listed client audit engagement since 2009: two as signing CPAs and one as a quality control reviewer.

The Big Four CPA firms in Taiwan

Andrew A.H. Chang founded KPMG in Taiwan in 1952. In 1971, the firm entered into an association with Peat Marwick Mitchell & Co., making it one of the oldest internationally affiliated CPA firms in Taiwan. T.N. Soong established T.N. Soong & Co (TNS, now Deloitte Taiwan) in 1960. TNS cooperated with Philippine SGV & Co in 1964. PricewaterhouseCoopers (PwC) Taiwan was established in 1970 under the name of Chen Chu & Co. In 1972, PwC Taiwan joined with Hong Kong Lowe and Bingham & Matthews (LB&M), which then became associated with Price Waterhouse (PW) in 1973 via LB&M. PwC Taiwan became a member firm of PW in 1988. These are the three largest CPA firms in Taiwan.

After TNS became a member of AA in 1985, the other five global CPA firms represented by TNS searched for other firms in Taiwan to help them to serve their multinational clients. By 1988, Taiwan's Big Eight CPA firms had all roughly been established. The global Big Eight CPA firms merged into the Big Six in 1989. Taiwan's Big Six CPA firms also emerged in 1991. Taiwan entered the Big Five era in 1999. After the demise of AA in 2002, the Big Four international CPA firms now operate in Taiwan.

Organizational forms of CPA firms in Taiwan

In the past, CPA firms in Taiwan were either single-person or joint organizations. Whether a joint CPA firm is equivalent to a partnership was legally ambiguous at the time. Although some law scholars argued that a joint CPA firm was certainly a partnership, most practising CPAs did not agree. Some joint CPA firms conducted businesses that were run together by co-located practitioners who accepted business separately and assumed liabilities separately. Therefore, whether CPAs in a joint audit firm are jointly liable for the civil actions against any CPA in the same firm was then debatable.

In order to resolve the dispute, the 2007-amended CPA Act classifies CPA firms into four types: 1) single-person, 2) co-located, 3) joint and 4) incorporated CPA firms. In addition, a joint CPA firm is specified as a partnership, and a co-located CPA firm cannot conduct the attestation of the financial statements of public companies.

Table 11.2 shows the number of CPA firms in Taiwan from 2009 to 2013. Most of them are single-person firms. Co-located CPA firms have existed since 2012. Although incorporated CPA firms are acceptable under the CPA Act, there are as yet no such firms in Taiwan.

Functions of Taiwanese CPA associations

According to the Taiwanese Certified Public Accountant Act of 1945, CPAs had to form provincial or municipal CPA associations, which were further organized into a national

Table 11.2 The number of CPA firms in Taiwan from 2009 to 2013

	2009	2010	2011	2012	2013
Single-person CPA firm	1,055	1,114	1,318	1,393	1,446
Joint CPA firm	341	313	384	346	368
Co-location CPA firm	—	—	—	47	47
Incorporated CPA firm	—	—	—	—	—
Total	1,396	1,427	1,702	1,786	1,861

Source: The FSC inspection reports of CPA firms.

federation wherever the central government was located. The NFCPAA was founded in Nanjing, Mainland China, in 1946 and moved to Taiwan in 1949. The Taiwan Provincial CPA Association was established in Taipei City in 1950. In 1967, the Taipei Municipal CPA Association was founded and it shared an office with the Taiwan Provincial CPA Association. Similarly, Kaohsiung was reformed directly under the Executive Council, and the Kaohsiung Municipal CPA Association was founded in 1979. In 2010, Taichung County and Taichung City were combined and administered directly by the Executive Council, then the Taichung Municipal CPA Association was founded.

In their early years, Taiwanese CPA associations were responsible for formulating accounting principles, auditing standards and codes of professional ethics. In 1970, the Taipei Municipal CPA Association and the Taiwan Provincial CPA Association jointly developed the generally accepted accounting principles, the generally accepted auditing standards and the code of ethics for professional accountants. In 1982, NFCPAA was reorganized, taking on the task of developing new accounting principles and auditing standards and a new code of ethics. In 1984, the Accounting Research and Development Foundation (ARDF) was established to be responsible for setting standards for both accounting and auditing in Taiwan.

Currently, the NFCPAA is responsible for establishing the code of ethics for CPAs. The other important functions of the NFCPAA include professional education, periodical publications, professional liability assessments and peer reviews.

Standards setting in Taiwan

Setting Taiwanese accounting standards

In 1970, the Taipei Municipal CPA Association and the Taiwan Provincial CPA Association jointly compiled and translated the Elements of Generally Accepted Accounting Principles issued by the American Institute of Certified Public Accountants. However, without financial accounting standards, the financial reports in Taiwan were mainly generated to meet the requirements of income tax reporting.

In 1981, the Taiwan Provincial CPA Association, the Taipei Municipal CPA Association and the Kaohsiung Municipal CPA Association jointly established the Financial Accounting Board. In 1982, the Financial Accounting Board was reorganized under the NFCPAA. When the ARDF was established in 1984, the Financial Accounting Board was replaced by the Taiwan Financial Accounting Standards Board (TFASB) under the ARDF.

Initially, the Taiwan Statements on Financial Accounting Standards were formulated based on the US Statements of Financial Accounting Standards (SFASs), set by the Financial Accounting Standards Board in the US. However, the TFASB changed its direction for setting accounting standards to converge with the International Financial Reporting Standards (IFRSs) in 1999. Thus, accounting standards setting in Taiwan entered into a new stage of reliance on IFRSs, supplemented with the SFASs. In 2001, at the Economic Development Advisory Conference, the Taiwanese government decided that Taiwan's financial accounting standards would fully converge with the IFRSs. In 2005, the European Union's adoption of the IFRSs accelerated Taiwan's convergence process. In 2009, the FSC decided that public companies in Taiwan should adopt the IFRSs in two phases. In the first phase, all listed companies and financial institutions under the supervision of the FSC, except for credit cooperatives, credit card companies and insurance intermediaries, would be required to prepare financial reports in accordance with the Taiwan-IFRS from 1 January 2013. In the second phase, unlisted public companies, credit cooperatives and credit card companies had to prepare financial statements in accordance with the Taiwan-IFRS from 1 January 2015 onwards.

With the FSC's decision to adopt IFRSs, the Taiwan Statement on Financial Accounting Standard No. 41 became the last accounting standard set by the ARDF. In order to continuously update the Taiwan-IFRSs, the ARDF established the Taiwan Financial Reporting Standards Committee (TFRSC) in 2013. The new IFRSs are translated by the staff of the ARDF and reviewed by the TFRSC. Once approved by the FSC, the Chinese-language versions of the Taiwan-IFRSs are made available on the FSC Securities and Futures Bureau website.

Setting Taiwanese auditing standards

In 1970, the Taipei Municipal CPA Association and the Taiwan Provincial CPA Association jointly formulated the earliest version of the generally accepted auditing standards for their members to follow. In 1982, the NFCPAA set up the Auditing Standards Board to be responsible for formulating auditing standards in Taiwan. In 1984, the ARDF set up another Taiwanese Auditing Standards Board (TASB), which took over the task of setting auditing standards in Taiwan.

In the past, TSASs were based mainly on the US Statements of Auditing Standards and the International Standards on Auditing (ISAs) to adopt them with local practical conditions. However, in order to converge with ISAs, over a decade ago TSASs changed to using ISAs as their main reference. After the International Auditing and Assurance Standards Board (IAASB) completed the Clarity Project in 2009, the TASB of the ARDF pronounced several TSASs in a short period to speed up ISA convergence. Table 11.3 is a list of TSASs and their corresponding ISAs.

On 19 December 2001, the Ministry of Economic Affairs promulgated the Auditing Regulations, which were applicable to audits of private companies' financial statements. On 8 November 2002, SFC promulgated further Auditing Regulations applicable to financial statement audits for public companies. Since then, CPAs in Taiwan have to follow the Auditing Regulations and the auditing standards at the same time.[1]

Setting the code of professional ethics in Taiwan

The Taipei Municipal CPA Association and the Taiwan Provincial CPA Association formulated the earliest code of ethics in 1970. In 1983, the NFCPAA promulgated the Norm of Professional Ethics for CPAs. After the Enron scandal in the US, the NFCPAA comprehensively reviewed and revised the ethics norm in 2003, based mainly on the Code of Ethics of Professional Accountants set by the International Federation of Accountants (IFAC).

Enhancing auditor independence in Taiwan

Following the Sarbanes–Oxley Act of 2002 in the US, most countries created regulations on auditor independence. Three auditor independence regulations have been introduced in Taiwan.

Regulations on professional fees

Historically, practising CPAs in Taiwan could not charge service fees lower than the professional fee standards set by Taiwanese CPA associations in 1978 in order to prevent audit

Table 11.3 The convergence of Taiwan Statements of Auditing Standards (TSASs) and International
Standards on Auditing (ISAs)

TSAS	Pronounced date	Pre-clarity ISA	Clarity ISA
43 (The Auditor's Responsibility to Consider Fraud in an Audit of Financial Statements)	09/01/2006	ISA 240	
44 (Quality Control for Audits of Historical Financial Information)	09/01/2007	ISA 220	
45 (Audit Documentation)	02/26/2008		ISA 230
46 (Quality Control for Firms)	12/16/2008		ISQC 1
47 (Planning an Audit of Financial Statements)	10/01/2009		ISA 300
48 (Identifying and Assessing the Risks of Material Misstatement Through Understanding the Entity and its Environment)	11/15/2010		ISA 315
49 (The Auditor's Responses to Assessed Risks)	03/15/2011		ISA 330
50 (Analytical Procedures)	03/31/2011		ISA 520
51 (Materiality in Planning and Performing an Audit)	09/13/2011		ISA 320
52 (Evaluation of Misstatements Identified During the Audit)	10/18/2011		ISA 450
53 (Audit Evidence)	04/24/2012		ISA 500
54 (Special Considerations – Audits of Group Financial Statements)	08/20/2013		ISA 600
55 (Subsequent Events)	09/17/2013		ISA 560
56 (Auditing Accounting Estimates and Related Disclosures)	11/11/2014		ISA 540
57 (Forming an Opinion and Reporting on Financial Statements)	09/22/2015		ISA 700

Sources: The convergence to ISAs before TSAS 54 is adapted from Wu (2013), while this study updated the convergence status after TSAS 55.

quality impairments and fee-cutting competition. Sanctions may be imposed in the case of violation. However, the standards caught the attention of the Fair Trade Commission in 1998 when a practising CPA acquired the audit engagement of the Taiwan Fertilizer Company with a bidding price lower than the set fees standards. In exchange for not being professionally sanctioned for his violation of the professional fee standards, the Taipei Municipal CPA Association required the CPA to give up his audit engagement for this client the following year. In response, the CPA made an appeal to the Fair Trade Commission, which determined that the professional fee standards were in violation of the Fair Trade Act of 1991. Without the support of the competent authority of CPAs, the long-standing professional fee standards were abolished in 1998.

After the Enron scandal in the US in the early 2000s, the SFC amended the Regulations Governing the Preparation of Financial Reports by Securities Issuers (the Preparation Regulations) in 2002 in order to prevent the impairment of auditor independence by lucrative non-audit fees and fee-cutting competition. These regulations stipulate that public companies should disclose CPA professional fees when: 1) non-audit fees paid to the CPA are a quarter or more of the audit fees paid, or the amount of non-audit fees is more than NTD500,000; 2) when the company changes its CPA firm, and the audit fees paid to the successor CPA firm were lower than those paid to the predecessor CPA firm; and 3) the audit fees paid for the current fiscal year are 15 percent or more lower than those for the previous fiscal year. Since 2007, the disclosure of CPA professional fees has been regulated under the Regulations

Governing Information to Be Published in Annual Reports of Public Companies (the Annual Report Regulations). In addition, the disclosure threshold of NTD500,000 for non-audit fees has been removed. In 2009, the FSC amended the Annual Report Regulations to allow public companies to disclose CPA professional fees either by fee range or by individual amount.

Liao *et al.* (2012) found that, from 2002 to 2008, only 24 percent of Taiwanese listed companies had disclosed CPA professional fee information. However, the Information Disclosure and Transparency Rank System of 2006 encouraged voluntary disclosure of CPA professional fees. In addition, Taiwan's preparation for IFRSs adoption has increased non-audit fees, which has resulted in meeting the threshold of disclosure. These two factors led to 90 percent of listed companies in Taiwan disclosing CPA professional fee information for 2009 and 2010.

The 2007-amended CPA Act mandates that, if CPAs provide management consulting or other non-attestation services that may compromise their independence, they should not perform attestation on financial reports. In addition, if a CPA serves as an employee, officer, director or supervisor of a client or has financial relationships with a client, the CPA and other CPAs at the same CPA firm may not be contracted to perform attestation on financial reports.

Regulations on CPA rotation

CPA rotation is not mandatory in Taiwan. However, inspired by the Sarbanes–Oxley Act of 2002 in the US, the TWSE and the Taipei Exchange (TPEx) stated that financial statements were subject to the 'substantive review' procedure of the stock exchange if a lead or concurring CPA audited the same client for five consecutive years. Substantive reviews on audit documentation increase the chance of discovering audit deficiencies by regulators, thus increasing the likelihood of CPA sanctions. In order to reduce the risk of being sanctioned, the 'substantive review' mechanism, in effect, mandates a five-year rotation for CPAs (Chi et al., 2009). The substantive review rules of the TWSE and TPEx went into effect in 2003 and were implemented in two stages. Annual financial reports of 2003 were subject to the substantive review rules if they were audited by the same pair of CPAs for five consecutive years. After 2003, the rules were extended to those audits for which any signing CPA had audited the same client for five consecutive years. The rules do not specify the time interval during which the CPAs can audit the same client again. In 2009, Article 68 of TSAS No. 46 (ARDF, 2008) replaced the aforementioned rules. TSAS No. 46 mandates a seven-year rotation and an interval of at least two years before rotated CPAs may audit the same client again.

Regulations on the 'revolving door'

In Taiwan, when a company hires a senior financial reporting executive directly from its external audit firm, disclosure is required instead of a cooling-off period under the original regulations on the 'revolving door'. The SFC amended the Preparation Regulations in 2002, stipulating that, where the company's chairperson, general manager or any managerial officer in charge of finance or accounting matters has in the most recent year held a position at the CPA firm or at an affiliated enterprise of such accounting firm, the name and position of the person, as well as the period during which the position was held, must be disclosed. Similar to the aforementioned regulation on CPA professional fees, the regulation on the revolving door was moved in 2007 to the Annual Report Regulations.

Supervision and disciplinary mechanisms in Taiwan

Peer reviews in Taiwan

In the past, when an enterprise applied to a bank for a loan, local banks considered collateral as the main basis for their loan decisions. In contrast, foreign banks would make a loan decision based on the company's financial statements that were audited by CPAs. From 1982 to 1983, several financial crises in Taiwanese listed companies occurred in succession, as some companies' financial statements were fraudulent, causing foreign banks to suffer huge bad debts. Therefore, foreign banks, in a joint effort, classified the more than 500 CPAs in Taiwan into five grades: A, B, C, D and E. Foreign banks would always accept the financial statements audited by grade-A CPAs (16 CPAs in total) as a reference for loan decisions. The financial statements audited by grade-B and grade-C CPAs (18 and 400 CPAs, respectively) were accepted with prudence. If foreign banks discovered any defective financial statements audited by grade-B or grade-C CPAs, applicant companies would be required to engage a grade-A CPA for an additional audit. The financial statements audited by grade-D and grade-E CPAs (32 and 47 CPAs, respectively) would be rejected.

Practising CPAs were outraged by this grading system. As a result, foreign banks and the Ministry of Finance reached an agreement, replacing the grading system with the CPA evaluation results made by the Ministry of Finance (*CommonWealth Magazine*, 1985). From 1989 to 1993, the Ministry of Finance conducted CPA evaluations three times (Chen, 2003). It planned to publish the evaluation results, but received strong objection from some CPAs. Consequently, the results were simply used as an internal reference by the competent authorities (Yeh, 1991).

The NFCPAA was also active in promoting peer reviews while the Ministry of Finance was conducting its CPA evaluations. In 1992, TSEC approved the Method of Peer Review of CPAs, which was drafted by NFCPAA. Thus, CPA evaluations have been handed over to the NFCPAA since 1993.

The NFCPAA has two kinds of peer review: evaluation of overall audit quality of a CPA firm and evaluation of audit quality of an audit engagement. The cases reviewed by the NFCPAA include those cases submitted by government agencies, submitted by a provincial or a municipal CPA association under certain circumstances, and submitted by individual CPAs or CPA firms or by interested parties at their own expense.

Most cases reviewed by NFCPAA involved audit engagement quality as required by the competent authorities, and the number of CPA firms being reviewed was low. Therefore, the NFCPAA's peer review process was not fully functional. In 2003, the SFC encouraged CPA firms to follow overall audit quality reviews during the reform wave of corporate governance. In 2004, 29 CPA firms took part in the overall CPA firm quality reviews.

The FSC's inspections

The Taiwanese Certified Public Accountant Act regulated individual CPAs rather than CPA firms. After the 2007 amendment to the Taiwanese CPA Act, FSC could dispatch personnel to inspect the operations and operations-related financial status of any CPA firm that had been approved to provide attestation services to public companies. The FSC's inspection included quality control of CPA firms and their audit engagements.

The FSC began to inspect CPA firms in 2009. In 2011, the FSC signed the Statement of Protocol with the Public Company Accounting Oversight Board (PCAOB) in the US

Table 11.4 The number of CPA firms inspected by the Financial Supervisory Commission (FSC)

	2009	2010	2011	2012	2013	2014
Number of CPA firms inspected	3	3	2	6	3	3
Number of CPA firms approved to provide attestation services to public companies	83	83	83	NA	NA	NA

NA: not provided in the FSC inspection reports.
Source: FSC inspection reports of CPA firms

regarding cooperation and the exchange of information related to the oversight of auditors. As of 2012, FSC had completed the first round of inspections, including the Big Four CPA firms as well as 10 medium-sized CPA firms in Taiwan. In 2013, the FSC began a second round of reviews. Table 11.4 shows the number of CPA firms inspected by the FSC between 2009 and 2014.

CPA sanctions in Taiwan

Two authoritative agencies exercise sanctions against CPAs in Taiwan. The first is the CPA Discipline Committee, which can impose disciplinary sanctions under the CPA Act. The second is the FSC, empowered by the Taiwanese Securities Exchange Act, which imposes administrative sanctions. Disciplinary sanctions under the CPA Act include warnings, reprimands, suspensions and disbarments. The 2007-amended CPA Act adds administrative fines as a new type of sanction. In addition, the amended CPA Act stipulates that an incorporated CPA firm may be subject to four types of sanctions, including a warning, a prohibition from accepting new business for up to six months, a suspension of the whole or part of its business for not more than six months and the revocation of the firm's registration.

When a CPA subject to disciplinary proceedings under the CPA Act disagrees with the resolution of the CPA Discipline Committee, he or she may appeal to the CPA Disciplinary Rehearing Committee. In the past, CPAs' disciplinary sanctions were treated as a special power relationship; therefore, CPAs were not allowed to file an administrative appeal, administrative re-appeal or administrative litigation after receiving a rehearing resolution. However, the Justice of the Constitutional Court pronounced the Judicial Council Interpretation No. 295 in 1992 because a disbarred CPA applied for an interpretation. According to this interpretation, the resolution of the rehearing is equivalent to the final decision of administrative appeal and cannot be appealed via administrative appeal and re-appeal. In addition, the subject of the disciplinary proceedings should be allowed to bring administrative litigation to the institute as guaranteed by the constitution if he or she deems the said resolution to be illegal and damaging to his or her rights. Thus, since 1992, CPAs may litigate at the administrative court if they disagree with a resolution from the Rehearing Committee. After a disciplinary action against a CPA becomes final, the CPA Discipline Committee or the CPA Disciplinary Rehearing Committee may publicly announce and publish the results of its resolution in a government gazette.

To ensure a timely process, Article 37 of the Taiwanese Securities Exchange Act empowers the FSC to impose sanctions against CPAs providing attestation services to public companies regardless of the CPA Discipline Committee's processes. Sanctions under the Securities Exchange Act include a warning, a suspension from providing attestation services to public companies for up to two years and a revocation of permission to provide attestation services to public companies. An administration sanction is effective immediately after the FSC passes it.

The sanctioned CPAs can appeal to the FSC if they disagree with the decision and file an administrative action at the administrative court if they are dissatisfied with the result of the appeal.

The efficacy of the sanctions imposed by the two agencies differs. The Securities Exchange Act only applies to public companies. Therefore, sanctioned CPAs under FSC suspension or revocation are not allowed to render attestation services to public companies, but they can still render services to non-public companies. On the other hand, if CPAs are suspended or disbarred under the CAP Act, they are prohibited from practising all public accounting services during the sanction period.

The FSC placed sanctions on CPAs when material financial scandals occurred in Taiwan. Table 11.5 displays the CPA sanctions under the CPA Act. Four CPAs were disbarred until 2015. The first administrative fine occurred in 2010.[2] Table 11.6 shows the CPA sanctions under the Taiwanese Securities Exchange Act.

CPA legal liability in Taiwan

Regarding civil liability for third parties, CPAs are liable to compensate for any damages incurred as a result of their misconduct or negligence in Taiwan. When CPAs audit the financial reports of private companies, they are liable under the CPA Act and the Taiwanese Civil Code. In the 2007-amended CPA Act, a CPA's liability for damages could be no more than 10 times the total amount of the professional fees received from his/her client except where providing attestation services to a public company. In other words, the amended CPA Act put a ceiling of damage compensation in place for CPAs providing attestation services to private companies.

Table 11.5 CPA sanctions under the Taiwanese Certified Public Accountant Act

Year	Fine	Warning	Reprimand	Suspension	Disbarment	Total
1965–1971	0	7	2	0	0	9
1972–1980	0	39	20	13	1	73
1981–1990	0	54	37	13	2	106
1991–2000	0	28	48	189	1	266
2001–2009	0	21	22	52	0	95
2010–2015	18	4	7	25	0	54
Total	18	153	136	292	4	603

Sources: The sanctions before 1987 were sourced from Lin and Liu (1999). The sanctions for the period of 1988–2008 were sourced from Lin and Lin (2010). The sanctions after 2009 were taken from the website of the Bureau of Securities and Futures of the FSC: www.sfb.gov.tw/ch/home.jsp?id=601&parentpath=0,8,594.

Table 11.6 CPA sanctions under the Taiwanese Securities Exchange Act

Year	Warning	Suspension	Revocation of Permission	Total
2000	1	5	0	6
2001	0	2	0	2
2002	1	5	0	6
2004	4	12	0	16
2007	0	7	4	11
Total	6	31	4	41

Adapted from Lin and Lin (2010).

According to Article 32 of the Taiwanese Securities Exchange Act, when prospectuses contain false information or omissions, CPAs are jointly liable with the issuers within the scope of their responsibility. However, CPAs are not liable if they can prove that they have made reasonable investigations and have a just cause to believe that the audit opinions rendered thereto are accurate. In other words, CPAs in Taiwan bear the burden of proof that an adequate audit has been conducted in the situation of a company issuing new securities.

According to Article 20 of the Securities Exchange Act, financial reports filed by an issuer must contain no misrepresentations, and violators are held liable for the resulting damages. Since the provisions of Article 20 are ambiguous, debates are inevitable on whether CPAs are liable. What is the liability if CPAs are liable? In other words, is it an intentional liability or a negligent liability? In 2006, the Securities Exchange Act added Article 20-1 to stipulate that CPAs who negligently perform the attestation of financial reports of public companies shall be liable for damages in proportion to the degree of their responsibility. Thus, plaintiffs bear the burden of proving that CPAs are negligent or fraudulent when doing the attestations. In addition, a separate and proportionate liability clause was introduced in 2006.

From the establishment of the TWSE in 1962 until 1997, only one lawsuit was filed against a CPA. The court ruled that the CPA was not guilty and did not have to compensate the plaintiff. Following the 'landmine shares' crises in 1998, the Securities and Futures Institute established the Investor Service and Protection Centre (ISPC) to provide litigation services on behalf of investors. The Securities and Futures Investors Protection Centre (SFIPC) was founded in 2003 under the Securities Investor and Futures Trader Protection Act of 2002 to replace the ISPC. From 1998 to 2009, the ISPC and the SFIPC had 32 class-action lawsuits involving financial statements or prospectuses, with 22 CPAs as defendants (Lin and Lin, 2010).

As of June 2007, the courts had heard a total of eight civil lawsuits against CPAs, in which the court ruled against two signing CPAs and ordered the CPAs to compensate the plaintiffs (Liao *et al.*, 2007). Civil lawsuits are a lengthy process for plaintiffs in terms of receiving compensation for their investment losses.[3] For instance, Procomp Informatics was involved in accounting fraud in respect of fictitious transactions in 2004. Under pressure from the public and the expectations of the FSC to ensure that investors received proper compensation quickly, the SFIPC began to settle lawsuits out of court on behalf of investors. From 2004 to the end of 2007, SFIPC reached out-of-court settlements of NTD1.147 billion with criminal defendants, directors and supervisors, CPAs and underwriters.

As for the proportion of compensation, the court ruled that 3 percent was the appropriate amount of civil compensation if there had been no settlement before the court's judgment. For example, the judgment in the *Procomp Informatics* case was concluded in 2008. The total amount of compensation exceeded NTD5.5 billion, and the defendant CPAs had to bear about NTD170 million in costs. However, because of prior settlement, the defendant CPAs only paid the plaintiff NTD80 million in compensation (Huang, 2008).

There are five cases in which CPAs were criminal defendants: *Wanyi, Tong Lung Metal, Shmidt, Pacific Construction* and *China Rebar* (Lin and Lin, 2010). In three of these cases, the CPAs were sentenced to fixed-term imprisonment (more than six months and less than two years) for the offences of certifying clients' false financial statements, creating fraudulent business documents and breach of trust.

Summary and conclusion

This chapter has outlined the development of the auditing profession in Taiwan after World War II, describing the requirements for becoming a CPA, the size and organization of CPA firms and the role of CPA associations in Taiwan. The regulations and standards that influence CPA performance, as well as the supervision and disciplinary mechanisms in Taiwan, are also examined.

Whenever material financial scandals occur, the Taiwanese government has taken action to reform its financial regulations. For instance, inspired by the Sarbanes–Oxley Act of 2002 in the US, the regulatory agencies in Taiwan have strengthened regulation on auditor independence. In addition, the Taiwanese CPA Act was materially amended in 2007 to respond to the changed environment faced by CPAs and to enhance audit quality. In response to economic globalization, for a number of years the ARDF has been developing accounting and auditing standards using the IFRSs and the ISAs, respectively, as a primary reference. As a result, the FSC decided to fully adopt IFRSs in Taiwan in 2009.

The capital market in Taiwan has become prosperous over the last 60 years, making CPA services more important. The regulations on CPAs have also expanded and become more stringent. The Taiwanese government has continuously reviewed relevant laws and regulation and supported standards setters consistently to maintain a high quality of practitioners and their services, ensuring the sound development of the accounting profession in Taiwan to keep up with the international trend.

Notes

1 Ming-Cheng Chang, the current director of the TASB of ARDF, explains that the Auditing Regulations focus on substantive audit procedures, while auditing standards focus on three parts: risk assessments, tests of control and substantive audit procedures (ARDF 2014).
2 Until now, no incorporated CPA firm exists in Taiwan, and thus no sanction has been placed on incorporated CPA firms.
3 For example, the plaintiffs of the *Cheng I Food* case waited eight years to receive the first-instance court's judgment (it lasted from 1998 to 30 November 2006).

References

Accounting Research Development Foundation (ARDF) (2008) *Taiwan Statements of Auditing Standards No. 46: Quality Control for Public Accounting Firms*. Taipei: ARDF (in Chinese).

Accounting Research Development Foundation (ARDF) (2014) *Special Issue of the 30th Anniversary for the Accounting Research Development Foundation*. Taipei: ARDF (in Chinese).

Chen, C.C. (1986) *The Deficiencies of Financial Attestation by Certified Public Accountants in Taiwan*. Unpublished thesis, National Chengchi University, Taipei (in Chinese).

Chen, H.R. (2003) Introduction to the exposure draft on the amendment to the Taiwanese Certified Public Accountant Act and discussion of the future direction of regulation on certified public accountants. *Securities and Futures Management*, 21(5), 1–11 (in Chinese).

Chi, W., Huang, H., Liao, Y. and Xie, H. (2009) Mandatory audit partner rotation, audit quality, and market perception: Evidence from Taiwan. *Contemporary Accounting Research*, 26(2), 359–391.

CommonWealth Magazine (1985) Which certified public accountants do foreign banks trust? *CommonWealth Magazine*, 50, 150 (in Chinese).

Huang, S.K. (2008) Compensation for landmine shares, with certified public accountants bearing 3%. *Commercial Times*, April 12, 2008, p. B2 (in Chinese).

Liao, D.Y., Lin, C.F. and Ku, H.Y. (2007) *Research on Responsibility Division of Underwriters, Certified Public Accountants and Attorney Experts*. Unpublished research report, Financial Supervisory Commission, Taipei (in Chinese).

Liao, H.M., Wang, C.C. and Chi, W.C. (2012) What does the complete disclosure of audit fee information tell us in Taiwan? *Taiwan Accounting Review*, 8(1), 49–88 (in Chinese).

Lin, C.C. and Lin, H.L. (2010) Auditor's liability for financial statement fraud in Taiwan from Rebar verdict: An empirical analysis, *National Taiwan University Law Journal*, 39(3), 223–288 (in Chinese).

Lin, C.C. and Liu, C.W. (1999) *Comparison on CPA's Sanction System between Taiwan and Developed Countries*. Unpublished research report, National Federation of CPA Associations, Taipei (in Chinese).

Wan, R.H. (1983) Research on the systems of CPA examination and of CPA qualification screening examination and CPA education in Taiwan. *Audit Journal*, *14*(2), 69–97 (in Chinese).

Wu, C.F. (2013) *Auditing* (2nd ed.). Taipei: Best-Wise (in Chinese).

Yeh, R.P. (1991) *The Qualities of Certified Public Accountants: Evidence from the Ways to Obtaining a CPA Designation and from the Audit Firm Peer Reviews*. Unpublished thesis, National Taiwan University, Taipei (in Chinese).

Part IV
Governmental and public-sector accounting

Historically, ancient accounting activities were derived mainly from the needs of recording and reporting for rulers of empires or owners of manors, thus governmental accounting or accounting in the public sector is an important branch of accounting. Even nowadays, a great portion of social resources are spent by governments and public-sector institutions, and their accountability as well as the adequacy and justification of their revenues and expenditures are the key objectives of governmental or public-sector accounting. Governments and public-sector institutions are different from business entities in that they are not profit-seeking in their operations, thus there are substantial differences in their objectives, accounting subjects and methods, as well as the reporting formats between business accounting and governmental and public-sector accounting. In general, the focus of governmental or public-sector accounting is on the rational allocation and spending of different funds in terms of specified operating purposes (i.e. running governmental functions or fulfilling pre-set missions), thus the 'fund accounting' method is applied to accounts and reports for the execution of operating budgets in each pre-set fund. Budgeting is thus a major tool for accounting and control in governmental and public-sector accounting, which can also be called 'budgetary accounting'. However, with increased participation in the capital markets of external financing by governments and other public-sector institutions, governments and public-sector institutions have now been required to provide understandable and comparable accounting information to capital market investors and creditors in addition to the traditional objective of discharging their accountability to legislative authorities or fund providers. Therefore, there have in recent years been reforms in governmental or public-sector accounting in most countries, and the direction of the reforms has been to gradually adopt some fundamental concepts and methods in business accounting such as a shift from traditional cash accounting to accrual accounting in varied forms and the provision of consolidated financial statements (e.g. whole-of-government consolidated financial statements), and so on. This trend of change has also been witnessed in Asian countries.

Part IV covers the development of governmental and public-sector accounting in three Asian countries, China (Chapter 12), India (Chapter 13) and Nepal (Chapter 14).

There is a consensus among accounting historians that China had the most sophisticated governmental accounting and auditing systems of the ancient civilizations of the world (Chatfield, 1977). Chapter 12 presents a historical review of Chinese governmental accounting from ancient feudal dynasties to the contemporary China. It is interesting to learn how governmental accounting was invented and has continually evolved to sophisticated levels over the long period of feudal dynastic society in China, for the purpose of serving mainly the purposes of monitoring and control of revenues and expenditure (including flows and storage of physical grains and properties) for the emperors of the ruling dynasties. Substantial changes in Chinese governmental accounting were however witnessed in the periods of the Republic of China (1911–1949) and the People's Republic of China (1949–present), as some contemporary governmental accounting methods and practices were accepted or adapted to accommodate the significant changes in the social, political and economic systems in China.

The authors have elaborated in detail the original practices of the 'budgetary accounting system' that was in use in Chinese governments and public institutions under the former Soviet-style centrally planned economic administrative systems in the 1950s to the 1970s and their changes during the course of China's comprehensive economic reforms towards market orientation one since the beginning of the 1980s. In particular, the current round of governmental and public-sector accounting reforms with an inheritance of successful experience in budgetary accounting practices in past decades and the adoption of international governmental and public-sector accounting practices are under way. The Chinese government has set a clear timetable and taken concrete measures, such as formulating new governmental accounting standards and regulations to adopt accrual accounting and consolidated governmental financial statements, to revamp the accounting systems for governments and public institutions in China, aiming at a convergence with international norms in the very near future. This chapter provides strong evidence to demonstrate that substantial changes in government will occur whenever there is a significant change in the political, economic and social environment, such as is the case in China.

India is the second largest country in Asia, and in the world, by population. It is also the seventh largest economy in the world. As one of the BRICS countries, India has maintained a rapid economic growth over the last decade. As a result, India is a key player in social and economic development in Asia and the world. As stated in Chapter 13, unlike many developed countries, there is a huge section of government and public-sector institutions in Indian economy. For instance, public-sector undertakings (i.e. corporations and enterprises in the public sector) contribute more than 22 per cent of Indian GDP. Thus, accounting and financial reporting are important means for resource distribution and governance efficiency for governments and public-sector institutions in India.

Chapter 13 introduces the development of accounting and reporting for governments and public-sector institutions (PSUs) in India. There are three levels of government in India: union (central), state and local. In order to provide uniform accounting information and ensure its usefulness, the Indian government, through the comptroller and auditor general (the CAG), established the Government Accounting Standards Advisory Board (GASAB) in 2002 to promulgate nationwide governmental accounting standards. Under India's constitution, the CAG is responsible for compiling and audit of the financial statements of the union government, while the accountants general at the state level prepare the financial statements for state governments. In addition, the CAG jointly audits financial reports (which must be prepared in accordance with the governmental accounting standards issued by the GASAB) of all public-sector entities administered at either the central or the state level.

Currently, the GASAB adopts case-based accounting for Indian governments and public-sector entities. However, following a request from the government of India, the GASAB has also committed to developing a new set of governmental accounting standards with an accrual base, to be consistent with the international trend towards governmental accounting reforms.

Several new government accounting standards – the Indian Government Financial Reporting Standards (IGFRS) – have been drafted by the GASAB in recent years, pending approval by central government. Nonetheless, as pointed out by the authors, the GASAB has a long road ahead in terms of formulating a complete set of new accounting standards for governments and public-sector entities in India, especially compared to standards in the developed countries (e.g. the USA). Surely, with continuous progress in the new efforts for governmental accounting reforms, a significant improvement in the governance and financial reporting for governments and public-sector entities in India will be witnessed in the coming decade.

Chapter 14 describes the Nepalese public-sector accounting practices and reforms from the perspective of accounting as a social and institutional practice. The authors state that the Nepalese government has promoted the New Public Management movement and enacted a new constitution and related financial laws and regulations to ensure the proper operation of governmental funds and effective budget implementation. As indicated, budgeting and budgetary control are the key components in Nepalese public-sector accounting. The current reforms include a change from traditional cash accounting towards a certain kind of accrual accounting (e.g. Cash Basis International Public Sector Accounting Standards) and the provision of consolidated financial statements at varied jurisdictional levels, following the recommendations of the World Bank and the Asian Development Bank to better ensure the accountability of the public sector and report the effectiveness of foreign aid and donation projects. The state budgets and their implementation results remain at the core of public-sector accounting in Nepal. At present, foreign financial consultants and domestic professional accountants are allowed to participate in the ongoing public-sector accounting reforms, including the development of Nepalese Public Sector Accounting Standards. It is expected that Nepalese public-sector accounting will move towards international norms, as the reforms progress is designed to ensure.

12

The evolution and reforms of governmental accounting in China

Zhibin Chen, Yan Wang, Ying Wang and Z. Jun Lin

Introduction

We cannot depart from a historical review in the study of any important accounting issues. Similarly, our understanding of significant accounting development should start with a historical review, analysis and probing (Guo, 1999). Governmental accounting has evolved in various forms or shapes over the long history of China, such as accounts for feudal dynasties, governmental accounting, budgetary accounting and the reshaped governmental accounting of the present time, which has been determined by the specific forms of imperial power and governmental authority and closely associated with the development of political and economic systems (Fang, 2001). Every significant change in the ruling regime and political or economic system has greatly prompted the evolution of governmental accounting with enriched practices and theories. Therefore, a historical examination of the evolution process will help our understanding of the essentials of governmental accounting, exploring the root causes and the trends of its development, assessing governmental accounting practices and the further reforms of governmental accounting in China.

This chapter presents a historical review of governmental accounting evolution in China and it is organized as follows: the second section briefly illustrates ancient governmental accounting in China, i.e. the development of governmental accounting during various feudal dynasties from *the West Zhou dynasty* (1046–256 BC) to the *Qing dynasty* (AD 1644–1911). The third section describes the major changes of governmental accounting in the period of the Republic of China (1911–1949). The fourth section sets out the development of new governmental accounting, that is, the budgetary accounting system installed after the founding of the People's Republic of China in 1949, as well as the most recent reforms of accounting for governments and public institutions in the course of China's transition towards a market-oriented economy and the internationalization of Chinese accounting. The fifth section presents a conclusion.

Ancient governmental (dynastic) accounting

In most Western countries, accounting practices have stemmed mainly from business entities in the private sector before their application to governmental entities. However, ancient accounting in China emerged from the accounts of various feudal dynasties and later proliferated to business entities in the private sector (Sun, 1989). Thus, accounts systems in the ancient dynasties of China were much more complete and sophisticated than accounting practices in the private sector. Therefore, research on Chinese accounting development cannot neglect the early accounting activities in various ancient dynasties. For instance, in the *Xia dynasty* (2100 BC), detailed records, calculations and supervision methods were used to keep track of the tributes submitted by subordinate tribes, affiliated kingdoms and officials, as well as tax revenues, to the rulers of the empire. In the *Shang* and *Ying* dynasties (1600–1100 BC), records were also kept for all tribute income, spending on sacrifice ceremonies and wars by the dynastic empires, which was the origin of a crude form of governmental accounting in China.

According to *The Rites of Zhou Dynasty* (Zhou Li),[1] the governmental accounting system reached completion in *the West Zhou dynasty* (1066–771 BC) (Fu, 1971; Li, 1982a, 1982b, 1982c). The *Zhou dynasty* installed a centralized accounting system and set up a post of *Sikuai* (similar to a chief comptroller), who was in charge of promulgating rules on accounting and reporting, overseeing fiscal revenue and expenditure and performance assessment of government officials. Thus, '*Sikuai* is responsible for Six Codes, Eight Laws and Eight Rules . . . and annual accounts'. The earliest accounts reporting system was also created in the *Zhou dynasty*. '*Sikuai* . . . must check account records daily, monthly and annually', so the daily records (*richeng*), monthly summary (*yueyao*) and yearly accounts (*shuikuai*) were the accounting records and reports of the dynasty. There were specific regulations on the special use of specialized funding and complete accounts systems for tribute revenues and official expenditures in the *West Zhou dynasty*. In addition, there was a governmental audit function so that the dynastic accounts and audits were used to prevent or restrain the behaviour of officials at various ranks. There is a description of the official position of *Daizai* in the Chapter of Offices of the Heaven (*Tian Guan*) in *The Rites of Zhou Dynasty*: 'the Eight Laws were used to govern the operation of governmental offices . . . . Accounts were used for control of officials . . . and for prevention officials from corruptions.' The governmental accounting system created in the *Zhou dynasty* played a significantly role in supporting the fiscal operation of the dynasty and become an institutional prototype in governmental accounting, followed continuously by subsequent dynasties until the *Qing dynasty* (AD 1644–1911).

The first Great Emperor in China, *Qin Shi Huang*, unified the whole country by defeating all of the small kingdoms and warlords in 475 BC, and built up the first centralized feudal imperial dynasty in China. The governmental accounting system was then developed and improved following the establishment of the centralized fiscal and legal administrative systems. Thus, the bookkeeping method with *Ru* (in) and *Chu* (out) recording symbols was invented in governmental accounting at that time (Liu, 2009). The premier of the dynasty was in charge of fiscal and accounting administration, and set up subordinate offices in lower governments. Later, two sets of accounts were created to record and report the revenues and expenditures of the government and of the imperial household separately. Different accounting books were created for governmental operations (*yuanji*), army provisions (*liangji*) and account summaries (*hengji*), implementing account recording by classification (e.g. governmental functions).

Until the later *Han dynasty* (206 BC–AD 220), accounting records were called 'recording books' (*bu*); the main recording books used in governmental accounting include 'treasury books' (*qian gu bu*), with subsidiary books to record the flows in and out of money (*qian chu-ru bu*), grains (*gu chu-ru bu*) and other goods and properties (*cai wu bu*), which could be seen as a primitive form of the 'receipts and payments' bookkeeping method (*shou-fu fa*) in traditional Chinese accounting, along with the use of transaction vouchers, books and account statements.

The central government of the dynasty established an annual reporting system to monitor the fiscal revenues and expenditures of governmental offices and local governments, following the early practices adopted in previous dynasties. However, such a system became more form than substance owing to the emperors losing power to local warlords in the late *Han dynasties*.

In the *Tang dynasties* (618–907), commercial activities and foreign trade increased substantially in the country, and governmental accounting evolved correspondingly as the emperors regained ruling power. A fiscal budgeting system was created in the Tang dynasty, with separate government offices of revenues, treasury, cashier and storage to control government revenues, accounting and treasury functions. In addition, the government audit office (*bi bu*) was set up to exercise fiscal monitoring and supervision. In the *Song dynasty* (960–1279), governmental accounting and auditing systems became more stringent to discipline the corruption of officials, with the setting up of the Office of Accounts in 1074 and the Office of Audit in 1127. Governmental accounting in the *Song dynasty* went through several rounds of restructuring and the Chinese bookkeeping system of 'four pillar bookkeeping' (*si zhu qian ce*) was then invented, including specific formats for accounts and books as well as systematic recording, calculation and reporting methods, which was a significant innovation in the governmental accounting in the *Song dynasty*.

The emperors in the later *Ming* and *Qing dynasties* (around the fifteenth century) inherited the bureaucratic governing systems from the Song dynasty. The Department of Revenues was set to exercise fiscal management and accounting. In particular, annual financial audits were in practice for governmental offices in the *Qing dynasty* (1644–1911). Governmental accounting was quite sophisticated, although accounting in the private sector remained less developed in China. All government offices received funding from the Department of Revenues according to centrally set fiscal budgets, and the officials in charge of governmental offices or departments had to submit summary revenues and expenditure accounts to the Department of Revenues at the end of each year (Song, 2009).

In sum, the governmental accounting in the long period of feudal dynastic society in China evolved continuously to a pretty sophisticated level, serving mainly the purposes of monitoring and control of revenues and expenditure (including flows and storage of physical grains and properties) for the emperors of the ruling dynasties. Chinese ancient governmental accounting was an important instrument to implement fiscal control for the ruling authorities and became a fundamental set-up for the development of contemporary governmental accounting in China (Li, 1999).

Governmental accounting in the Republic of China (1911–1949)

Governmental accounting in the early twentieth century

The Chinese feudal society was ended by the overturn of the *Qing dynasty* in the *Xin Hai* (*Hsin-hai*) Revolution in 1911. The provisional Nanjing government established the Ministry of Finance (MoF), with expanded responsibilities to centralize the administrative functions of state fiscal revenues and expenditures, preparing state budgets and annual final accounts, and formulating accounting and auditing regulations. Five departments were set under the MoF: tax revenues, accounting, cashier, government bonds and state treasury. The Department of Accounting was in charge of the preparation of state budgets and annual final accounts and maintaining accounting records and reports of the revenues and expenditures of all governmental departments, following the ancient Chinese governmental accounting systems and the governmental accounting practices of some industrialized countries (Song, 2009).

To build up the legal framework for accounting work, the MoF formulated the *Accounting Law*, with a reference to the experience in Japan, which was the first national accounting code in China, and it set out detailed provisions on government annual fiscal revenues and expenditures, tax collection, budgeting and budgetary control, government borrowing for significant construction projects and cashier and treasury functions etc. (Chu, 1990). However, this accounting law was not effectively implemented owing the civil wars among various warlords in the early twentieth century. Nonetheless, the introduction of the Western 'debit and credit' bookkeeping system in this period set the direction for governmental accounting developments by subsequent governments.

Governmental accounting in the Republican government (1927–1949)

The Republican government in China gained power in the late 1920s before it was replaced in 1949 by the People's Republic. During this period, many Chinese scholars proposed to improve the traditional Chinese accounting systems, which had developed in China over a long time, and to establish contemporary governmental accounting, modelled on that in industrialized Western countries. The improved governmental accounting system was in fact a combination of governmental budgeting, accounting and statistics, with centralized administration on the appointment, promotion and relocation of governmental accountants by the MoF, in order to reduce fiscal risks, deficiencies and corruption by government officials (Fang, 2001).

The Republican government promulgated the Accounts Organization Act in 1931, which mandated the National Accounts Administration as the highest government authority in charge of accounting work, with the three subordinate departments of fiscal revenues, accounting and statistics being set up. An Audit Bureau was established under the National Legislative Council to exercise accounting monitoring, while the offices of chief accountant were also set up at the provincial level. A series of laws was formulated by the central government, including the Auditing Act in 1928, the Uniform Accounting System for Central Government and Subordinate Organizations in 1932 and the amended Accounting Law in 1936. It should be noted the Chinese governmental accounting and auditing systems in the Republican government ruling period were sophisticated but they were not implemented effectively owing to the war against Japanese invasion and the subsequent civil war, along with severe corruption on the part of government officials.

Governmental accounting in the People's Republic of China (1949–present)

The communists won the civil war and established the People's Republic of China in 1949. The new government adopted a centrally planned economic administrative system with assistance from the former Soviet Union in the early 1950s. Governmental accounting was changed to 'budgetary accounting' and placed on a cash basis, which was originally developed during the civil war period to establish uniform fiscal control and accounting monitoring, to ensure the logistic supply for the revolutionary war to gain national power. Nonetheless, budgetary accounting has experienced three major evolution stages and taken a winding course over the last six decades in China.

Budgetary accounting in the planned economy (1949–1978)

After the founding of the People's Republic, the government introduced a fiscal policy of 'centralized fiscal revenues and expenditures', with all revenues being submitted to the central government and all spending being provided by central allocation of fiscal appropriations. The MoF started the preparation of the State Fiscal Budgets in 1950 to implement the centralized economic and fiscal administration. All governmental and public institutions (even business enterprises) were treated as budgetary units as their revenues and expenditures had to be determined through the comprehensive budgets set out by the MoF in central government. To satisfy the needs of budgetary control by the central government, in December 1950 the MoF issued the Provisional Comprehensive Budgetary Accounting System for Governments and the Budgetary Accounting System for Budgetary Units of Governments at Varied Levels, and regulated the accounting work for all governments and their subordinate organizations in the country, representing the instalment of nationwide budgetary accounting in the public sector. In 1953 the MoF revamped the budgetary accounting systems and methods by adopting Soviet models and implemented the Uniform Chart of Accounts and Uniform Format of Accounting Reports, with a few amendments in 1954 and 1956. Thus, the chart of account, bookkeeping methods, and format and content of accounting reports (including some statistical data) for all governmental organizations and public institutions were uniformly specified by the MoF to meet the needs of preparing, executing and evaluating the state comprehensive budgets. In fact, Chinese governmental accounting practice and its reporting format and content were substantially different from those in governmental accounting in Western countries during this period, but, in general, the budgetary accounting systems ran relatively smoothly to serve the government's centralized economic planning and administration.

China took a 'Great Leap Forward' in 1958 in order to achieve unrealistic growth goals. Under the influence of overheated growth ideology and a break away from the former Soviet Union (i.e. abandoning Soviet influences), governmental accounting work was disrupted, as many accounting setups were dismantled and accountants were dismissed; the idea of 'accounting without books' was even proposed. The central government's fiscal control was delegated to lower authorities, and budgetary accounting could no longer be executed effectively. The chaos in governmental accounting was ended when the Chinese government revised the development policy and reemphasized the important role of accounting in economic growth in the early 1960s. The MoF convened the National Conference of Budgetary Accounting in 1965, aiming to restore the budgetary accounting systems in use before the 'Great Leap Forward' movement, with amendments to the Comprehensive Accounting System for Fiscal Organizations and the Accounting System for Governmental and Public Institutions and the implementation of the unique 'fund receive and payment' bookkeeping method in Chinese government accounting (Pu, 2003).

However, budgetary accounting in China was disrupted again in 1966 when the 'Cultural Revolution' started, which led to 10 years of chaos in all aspects of social and economic lives in China. Accounting work for governments and public institutions was severely damaged and accounting records and reports could barely be used in decision-making in governments and public institutions until 1978.

Reform of budgetary accounting (1979–2000)

The government ended the 'Cultural Revolution' in 1978 and introduced comprehensive economic and political reforms to transform the poorly performing centrally planned economy to a market-oriented one. With the 'splitting revenues and expenditures and segregating fiscal responsibilities' reform of fiscal administration, the local governments became the main budgetary control units, with corresponding fiscal administrative power and responsibility. Thus, significant amendments were made to the Comprehensive Budgetary Accounting

System, Accounting Systems for Government Organizations and the Accounting System for Public Institutions in 1983 and 1988, respectively, in order to accommodate the new fiscal administration systems being implemented. The Regulation on State Budgetary Administration and the Decisions on Tax Revenue-Sharing Fiscal Administrative System had been promulgated in 1991 and 1994, respectively, by the central government and related changes in Chinese budgetary accounting (including revision of the chart of accounts and accounting statement formats) had been adopted accordingly in the early 1990s.

China entered a period of market-oriented economic administration after 1993. The government's fiscal administrative system had again been significantly revamped, so the original budgetary accounting system for governments and public institutions became outdated. In particular, the People's Congress enacted the new Law on Budgets in March 1994 so the MoF had to initiate reform of budgetary accounting. With a few years of studies of historical experience and the progress of business accounting reform in China, as well as the international norms on government and public-sector accounting reforms, the MoF issued the Accounting Standards for Public Institutions (Provisional), the Accounting System for Public Institutions, the Comprehensive Fiscal Accounting System and the Accounting System for Governments in 1997 and 1998, laying out a new framework for accounting and reporting for governments and public-sector institutions that could satisfy the need for fiscal reform in the late 1990s. Thus, bookkeeping methods and formats of accounting statements in the public sector had all been significantly altered, including the re-adoption of 'debit and credit' bookkeeping method and the internationally accepted accounting statement formats, in light of the economic transition towards a market-oriented economy in China. Obviously, budgetary accounting reform in this period was a move to accommodate the external environmental changes, e.g. the progresses of comprehensive economic reforms in the country.

New round of governmental accounting reforms (2000–present)

The MoF initiated a joint study project with Hong Kong Polytechnic University, of Budgetary Accounting System Reforms for Chinese governments: From Cash Accounting Towards Accrual Accounting, in 2000, to embark a new round of reforms for accounting for governments and public institutions in China in light of the international accounting convergence (Lu and Liu, 2014). To establish the new regulatory framework for governmental and public-sector accounting, in August 2004 the MoF issued the Accounting System for Non-profit Organizations, which was the first accounting regulation for non-profit organizations in the public sector in China, with references to the experience of business accounting reforms in the country and the internationally accepted public-sector accounting practices. The Chinese central government set out the requirement to establish accounting standards for governments and public-sector institutions and to develop consolidated governmental financial statements in the 11th Five-year National Economic and Social Development Plans, released in 2006. The MoF then issued the drafts of Accounting System for Tertiary Institutions and Accounting System for Public Hospitals in 2009, and set the road map for building up the new governmental and public-sector accounting systems in China. The Decision on Significant Issues in Promoting Comprehensive Reforms by the Central Committee of the Chinese Communist Party in 2013 required specifically that experiments of preparing the balance sheet for central and local governments and governmental consolidated financial statements based on accrual accounting, as well as establishing cross-years budgetary balancing mechanism, should be carried out in the country.

In August 2014, an amendment to The Budget Act was approved by the national legislative authority, adding a new Article 97, which required all governments to prepare accrual-based consolidated financial statements to the corresponding legislatures to reflect the overall financial positions, operating results and long- and mid-term fiscal sustainability of governments at all administrative regions. The State Council approved the Reform Proposal for Accrual-based Governmental Consolidated Financial Reporting in China, prepared by the MoF in December 2014, which presents the timetable for setting a series of accounting standards for governments and public institutions in the following five to six years. On 23 October 2015, the minister of finance signed Instruction No. 78 to issue The Governmental Accounting Standards: Basic Standards, which went into effect on 1 January 2017. The promulgation of this new governmental accounting standard heralds the internationalization of Chinese governmental and public-sector accounting to adapt to changed economic and fiscal administrative systems, as well as changing governmental functions, in recent years. On 3 August 2016, the exposure draft of Governmental Accounting System: Chart of Accounts and Accounting Statements for Governments and Public Institutions was issued by the MoF for public consultation, revealing that the construction of new governmental and public-sector accounting systems, which are much in line with international standards, has entered a substantial development phase in China.

Conclusion

With a historical review, we can see that governmental accounting has been through a long and winding period of evolution in China. It is well recognized in the literature that ancient Chinese government accounting was very sophisticated (Chatfield, 1977). Substantial changes in governmental accounting occurred whenever there was a significant change in the political, economic and social environment. The root cause of governmental accounting reforms and development is the urgent need derived from environmental or institutional changes in China. There is an inheritance in the reform of Chinese governmental accounting in the long course of evolution, as the useful experiences are maintained while new or more advanced practices are continuously adopted to accommodate changing institutional demands, including accepting or adopting the successful governmental accounting practices in other countries, in particular the adoption of the international norms in the current economic transition towards a market-oriented economy in China. However, the adoption of international governmental accounting standards or norms should not just be a simple transplantation, as there are substantial differences between the political and economic environment and governmental institutions of China and those of other developed countries in the West. Even in the current course of internationalization of Chinese accounting, reforms of Chinese governmental and public-sector accounting must take into consideration the specific environmental and institutional settings in the country and the useful experiences and practices that have stemmed from a long history of evolution in China.

It is evident that the Chinese government is now actively promoting the reforms of governmental and public-sector accounting, and new accounting and reporting standards are being promulgated by reference to international norms for governments and public-sector institutions in China, which will substantially improve the practices of government accounting and promote the restructuring of the government's fiscal administration systems to facilitate the development of market-oriented economic transition in China.

Note

1 *The Rites of Zhou* is a comprehensive official text on bureaucracy and governing organizational theory, compiled by the *Duke of Zhou* in the *Zhou dynasty*, which has had a profound influence on subsequent dynasties in China.

References

Chatfield, M. (1977) *A History of Accounting Thought* (rev. ed.). Huntington, NY: Robert E. Krieger.

Chu, C. (1990) A survey of accounting practices in 1920–1949. *Correspondence on Finance and Accounting*, *1*, 61–66 (in Chinese).

Fang, Z.J. (2001) A historical review of the accountant assignment system in China. *Auditing Research*, *2*, 40–44 (in Chinese).

Fu, P. (1971) Governmental accounting in China during the Chou Dynasty (1122 B.C.–256 B.C.). *Journal of Accounting Research*, *9*(1), 40–51.

Guo, D.Y. (1999) *Textbook of Accounting History*, Volume 1 (in Chinese). Beijing: China Finance and Economics Press.

Li, B.Z. (1982a) Historical review of accounting in China, I. *Correspondence on Finance and Accounting*, *7*, 56–57 (in Chinese).

Li, B.Z. (1982b) Historical review of accounting in China, II. *Correspondence on Finance and Accounting*, *8*, 52–53 (in Chinese).

Li, B.Z. (1982c) Historical review of accounting in China, III. *Correspondence on Finance and Accounting*, *10*, 56–57 (in Chinese).

Li, J.F. (1999) *Governmental Accounting in China* (in Chinese). Xiamen: Xiamen University Publishing House.

Liu, W.W. (2009) A study on Chinese accounting history. *Journal of Tianjing University of Finance and Economics*, *2*, 56–63 (in Chinese).

Lu, J.W. and Liu, Z.K. (2014) The weak impetus phenomenon of governmental accounting reforms and its cause analysis. *Journal of China University of Mining* (Social Science version), *2*, 74–78 (in Chinese).

Pu, D.L. (2003) *Study on the Reforms and Development of Budgetary Accounting in China* (in Chinese). Changsha: Hunan University Publishing House.

Song, L.Z. (2009) *Study on Accounting Thoughts in the Republic of China (1912–1949)* (in Chinese). Wuhan: Wuhan University Publishing House.

Sun, B.Z. (1989) *History of Accounting Development* (in Chinese). Beijing: Guanming Daily Press.

13

Accounting for governments and organizations in the public sector in India[1]

Saleha B. Khumawala and Arpita Shroff

Introduction

With globalization of economies and the rising economic power and rapid growth in the developing world, accounting and financial reporting of public-sector entities has been of great current research interest. Literature to date has primarily focused on the private sector (corporate financial reporting systems) and examined the accounting systems in countries with market-oriented economies. The accounting systems of emerging markets such as India, China, Indonesia, Malaysia, Singapore and Thailand, while not fully in conformity with the International Accounting Standards (IAS/IFRS) set by the International Accounting Standards Board (IASB), or the Generally Accepted Accounting Principles in the United States (US GAAP), are sometimes more accurate[2] in the presentation of financial statements than many markets from developed countries owing to accounting practices that are more strictly regulated than those enforced by industrialized nations.

The relatively little research coverage on governmental accounting also has focused on the industrialized nations (Hardman, 1982; Luder, 1989). Most researchers have virtually ignored the governmental accounting systems in the emerging and developing countries, which is unfortunate because the emerging economies are the fastest growing economic segment of the world economy, and they also tend to have very large or dominant governmental entities. The accounting developments in the public sectors of these growing economies can therefore provide excellent material for research on this regard.

Despite rapid economic growth, the awareness of problems of public-sector accounting in developing countries has generally been lacking (Enthoven, 1988). For example, India's government did not establish its Government Accounting Standards Advisory Board until 2002, despite India being the second largest country in the world in terms of population (about 1.3 billion people).[3] India is indeed representative of South East Asian countries.[4] Unlike Western countries, its public sector (with a large number of governmental entities) is a very significant part of the Indian economy. Thus, government and public-sector accounting plays an important role in economic development in India.

The objective of this chapter is to provide an analysis of accounting for governments and organizations in the public sector in India. First, the scope of the public sector of India is defined. The public sector encompasses the central government (the equivalent of the US federal government), state governments, union territories, government agencies and departments, public-sector enterprises (PSEs) and non-governmental organizations such as hospitals and schools.[5]

The progressive stages of economic development and reforms in India are also discussed as they are relevant and can form an underlying premise for governmental accounting standards and practices. In addition, a brief history of India is provided since its cultural and political heritage has influenced not only the governance structure but also the accounting and financial reporting of governmental entities. The rest of this chapter is organized as follows.

The second section briefly traces the development of governmental accounting systems from before national independence to the current structure of governmental accounting. The third section describes public-sector undertakings in India while the fourth introduces the government accounting standards-setting bodies and the role of auditors in India. The fifth section elaborates the accounting policies and procedures in the public sector and discusses the accounting standards that must be followed in the preparation of the financial statements of governments and governmental entities. We also introduce the existing system of account classification, the proposed new accounting systems in the public sector and the underlying reasons why it must be amended. In the sixth section, we evaluate the compilation of the financial reports of the central public-sector enterprises (CPSEs) administered at the union and state levels of government. A conclusion with a summary of our findings in comparison with developed countries (e.g. the USA) is presented in the seventh section.

History and structure of governmental accounting in India

The British-owned East India Company introduced international trade and commerce activities (including commercial accounting) to most parts of India in the seventeenth century. Thus, the strong common law-based accounting system still influences India. After national independence in 1947, India was constituted as a union of states, and it currently has 29 states and seven union territories. All states, as well as the union territories of Puducherry and the National Capital Territory of Delhi, have elected legislatures and governments, both patterned on the British Westminster model, with the governmental accounting systems being under the control of the executive branch of the central government. The beginning of India's highly stratified system was initiated by Article 150 of the Act of the Constitution, which granted the president and the comptroller and auditor general (CAG) the authority to set accounting standards. The Indian government then proceeded on a gradual basis to develop governmental accounting systems with an accompanying body of rules. The forms of accounts to be followed by all governmental entities were prescribed by the president on the recommendation of the CAG. Section 22 of the Act authorized the central government to develop guidance and rules regarding the maintenance of governmental accounts.

The conventional pattern of classification of accounts, which primarily ran along organizational lines, was followed by all governmental authorities. But, with phenomenal growth and diversity in the functions of governments, involving huge outlays of cash flows, the initial system of governmental accounts became outdated and irrelevant. The need for a more meaningful classification of transactions for the presentation of government operations in terms of functions, programmes and activities then emerged. Thus, in 1974–1975 the CAG, with the approval of the president, issued a revised classification of accounts for government transactions. Accordingly, the system was consolidated into three governmental funds: 1) the consolidated fund, 2) the contingency fund and 3) the public account fund.

Besides providing a uniform classification for government budgets, accounts and planning, the important objectives to be achieved under the revised classification of governmental accounts included: 1) presenting and compiling government expenditure clearly in terms of functions, programmes and activities irrespective of the administering organizations, 2) providing administrative authorities with timely and detailed financial data to help with monitoring and analysing expenditure on these pre-set activities and 3) facilitating the introduction of performance budgeting.

Major revisions were again made in 1976, in order to combine the accounting and administrative functions of the government's ministries and departments. The main objective was to integrate the accounting function with the administrative function of the ministries and departments so that the accounting and finance function would form an integral part of the overall government administration. As a result, the Department of Expenditures was created by the Ministry of Finance in 1980, under the controller general of accounts (CGA). This organization was then separated from the Audit Department and made to report directly to the CAG. As the centralized accounting authority, the CGA has responsibility for establishing and maintaining technically sound accounting systems in the departmentalized Accounts Office. On behalf of the functional departments within each ministry, the Department of Railways, Defence, Posts and Telecommunications, and union territory administrations, the CGA acts as the liaison between the Budget Division and the comptroller auditor general over all accounting matters.

Having long been under British rule, India follows the parliamentary system, by which the overall process of control over the fiscal administration of the government is threefold: 1) legislative control, 2) administrative control and 3) audit control.

Legislative control over the finance of the government is exercised primarily in two stages: in policymaking and in the implementation of the policy. The legislature controls the funding and determines not only the amount and the manner of raising resources (revenues or appropriations) but also how expenditures can be made. The initial control is exercised when the annual government budgets, more commonly known as annual financial statements, showing the estimated receipts and proposed expenditures for the fiscal year, are presented. The second stage of control is over the implementation of policies, which is exercised using a standardized set of parliamentary procedures and a system of committees.

Administrative control is exercised by holding government administration accountable to the legislature for inflows and outflows of funds. Similar accountability is carried out at each level of government in the hierarchy of delegation.

Audit control is carried out through: 1) fiscal accountability, which includes the stewardship of governmental funds and compliance with the related laws and regulations, 2) managerial accountability, which is concerned with the efficiency of the resources being employed and 3) programme accountability, which is to determine whether government programmes have achieved the objectives for which they were established.

Public-sector undertakings in India

India has established three tiers of governance, in which the union (i.e. the federal level) is at the top, followed by the states in the middle and the local governing bodies (namely the Panchayat Raj institutions and urban local bodies) are at the bottom level. As a developing country, the role of the government is pertinent at all levels. Accordingly, at each level, the government plays a substantial role in economic development and maintaining the welfare of citizens and residents directly, as well as indirectly through public-sector undertakings (PSUs). Appendix 1 provides a list of some typical PSUs at each governance level.

A PSU, a government undertaking, is defined as an enterprise for which the government (either union, state or local) owns a majority share of 51 per cent or more (as defined in Section 2(45) of the Companies Act, 2013). These PSUs can be classified as state public-sector enterprises (PSEs), central public-sector enterprises (CPSEs) and public-sector banks (PSBs).[6] The term CPSEs encompasses government-owned companies established under the Companies Act, 2013. The statutory corporations are CPSEs set up by a special Act of Parliament, which defines their powers and functions, rules and regulations governing their employees and their relationship with government departments. The performance of these entities is also consolidated with that of other CPSEs each year. Since these corporations are created by special legislation, they are autonomous in their functions and are fully funded by the central government. Not only do they have the power of the government but they also have a considerable amount of operating flexibility, similar to private companies. Appendix 2 lists some of the statutory corporations in India.

The PSUs were set up to create and maintain the infrastructure necessary for economic development, as well as to provide public services such as utilities, transportation, education, fresh air, clean water etc. From a mere five CPSEs in the first five-year plan after India's independence, the sector has grown to 260 CPSEs, amounting to a total investment of 13,33,261 crore Indian rupees (1 rupee = 0.02175 US dollar) as of 31 March 2015.[7] In 2012, the PSUs contributed 22 per cent of total Indian GDP.[8] The PSUs play a significant role in the industrial development of the country. Profitability is not the primary objective of the PSUs; their success is measured by the increase in economic development of the nation. One of the key objectives of the PSUs is to provide the government (central, state or local) the leverage to influence the economy (indirectly or directly) and to achieve its designated socio-economic development objectives. The PSUs also provide basic infrastructure services (roads, transportation, utilities, fresh water etc.) to citizens. On the other hand, the PSBs provide low- (or no-)interest funds to farmers to help develop the agricultural economy (the largest sector in India). In sum, the seventh largest economy in the world is significantly impacted by the investment and outreach of these governmental entities (CPSEs and PSBs).

Standards-setting bodies

The two primary standards-setting bodies that provide accounting policy guidance to the government of India are the Government Accounting Standards Advisory Board (GASAB or 'the board') and the Institute of Chartered Accountants of India (ICAI). While the ICAI mainly provides accounting guidance (standards and rules) for non-governmental entities, the primary purpose of the GASAB is to provide guidance to the Indian government and public-sector undertakings. The comptroller and auditor general of India (CAG) established the GASAB with the support of the Indian government on 12 August 2002. The board's mission is:

> to formulate and recommend Indian Government Accounting Standards (IGASs) for cash system of accounting and Indian Government Financial Reporting Standards (IGFRS) for accrual system of accounting, with a view to improving standards of Governmental accounting and financial reporting which will enhance the quality of decision-making and public accountability.

The composition and responsibilities of the GASAB are listed in Appendix 3.

Currently, the union, state and local governments follow cash-based accounting. The union government's financial statements are prepared by the controller general of accounts (CGA).

The CGA reports to the Ministry of Finance and is responsible for 'establishing and maintaining a technically sound management accounting system'. The accountant general (AGs) of each state prepares the financial statements for the state government.[9] The central government supports the state's operations and in return receives payments by way of dividends, interest on government loans and payment of taxes and duties.

The comptroller and auditor general of India (CAG) is the supreme audit institution of India. Its mission, mandated by the constitution of India, is to 'promote accountability, transparency and good governance through high quality auditing and accounting and provide independent assurance to our stakeholders, the Legislature, the Executives and the Public, that public funds are being used efficiently and for the intended purposes'.[10] The CAG is responsible for auditing the financial statements of the governments (union and state), as well as the PSUs.[11] Furthermore, the CAG is also responsible for combining the annual finance and revenue accounts of the union and state governments. Their final annual report 'incorporates comparable information relating to the accounts of the Union and all the States for a year, together with their balances and outstanding liabilities and other information relating to the financial health of the Union and the States' (http://cag.gov.in). The CAG also prepares the annual 'appropriation accounts and finance accounts' for all 29 states in India. Appropriation accounts are a grant-wise tabulation of the final appropriated amounts and actual expenditures against that, with justifications for savings or deficits. Appendix 4 states the duties powers of the CAG.

Accounting policies and procedures for governments and public-sector undertakings

The fiscal year end for all government entities in India is 31 March. On 12 August 2002, the government of India voted to set up an advisory board for governmental accounting (the GASAB). The government's objective in setting up the board was to 'keep pace with international trends'. The board's priorities are to 'focus on good governance, fiscal prudence, efficiency and transparency in public spending . . . and migration from cash to accrual-based system of accounting'.

In this section, we discuss some of the significant accounting policies and procedures currently employed in the preparation of financial statements by governments (state and union). We will also discuss the board's proposed accounting standards, which are based on the accrual method, as consistent to the international trend of governmental accounting reforms.

Indian Government Accounting Standards (IGAS)

The Indian Government Accounting Standards (IGAS) were formulated by the GASAB for cash-based accounting and are mandatory for all government entities. IGAS provides detailed guidance on the recognition, measurement and disclosure of various elements in the preparation of annual financial statements for the union, state and union territory governments. In particular, the IGAS specify the objective, scope and definitions of the terms included in the standards: recognition, measurement and valuation, disclosure, effective date and format of disclosure. These standards are established to ensure that all government bodies follow uniform accounting practices to enhance the comparability of their financial statements. The GASAB, since its inception in 2002, has issued six Indian Government Accounting Standards, three of which were approved by the central government between 2010 and 2012. The remaining three have been approved by the board but have not yet been approved by central government. The objective and scope of the six standards approved by the board are provided below:

1   IGAS 1 – The objective and scope of this first standard is to set out disclosure norms in respect of guarantees given by the governments in their respective financial statements to ensure uniform and complete disclosure of such guarantees. Hence, this standard is applicable to the preparation of the Statement of Guarantees, which must be included in the financial statements of all three levels of government in India. This accounting standard was published on 20 December 2010.

2   IGAS 2 – The second accounting standard provides guidance on accounting and classi-fication of the grants-in-aid section of the financial statements for the government, as both the grantor and the grantee.[12] Similar to the first government accounting standard, it is mandatory for the union government and all state governments to prepare the grants-in-aid section of their financial reports in accordance with the format of disclosure requirements being provided. This accounting standard was published on 19 May 2011.

3   IGAS 3 – The objective of this governmental accounting standard is to provide guidance for the recognition, measurement, valuation and reporting of loans and advances made by the union and state governments. This applies to all loans, including loans to other governing agencies, local bodies and private companies, nationally as well as internationally. This governmental accounting standard was published on 13 February 2012.

4   IGAS 7 – This standard provides guidance for accounting and the disclosure of transactions in foreign currencies, reporting of losses and gains due to exchange rate variation and the disclosure of foreign currency external debts and rates applied therein.

5   IGAS 9 – This standard provides guidance for the recognition, measurement and reporting of equity investment made by governments in the investee entities.

6   IGAS 10 – The objective of this standard is to lay down the accounting principles for the measurement, recognition and disclosure of public debts and other obligations of the governments in the preparation of their financial statements.

Accounting policies

The government of India currently follows cash-based accounting, whereby transactions in government accounts represent actual cash receipts and disbursements during a fiscal year, instead of the amounts due to or owed by the government during the same period. The accounts are kept in three main funds:

1   The consolidated fund – established under Article 266(1) of the constitution of India.

   i   Revenue – taxes, fines, public services etc.
   ii   Receipts – loans raised by the issue of treasury bills, internal and external loans etc.
   iii Expenditures – loan repayments.

2   The contingency fund – The contingency fund, established under Article 267(1) of the constitution, is in the

   nature of an imprest placed at the disposal of the President to enable him/her to make advances to meet urgent unforeseen expenditure, pending authorization by the Parliament. Approval of the Legislature for such expenditure and for withdrawal of an equivalent amount from the Consolidated Fund is subsequently obtained, whereupon the advances from the Contingency Fund are recouped to the Fund.

3   The public fund – for transactions relating to debt (other than those included in Part I) and the 'deposits', 'advances', 'remittances' and 'suspense' accounts are recorded.

Proposed standards: Indian Government Financial Reporting Standards (IGFRS)[13]

To be consistent with the recent international trend of governmental accounting reform, the Indian government has recently commenced the move towards governmental accounting systems with accrual-based accounting. The GASAB states that:

> However, there is a much felt need for accounting framework and accounting standards on the accrual base to facilitate pilot studies and research efforts on migration to accrual accounting at Union and State level. To facilitate pilot studies and for scale up of activities, GASAB has taken a decision to develop accrual-based accounting standards alongside cash- based standards. The accrual-based standards are issued under the title of 'Indian Government Financial Reporting Standards' (IGFRSs).

The board is working towards migrating to an accrual-based accounting system for the governments. To date, it has already approved the following five accrual-based accounting standards, which are pending approval from the president of India:

IGFRS 1 (*Presentation of Financial Statements*)
IGFRS 2 (*Property, Plant and Equipment*)
IGFRS 3 (*Revenue from Government Exchange Transactions*)
IGFRS 4 (*Inventories*)
IGFRS 5 (*Contingent Liabilities (other than guarantees) and Contingent Assets: Disclosure Requirements*)

In addition, the board has issued an exposure draft in June 2012 that was titled *Accounting Policies, Changes in Accounting Estimates and Errors*.[14]

Financial reporting practices

Union and state governments

Central government: The financial statements of the union government are jointly compiled by the controller general of accounts and the secretary to the government of India, Ministry of Finance and Department of Expenditure. The comptroller and auditor general of India (CAG) has the obligation of auditing and certifying these statements in accordance with the requirements of Articles 149 and 151 of the constitution of India and the Comptroller and Auditor General's (Duties, Powers and Conditions of Service) Act, 1971. The final accounts of the union government present the receipts and disbursements for the purpose of the union government. The financial reports include revenues, capital accounts, public debts, liabilities and assets. The report also includes a section on the appropriation account for grants and charge appropriations. The financial reports are prepared in accordance with the Indian Government Accounting Standards discussed in the earlier section.

State governments: The financial statements of the state governments are prepared by the accountant general (A&E) of the state in accordance with the standards formulated by the GASAB. Their finance accounts come in two volumes. Volume I contains several statements that depict the financial position (e.g. the balance sheet) of the state government, including the notes to the accounts. Volume II contains statements such as borrowings and liabilities, loans and advances extended, guarantees given, investments, capital, revenue and expenditure etc. Both of these annual accounts must be laid before the state legislature for approval.

Public-sector undertakings

Central level: The CAG is responsible for the compilation and audit of the financial statements of *all* public-sector enterprises at the union level. We examined the report of the CAG for the fiscal year ending 31 March 2015. This report was prepared by the CAG based on the financial reports provided by each entity. In the referenced fiscal year, there were 564 central public-sector enterprises (CPSEs).[15] These enterprises were required to prepare and submit their financial statements in accordance with the format specified in Schedule III to the Companies Act, 2013, and in adherence to the IGAS set out above. The statutory corporations are required to prepare their accounts in the format prescribed by the rules, framed in consultation with the CAG and any other specific provision relating to accounts in the Companies Act governing such corporations.[16] These submitted financial reports must be audited by statutory auditors appointed by the CAG. The CAG Report (2014–2015) starts with an executive summary regarding a comprehensive report of the performance of those CPSEs. The highlight of this summary section describes the impact of the introduction of the three-phase audit of accounts of public entities, which contained the CAG's interim feedback to the entities. This led to a net impact of 8,387.82 crore Indian rupees on profitability and 16,394.97 crore Indian rupees on assets/liabilities. The pie chart below provides a summary of government investment in the 156 other government-controlled companies. The equity increased to 29,786 crore Indian rupees in 2014–2015 compared to the investment of *Rs.* 2 7,001 in the previous year.[17]

The chart below provides a comparative analysis of the value, production and capital employed by CPSEs in the past three years.

State level: The auditor general of each state and the CAG jointly compile and audit the financial reports of all public-sector entities administered at the state level. We examine the recent (fiscal year 2013–2014) report of the comptroller and auditor general of India on public-sector undertakings,[18] which encompasses the audit results of 80 governmental companies and four statutory corporations.[19] In the same vein as the union-level report, the accounts of governmental companies are audited by the statutory auditors appointed by the CAG. The companies must adhere to the Indian Governmental Accounting Standards. As a result of the audits, only 46 companies received an unqualified audit statement. The report provides

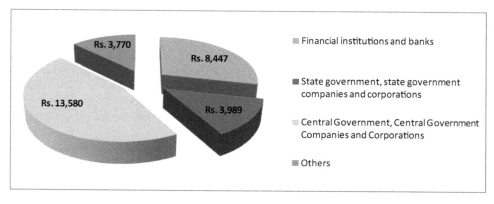

Figure 13.1 Composition of share capital in government-controlled other companies

Source: CAG Annual Report #9 – General purpose financial reports of CPSEs, page 7.

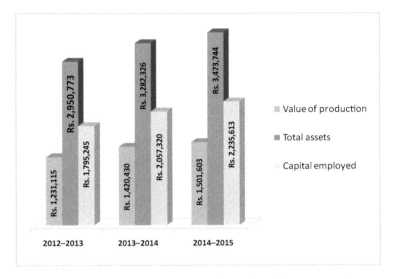

Figure 13.2 Value of production, assets and capital employed (crore rupees)
Source: CAG Annual Report #9 – General purpose financial reports of CPSEs, page 14

an in-depth analysis of the use of public funds and the deficiencies in the public services. The report also highlights some significant errors in reconciling the outstanding loans and guarantees in the state financial accounts and the financial reports of PSUs. The summary of the combined financial performance of the PSUs is that only 46 PSUs reported a profit, netting 3,363.96 crore rupees, whereas 20 PSUs incurred losses of 1,111.85 crore rupees in the fiscal year.

Conclusion

The GASAB was formed in 2002 and it has since approved six Indian Governmental Accounting Standards. Of these six standards, the central government has since endorsed only three standards. As a result, the GASAB has a long road ahead in terms of formulating a complete set of standards for the governments in India. In comparison, since its inception in 1984, the Governmental Accounting Standards Board (GASB) in the United States of America has issued six concept statements, 82 accounting standards, six interpretations and numerous technical bulletins.

On the recommendation of the Indian government, over the last three to four years the GASAB has undertaken the mammoth task of developing a new governmental accounting framework and accounting standards on an accrual basis to help migrate the Indian governmental financial reporting from cash-based to accrual-based, and there has been modest progress on formulating a comprehensive set of accrual-based governmental accounting standards in India.

In our study of the financial reports provided by the CAG at the union and state levels, we conclude that the transparency of financial reporting for governments and public-sector undertakings has come a long way in the past decade. However, a significant number of

PSUs in India have still not completely submitted their annual financials as required. We did not further explore the legal consequences of this deficiency in the comparison of the financial reporting practices over recent years, but we have witnessed a certain improvement in governmental accounting and reporting very recently. We anticipate that there will be a substantial improvement in the governance and financial reporting of these public-sector undertakings so long as the government of India and the GASAB continue to commit to and pursue the international trend of accounting and reporting reforms for governments and public-sector institutions in the coming decade.

Appendix 1 – Three levels of Government in India

1   Union – The union (i.e. the central government) consists of several administrative ministries and other public-sector units (PSUs), including:

       i   Agriculture and rural development
      ii   Art, culture and sports
     iii   Commercial
      iv   Communications and IT
       v   Education, health and family welfare
      vi   Defence and national security
     vii   Taxes and duties
    viii   Industry and commerce
      ix   Information and communication
       x   Post and telegraph
      xi   Power and energy
     xii   Railways
    xiii   Social welfare
     xiv   Social infrastructure
      xv   Science
     xvi   Transport and infrastructure

2   State – There are 29 states and each one has one or more PSUs similar to the union's, albeit at the state level.
3   Local – Local governing bodies include:

       i   Panchayat Raj institutions
      ii   Rural local bodies
     iii   Urban local bodies

Appendix 2 – Partial list of statutory corporations in India

- Airports Authority of India (www.aai.aero)
- National Highways Authority of India (www.nhai.org)
- Food Corporation of India (fciweb.nic.in)
- National Human Rights Commission (www.nhrc.nic.in)
- Central Warehousing Corporation (cewacor.nic.in)
- Damodar Valley corporation (www.dvcindia.org)
- Inland Waterways Authority of India (www.iwai.gov.in)

Appendix 3 – the Government Accounting Standards Advisory Board (GASAB)[20]

Structure of the board

The board has high-level representation from the senior accounting heads in government, such as the Ministry of Finance, the Department of Post, the finance secretaries of states, the RBI and heads of premier accounting and research organizations. The board's composition includes the following members:

1. Deputy comptroller and auditor general (government accounts) as the chairperson
2. Financial commissioner, railways
3. Member (finance) telecom commission, Department of Telecom
4. Secretary, Department of Post
5. Controller general of defence accounts
6. Controller general of accounts
7. Additional/joint secretary (budget), Ministry of Finance, government of India
8. Deputy governor, Reserve Bank of India or his nominee
9–12. Principal secretary (finance) of four states by rotation
13. Director general, National Council of Applied Economic Research (NCAER), New Delhi
14. President, Institute of Chartered Accountants of India (ICAI) or his nominee
15. President, Institute of Cost and Works Accountants of India
16. Principal director of the GASAB as member secretary.

Responsibilities of the board

1. To formulate and improve the standard of government accounting and financial reporting in order to enhance accountability mechanisms.
2. To formulate and propose standards that should improve the usefulness of financial reports based on the users' needs.
3. To keep the standards current and reflect changes in the governmental environment.
4. To provide guidance on the implementation of the governmental accounting standards.
5. To review and consider significant areas of accounting and financial reporting that can be improved through the standard-setting process.
6. To improve common understanding of the nature and purpose of information contained in the financial reports.

Appendix 4 – Duties and powers of the CAG (comptroller and auditor general of India)

The Comptroller and Auditor General's (Duties, Powers and Conditions of Service) Act, 1971, authorized some important duties of the CAG:

- To compile the financial statements of the union, states and union territories. To report the financial results directly to the head of each level government (e.g. the president and the governors).

- To be responsible for all audit requirements with respect to the government and the public-sector units.
- To jointly compile and audit the financial reports of all public-sector entities at the state level.
- To compile the financial accounts of the union government by presenting the receipts and the disbursements for the purpose of the union.
- The CAG has the power to audit all receipts of all governments in India. The CAG also has the power to demand reconciliation of the loans provided by the central government to the state/local governments.
- The CAG has the power to audit the grants or loans given to other authorities or bodies.

Notes

1 We gratefully acknowledge the assistance of Chandra Mauli Singh, Indian consul general, and Anupam Ray.
2 Karmin (2002), along with the CLSA Emerging Markets survey, presented empirical evidence regarding improved accuracy in Asian accounting systems over those of the United States.
3 http://countrymeters.info/en/India, accessed 10 September 2016.
4 Prior to independence from the British in 1947, 'British India' comprised what is presently Pakistan, India and Bangladesh.
5 Public-sector enterprises (PSEs) are grouped into one of three categories: 1) departmentally managed PSEs, which form part and parcel of government activities, 2) a government company registered and incorporated under the Companies Act of 1956 and 3) a statutory corporation that is not a government company though all the shares in it are held and owned by the government. These are corporations, as distinguished from government companies, and are incorporated under separate Acts of Parliament.
6 In this chapter we use the term PSU and PSE interchangeably.
7 Financial performance of CPSEs: www.cag.gov.in/sites/default/files/audit_report_files/Chapter_1-%20 Report%20No.%209%20of%202016.pdf (accessed 10 February 2016).
8 https://data.gov.in (accessed 15 July 2016).
9 Based on 2016 data, India comprises 29 states and seven union territories
10 http://cag.gov.in/content/our-vision-mission-and-values (accessed 1 August 2016).
11 All these documents are available on the CAG website, http://cag.gov.in (accessed 1 August 2016).
12 Grants-in-aid are defined in the standard as the 'payments in the nature of assistance, donations or contributions made by one Government to another Government body, institution or individual for the specified purpose of supporting the institution or individual'. Such grants can be in cash or kind.
13 http://gasab.gov.in/gasab/igfrs.aspx (accessed 6 August 2016).
14 http://gasab.gov.in/gasab/pdf/Accrual_Exposure_Draft6.pdf (accessed 6 August 2016).
15 Included in the report are 365 government companies and corporations (including six statutory corporations) and 156 government-controlled other companies. Forty-nine companies whose accounts were in arrears for three years or more or were defunct/under liquidation are not included in the report. Out of 564 CPSEs, annual accounts for the year 2014–2015 were received from 483 CPSEs in time (i.e. by 30 September 2015). Of these, the accounts of 277 CPSEs were reviewed in audit.
16 Examples of statutory corporations are: the Airport Authority of India, the National Highways Authority of India, the Inland Waterways Authority of India, the Food Corporation of India etc.
17 Company details are available on CAG website, www.saiindia.gov.in (accessed 6 August 2016).
18 We could not find any public record of the financial report for year 2014–2015.
19 The four statutory corporations are the Gujarat Industrial Development Corp., the Gujarat State Road Transportation Corp., the Gujarat State Warehousing Corp. and the Gujarat State Financial Corp.
20 http://gasab.gov.in/gasab/about.aspx (accessed 6 August 2016).

References

Enthoven, A.J.H. (1988) The future of international standards in government accounting. *Advances in International Accounting*, 2, 207–230.

Hardman, D.J. (1982) Models of government accounting. In *Government Accounting and Budgeting*. Sydney: Prentice-Hall.

Karmin, C. (2002) Asian firms avoid U.S.-style accounting woes. *The Wall Street Journal*, 29 May 2002, p. C14.

Luder, K.G. (1989) *Comparative Governmental Accounting Study*. Speyerer Forschungsberichte.

Public information websites from the government of India referenced:

Comptroller and auditor general of India: http://cag.gov.in.

The controller general of accounts (Ministry of Finance): www.cga.nic.in/forms/Publication.aspx.

Archives of documents of the government of India: www.archive.india.gov.in/spotlight/spotlight_archive.php?id=78.

Department of Public Enterprises: http://dpe.nic.in/publications/pesurvey_2011-12.

Public-sector undertakings: http://business.mapsofindia.com/sectors/public/ (accessed 6 August 2016).

14

Public-sector accounting practices and reforms in Nepal

Pawan Adhikari

Introduction

In the aftermath of the New Public Management (NPM) movement, public-sector accounting has become a fertile ground for critical and interpretative researchers (Adhikari and Gårseth-Nesbakk, 2016). The key issue of the NPM reforms is the move away from cash accounting while adopting various forms of accrual accounting at different administrative levels (Guthrie *et al.*, 1999). The importance of accrual accounting is predicated on its ability to engender more comprehensive information for financial decision-making and to promote efficiency, effectiveness and transparency in public service delivery (IFAC, 2011; PwC, 2013; Carlin, 2005). Literature has brought about the efforts of many Western countries to streamline their accounting practices and the varied paths and paces that they have adopted in embarking towards accrual accounting in the public sector (Ezzamel *et al.*, 2014; Hyndman and Connolly, 2011).

There has in recent years been a steady upsurge in the volume of public-sector accounting literature delineating the attempts made by many developing countries to embrace globalized accounting techniques such as International Public Sector Accounting Standards (IPSAS) and accrual accounting (Lassou and Hopper, 2016; Goddard *et al.*, 2015; Harun *et al.*, 2012). Prior studies on public-sector accounting in developing countries are, however, narrowly focused in that they are primarily unfolding the adoption of globalized public sector reforms in the specific contexts of developing countries, and the challenges that these countries are encountering in implementing those reforms (Adhikari *et al.*, 2013). Less attention has been paid to unveiling how public-sector accounting is practised, accountability rendered and reform ideas articulated in developing countries. However, such a comprehensive insight into public-sector accounting in developing countries is paramount at present, given that so much effort and so many resources are being spent in the reconstruction of accounting and accountability in these countries, mainly by international monetary organizations such as the World Bank, the Asian Development Bank (ADB) and the International Monetary Fund (IMF) (Adhikari and Mellemvik, 2011). Improved accounting has become a key ingredient of the public finance reform agenda of these international organizations, through which they intend to improve governance and accountability and stimulate economic growth in developing countries (Allen, 2009). By examining the three aspects of government accounting in Nepal, i.e. contemporary practice, accountability mechanisms, and the way the reform ideas are being articulated, this chapter intends to fill the perceived lacuna in the public-sector accounting literature.

The chapter draws on the perspective of accounting as a social and institutional practice entailing three interrelated approaches – accounting as a technology, the rationales of accounting and the domain of accounting (Miller, 1994). The essence of this perspective is its ability to address the multifaceted picture of accounting practice, the way accountability is maintained and the manner in which new accounting ideas are circulated within a country (Potter, 2005). Moreover, this perspective of accounting as a social and institutional practice has proved to be valuable in elucidating how the context in which accounting is enmeshed has led to diversity in accounting practices despite the adoption of similar globalized accounting thought (Miller, 1994; Timoshenko and Adhikari, 2009).

The remainder of this chapter is structured as follows. The second section elaborates in detail the perspective of accounting as a social and institutional practice. Thereafter, an observation of public-sector accounting in Nepal is presented in the third section, covering its accounting practices, existing accountability patterns and the changes that are being proposed and carried out. The fourth section analyses and then draws conclusions on how the use of the perspective of accounting as a social and institutional practice has contributed to a better understanding of the multifaceted aspects of Nepalese public-sector accounting and its ongoing reforms.

The perspective of accounting as a social and institutional practice

This chapter aims at providing an understanding of how accounting as a social and institutional practice can contribute to generating more complete and comprehensive knowledge about the application of accounting within a particular organizational context, with implications for governance, accountability and dissemination of new accounting thought (Miller and O'Leary, 1987; Hopwood, 1990). Miller (1994) outlines three distinctive aspects of the view of accounting as a social and institutional practice, i.e. accounting as a technology, the rationales of accounting and the domain of accounting. Potter (2005) further discussed the pertinence of these distinctive aspects to provide a broader understanding of the application of accounting practice and the ways in which accounting practices enable the governance of people, processes and societies. Presenting the case of Nepal, this chapter should make a further contribution to the public-sector accounting literature, drawing on these three aspects of accounting as a social and institutional practice.

Accounting as a technology

Miller (1994, p. 2) emphasizes accounting as a technique/technology in that it offers 'a way of intervening, a device for acting upon activities, individuals and objects in such a way that the world may be transformed'. The underlying idea is that accounting technologies facilitate the governance of people, organizations and societies by transforming economic and financial activities into numbers and portraying them in the form of standardized reports (Miller and O'Leary, 1987; McKernan, 2007). In the public sector, the budget system has been suggested to be an indispensable part of accounting technology on the grounds of its ability to control individuals and their activities in a particular organizational manner (Timoshenko and Adhikari, 2009). Government plans and policies, which are represented in the budgets, are made visible to the public through the assignment of numbers to each event and activity, i.e. through the application of accounting (Caiden and Wildavsky, 1974). Given this close relationship between accounting and budgeting, public-sector accounting has often been referred to in the literature as 'budgetary accounting' (Lüder and Jones, 2003). This extensive focus on budgetary control is also reckoned to be a factor, which has led to budgets being central to the financial and administrative control in many Western governments. Moreover, with the exception of the UK, Australia and New Zealand, most countries that have embarked on accrual accounting and reporting reforms in their public sectors have continued to use traditional cash basis budgets, signalling the importance of budgetary control in the political negotiation process (Adhikari and Gårseth-Nesbakk, 2016).

The rationales of accounting

Miller (1994) states that accounting practices are not confined to numerical computation of profits and losses, but are also inherited through discursive representations and vocabularies, symbolizing, amongst other things, costliness, efficiency, decision-making, accountability and transparency. The appreciation of such rationales is argued to be imperative in that they can provide an insight into the articulation of a particular accounting technique in a specific organizational setting (Potter, 2005). The notion of democratic accountability is probably one of the most important rationales in the public sector in terms of which public-sector entities are to be restructured and which individuals controlled (Timoshenko and Adhikari, 2009). The whole idea behind democratic accountability, especially in developing countries, is that public money should not be misappropriated and misused. In many countries that have embraced a parliamentary form of democracy, e.g. the UK and India, money can only be issued out of the consolidated fund with specific statutory authority, i.e. annual budgets (Jones, 2012), which must be presented to the parliament and codified in law, i.e. through an appropriation act, once they receive parliamentary approval. It is for this reason that the cash basis of accounting has remained a preferred technique for many governments, not least in the developing world but also in some developed countries, for instance in Germany, Austria, and Norway (Adhikari and Gårseth-Nesbakk, 2016). One of the essences of cash basis accounting is that it enables governments to secure parliamentary (i.e. democratic) accountability by assuring the legislative branch that no money has been collected and spent in ways and amounts other than those approved through budget appropriations (Barton, 2007).

The domain of accounting

Miller (1994) has given special attention to the domain in which accounting is implicated and the way such a domain is (re)constituted in an attempt to define accounting as a social and institutional practice. Potter (2005, p. 272) states that this acknowledgement of the pertinence of accounting domain has resulted in the emergence of two categories of accounting research, one focusing on the implications of changing the accounting domain and another exploring the processes that lead to a change of the domain in a particular context. The former is mainly concerned with the manner in which the actions of individuals are brought into a specific calculative regime through the use of certain accounting practices/technologies. The underlying idea is that a change in accounting practice, i.e. accounting domain, is often meant to shift the forms of discussion and debate that accompany organizational and social action, providing an alternative way of measuring and restructuring organizational actions (Miller, 1994). The changing nature of the accounting domain has led to another stream of research examining the process through which the domain of accounting is reconstructed in a specific context. It is argued that a particular accounting practice and rationale may, over time and space, turn out be problematic, creating an avenue for new accounting technologies to evolve in the resolution of these problems. In the context of developing countries, the process of problematizing accounting practice can be externally driven. Studies drawing on the neo-institutional perspective have for instance demonstrated that resource providers such as the World Bank and the IMF tend to problematize the existing cash accounting of developing countries using various mechanisms, indicating coercive, mimetic and normative mechanisms (Adhikari *et al.*, 2013).

To sum up, accounting technologies are important in the sense that they provide a means for making individuals and activities calculable and accountable, without which governance is simply not possible (Miller, 1994). Accounting practices, however, depend on rationales, implying that different rationales will appeal for different ways of mobilizing calculative practices. As stated by Burchell *et al.* (1980, 1985), one reason why accounting systems function diversely across varied contexts despite the adoption of similar reforms across organizations/countries is anchored on analogous rhetoric such as efficiency, rationality and relevance. Moreover, both accounting technologies/practices and rationales tend to constitute and reconstitute over time. We thus argue that the synthesis of the three interrelated approaches to accounting, embedded within the notion of accounting as a social and institutional practice, will enable us to examine Nepalese public-sector accounting practice, accountability and the adoption of reforms from a broader perspective.

Observation of public-sector accounting in Nepal

Research method: a triangulation approach

We adopt a triangulation approach to data collection for the study of public-sector accounting in Nepal, encompassing document analysis, semi-structured interviews, and observation. At the outset, accounting regulations and reports issued by government agencies and international organizations regarding various aspects of Nepalese public-sector accounting and recommending changes were all reviewed. Thereafter we conducted informal interviews with 20 Nepalese public-sector accountants at the Financial Comptroller General Office (FCGO), a key organ for government and public-sector accounting in Nepal. During the interviews, those government accountants were requested to comment on three main issues: 1) the objectives of the Nepalese government and public-sector accounting; 2) the way accounting is practised and accountability discharged; and 3) the manner in which new accounting ideas have been proposed and changes have taken place in Nepalese public-sector accounting. Upon the requests of the respondents, the assurance of anonymity has been preserved when we present their statements. In addition, an author was allowed to observe the activities of the FCGO, as well as the day-to-day operations of Nepalese public-sector accounting for a week in late 2015. This observation is valuable, not only in ensuring the reliability and authenticity of the interview data but also in extending an understanding of how accounting is currently being practised in the Nepalese government and the public sector. Having completed the observation, the obtained data were grouped into the three major themes of this study – accounting practice, accountability mechanism and accounting changes – so as to provide a much clearer picture of Nepalese public-sector accounting. Narratives were then constructed and attempts were made to interlink them with the theoretical perspective applied.

Prevailing public-sector accounting practices

Miller (1994) mentioned that the use of a particular accounting technology is meant to quantify events and activities that are pertinent to a specific organizational setting. Those events and activities that have been made visible using accounting technologies are important as they provide a mechanism for acting upon individuals and entities, i.e. for controlling and transforming them (Potter, 2005; Timoshenko and Adhikari, 2009). In the context of the public sector in Nepal, the use of accounting technologies is apparently intended to underpin the implementation of annual budgets. The budgets have remained a key instrument in the Nepalese public sector since the 1960s in terms of facilitating day-to-day activities, maintaining control over bureaucrats and discharging accountability to the legislative authority in the country.

The operation of government funds and budget implementation are mandated by the financial regulations of the 2015 constitution of Nepal and the 2007 Financial Procedures Rules (FPR). The constitution and the FPR demand that each government transaction be channelled through the consolidated fund. The FCGO is the custodian of the consolidated fund. The local branches of this office are referred to as the 'district treasury control offices' (DTCOs) at jurisdictional district levels. Money collected in the form of revenues, loans and loan repayments, except those from religious endowments, is directly credited to this fund. Similarly, expenditures incurred from the consolidated fund are represented in the annual budgets of government entities, which requires parliamentary approval. Money not spent during the budget year cannot be carried forward to subsequent years and must be paid back into the consolidated fund. The operation of the consolidated fund by the government of Nepal is clearly analogous to many other countries, in particular those that have been influenced by Westminster-style financial administration, such as India and Sri Lanka. An important aspect of the financial regulations incorporated in the Nepalese constitution and the FPR is, however, the requirement that the results of spending in the previous year should be reported in parallel to the budget requests for the next year. A senior accountant at the FCG commented on this requirement:

> We need to forward our budget request for the next year with the accounts of whether the targeted objectives set for the current year are likely to be achieved. The problem is how we would know whether we will be able to meet the targets without even spending the allocated budget.

During the interviews, several government accountants mentioned that an assurance of budget spending and compliance is crucial in order to be eligible for an annual increment to their budget allocation. The fact that the performance evaluation of public-sector entities and accountants is based on their success in spending the budgeted appropriations and maintaining budgetary compliance has resulted in public-sector accountants rushing with the budget release as well as its implementation, particularly in the last few months of the fiscal year. Claims have been made that money is often released to projects/programmes without adherence to procedure, and that accounts of such expenditures have been kept without adequate supporting evidence, e.g. receipts and contracts (Government of Nepal, 2008). Such accounts lacking supporting evidence are termed irregularities, which is evident in the annual auditor general's reports (AGO, 2014). In its fifty-first annual report, the AGO (2014) states that accounting irregularities have been increasing annually at a rate of 4 per cent. This was also evident in the following statement of a public-sector accountant at the FCGO:

Sometimes the budgets are realised to activities and projects only six months from the commencement of the fiscal year. Accountants had to release the money to the concerned offices and programmes even though they knew that these offices had not adhered to the budgetary guidance such as inviting contractors to bid for services, etc. Otherwise, the whole budgeted fund would have remained unspent.

The extensive focus on the approved budget, and the established perception that accounting is considered an element of budgetary control system rather than an independent discipline, has been argued to be a key factor stifling the development of the public-sector accounting system in Nepal (Adhikari and Mellemvik, 2011). There is a lack of clarity over whether budget implementation would be impaired if there were no adequate accounting system to represent the results and outputs of expenditures and to measure the performance of accountants based on their capacity to engender outputs rather than to incur budget inputs. The new budgetary measures introduced in recent years, for instance the Medium Term Expenditure Framework (MTEF), the Gender Responsive Budget (GRB) and the Climate Change Budget Code (CCBC), without parallel improvements in the supporting accounting systems, serve as evidence. A senior accountant at the FCGO, previously employed in a project management unit, commented on the donors' emphasis on budgetary reforms:

> Donors and international organisations often provide us with separate reporting requirements and ask for the auditing of their resources by independent auditors. Many of them have also established a separate unit for the implementation of the projects they have funded, as well as for adequate accounting and auditing of their resources. But they have neither asked for our accounting statements nor submitted their statements to the FCGO.

The role of accounting in the Nepalese public sector has been confined primarily to making budget implementation visible. As stated in the literature, such accounting representation has, however, been partial and biased in that it is aimed at ensuring the performance of accountants and spending units so that they continue to get a share of the annual budget increment. Accounting has been seen as an indispensable part of the budgets rather than an independent discipline, and such a lack of understanding can be observed regarding the capacity and use of accounting beyond budgetary compliance and implementation. Reforms in the budgeting process are envisaged as self-evident improvements in the accounting systems as part of a budgetary control. The fact that donors and international organizations have channelled almost 60 per cent of their grants and aid to this country through the budgets has led these donors and international organizations to pay increasing attention to budgetary reforms than to the improvements in accounting practice.

Discharging the accountability

An underling rationale for Nepalese public-sector accounting is to discharge the government's accountability to parliament as well as to international donor organizations for the use of resources obtained in the forms of loans, grants and aid. Various reports published over time have shown that almost 50 per cent of the Nepalese government development budgets in the 1990s were funded through external resources, accounting for over 10 per cent of the country's total GDP (ADB, 2005; World Bank, 2002; IMF, 2007). In the last few years, almost 25 per cent of total government expenditure has been funded through foreign grants and loans (MoF, 2015). Ensuring external accountability has therefore become a key concern of the Nepalese government, which has set out a range of new public-sector accounting reporting initiatives, including performance-oriented reporting, especially for those projects/programmes funded through development aid, grants and loans.

The government's internal accountability, i.e. its accountability to parliament, is discharged only after the auditor general's report on the FCGO's consolidated statements has been approved by parliament. Based on the views expressed by the interviewees, a key concern of the AGO's external auditing is to identify and provoke discussion of the budget variations, i.e. differences between the budgeted and actual expenditures and revenues, and irregularities. The fact that only irregularities will be brought up for discussion in parliament and its Public Accounts Committee (PAC), and covered by media, also signals the importance of budgetary compliance in discharging accountability (World Bank, 2002). The PAC will organize a separate meeting with the secretaries of each ministry after the issuance of the auditor general's report, and to scrutinize the budget variations and irregularities. The PAC is also authorized to provide parliament with an assurance that the ministries will undertake appropriate measures to settle their accumulated irregularities.

The fact that discharging accountability in the Nepalese public sector is concerned with avoiding irregularities and variations has led the accounting statements of every public entity to be scrutinized and consolidated at each successive level. In particular, public units are required to forward their monthly and annual budget statements to the respective departments, line ministries and DTCOs. The line ministries are required to prepare ministerial consolidated statements, amalgamating the reports of all their subordinate agencies and forwarding those reports to the Ministry of Finance (MoF), the respective DTCOs and the FCGO within four months of the fiscal year end. The ministerial consolidated statements, the so-called central-level accounts, consist of budget allocations, release of appropriations, expenditures and unspent money of all subordinate agencies. The DTCOs are mandated to maintain district-level accounting, which is concerned with accumulating the monthly statements of public entities operating under their jurisdiction, facilitating internal auditing so as to identify variations between the actual and budgeted expenditures, and preparing the monthly and annual consolidated statements for the jurisdictional district as a whole. Such integrated district reports are to be forwarded to the FCGO, line ministries and the AGO on a monthly and an annual basis. The underlying justification is that the FCGO should reconcile the consolidated statements it receives from the line ministries and DTCOs prior to preparing the consolidated statements for the country as a whole, which is then to be submitted to the AGO within six months of the end of the fiscal year. Although this reconciliation of the consolidated statements forwarded by the line ministries and the DTCOs is deemed important for budgetary compliance, it was observed during the interviews that such a reconciliation requirement has remained ineffective in practice. A senior accountant at the FCGO remarked:

> It is very difficult to consolidate the central-level statements, as they are incomplete and heterogeneous. We have online access to the accounting data of district treasuries. It is therefore much easier for us to compile the statements provided by the DTCOs. We do not use the central-level reporting any more for consolidation.

A rather different, and more comprehensive, approach has been taken, however, in discharging the accountability of donor-funded projects. Rendering the accountability of externally funded projects in fact extends beyond the monitoring of budgetary compliance to the demonstration of performance and results. The projects embedded in the MTEF serve as an example in this regard. Most of the MTEF projects are development-focused and funded by international organizations, so the beneficiary public entities must submit an additional progress report for each of these projects to the DTCOs on a quarterly basis (Pradhan, 2013). The continuation of the projects should rely upon the results as demonstrated in the progress reports. In fact, the DTCOs are allowed to release money (funding) to the projects without any further investigation/inquiry only if the demonstrated progress is at least 80 per cent of the targets set out for that quarter (National Planning Commission, 2002). The budget release will be subject to further scrutiny if the projects achieve within 50 to 80 per cent of the targets. The DTCOs are authorized to suspend the budget release for those projects that achieved less than 50 per cent of their target progress.

In summary, our findings show that the underlying rationale for the use of cash basis accounting in the Nepalese public sector has been inextricably linked to the notions of accountability. While internal accountability to the parliament has been discharged by maintaining budgetary compliance, a system of performance reporting has been introduced within the ambit of cash accounting to ensure the accountability of external resources. As claimed by the neo-institutional-based literature (Carpenter and Feroz, 2001), accounting in the public sector in Nepal has become a legitimizing device through which the constitutional requirements are tackled and the external pressures to ensure the performance of public expenditure is addressed. The prevailing cash basis accounting has, however, been problematized, and new accounting technologies, e.g. the Cash Basis IPSAS, have been imposed using various accounting and reporting mechanisms – coercive, mimetic and normative – over time.

Reforms of public-sector accounting

In the context of Nepalese public-sector accounting, accountants are controlled and accountability is discharged through the mobilization of budgetary accounting. However, accounting representations have been partial and biased as they have been fabricated to ensure budgetary compliance, which has been acknowledged in a range of reports published jointly by the government and international organizations (World Bank, 2007, 2010; MoF, 2015). The prevailing accounting practices in the public sector have also been criticized in these reports for the way certain accounting transactions, in particular, advance payments and inventories, have been handled and reported. Such elements continue to be recognized and presented in the financial statements as government expenditures. It has also been claimed that the prevailing accounting systems lacks both instructions and reporting formats for recording and reporting direct payments and commodity grants offered by donors (World Bank, 2007). Government statistics show that almost 30 per cent of foreign aid, mostly technical assistance, is beyond the purview of the FCGO and has therefore not been included in the budgets (FCGO, 2014).

Adhikari *et al.* (2013) argue that the concept of accrual accounting has been featured in the Nepalese financial administration throughout the 1980s and 1990s, as a panacea for coping with the weaknesses inherent in cash accounting. Reforms emerged, however, in 2007 after the World Bank published a report comparing Nepalese public-sector accounting and auditing practices to international standards. The World Bank and its allies, such as the ADB, are now urging developing countries to take a sequential approach to public-sector accounting reform, commencing with the adoption of the Cash Basis IPSAS and advancing towards accrual accounting (Bietenhader and Bergmann, 2010; World Bank, 2007, 2010). The importance of adopting the Cash Basis IPSAS has been propagated in Nepal not only as a means of rectifying the perceived deficiencies of the existing accounting practices but also of enhancing the country's capabilities in terms of infrastructure (e.g. supporting IT systems) and well-trained accountants that will be crucial for implementing accrual accounting reforms in the future.

At the same time, the World Bank has attempted to disseminate IPSAS ideas using a combination of coercive, mimetic and normative mechanisms. Promoting the adoption of the Cash Basis IPSAS by Nepalese public entities has become one of the high-priority projects of the World Bank, which is evidence of the existence of coercive pressure. It has been witnessed in recent years in Nepal, and perhaps also in other developing countries, that there has been a change in the way the World Bank, the ADB and development partners provide financial support for the execution of development programmes/projects. Under the lead of the World Bank, these donor organizations have introduced a joint fund, i.e. the so-called 'multi-donor trust fund' (MDTF), so as to coordinate their aid and grants to the country. The intention is to hold a joint meeting either annually or semi-annually to determine the projects that should be a priority for the country, and the amounts each donor can contribute to each specific project. A Nepalese accountant commented as follows about the coercive pressure to implement the Cash Basis IPSAS:

> The World Bank has now proposed a grant for implementing public sector accounting standards, as part of a broader public financial management reform. The proposed grant will come from a multi-donor trust fund. This means most of our donors are supporting this project. Whether we like it or not, or whether we are ready or not, we have no other options. If we reject this proposal, there will be an impact on overall donor-funded projects.

This statement clearly suggests that any attempt to oppose the World Bank's proposal may jeopardize not only its contribution but also the donors' funding, which accounts for approximately 20 per cent of the total annual public expenditures in Nepal (FCGO, 2014). Apart from making the adoption of the Cash Basis IPSAS a condition for its further support, the World Bank has also adopted the strategy of persuading government officers and senior-level accountants at the FCGO to accept the IPSAS by hiring professional accountants as local consultants. Consultants appointed by the World Bank have been involved in organizing workshops and seminars for Nepalese government officers and accountants and have used such seminars/workshops to emphasize the widespread use of the Cash Basis IPSAS in other South Asian countries. In doing so, the consultants have made it very clear to the Nepalese accountants and officers that the adoption of the Cash Basis IPSAS would allow the country to emulate the best accounting practices prevailing in other South Asian countries. A senior accountant at the FCGO elaborated on this:

> It was suggested by the World Bank's consultants that we form a core team to make a study visit to Sri Lanka and other South Asian countries. We were very eager to learn how other South Asian countries had approached international standards and to follow their footsteps in developing and adopting the cash basis international accounting standards in Nepal.

The World Bank's attempt to involve professional accounting institutions, i.e. the Institute of Chartered Accountants (ICAN) and the Accounting Standards Board (ASB), in the IPSAS project can be seen as part of its normative approach to disseminating international standards in the country. The World Bank has offered grants to the ASB through the MDTF in order to enhance its institutional capacity to facilitate training on various aspects of the IPSAS for government accountants. A government accountant commented on the participation of professional accountants in ongoing public-sector accounting reforms: 'There has been increasing collaboration between professional accounting institutions and international organisations in public finance reforms. Both types of institutions have echoed the necessity and benefits of accounting standards, creating the perception that accounting standards are a panacea.'

The way the World Bank has propagated the Cash Basis IPSAS in Nepal has resulted in the involvement of the ASB in the development of the Nepal Public Sector Accounting Standards (NPSAS), corresponding to the Cash Basis IPSAS (ASB, 2009). In September 2009, the government of Nepal announced that the Cash Basis NPSAS developed by the ASB would be implemented in Nepali public entities within the next few years. It was mentioned during our interviews that the NPSAS are being piloted in 14 ministries and that all public entities would be required to prepare their financial statements adhering to the NPSAS in the next three years. In this regard, Nepalese public-sector accounting has been evidenced how and to what extent accounting changes are intertwined with the environment in which accounting operates. An attempt to disseminate IPSAS ideas has apparently led to a significant change in the domain of Nepalese public-sector accounting. The participation of professional accounting institutions and international donors in the reform process implies that the scope of accountability for public-sector entities has now been extended beyond the implementing of annual budgets and the discharging of accountability to parliament. The emergence of a new accounting domain has been observed, underpinning new rationales, namely to discharge a wider form of accountability based on performance to a broader user groups, not limited to parliament members but covering accounting professionals and international donors as well.

Discussion and conclusions

The perceived diversity in the implementation of public-sector accounting reforms, along with the proliferation of interpretative research, has raised concerns in the literature on the need to understand the practices of accounting in a broader sociopolitical and institutional context. This chapter has addressed such a concern. Our study findings demonstrate that public-sector accounting in Nepal has been functioning as a technology with a special focus on legal and budgetary compliance. This emphasis on input side of the budgets has led to the establishment of stewardship-oriented accounting and hierarchical reporting, in which the accounting of public entities is to be scrutinized and consolidated at successive levels. In addition, internal and external auditing, another important element of public finance, is devoted to identifying budget variations and irregularities rather than examining the results and outcomes of public spending. Budgetary compliance is currently the only issue that is discussed in the parliament, by its PAC and by the media. Of the two major objectives of accounting summarized in the literature, i.e. facilitating financial decision-making and maintaining financial control (Mellemvik et al., 1988), only the latter is emphasized in Nepalese public-sector accounting practice. The underlying rationale for public-sector accounting practice has been to fulfil the constitutional requirement of discharging the accountability of public-sector entities, and that cash basis accounting has been the vehicle through which this objective is fulfilled.

The addition of performance-oriented reporting within cash basis accounting has enabled public-sector entities to discharge their external accountability to international organizations and donors for their contributions to the development projects using the same cash basis technology. The inadequacy of cash accounting for cost and performance analyses has, however, led public-sector entities to fabricate the achievements of the externally funded projects and programmes. The fact that donors and international organizations have set up their own accounting and auditing mechanisms for the projects they support, and the criteria for reimbursing their commitments to such projects had, however, further elucidated the weaknesses of Nepalese public-sector accounting. Such deficiencies in accounting practice have provided an impetus for international organizations and donors to exert pressures of varying potency on Nepal to embrace the globalized accounting reform initiatives, mainly the Cash Basis IPSAS, at present.

International organizations are championing the construction of a new Nepalese public-sector accounting domain, which should be able to provide more accurate results and outcomes regarding the resources they offer to the Nepalese government. A rhetoric has been constructed proclaiming the Cash Basis IPSAS as an initial step towards accrual accounting, but we argue that it is this rhetoric has led to the change in the Nepalese public-sector accounting reform agenda from accrual accounting to the Cash Basis IPSAS. The inclusion of the Cash Basis IPSAS as part of the MTDF, the issuance of reports heralding the success of the IPSAS in other contexts, and the financial support provided to the ASB to promote the IPSAS project are evidence of the coercive, mimetic and normative attempts of international organizations and other donors to disseminate the Cash Basis IPSAS in the public sector in Nepal.

The commitment by the government to implement Cash Basis IPSAS means that the domain in which Nepalese government accounting is embedded is at the state of flux. However, it is difficult to argue whether this change in the accounting domain or the adoption of the Cash Basis IPSAS will actually result in improvements in public-sector accounting practice in this country. For instance, it has been argued in the literature that the attempts of many African countries to embrace the Cash Basis IPSAS have remained futile owing to their failure to address a number of the essential requirements of the IPSAS, e.g. the preparation of whole-of-government financial statements, the treatment of third-party payments and the disclosure of external assistance (Wynne, 2013; Parry and Wynne, 2009). This also signals the importance of understanding the public-sector accounting context in developing countries, as well as the existing accounting practices and their objectives prior to the dissemination of radical reform programmes, which would generate significant consequences in the accounting domain (Timoshenko and Adhikari, 2009; Potter, 2005). We therefore call for public-sector accounting researchers in Asia to extend their studies to cover other countries, so as to unfold the similarities and differences in accounting practices and challenges in order to effectively implement the needed accounting reforms in the public sector.

References

Accounting Standards Board (ASB) (2009) *Nepal Public Sector Accounting Standard*. Kathmandu: ASB.

Adhikari, P. and Mellemvik, F. (2011) The rise and fall of accruals: a case of Nepalese central government. *Journal of Accounting in Emerging Economies*, 1(2), 123–143.

Adhikari, P. and Gårseth-Nesbakk, L. (2016) Implementing public sector accruals in OECD member states: major issues and challenges. *Accounting Forum*, 40(2), 125–142.

Adhikari, P., Kuruppu, C. and Matilal, S. (2013) Dissemination and institutionalization of public sector accounting reforms in less developed countries: A comparative study of the Nepalese and Sri Lankan central governments. *Accounting Forum*, 37(3), 213–230.

Allen, R. (2009) *The Challenge of Reforming Budgetary Institutions in Developing Countries*. IMF Working paper (WP/09/96). Washington, DC: IMF.

Asian Development Bank (ADB) (2005) *Nepal: Public Finance Management Assessment*. Manila: ADB.

Auditor General's Office (AGO) (2014) *Fifty-first (51ˢᵗ) Annual Report of the Auditor General 2070*. Kathmandu: AGO.

Barton, A. (2007) Accrual accounting and budgeting systems in Australian governments. *Australian Accounting Review*, 17(1), 38–50.

Bietenhader D. and Bergmann A. (2010) Principles for sequencing public financial reforms in developing countries. *International Public Management Review*, 11(1), 52–66.

Burchell, S., Clubb, C., Hopwood, A.G., Hughes, J. and Nahapiet, J. (1980) The roles of accounting organizations and society. *Accounting, Organizations and Society*, 5(1), 5–27.

Burchell, S., Clubb, C., Hopwood, A.G., Hughes, J. and Nahapiet, J. (1985) Accounting in its social context: Towards a history of value-added in the United Kingdom. *Accounting, Organizations and Society*, *10*(4), 381–413.

Caiden, N. and Wildavsky, A. (1974) *Planning and Budgeting in Poor Countries*. New Brunswick, NY: Transaction.

Carlin, T. (2005) Debating the impact of accrual accounting and reporting in the public sector. *Financial Accountability & Management*, *21*(3), 309–336.

Carpenter, V. and Feroz, E. (2001) Institutional theory and accounting rule choice: an analysis of four US state governments' decisions to adopt generally accepted accounting principles. *Accounting, Organizations and Society*, *26*(7–8), 565–596.

Ezzamel, M., Hyndman, N., Johnsen, A. and Lapsley, I. (2014) Reforming central government accounting: An evaluation of an accounting innovation, *Critical Perspectives on Accounting*, *25*(4/5), 409–422.

Financial Comptroller General Office (FCGO) (2014) *Consolidated Financial Statements: Fiscal Year 2012/2013*. Kathmandu: FCGO.

Goddard, A., Assad, M., Issa, S. and Malagila, J. (2015) The two publics and institutional theory: A study of public sector accounting in Tanzania. *Critical Perspectives on Accounting*. doi:10.1016/j.cpa.2015.02.002 (in press).

Government of Nepal (GoN) (2008) *An Assessment of the Public Financial Management Performance Measurement Framework (As of FY 2005/06)*. Kathmandu: Financial Comptroller General Office.

Guthrie, J., Olson, O. and Humphrey, C. (1999) Debating developments in New Public Financial Management: The limits of global theorizing and some new ways forward. *Financial Accountability and Management*, *15*(3/4), 209–228.

Harun, H., Peursem, K. and Eggleton, I. (2012) Institutionalization of accrual accounting in the Indonesian public sector. *Journal of Accounting & Organizational Change*, *8*(3), 257–285.

Hopwood, A.G. (1990) Accounting and organization change. *Accounting, Auditing & Accountability Journal*, *3*(1), 7–17.

Hyndman, N. and Connolly, C. (2011) Accruals accounting in the public sector: a road not always taken. *Management Accounting Research*, *22*(1), 36–45.

International Federation of Accountants (IFAC) (2011) *Transition to the Accrual Basis of Accounting: Guidance for Public Sector Entities, Study 14* (3rd ed.). New York: IFAC.

International Monetary Fund (IMF) (2007) *Nepal: Report on Observance of Standards and Codes—Fiscal Transparency Module*. Washington, DC: IMF.

Jones, R. (2012) Budgetary accounting in national governments: Anglo versus American Accounting. *Financial Accountability and Management*, *28*(3), 286–305.

Lassou, P. and Hopper, T. (2016) Government accounting reform in an ex-French African colony: The political economy of neo-colonialism. *Critical Perspectives on Accounting*, *36*(April), 39–57.

Lüder, K. and Jones, R. (2003) The diffusion of accrual accounting and budgeting in European governments – a cross-country analysis. In K. Lüder and R. Jones (Eds), *Reforming Governmental Accounting and Budgeting in Europe* (pp. 13–58). Frankfurt am Main: Fachverlag Moderne Wirtschaft.

McKernan, J.F. (2007) Objectivity in accounting. *Accounting, Organizations and Society*, *32*(1–2), 155–180.

Mellemvik, F., Monsen, N. and Olson, O. (1988) Functions of accounting – a discussion. *Scandinavian Journal of Management*, *4*(3/4), 101–119.

Miller, P. (1994) Accounting as social and institutional practice: an introduction. In A. Hopwood and P. Miller (Eds), *Accounting as Social and Institutional Practice*. Cambridge: Cambridge University Press.

Miller, P. and O'Leary, T. (1987) Accounting and the Construction of the Governable Person. *Accounting, Organizations and Society*, *12*(3), 235–265.

Ministry of Finance (MoF) (2015) *Nepal Portfolio Performance Review (NPPR)*. Kathmandu: Government of Nepal.

National Planning Commission (NPC) (2002) *Medium Term Expenditures Framework: Fiscal Year 2002/03-04/05*. Kathmandu: NPC.

Parry, M. and Wynne, A. (2009) The cash basis IPSAS: an alternative view. *International Journal on Governmental Financial Management*, *IX*(2), 23–29.

Potter, B. (2005) Accounting as a social and institutional practice: Perspectives to enrich our understanding of accounting change. *ABACUS*, *41*(3), 265–289.

Pradhan, S. (2013) Budgetary reform: Implementing medium term budgeting framework (MTBF) in Nepal. *The Nepalese Journal of Public Financial Management (PEFA Journal)*, *2*(1), 1–10.

PwC (2013) *Towards a New Era in Government Accounting and Reporting*. PwC Global survey on accounting and reporting by central governments.

Timoshenko, K. and Adhikari, P. (2009) Exploring Russian central government accounting in its context. *Journal of Accounting & Organizational Change*, 5(4), 490–513.

World Bank (2002) *Financial Accountability in Nepal: A Country Assessment*. Washington, DC: World Bank.

World Bank (2007) *Nepal Public Sector Accounting and Auditing: A Comparison of International Standard*. Washington, DC: World Bank.

World Bank (2010) *Public Sector Accounting and Auditing in South Asia (Report no. 54606-SAS)*. Washington, DC: South Asia Region Financial Management Unit.

Wynne, A. (2013) *International Public Sector Accounting Standards: Compilation Guide for Developing Countries*. International Consortium on Governmental Financial Management. Retrieved from www.scribd.com/doc/134603499/ICGFM-Compilation-Guide-to-Financial-Reporting-by-Governments (accessed 29 August 2014).

Part V

Accounting education

Accounting education is crucial to the supply of professional accountants and to the improvement of accountants' professional qualifications and practising skills. Constrained by varied social, political, cultural, economic and legal institutions in different countries, there are distinct differences in accounting education in individual countries, and varied models and experience of accounting education are available. This section covers the development of accounting education in two Asian countries, Japan (Chapter 15) and Singapore (Chapter 16), to provide an insight into the roles and changes in accounting education in the changing business environment in Asia.

Japan is a developed country and its accounting development is at an advanced level compared to most countries in Asia. However, Japan is also a country with relatively conservative cultural traditions. The entire education system, including tertiary education and professional education, is under the direct influence of the government and its agencies. At present, accounting education in Japan aims mainly at supplying pre-entrance candidates to the accounting profession. Unlike most countries, the Japanese accounting profession has not required a minimum tertiary education (i.e. an undergraduate degree) as a prerequisite for entrants to join the profession. Thus, in Japan candidates can have two pathways to become professional accountants. First, in the ordinary pathway, students must take a two-stage nationwide examination for professional accountants (e.g. the CPA examination). Stage 1 of the examination contains multiple-choice questions. Students successful at this stage can take the Stage 2 examination, which asks essay-style questions. These students will become provisional members of the Japanese professional accounting association, the Japan Institute of Certified Public Accountants (JICPA), if they pass the second stage of the examination. After fulfilling the two-year practical experience requirement and successful completion of the requirements to be qualified for full membership of the JICPA, they can be awarded CPA certificates by the government authority in charge. The second pathway to becoming a professional accountant is to take studies at a specialized vocational professional school of accountancy, which have been accredited by the government educational authorities since 2003. Degree holders (regardless of their study major) can take professional studies in accounting at these vocational schools and graduates can be exempted from three of the four multiple-choice sessions required at Stage 1 of the CPA examination; they must still sit the Stage 2 examination. Accounting schools are under the direct supervision of the Accreditation Organization for Professional Accounting Schools (AOPAS), which was set up by the Ministry of Education, Culture, Sports, Science and Technology of Japan. It is interesting to note that the CPA examination and the accounting profession have become less attractive in Japan and the numbers of candidates or new entrants have declined substantially in recent years. The authors of this chapter attribute the decline to the negative impact of the financial crisis of 2008–2009 as accounting firms in Japan have since significantly reduced their recruitment.

It is noted that Japan took a lead in Asia in promoting the global convergence of accounting education by adopting the international education standards (IES) jointly formulated by the IFAC and the IASB, in order to: 1) increase the global mobility of accountants, and 2) reduce inter-country differences in the requirements for becoming a professional accountant together with their ongoing professional development, which have been adopted by several accounting education programmes in Japan, although the adoption rate is not high enough owing to the constraints in supporting educational resources and insufficient exchanges with international educational communities. In the meantime, Japanese educational institutions are bringing various forms of active learning approaches (ALA) into accounting programmes; these are the instructional methods that engage students in the learning process to raise the quality and effectiveness of accounting education. Chapter 15 also outlines the characteristics and key requirements for the continuing professional education (CPE) programme for professional accountants in Japan.

Singapore is an Asian country that shows high economic growth; in particular, it is well positioned as a key business and financial hub in South East Asia. The Singapore government has long emphasized fostering specialized talents and promoted accounting education to support rapid economic growth in Singapore. In particular, in 2008 the Singapore government started an ambitious initiative to transform the country into the leading global accountancy hub and to enhance the competitiveness of Singapore in regional and global economic development. Thus, in late 2008 the government established the Committee to Develop the Accountancy Sector (CDAS) under the Ministry of Finance and in 2013 the Singapore Accountancy Commission (SAC), and promulgated the vision and strategies to reach this goal in the following 10 years. The CDAS issued a series of recommendations, aiming to: 1) develop a Singapore-branded post-university accounting qualification programme; 2) develop Singapore into a centre of excellence for the professional development of chief financial officers (CFO); and 3) boost accounting-sector research. It should be pointed out that these strategies and measures on promoting accounting education proposed by the Singapore government are forward-looking and will have a significant impact on the development of professional accounting in the country and the region.

This chapter introduces not only the various stakeholders who have participated in and contributed to the development of accounting education, but also the structural characteristics and requirements of accounting education and professional training in the country. At the same time, the knowledge and skill requirements in accounting programmes or curriculum design at leading tertiary institutions in Singapore are illustrated in detail. The innovative effort and experience in accounting education in Singapore should be a valuable reference for other countries in the region.

15

Accounting education in Japan

Satoshi Sugahara

Introduction

The purpose of this chapter is to introduce recent developments in accounting education in Japan. Japan is the leading developed country in Asia, thus the quality of accounting professions is important to achieve higher levels of social and economic activities in both the domestic and the global contexts. However, little literature in the accounting field to date has been published to explain education for accounting professionals in this country. One key study among the literature is Watty *et al.* (2012)—the author of this chapter was one of the project members—which addressed broader issues of accounting education provided by professional bodies and formal colleges or schools in Japan. However, the data of the prior study have become obsoleted and should be updated with related developments after 2012.

The primary topics covered by this chapter cover: 1) the development of the Japanese accounting profession system; 2) initial professional development (IPD); 3) continuous professional development (CPD); 4) statistics of CPA examinees in Japan; 5) the global convergence of accounting education in Japan; and 6) the latest trends in accounting education in Japan. A descriptive case study approach is used here to analyze the data and statistics collected from the extant literature and official documents associated with accounting education in Japan. This chapter concludes with a brief summary and discussion of several implications for the future development of accounting education in Japan.

Development of the accounting profession system

The education system for the accounting profession in Japan

The educational structure of the accounting profession in Japan is unique among developed countries. In Japan, the CPA designation is regulated by the Certified Public Accountants (CPAs) Law. Japanese CPA examinations have been open to college graduates and other nongraduates who wish to become CPAs. The CPA examination scheme in Japan allows candidates to attempt CPA examinations without any dedicated accountancy education or without any degree as a prerequisite for entry.[1] For example, a 16-year-old secondary school student passed the CPA examination in 2010 and qualified as a provisional member of the Japanese Institute of Certified Public Accountants (JICPA).[2] To pass the CPA examination, the secondary school student studied all accounting subjects at a vocational school[3] and undertook community college courses provided by a university. While this is a rare case, it does provide an insight into the current accounting education system in Japan. More generally, only a small number of examinees have passed the CPA examinations without having attended tertiary school programs. Table 15.1 shows the breakdown of the successful 2015 examinees in terms of their academic credentials. As shown, only 57 examinees (5.4 percent) passed the CPA examinations in the year they completed their secondary school education.

This lack of a requirement for a tertiary degree is one of the particular features of the Japanese accounting education system (Sugahara and Boland, 2009), but this gives rise to some controversial discussions among academics and policymakers about the validity of this qualification mode (FSA, 2010). As a result, an agenda was raised in the parliament in April 2011 to discuss the prerequisite requirements for CPA examinees owing to the impact of the international convergence of accounting education in Japan. It has been proposed that candidates be required to complete some modules at tertiary institutions before sitting CPA examinations.[4] However, this proposal was rejected on April 27, 2012.[5]

Specific education and accounting education standards in Japan

There is ongoing discussion about accounting education standards specifically applicable to Japan. Initially, the Ministry of Education, Culture, Sports, Science and Technology (MEXT) began with the development of general quality assurance standards for the tertiary sector in 2008. Accounting education standards in Japan have also been reviewed as part of this project.

Based on the policy report *Towards the Development of Bachelorship Education Scheme*, which was issued by the Central Council on Education (CCE) in 2008,[6] MEXT required the Science Council of Japan (SCJ) to design a framework for sectorial quality assurance for undergraduate degree programs. This is because the CCE policy report simply proposed a set of fundamental concepts of "bachelorship," which outlines the abilities and skills that are commonly demanded for all undergraduate degree holders regardless of their major(s). Thus, MEXT intended to promulgate more specific standards to assure the quality of graduates in terms of their particular specialized majors. As a result, the SCJ issued a recommendation

Table 15.1 Academic credentials of CPA examinees in 2015

	Number of graduates	Number of successful CPA examinees
Graduates from postgraduate institutions	645	42 (4.0%)
Graduates from accounting school (AS)	930	75 (7.1%)
Postgraduate students	92	8 (0.8%)
AS students	154	29 (2.8%)
Graduates from undergraduate institutions	5,001	498 (47.4%)
Undergraduate students	2,219	307 (29.2%)
Graduates from secondary school	853	57 (5.4%)
Others	286	35 (3.3%)
Total	10,180	1,051 (100.0%)

Source: CPAAOB website, www.fsa.go.jp/cpaaob/kouninkaikeishi-shiken/ronbungoukaku_27/03.pdf (accessed February 17, 2016).

report, *The Future Shape of Sectorial Quality Assurance for the Tertiary Educations*, in July 2010.[7] However, the SCJ report did not specify sectorial education benchmark standards for each specialized discipline (study major), but simply illustrated the basic framework and premises of the sectorial quality assurance for liberal courses at the undergraduate level. Nonetheless, the SCJ report indicated an intention to design and issue specific education benchmark standards for 30 different disciplines in the next three years. In the SCJ report, the 'Subject Benchmark Statement' in the United Kingdom (UK) was often referred to as an example of sectorial quality assurance standards.[8] The SCJ report also mentioned that the UK's QAA benchmarks should not be simply duplicated, but that they would be the best examples to use in the process of developing specific education standards for Japan.

One of the distinguishing traits for accounting education standards specific to Japan is that the benchmark in the Japan University Association for Computer Education (JUACE) prescribes accounting students' competencies to understand, process, and disseminate accounting information in order to make appropriate economic decisions (see www.juce.jp/gakushiryoku/2009/#kaikei, accessed April 24, 2017). In contrast to this Japanese benchmark, the QAA in the UK views generic competencies as equally important for accounting students, together with other technical and subject-specific knowledge and skills (QAA, 2016). The QAA's benchmark for the accounting discipline released in 2016 articulates the importance of cognitive abilities and generic skills including communication skills, teamwork skills, and interpersonal skills.

The International Education Standards for Professional Accountants (IES) has also set the fundamental premise that communication and interpersonal skills are required to work effectively in a cross-cultural setting, rather than in a domestic setting only (IFAC, 2003). In this context, the 2003 amendment to the CPA Law in Japan attempted to address and articulate the importance of a global horizon and foreign language capabilities in the official report of the Subcommittee on the Certified Public Accountants System led by the Financial System Council (FSC, 2002). However, this signal has not been reflected adequately in either the CPA Law or the educational benchmarks (Sugahara and Coman, 2010).

Initial professional development (IPD) programs

Provisional professional association membership

In Japan, degrees granted by universities are not necessary to qualify as a CPA and become a member of the JICPA, because there is currently no degree prerequisite for students to sit in the CPA examinations. In fact, there are two pathways for applicants to obtain the CPA qualification.

1 Ordinary pathway: CPA examination scheme

There currently are two types of examinations that candidates must sit for the CPA examination scheme in Japan. These examinations, which are commonly referred to as the CPA examination, consist of a multiple-choice test at the first stage; successful examinees from this first step are able to go forward to the essay-style questions in the second stage. A pass must be achieved in these two CPA examinations in order to qualify as a provisional member of the JICPA. All successful examinees in the CPA examinations are permitted to be provisional members. The provisional members are awarded CPA certificates by the government after a total of two years' practical experience and successful completion of the requirements to qualify for full membership of JICPA. During the two years of practical experience, a JICPA provisional member needs to successfully complete multiple special training courses offered by JICPA.

The CPA examination process is undertaken by the Certified Public Accountants and Auditing Oversight Board (CPAAOB) in Japan. The CPAAOB is authorized under the CPAs Law as an advisory board of the Financial Service Agency (FSA), which is responsible for the CPA examination and some related work. The CPAAOB recommends a certain number of examiners for the CPA examinations from academia and practicing CPAs and their appointments should be endorsed by the Prime Minister of Japan (CPAs Law, Article 38.2). Thirty-six academics and nine CPAs were appointed as the examiners for the CPA examination in 2016.[9] The JICPA also has strong connections with the CPAABO, because all successful CPA examinees can be provisional members of the JICPA.

Generally, before attempting the CPA examinations, students will have either studied at a university in any discipline or attended a vocational school (preliminary private school) to support their self-learning. Many believe that the university curriculum in accounting/business courses does not sufficiently prepare candidates to pass the two stages of the CPA examination, so students usually go to vocational schools on a voluntary basis.

Table 15.2 below shows the list of subjects covered in the CPA examination. A summary of the contents of the CPA examination are set out on the CPAAOB website.[10]

Multiple-choice-type questions are given to examinees in the first stage of the CPA examination. The duration of the examinations varies depending on the subject. For example, financial accounting is a two-hour examination, while the other three subjects are one-hour examinations. At the second stage, essay-type questions are provided, though only for examinees who have passed the first stage of examination. Five hours are allocated for a joint examination of financial accounting and management accounting. Two hours each for the other four subjects are allocated.[11]

There is a wide variety of content for each subject, making the preparatory study very intensive. This is why self-learning at colleges is not enough for applicants to pass the entire examination process. Some information on the contents covered in the CPA examinations is released by the CPAAPB.[12]

2 Alternative pathway: accounting school

New professional schools, called "accounting schools (AS)," were established in 2003. The accounting schools offer a two-year postgraduate degree program designed for students who already have undergraduate degrees in any discipline. Graduates from the accounting schools can apply for exemptions in three of the four multiple-choice sections of the CPA examination

Table 15.2 The subjects in the CPA examination in Japan

Examination subject	Stage of the CPA examination
Financial accounting	First and second stages
Management accounting	First and second stages
Auditing	First and second stages
Company law	First and second stages
Tax law	Second stage only
Business administration	Elective among four subjects at second stage
Economics	Elective among four subjects at second stage
Civil law	Elective among four subjects at second stage
Statistics	Elective among four subjects at second stage

at the first stage; however, they cannot be exempted from any of the essay-type questions at the second stage. Currently 13 accounting schools operate within Japan (see Table 15.3), each affiliated with the business or accountancy faculty of a university (MEXT, 2010). Since 2007, the Accreditation Organization for Professional Accounting Schools (AOPAS) has been authorized by MEXT to be in charge of the quality assurance activities for accounting schools in Japan. This Institute is a nonprofit organization that undertakes the quality assurance role for accounting schools, such as assessing educational programs, issuing evaluation reports, setting assessment criteria, etc.

Further, the Japan Association of Graduate Schools for Professional Accountancy (JAGSPA) has also been established as the self-assessment institute to oversee educational activities at accounting schools.[13] The JAGSPA is a private institute funded by all accounting schools and other possible universities that intend to open new accounting schools in the future. This association is responsible for faculty development, quality control of curriculum, and objective evaluation as a third party.

Full professional association membership

The JICPA is the official accounting professional body in Japan, and it is the sole Japanese member of the IFAC. The requirement for becoming a member of the JICPA is passing the CPA examination explained above. Upon satisfactory completion of the CPA examination, successful examinees first become provisional members of the JICPA. They are then required to complete training courses offered by the JICPA and participate in a two-year work experience program in an accounting firm or a business enterprise. After that, provisional members will be certified by the government and given CPA licenses, which allow them to practice audits and other related activities as a CPA. At this stage, they become full members of the JICPA and may also use their specific professional CPA designation.

Table 15.3 Accounting schools in Japan

	University	Website	Enrollment limit
1	Aoyama Gakuin University	www.gspa.aoyama.ac.jp	80
2	Ohara Graduate University	www.o-hara.ac.jp/grad	30
3	Kansai University	www.kansai-u.ac.jp/as	70
4	Kwansei Gakuin University	www.kwansei-ac.jp/iba	70
5	Kumamoto Gakuen University	www.as.kumagaku.ac.jp	30
6	Chiba University of Commerce	www.cuc.ac.jp/prospective/graduate/ accounting/index.html	70
7	Chuo University	www.chuo-u.ac.jp/chuo-u/cgsa/index_j.html	80
8	Tohuko University	www.econ.tohoku.ac.jp/econ/kaikei/index.html	40
9	University of Hyogo	www.acs.u-hyogo.ac.jp	40
10	Hokkaido University	www.haccs.hokudai.ac.jp	20
11	Meiji University	www.meiji.ac.jp/macs	80
12	LEC Graduate School of Accounting	www.lec.ac.jp/graduate-school/accounting	60
13	Waseda University	www.waseda.jp/accounting	100
Total			770

* Based on data in July 2015
Source: The website of the Ministry of Education, Culture, Sports, Science and Technology, www.mext.go.jp/a_menu/ koutou/senmonshoku/08060508.htm (accessed February 17, 2016).

In Japan, there are other accounting bodies such as the Japan Federation of Certified Public Tax Accountants Association and TKC Corporation, which deal specifically with tax accounting for small and medium-sized enterprises but are not allowed to audit listed companies. These bodies are not members of the IFAC. Thus, only the JICPA is recognizable as an equivalent to the professional accounting bodies in other countries.

It is relatively rare for a Japanese accounting professional with a government CPA license to join international professional accounting bodies such as the American Institute of Certified Public Accountants (AICPA) or the Institute of Chartered Accountants in Australia (ICAA). However, the numbers of these professional accountants are gradually increasing year by year. Recently, the JICPA joined the Global Accounting Association (GAA), which opens more flexible interaction between Japanese and international accountants.

Continuous professional development (CPD)

The CPAs Law requires all CPAs to complete CPD (continuous professional development) programs provided by the JICPA. Each JICPA member (who is a CPA) needs to obtain 120 CPD credits over a three-year period. JICPA offers a variety of CPE educational methods such as group learning seminars, CD-ROMs, e-learning, distance learning, small groups of self-study, and so on. JICPA members also can obtain credits by publishing papers relating to the profession and by giving public lectures/speeches.[14] The number of credits obtained from each learning mode varies. The JICPA expects its members to keep up to date on the following subjects and contents through the CPD program.

- Auditing
- Accounting
- Taxation
- Consulting
- Information technology
- Professional ethics
- Related laws and regulation (e.g. the Commercial Code)

More specifically, members are required to complete four credits of professional ethics and four credits of audit quality control as part of the annual 40-credit requirement.

Statistics on CPA examinees in Japan

Brief profile of statistics

In January 2016, the JICPA had 28,455 CPA full members. In addition, 6,328 individuals were qualified as provisional members of the JICPA.[15] The annual number of successful CPA examinees was 1,051 in 2015 while there were 10,180 original applicants (from the first stage), indicating a pass rate of 10.3 percent.

There are no statistics to show the number of students who majored in accounting. Instead, the CPAAOB presents some demographic data about CPA examinees each year. For example, Table 15.4 exhibits profiles of CPA examinees in 2015. The largest group of persons who sat in the CPA examination in 2015 were university students (including postgraduate students), followed by persons working in private companies and vocational school students. Most interestingly, academics teaching accounting at university made up only two (0.2 percent) of all successful examinees. The data for previous years demonstrates that the number of full-time academics who had passed the CPA examinations was only two (0.2 percent) in 2015, five (0.5 percent) in 2014, one (0.1 percent) in 2013 and three (0.2 percent) in 2012.[16]

Decreasing numbers of CPA examinees

For the supply side of professional accountants in Japan, it is observed that the number of CPA examinees has dropped substantially in Japan in recent years. Figure 15.1 shows the numbers of both total CPA examinees and successful examinees over the past 10 years. It is obvious that the number of CPA examinees had dramatically decreased, being half as many in 2015 than in the years before 2012.

Accounting firms and the JICPA are worrying about the recent decline of entrants to the profession. This unfavorable situation is thought to be caused by accounting firms drastically reducing the intake of new employees after the financial crisis in 2009 (Anon, 2015). CPA examinees who seek job opportunities in accounting firms basically need to dedicate more than a few years of intensive studies to pass the relatively rigorous CPA examination, while nearly half of successful CPA examinees subsequently failed to be hired by accounting firms owing to their downsized employment after the financial crisis. Such a deep drop in demand by accounting firms has given future professional candidates an unfavorable perception of the CPA profession. The unpopularity of the CPA career also affects the education systems for accounting schools. In 2015, three out of the initial 16 accounting schools in Japan had announced the suspension of their application operations from 2016 (Anon, 2015). Furthermore, nine of the other 13 schools failed to reach the minimum number of applicants for their enrollments in 2016 (Anon, 2015).

Global convergence of accounting education in Japan

The literature in accounting education has actively argued the impact of globalization on accounting education across countries. This section provides a brief summary of relevant previous studies in an attempt to understand the progress of globalizing accounting education in Japan.

Table 15.4 Profile of CPA examinees in 2015

Category	Number of applicants	Number of successful CPA examinees
Provisional member who passed CPA exam subjects	109	16 (1.5%)
Accounting staff who work for accounting firms	456	48 (4.6%)
Tax accountants	78	6 (0.6%)
Practitioners working for private companies	2,046	94 (8.9%)
Public servants	322	20 (1.9%)
Full-time teachers (including academics at university)	45	2 (0.2%)
Part-time teachers (including casuals)	55	2 (0.2%)
University students (including postgraduate)	3,122	438 (41.7%)
Cram school students	1,812	280 (26.6%)
Non-occupation	1,874	137 (13.0%)
Others	261	8 (0.8%)
Total	10,180	1,051 (100.0%)

Source: CPAAOB website, www.fsa.go.jp/cpaaob/kouninkaikeishi-shiken/ronbungoukaku_22a.html (accessed February 17, 2016).

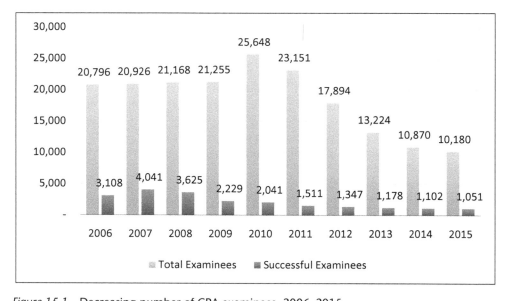

Figure 15.1 Decreasing number of CPA examinees, 2006–2015

Source: CPAAOB website, www.fsa.go.jp/cpaaob/kouninkaikeishi-shiken/ronbungoukaku_27/03.pdf (accessed February 17, 2015).

One of the key issues about the international convergence of accounting education is the global framework of accounting education known as the International Education Standards (IES) (IAESB, 2010). The IES have been released by the International Federation of Accountants (IFAC) and the International Accounting Education Standards Board (IAESB) in order to 1) increase the global mobility for accountants and 2) reduce cross-country differences in the requirements for becoming a professional accountant together with their ongoing professional development.

An earlier study to deal with the IES issue in Japan was Sugahara and Boland (2011), who examined the degree to which Japanese accounting academics were exposed to the IES in terms of quality assurance in the accounting profession. Their questionnaire-based research revealed that only one-fourth of the participants had previously read about IESs and concluded that such low exposure rate to the IESs did not contribute to developing academics with clear views on the global convergence of accounting education. Further, Sugahara (2013) investigated the perceptions of Japanese academics toward the global convergence of accounting education. With 87 accounting academia respondents, this study reported that the majority of Japanese academics did not believe that the IES would have a substantial effect on accounting education in Japan. This passive view of the IES is regarded to be determined by a unique education system in Japan where the professional IFAC member body (i.e., the JICPA) has no formal networks with the Japanese educational community in terms of developing the accounting curriculum for undergraduate education (Sugahara et al., 2009). This peculiar structure in Japan hampers the possibility for academics to incorporate the IES into accounting programs, which even discourages them from holding positive views toward the effectiveness of the IES.

With regard to the negative view toward the effectiveness of the IES, Sugahara (2013) also found statistically that a lack of knowledge about the IES among academics was not the primary perceived obstacle for the successful international convergence of accounting education, rather the main obstacles inhibiting the global convergence of accounting education were differences in culture, educational systems, and languages across countries. However, this study reports that academics did not know how they could ever confront these obstacles to achieve international convergence. It is therefore suggested that the IAESB should further increase the promotion of the IES among accounting academia in Japan. Without an accreditation system, it is suggested that the IAESB should improve dialogue with domestic accounting professionals and academics in Japan via organizing more symposiums and conferences.

Latest trends in accounting education in Japan

The most prominent trend in accounting education in Japan is to bring active learning approaches (ALA) into accounting classroom. ALA are defined as the instructional methods that engage students in the learning process (Prince, 2004). ALA require students to do meaningful learning activities and think about what they are doing (Prince, 2004). ALA have been applied in various disciplines such as science, criminal justice, information systems and technology, and business education, and in a similar way to accounting education programs (e.g. Jackson, 2014; Loeb, 2014).

Recently, several accounting researchers in Japan have invented self-developed innovative ALA and applied them as teaching materials in accounting programs. Some examples using ALA are "active learning class using monopoly game," "learning CVP analysis by paper tower" (Ushio, 2014), "learning financial accounting by paper aircraft" (Urasaki, 2010), "learning cost accounting and productivity by paper cranes" (Shima, 2013), and "LEGO simulation game for learning accounting." For instance, the ALA with paper cranes gives students an opportunity to operate their production activities effectively and efficiently so as to produce the largest number of paper cranes. Through this teaching approach, instructors provide technical concepts such as mass production, manufacturing management, cost accounting, and lean production systems, and explain how to apply these concepts to manage all activities. Such ALA materials are regarded as useful teaching/learning tools because they can: 1) enhance students' engagement and motives, 2) establish critical thinking skills, and 3) enable learning transfer through activities to application in practice (Anderson and Lawton, 2009).

Although Japanese accounting researchers and educators actively elaborate and introduce various ALA into accounting classroom, there is a lack of empirical evidence regarding the effectiveness of ALA to improve the actual abilities and competences of students. Sugahara (2016), for example, examined the effect of a program incorporated with several ALA among first-year business students and found significant evidence of improving students' attention and confidence to learning accounting by engaging ALA in the classroom, and also reported a significant association between higher degrees of motivational factors and students' work aspirations toward the accounting profession. However, the study failed to address the effect of ALA on students' critical thinking and professional judgment skills. Furthermore, almost all studies on ALA in Japan have been published only in Japanese academic journals, which are normally written in the Japanese language. Thus, the impact of these research outcomes is limited. Japanese accounting educators should engage dialogues about ALA with international communities to introduce and present their unique findings from the Japanese accounting education.

Conclusion

This chapter aims to elaborate the recent development of accounting education in Japan, addressing in particular the education processes and structures for accounting professionals.

It reveals that the educational structure of the Japanese accounting profession is unique, allowing candidates to sit CPA examinations without any dedicated accountancy education or without college degrees as a prerequisite for entry. This feature contrasts with to those of other developed countries, where a minimum requirement of formal tertiary education is now usually needed for new entrants to the profession.

Furthermore, the new professional schools (i.e., the accounting schools) have been established since 2003 for the education of professional development. However, it has recently been found that accounting schools have failed to attract a sufficient number of students and a few had to suspend their application processes in April 2016. This failure may be affected by reduced recruitment by accounting firms after the financial crisis in 2009.

Another critical finding from the recent literature in accounting indicates that the majority of Japanese academics perceive the differences in culture, educational systems, and languages across countries to be the main obstacles inhibiting the international convergence of accounting education. Further exposures on global convergence issues of accounting education should be enhanced among Japanese academics by the efforts of IAESB and other related international organizations.

We have seen various innovative approaches of active learning (ALA) applying for accounting education programs in Japan. This new trend of teaching/learning materials is expected to be used not only for training the generic skills needed for students' accounting practices but also encouraging their intrinsic motivation of learning accounting. This may help attract more students to come back to the accounting labor market in the near future.

Although this chapter prescribes accounting education and its system structure in Japan, the scope of this study is limited within the extant literature and the available statistics, and it does not reflect the perspective of accounting professionals. As primary stakeholders, their views and perceptions are of great importance in understanding the present and future shape of accounting education in Japan. Regardless of this limitation, this chapter contributes to the accounting literature by providing an in-depth description of accounting education in Japan.

Glossary

Initial professional development (IPD)
Continuous professional development (CPD)
Certified public accountant examination (CPA Exam)
Certified public accountant (CPA)
CPAs Law
Japanese Institute of Certified Public Accountants (JICPA)
Cram school
Qualification method
Prerequisite requirements
Ministry of Education, Culture, Sports, Science and Technology (MEXT)
General quality assurance standards
Central Council on Education (CCE)
Science Council of Japan (SCJ)
CCE policy report
Bachelorship
Sectorial education benchmark standards
Quality Assurance Agency for Higher Education (QAA)
QAA benchmarks

Japan University Association for Computer Education (JUACE)
Cognitive abilities
Generic skills
Communication skills
Teamwork skills
Interpersonal skills
International Education Standards for Professional Accountants (IES)
Financial System Council (FSC)
Provisional professional association membership
Certified Public Accountants and Auditing Oversight Board (CPAAOB)
Financial Service Agency (FSA)
Multiple-choice-type examination
Essay-type examination
Accounting school (AS)
Accreditation Organization for Professional Accounting Schools (AOPAS)
Japan Association of Graduate Schools for Professional Accountancy (JAGSPA)
Full professional association membership
Japan Federation of Certified Public Tax Accountants' Association (JFCPTAA)
TKC Corporation
Small and medium-sized enterprises (SMEs)
CPA license
American Institute of Certified Public Accountants (AICPA)
Institute of Chartered Accountants in Australia (ICAA)
Global Accounting Association (GAA)
Successful CPA examinees
Financial crisis
International Education Standards for Professional Accountants (IESs)
International Accounting Education Standards Board (IAESB)
International Federation of Accountants (IFAC)
Active Learning Approach (ALA)
Simulation game
Critical thinking skills
Engagement
Motives
Professional judgment skills

Notes

1 See the CPAs Law, Art.5, and CPAAOB website, www.fsa.go.jp/cpaaob.
2 Nihon Keizai Shimbun on November 16, 2011, www.chubu-gu.ac.jp/media/2010/101116-01 (accessed February 17, 2016).
3 In Japan, there are the three major cram schools for preparing for the CPA examination: TAC Co. Ltd (www.tac-school.co.jp/tac/english), O-hara (www.o-hara.ac.jp), and Tokyo Legal Mind K. K. (www.lec-jp.com/english). There are also countless other independent cram schools in all other local areas of Japan. In general, this type of school is referred to as a cram school.
4 FSA website, www.fsa.go.jp/common/diet/index.html (accessed February 17, 2016).
5 The Japanese Institute of Certified Public Accountants (JICPA) website, www.hp.jicpa.or.jp/ippan/jicpa_pr/news/post_1515.html (accessed February 17, 2015).
6 Source: www.mext.go.jp/component/b_menu/shingi/toushin/__icsFiles/afieldfile/2013/05/13/1212958_001.pdf (accessed February 17, 2016).

7 Source: www.scj.go.jp/ja/info/kohyo/pdf/kohyo-21-k100-1.pdf (accessed February 17, 2016).
8 This statement was issued by the Quality Assurance Agency for Higher Education (QAA) in the UK, which has released benchmark statements for a total of 59 subjects, including accounting. See www.qaa.ac.uk/en/Publications/Documents/SBS-Accounting-16.pdf (accessed February 17, 2016).
9 Source: www.fsa.go.jp/cpaaob/kouninkaikeishi-shiken/shikeniin29.pdf (accessed February 17, 2016).
10 See www.fsa.go.jp/cpaaob/kouninkaikeishi-shiken/hani.pdf (accessed February 17, 2016).
11 Source: www.fsa.go.jp/cpaaob/kouninkaikeishi-shiken/annai28a.pdf (accessed February 17, 2016).
12 Source: www.fsa.go.jp/cpaaob/kouninkaikeishi-shiken/hani28-b/01.pdf (accessed February 17, 2016).
13 Source: www.jagspa.org/university.htm (accessed February 17, 2016).
14 See www.hp.jicpa.or.jp/english/accounting/cpe/index.html (accessed February 17, 2016).
15 Source: www.hp.jicpa.or.jp/ippan/about/outline/pdf/kaiinnsu-201601.pdf (accessed February 17, 2016).
16 See CPAAOB website, www.fsa.go.jp/cpaaob/kouninkaikeishi-shiken/ronbungoukaku_22a.html (accessed February 17, 2016).

References

Anon (2015) Continuous miscalculation of accounting schools. *Nihon-Keizai-Shinbun*, June 12, 2015 (in Japanese).
Anderson, P.H. and Lawton, L. (2009) Business simulation and cognitive learning: Developments, desires and future directions. *Simulation and Gaming*, 40(2), 193–216.
Financial Service Agency (FSA) (2010) *2nd Round Table Conference for Certified Public Accountant Scheme held on 20 January 2010*. Retrieved from www.fsa.go.jp/singi/kaikeisi/gijiroku/20100120.html (accessed February 17, 2016).
Financial System Council (2002) *A Report of Subcommittee on Certified Public Accountants System: Vitalizing the Certified Public Accountants Audit System* (*Kohnin Kaikeishi Kansa Seido no Jyujitsu Kyouka*). Tokyo: Financial Service Agency, December 17, 2002. Retrieved from www.fsa.go.jp/news/newsj/14/singi/f-20021217-1.pdf (accessed February 17, 2016).
International Accounting Education Standards Board (IAESB) (2010) *Handbook of International Education Pronouncements 2010 Edition*. New York, NY: IFAC.
International Federation of Accountants (IFAC) (2003) *Introduction to International Education Standards*. Retrieved from www.ifac.org (accessed June 11, 2011).
Jackson, M. (2014) Accounting "boot camp". *Journal of Accounting Education*, 32(1), 88–97.
Loeb, S.E. (2014). Active learning: An advantageous yet challenging approach to accounting ethics instruction. *Journal of Business Ethics*. doi:10.1007/s10551-013-2027-1.
Ministry of Education, Culture, Sport, Science and Technology (MEXT) (2010/2011). Retrieved from www.mext.go.jp/english.
Prince, M. (2004) Does active learning work? A review of the research. *Journal of Engineering Education*, 93(3), 223–231.
Quality Assurance Agency for Higher Education (QAA) (2016) Subject benchmark statement, accounting. Retrieved from www.qaa.ac.uk/en/Publications/Documents/SBS-Accounting-16.pdf (accessed February 17, 2016).
Shima, Y. (2013) Learning cost management through the art of folding paper into a crane. *Shokei-gakuso*, 169, 395–403 (in Japanese).
Sugahara, S. (2013) Japanese accounting academics' perceptions on the global convergence of accounting education in Japan. *Asian Review of Accounting*, 21(3), 180–204.
Sugahara, S. (2016) *Bring Active Learning into the Accounting Classroom*. Paper presented at the European Accounting Association 2016 Annual Congress, Maastricht, the Netherlands, May 2016.
Sugahara, S. and Boland, G. (2009) The accounting profession as a career choice for tertiary business students in Japan – A factor analysis. *Accounting Education: An International Journal*, 18(3), 255–272.
Sugahara, S. and Boland, G. (2011) Effects of exposure to the international education standards on perceived importance of the global harmonization of accounting education among Japanese accounting academics. *Advances in Accounting, Incorporating Advances in International Accounting*, 27(2), 382–389.
Sugahara, S. and Coman, R. (2010) Perceived importance of CPA's generic skills: A Japanese study. *Asian Journal of Finance and Accounting*, 2(1), 1–24.

Sugahara, S., Hiramatsu, K. and Boland, G. (2009) The factors influencing accounting school students' career intentions to become a Certified Public Accountants in Japan. *Asian Review of Accounting*, *17*(1), 5–22.

Urasaki, N. (2010) Development of accounting courses at Japanese universities by teaching international financial reporting standards. *Shokei-gakuso*, *57*(2), 297–317 (in Japanese).

Ushio, S. (2014) Applying "paper tower" game in accounting education and its effectiveness. *Journal of Accounting Education and Research*, *2*, 22–31 (in Japanese).

Watty, K., Sugahara, S., Abayadeera, N., Perera, L. and McKay, J. (2012) Developing a global model of accounting education and examining IES compliance in Australia, Japan and Sri Lanka. *The Final Report for IAAER/ACCA Awards Grants for Research to Inform the International Accounting Education Standards Board (IAESB)*, October 2012. Retrieved from http://files.iaaer.org/research/Watty_et_al_Final_Report_submitted_to_funding_bodies_October_29_2012.pdf?1406817904 (accessed February 17, 2016).

16

Accounting education
in Singapore

Chan Yoke Kai, Uantchern Loh and Allene Ng Bee Lian

Introduction

Singapore is well positioned as a key business and financial hub in Southeast Asia. The business-friendly environment makes it attractive to corporations ranging from Fortune 500 multinationals to start-ups. The Singapore government is also working towards a vision to make Singapore the global accountancy hub by the year 2020. These factors have created strong demand for well-qualified accountancy professionals. As the profession continues to grow, there will be a significant demand for accounting education to train more qualified accountants. The annual cohort of accounting graduates from local universities has been stretched to meet the demands for talent. Accounting and finance recruitment in Singapore saw an 18 per cent increase in the number of job vacancies advertised in the first quarter of 2015, according to research from the Robert Walters Asia Jobs Index (Kan, 2015).

Full-time accounting education began in Singapore in 1956. Since then, remarkable progress has been made in the quality and complexity of accounting education. These developments have initially been documented in Tan *et al.* (1994). Since 2010, significant reforms in the accountancy sector have taken place. These changes in the accounting landscape are still evolving and have a significant impact on how accountants are educated and trained.

This chapter examines the general framework for accounting education in Singapore and the pathway to become a chartered accountant of Singapore, or CA (Singapore) This chapter is organized as follows. The next section traces the birth of the vision to make Singapore the leading global accountancy hub. The third section introduces the institutional framework and key stakeholders who collaborate together to drive the accounting profession towards achieving this grand vision. The fourth section examines the requirements to qualify as a CA (Singapore). The fifth section examines the accounting education curriculum for accredited degree programmes offered by Singapore universities. The sixth section describes the collaboration between Singapore and other international professional accounting bodies, and provides some insights into the future. The last section concludes.

The vision of accounting development in Singapore

Vision and strategy

The Singapore government recently started an initiative to transform the country into a leading global accountancy hub. This journey began in December 2008 when the Committee to Develop the Accountancy Sector (CDAS) was formed by the Ministry of Finance to undertake a holistic review of the Singapore accountancy sector and profession. The committee comprises leading members of the accounting profession, business community, academia and the public sector.

The first work that CDAS did was to solicit feedback and suggestions from a wide range of stakeholders, which included undergraduates, educators, public accountants, professional accountants, national and international professional bodies, company directors, chambers of commerce, chief financial officers and government agencies. With valuable input from the feedback, CDAS mapped out a vision to transform the Singapore accountancy sector into the leading global accountancy hub for the Asia-Pacific region by 2020.

CDAS specifies that a global accountancy hub should have some distinct characteristics. First, it has to have an accounting profession that embraces an international outlook with high value-adding expertise and professionals with uncompromising adherence to ethics and integrity. Second, it must have a professional development environment that is vibrant with a diversity of talents, skills and professional bodies with strong contributions in knowledge leadership, research and development. With this vision in mind, CDAS defines three strategic aims: 1) becoming a leading global centre for accountancy talent, education, thought leadership and professional development; 2) becoming a leading centre for high value-adding professional accountancy services; and 3) having strong accountancy-sector infrastructure and institutions.

In line with the above strategy, CDAS has set the following goals for the accountancy sector over the next 10 years: 1) doubling the accountancy sector's contribution to Singapore's Gross Domestic Product, from the existing 0.4 per cent to about 1 per cent over the next decade; and 2) to double the export contribution of professional accountancy services by the sector to the Asia–Pacific region from the current 22 per cent to 50 per cent.

Recommendations

More than a year after the issuance of this grand vision, CDAS submitted its final report, *Transforming Singapore into a Leading Global Accountancy Hub for Asia-Pacific* to the minister for finance on 12 April 2010. The final report contains 10 key recommendations, which set out the key focus areas to raise sector-wide professional capabilities and to strengthen the international outlook for accountancy sector. Three of the CDAS's recommendations under the first strategic aim – 'Leading global centre for accountancy talent, education, thought leadership and professional development' – are described here as they have a significant impact on accounting education.

To develop a Singapore-branded post-university accounting qualification programme[1]

This qualification programme, relevant for training auditing professionals and commercial accountants, should be globally recognized, with international portability and an 'Asian market value factor'. It would be administered by the Institute of Singapore Chartered Accountants (ISCA) under the independent oversight of the Singapore Accountancy Commission (SAC).

Admission criteria for this qualification programme should be robust, so applicants for the qualification programme should have accredited university degrees. One important element of the programme is mandatory structured practical experience, which should be acquired via employment-cum-training contracts with accredited training organizations (ATOs). In order to create a professional development environment that is vibrant with a diversity of talents, accountancy programmes should be developed to create pathways that facilitate the entry of degree holders from non-accountancy disciplines, as well as the re-entry of former professional accountants.

This Singapore Qualification Programme (Singapore QP) was launched in June 2013 and its details are described below.

To develop Singapore into a centre of excellence for the professional development of chief financial officers

The specialization pathways include internal audit and risk management, business valuation (especially in the areas relating to intellectual property, brands, corporate finance and arbitration proceedings) and international taxation. Under the SAC's oversight, steering committees should be set up for the development of these specialization pathways, which include the development of professional qualifications, job-specific competency frameworks, certification programmes and a regional examination centre.

In September 2011, the Singapore CFO Institute, for the professional development of chief financial officers, was officially established (Singapore Accountancy Commission, 2016a). In August 2014, in collaboration with the Tax Academy of Singapore,[2] the Singapore Management University launched the SMU–TA Centre for Excellence in Taxation (SMU–TA CET) (Singapore Management University and Tax Academy of Singapore, 2014).

To set up the Accountancy Sector Research Center (ASRC)

The ASRC's objective is to promote high-quality market-relevant research to position the Singapore accountancy sector strongly for new and emerging opportunities in the professional services markets. This is an integral part of the overall effort to promote and position Singapore as a leading global accountancy hub, and for attracting local and international talent from academia and professional practice.

The ASRC's research focus is on developing applied research capabilities in professional accountancy services, and on issues relevant to Singapore and the Asia-Pacific marketplace. Its research areas include application issues arising from developments in international accounting standards, and regulatory reforms that have practical impact in the Asia-Pacific marketplace. ASRC works closely with the Singapore Accounting Standards Council in research and developmental activities relating to financial reporting standards. It is proposed that a SAC research and practice professorship programme could be developed in conjunction with universities to incentivize researchers to conduct market-relevant research and publications. An accountancy research and development fund should be set up (CDAS, April 2010). The ASRC has now been established as the research arm of SAC. The diagram below illustrates the ASRC road map.

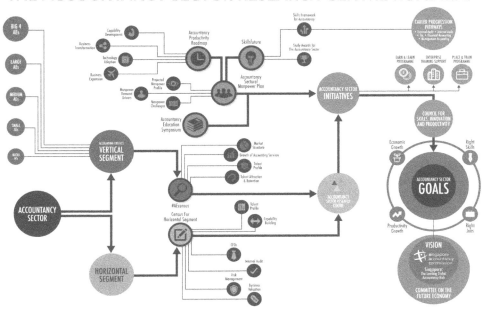

Figure 16.1 Accountancy Sector Research Center road map
Source: Singapore Accountancy Commission, 2016b.

Stakeholders for the accountancy sector

The key stakeholders who collaborate together to reshape accounting education in Singapore include the following.

Singapore Accountancy Commission

In the CDAS final report in April 2010, the tenth recommendation stated:

> To establish a Singapore Accountancy Council. The objective of [which] is to transform Singapore into a leading global accountancy hub through: overseeing the accountancy sector's strategic direction and ensuring the efficient and effective use of incentive programmes to develop the sector; establishing a strong network between Singapore and the international accountancy community and stakeholders; and fostering thought-leadership, research and development activities for accountancy services and their related fields.

In September 2010, a Pro Tem Singapore Accountancy Commission was formed to help realize the CDAS recommendations. Later, the SAC was established as a statutory body of the Singapore government in April 2013 with a mission to develop a vibrant accountancy sector for Singapore that enables the economy to grow, businesses to thrive and talent to flourish. SAC collaborates with local and international communities in order to drive accountancy excellence in Singapore through talent development, professional qualification, research and thought leadership.

237

According to the Singapore Accountancy CommissionAct 2013 (Republic of Singapore Government, 2013), the SAC functions include: 1) to oversee the strategic direction for, and promote, facilitate and assist in, the growth and development of the accountancy sector and related fields in Singapore; 2) to develop, provide or administer, or facilitate or collaborate on the development, provision or administration of programmes, qualifications, certifications, specializations and continuing professional development relating to the accountancy sector and related fields in Singapore; 3) to promote, develop, improve or maintain, or facilitate or collaborate on the promotion, development, improvement or maintenance of, competencies, expertise and professional standards in the accountancy sector and related fields in Singapore; 4) to promote, facilitate or collaborate on research and development activities for the advancement of the accountancy sector and related fields in Singapore; 5) to develop or manage cooperation and exchange with other persons and organizations, including foreign and international organizations, in respect of matters relating to the accountancy sector and related fields in Singapore; and 6) to advise the government on matters relating to the development of the accountancy sector and related fields in Singapore (Singapore Accountancy Commission, 2016i).

Accounting and Corporate Regulatory Authority (ACRA)

The Accounting and Corporate Regulatory Authority (ACRA) was formed as a statutory board on 1 April 2004, following the merger of the then Registry of Companies and Businesses (RCB) and the Public Accountants Board (PAB). It became the national regulator of business entities and public accountants in Singapore. The ACRA also plays the role of a facilitator for the development of business entities and the public accountancy profession. The mission of the ACRA is to provide a responsive and trusted regulatory environment for businesses and public accountants. The ACRA aims to achieve synergies between the monitoring of corporate compliance with disclosure requirements and the regulation of public accountants performing statutory audits with the following responsibilities.

1   To administer the Accounting and Corporate Regulatory Authority Act (Cap 2A), the Accountants Act (Cap 2), the Business Registration Act (Cap 32), the Companies Act (Cap 50), the Limited Liability Partnerships Act (Cap 163A) and the Limited Partnerships Act 2008 (Act 37 of 2008);
2   To report and make recommendations to, and advise the government on matters relating the registration and regulation of business entities and public accountants;
3   To establish and administer a repository of documents and information relating to business entities and public accountants and to provide access to the public to such documents and information;
4   To represent the government internationally in matters relating to the registration and regulation of business entities and public accountants;
5   To promote public awareness about new business structures, compliance requirements, corporate governance practices and any matter under the purview of the authority; and
6   To promote, facilitate and assist in the development of the accountancy sector, including study, report, make recommendations to and advise the government on all matters relating to the development and promotion of the accountancy sector.

Chapter 2 of the Accountants Act in Singapore states that ACRA shall be responsible for the administration of the Act as well as the registration of public accountants and the approval of accounting entities, and the control and regulation of the accounting profession (i.e. public accountants, accounting corporations and accounting firms) (ACRA, 2015).

Institute of Singapore Chartered Accountants (ISCA)

The ISCA is the national accountancy body of Singapore and it has undergone several name changes since 1963. It was originally called the Singapore Society of Accountants (1963), then the Institute of Certified Public Accountants of Singapore (1987) and has been known as the ISCA since 1 July 2013. The ISCA's vision is to be a globally recognized professional accountancy body, bringing value to its members, the profession and the wider community.

The ISCA is the administrator of the Singapore CA Qualification and the designated entity to confer the CA (Singapore) designation. The Singapore Accountancy Commission (SAC) announced on 1 April 2013 that new CA (Singapore) professional designation would be conferred on candidates who had completed the Singapore CA Qualification. The ISCA is responsible for programme admission, module enrolment, workshop arrangement, live examination organization, examination results assessment, candidate management and the accreditation of employers and universities.

The ISCA has three classes of membership: associate (ISCA), chartered accountant of Singapore (CA(Singapore)) and fellow chartered accountant of Singapore (FCA (Singapore)). The ISCA will launch a new membership class, affiliate (ISCA), in 2016. With the introduction of the new membership class in 2016, eligible individuals will have different options for entry into the ISCA, based on relevant pathways as shown in the map below.

Institutions of higher education

Local universities and polytechnics

Singapore's tertiary academic systems produce more than 1,000 accountancy graduates every year, 60 per cent of whom join the Big Four firms, while the rest join financial institutions and other corporations (Singapore Accountancy Commission, 2016c). Accountancy professionals in Singapore have a range of certification programmes to choose from. Among the professional bodies that offer certification programmes are the ISCA (with more than 28,000 members),[3] Certified Public Accountants (CPA) Australia (with 7,000 members)[4] and ACCA Singapore (with 10,000 members)[5] (Singapore Accountancy Commission, 2016c) and the Chartered Institute of Management Accountants (CIMA) (with 229,000 members and students worldwide)[6] (CIMA, 2016).

There are four local universities that offer accredited accountancy degrees with full exemptions from the Singapore CA Qualification foundation programme: Nanyang Technological University (NTU); National University of Singapore (NUS); Singapore University of Social Sciences (SUSS); and Singapore Management University (SMU).[7] In addition, there are four polytechnics that offer accountancy diploma programmes that are recognized by professional bodies: Nanyang Polytechnic (NYP); Ngee Ann Polytechnic (NP); Singapore Polytechnic (SP); and Temasek Polytechnic (TP).

The diplomas from local polytechnics are recognized by all local universities and many overseas universities. Diploma holders also enjoy module exemptions for courses and examinations offered by the ACCA, the CIMA, the Institute of Chartered Accountants in England and Wales (ICAEW) and the Singapore Association of the Institute of Chartered Secretaries and Administrators (SAICSA) (Ngee Ann Polytechnic, 2016).

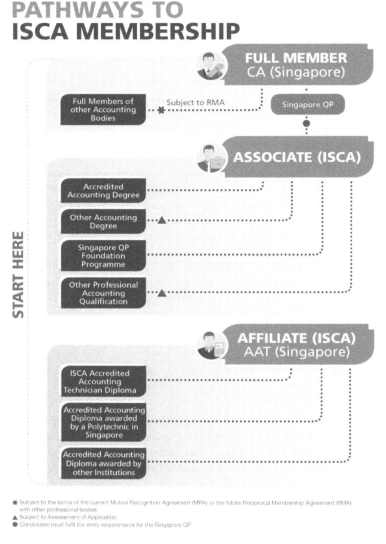

Figure 16.2 Pathways to ISCA membership

Source: Institute of Singapore Chartered Accountants, 2016.

Private-sector education providers

According to data from the Council for Private Education,[8] there are about 40 institutions in the private sector that provide accounting education for professional certification programmes (Council for Private Education, 2015). These private-sector providers collaborate with various foreign universities or professional bodies such as the ACCA and the CIMA. Together, they offer over 140 accounting-related courses at degree, diploma or postgraduate level. Degree holders who graduate from these private institutions are required to complete the Singapore

CA Qualification foundation programme partially or in full, depending on the number of exemptions granted before progressing to the Singapore CA Qualification professional programme.

Singapore CA Qualification (ISCA, 2015a)

The Singapore CA Qualification is a post-university professional accountancy qualification with three main components: academic base, professional programme and practical experience. The Singapore CA Qualification has been developed using the IFAC's International Education Standards as guidance.

Academic base

To satisfy the requirements of the academic base, candidates must have either: 1) an accredited accountancy degree with a five-year validity period commencing from the date of conferment; 2) an accredited degree and have completed the enhanced foundation programme for Singapore CA Qualification; 3) a non-accredited degree, which must be recognized by the SAC as at least

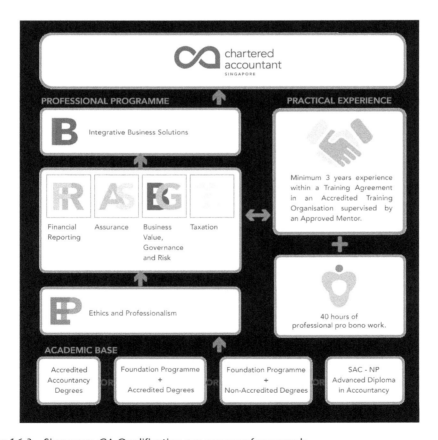

Figure 16.3 Singapore CA Qualification programme framework

Source: Singapore Accountancy Commission, 2016d.

comparable to a three-year undergraduate degree using internationally recognized reference sources, and have completed the enhanced foundation programme for the Singapore CA Qualification; or 4) completed the advanced diploma in accountancy offered by the Singapore Accountancy Commission–Ngee Ann Polytechnic (SAC–NP).

Accredited accountancy degree holders and the SAC–NP advanced diploma holders with full exemptions from the foundation programme would qualify for direct entry to the professional programme. Currently, there are six accredited accountancy degrees with full exemptions from the foundation programme.[9] The SAC–NP advanced diploma in accountancy is an eighteen-month work–study programme tailored to polytechnic graduates who hold a diploma in accountancy (or equivalent) from one of the four local polytechnics. Candidates who are enrolled onto the course will take the same centralized examinations for the Singapore CA Qualification foundation programme conducted by the SAC. These candidates must also work full-time with an accredited training organization (ATO) and accumulate 180 hours of supervised industry practice over a minimum period of eighteen months. Graduates from the advanced diploma in accountancy will be specialists in the domains of accounting, auditing and taxation. They may progress to the Singapore CA Qualification professional programme to attain the chartered accountant of Singapore designation (Singapore Accountancy Commission, 2016e).

Foundation programme

The foundation programme provides a pathway for applicants without accredited accountancy degrees to meet the entry requirements of the professional programme.

The existing foundation programme covers six core areas: financial accounting and reporting; management accounting; financial management; audit and assurance; Singapore law; and Singapore taxation.

Since the launch of the Singapore CA Qualification foundation programme in 2013, the SAC has been continuously seeking feedback from stakeholders on ways to improve the programme. The review has been conducted in consultation with the Singapore CA Qualification Academic Workgroup, which comprises leading employers, academics from local universities and industry practitioners. As a result, the enhanced Singapore CA Qualification foundation programme was proposed to be officially launched in August 2016, with the first Singapore CA Qualification foundation programme centralized examinations to be held in December 2016. The enhanced foundation programme covers a set of six core syllabus areas: principles of financial reporting (PFF); advanced financial reporting (AFF); accounting for decision making (ADF); assurance (ASF); financial management (FMF); and Singapore taxation (TXF) (Singapore Accountancy Commission, 2016f).

Professional programme

The professional programme consists of six modules, namely ethics and professionalism (EP); four technical modules (financial reporting (FR), assurance (AS), taxation (TX), business value, governance and risk (BG)); and integrative business solutions (IB) (Singapore Accountancy Commission, 2016g).

Practical experience

As part of the Singapore CA Qualification, candidates have to complete a mandatory structured practical experience component. They will have to accumulate three years of relevant practical experience within an ATO) under the guidance of a mentor and achieve: 1) a minimum of 450 days' (three years') practical experience; and 2) a minimum of five days' professional pro bono work over this period. The practical experience must be of a financial or business nature, and the pro bono work must be in areas of finance or accounting. The functional areas where practical experience can be gained includes, but is not limited to, finance, audit (internal or external), taxation, compliance and risk management, treasury, business recovery, restructuring and insolvency, and information technology. Practical experience can be gained in a range of functional areas or in one area. It would be expected that a significant proportion of experience should be spent in one or two specific key areas of competence relating to the candidate's role or roles within the ATO. If a candidate spends the bulk of the training in one area of work, it is necessary that the candidate gains an in-depth understanding in that specialized area.

Competence development

The competence development component consists of generic competences and technical competences. In order to satisfy the general skills required, candidates must demonstrate that they are competent in nine generic areas as shown in Figure 16.4.

Candidates will demonstrate different technical skills depending on their professional career plans. Candidates are required to be competent in basic accounting and finance in order to become a chartered accountant of Singapore. There are five areas of technical competence, each comprising three elements, making a total of 15 elements. Candidates are required to demonstrate effectiveness in a total of four elements, including one financial reporting element. The areas and elements of technical competence are shown in Figure 16.5.

Accredited training organization

An accredited training organization (ATO) is an employer that has been certified by the Singapore Accountancy Commission (SAC) to possess the appropriate standards of staff training, accountancy resources and development for Singapore CA Qualification candidates to fulfil their practical experience requirement. ATOs form a crucial part of the Singapore

A. ETHICS AND PROFESSIONALISM	B. ORGANISATION AND BUSINESS MANAGEMENT	C. PERSONAL EFFECTIVENESS
A1 Professional Ethics, Values and Judgement	**B1** Information and Technology	**C1** Self-Awareness
A2 Risk Management and Compliance	**B2** Critical Thinking, Reasoning, Analysis and Problem Solving	**C2** Manage Self and Others
A3 Business Awareness and Strategy	**B3** Manage and Deliver Activities	**C3** Business Communication

Figure 16.4 Generic competencies
Source: Singapore Accountancy Commission, 2015, p. 7.

243

FR FINANCIAL REPORTING	AS ASSURANCE	DSA DECISION SUPPORT AND ANALYSIS	GR GOVERNANCE AND RISK	TX TAXATION
FR1 Accounting for Transactions	AS1 Planning an Engagement	DSA1 Cost Management and Evaluation	GR1 Identifying and Managing Risk	TX1 Tax Computations
FR2 Preparing Financial Reports	AS2 Performing an Audit Engagement	DSA2 Cash Management, Planning and Budgetary Control	GR2 Designing Internal Controls	TX2 Tax Compliance
FR3 Analysing Financial Reports	AS3 Audit Review and Reporting	DSA3 Appraising Investments	GR3 Monitoring Performance and Accountability	TX3 Tax Planning

Figure 16.5 Technical competencies

Source: Singapore Accountancy Commission, 2015, p. 7.

CA Qualification, as they provide training and development opportunities for Singapore CA Qualification candidates to foster their competences and gain valuable experience in a professional environment. In order to hire, train and develop Singapore CA Qualification candidates, organizations must first be accredited by the SAC. The SAC first started accrediting ATOs in January 2013. There were about 299 ATOs as at the end of April 2017 (Singapore Accountancy Commission, 2016h).

New pathways

On 12 November 2015, the ISCA announced that it would create more pathways to enable more talents to enter the accounting profession, as a response to the government's skills future initiative,[10] as well as the shortage of skilled talent in accounting and finance in a tight labour market in the country.

Affiliate membership

As mentioned above, the ISCA has introduced a new affiliate membership class, which enables non-graduates to become ISCA members, providing them with professional support and recognition. The new affiliate membership class aims to professionalize the accounting technician segment and provide support in their continuing professional development. The ISCA is also offering the ISCA accredited accounting technician (ISCA–AAT) diploma in partnership with the Association of Accounting Technicians (AAT), the world's leading professional membership body dedicated to the education and development of accounting technicians. The ISCA–AAT diploma is a flexible skills-based programme that offers aspiring accounting technicians an opportunity to complement and give recognition to their experience with a structured and formal training programme that is internationally recognized.

The programme comprises three levels of practical skills training. To help students keep abreast of the latest technologies, the ISCA–AAT diploma programme includes a module on 'information technology for accountants', equipping them with the skills to interpret and analyse generated data. Apart from the latest digital skills, other skills that will be developed range from basic bookkeeping, accounting practices and techniques and preparation of reports to higher-level accounting tasks such as the drafting of financial statements, the evaluation of financial performance and auditing.

Individuals who are equipped with at least the Cambridge ordinary certificate or graduates in accounting from the Institute of Technical Education can enter the diploma programme. Upon completion of the programme and with one year's relevant work experience, they will attain the accredited accounting technician (Singapore) designation and be eligible to become ISCA affiliates. The ISCA is currently in discussion with the Association of Accounting Technicians to sign a mutual recognition agreement, which will enable graduates of the ISCA–AAT diploma to become full members of the AAT and achieve global recognition.

Applications to be ISCA affiliates commenced in June 2016. Applicants must hold accredited accounting diplomas awarded by local polytechnics, other institutes or the ISCA–AAT diploma which will see its first batch of graduates in 2019. Applicants will also need to have at least one year's practical experience verified by their employer. The ISCA is currently working with higher education institutions in Singapore and other professional bodies to accredit equivalent qualifications.

Associate membership

The ISCA also aims to expand the diversity as well as length and breadth of the talent pool by allowing accountancy graduates of foreign universities to become associate members. Previously, only graduates of local universities, those who had completed the ISCA professional examination or those with recognized accounting qualifications were eligible for associate membership. To be eligible for associate membership, an applicant must have an accredited accountancy degree or an accountancy degree recognized by ISCA, hold a recognized professional accountancy membership or be pursuing other recognized accountancy qualification programmes. In addition, current Singapore CA Qualification candidates will be eligible to apply for associate membership (ISCA, 2015b).

The educational curriculum – accredited accountancy degree programmes

This section provides an overview of the accredited accountancy degrees offered by four local universities: Nanyang Technological University (NTU), National University of Singapore (NUS), Singapore University of Social Sciences (SUSS) and Singapore Management University (SMU).

The programme requirements for all six accredited degrees are summarized in Tables 16.1 to 16.4, in Appendix I below. Table 16.5 in Appendix I lists the core accounting and business courses for each of these programmes.[11] All four universities cover accounting technical skills adequately in their degree programmes. The weights of accounting and business courses within each programme, measured as a percentage of the total credit requirements for each programme, range from about 56 per cent to 88 per cent, with the SUSS part-time accountancy degree programme having the highest weight of accounting core content. The SUSS part-time accountancy degree programme caters to working adults, hence it focuses more on developing depth in technical skills.

The full-time bachelor's degree programmes cater mostly to students who do not have working experience. Therefore, the curriculums of full-time programmes tend to be broader, to equip students with soft skills such as leadership and communication, which are essential for developing students to become well-rounded and socially responsible professionals. For example, the NUS has personal development and career management courses, where students learn job search strategies, CV writing, interviewing skills, the understanding of their strengths and job motivations, networking techniques and business etiquette and corporate dress.

To help students gain working experience, all full-time programmes in the four universities have compulsory internship or professional attachment, with duration ranging from eight to 24 weeks. SUSS has the longest professional attachment, which can be completed in either a continuous or a cumulative period of 24 weeks, with each period to be at least eight weeks in duration. The NTU has an experiential semester programme (NTU, 2016a), where students have the option of taking up a semester-long internship and still be able to complete their programme in the usual time span of three years.

In addition, some universities require students to work on community service projects as a graduating requirement. SMU requires students to perform 80 hours of community service. The SUSS full-time programme includes a service learning component, in which students are expected to research, discuss and propose a service learning collaboration in consultation with local community partners. Students work on a sustainable endeavour that meets the needs identified by the community partner over a period of two years or more.

Another interesting observation is that all four universities have overseas exchange programmes, whereby students can study or work overseas during their professional attachment. This is a reflection of Singapore's educational system, which places significant emphasis on helping students to gain overseas experience.

International collaborations and the future

Although the CA (Singapore) designation is the youngest professional CA designation in the world, it is also the fastest to be inducted into an international body. In June 2015, barely two years after its debut, Chartered Accountants Worldwide welcomed the ISCA as its first associate member. The original members of Chartered Accountants Worldwide are from five prestigious chartered accountancy professional bodies in the world – Scotland, England and Wales, Australia and New Zealand, South Africa, and Ireland. The move to include Singapore reflects the confidence that the global chartered accountancy community holds for the CA (Singapore) designation.

The SAC, together with the ISCA, has also signed expressions of intent to explore reciprocal membership with each of the five full members of Chartered Accountants Worldwide, which will ultimately provide CA (Singapore) title holders with international recognition and global mobility. In addition, the SAC has signed agreements with the CA ANZ and the ICAEW relating to the interchange ability of two professional level modules on the subjects of financial reporting and assurance. Thus, the financial reporting and assurance modules of the Singapore CA Qualification are interchangeable with their equivalent modules in the CA ANZ and ICAEW examinations. This allows Singapore CA Qualification and CA ANZ/ICAEW candidates choices on which examinations to take.

The vision for Singapore to be the leading global accountancy hub will start with the CA (Singapore) designation being globally recognized. With that as a foundation, there is an aspiration for accountants in the region and global markets to come to Singapore for their professional development and certification as CFOs and internal auditors, and to acquire specialized skills in risk management, taxation and business valuation.

Conclusion

As Singapore continues to attract multinational corporations as a key business and financial hub in the Asia-Pacific region, the growing demand for finance and accounting professionals has led to a talent crunch that is challenging the profession. The Institute of Singapore Chartered Accountants (ISCA) is addressing this challenge by creating new pathways to become a CA (Singapore), while concurrently implementing more stringent qualification criteria so as not to compromise the quality of accounting expertise.

The Singapore CA Qualification is still evolving, and as it evolves there may be opportunities to further enhance the programme so as to meet the changing demands of business and industry. The Singapore CA Qualification should continuously develop to support the growth of the accountancy profession. For example, the SAC can cast the net wider by involving more world-class corporations as ATOs. The current list of ATOs is relatively limited considering the size of the Singapore economy and the large number of corporate employers in Singapore. The number of ATOs needs to grow rapidly in order to expand the employment opportunities available for Singapore CA Qualification candidates.

Appendix I: accredited degree programmes

Table 16.1 Nanyang Technological University

Programme	Duration	Courses	Requirement
Bachelor of Accountancy (Nanyang Technological University, 2016b)	Full-time – three years Direct honours	Foundational core	10 courses
		Accounting core	Nine courses
		Career foundations	Two courses
		Strategic management	Capstone course
		General education requirements:	Six core courses
		Core	Three prescribed electives
		Prescribed electives	
		Unrestricted electives	Four to fve electives
		Total	35 courses
		Internship (Professional Attachment)	Eight to 10 weeks
Master of Science in Accountancy (Nanyang Technological University, 2016c)	Part-time – two years Full-time – one year	Business Core	Three courses
		Accountancy Core	Nine courses
		Total	12 courses

Table 16.2 National University of Singapore

Programme	Duration	Courses	Requirement
Bachelor of Business Administration (Accountancy) (National University of Singapore, 2016)	Full-time bachelor's degree – three years Note: bachelor's degree with honours requires 160 MCs and will usually take about four years to complete	University-level requirements • General education courses (at least eight MCs) • Singapore studies course (at least four MCs) • Breadth: electives outside business school (at least eight MCs)	20 modular credits (MCs)

		Programme requirements
		
		• Major requirements
		  (a) 15 core courses (worth 60 MCs)
		  (b) eight accounting essential courses (worth 32 MCs)
			92 MCs

		Unrestricted elective courses Five compulsory accounting courses	8 MCs
		Total	120 MCs
		Internship (National University of Singapore, 2013)	Eight weeks

Table 16.3 Singapore University of Social Sciences

Programme	Duration	Courses	Requirement
Bachelor of Accountancy (Singapore University of Social Sciences, 2016)	Part-time – four to eight years Direct honours	Accountancy courses	70 credit units (cu)
		Accounting theory and practice	10 cu Accountancy capstone course
		Business courses	50 cu
		Business strategy	10 cu
		Elective courses from accountancy, analytics or finance	10 cu
		General electives	10 cu
		University core courses	10 cu
		Total	170 cu

Bachelor of Accountancy (SSUS, 2016)	Full-time – four years Direct honours	Accountancy courses	75 cu
		Accountancy capstone course	10 cu
		Business courses	65 cu
		Common curriculum courses	40 cu
		Applied project	10 cu
		Total	200 cu
		Work attachment (SIM University, 2016)	24 weeks
		Service learning	Two years

Table 16.4 Singapore Management University

Programme	*Duration*	*Courses*	*Requirement*
SMU Bachelor of Accountancy (Singapore Management University, 2016a)	Full-time – three to four years Direct honours	Accounting core	Nine courses
		Accounting options	Three courses
		Foundation	Three courses
		University core	Four courses
		Business subjects	Eight courses
		General education	Four courses
		Modes of thinking	One course
		Asian studies	One course
		Entrepreneurship	One course
		Globalization	One course
		Technology studies	One course
		Total	36 courses
		Internship	12 weeks, of which two weeks must be spent in a voluntary welfare organization
		Community service	80 hours
		Finishing touch career workshops	Graduating requirement
SMU Master of Professional Accounting (Singapore Management University, 2016b)	Part-time – two years Full-time – one year	Accounting core	Six courses
		Business fundamentals	Three courses
		Professional services	Three courses
		Professional leadership development	One course
		Total	13 courses

Table 16.5 Compulsory accounting and business courses in accredited accountancy degree programmes in Singapore*

Content	NTU — Bachelor of Accountancy (Nanyang Technological University, 2016b)	NTU — Master of Science in Accountancy (Nanyang Technological University, 2016c)	NUS — Bachelor of Business Administration (Accountancy) (National University of Singapore, 2016)	SMU — Bachelor of Accountancy (Singapore Management University, 2016a)	SMU — Master of Professional Accounting (Singapore Management University, 2016b)	SUSS — Bachelor of Accountancy (SUSS, 2016)
Accounting courses:						
Accounting	Compulsory					
Accounting theory and practice	Compulsory	Compulsory	Compulsory	Compulsory		Compulsory
Assurance, attestation and auditing				Compulsory	Compulsory	Compulsory
Financial accounting		Compulsory	Compulsory	Compulsory	Compulsory	Compulsory
Intermediate financial accounting				Compulsory		
Advanced financial accounting				Compulsory	Compulsory	
Managerial accounting			Compulsory	Compulsory	Compulsory	Compulsory
Corporate accounting/financial reporting/accounting recognition and measurement	Compulsory	Compulsory	Compulsory	Compulsory	Compulsory	Compulsory
Corporate governance and risk management	Compulsory	Compulsory	Compulsory			Compulsory
Accounting for decision making, planning and control	Compulsory	Compulsory				Compulsory
Risk reporting and analysis	Compulsory	Compulsory				Compulsory
Taxation	Compulsory	Compulsory	Compulsory	Compulsory	Compulsory	Compulsory

Content		*included in the Financial management course			
Valuation	Compulsory			Compulsory	Compulsory	Compulsory
Corporate advisory		Compulsory			
Integrated perspectives in accounting and business				Compulsory	
Business courses:					
Economics	Compulsory	Compulsory	Compulsory	Compulsory		Compulsory
Business analytics – data and decisions			Compulsory	Compulsory	
Management/organization	Compulsory	Compulsory	Compulsory	Compulsory		Compulsory
Operations management			Compulsory	Compulsory	
Marketing	Compulsory			Compulsory		Compulsory
Statistics and quantitative methods	Compulsory	Compulsory	Compulsory	Compulsory		Compulsory
Decision analysis			Compulsory		
Strategy	Compulsory	Compulsory	Compulsory	Compulsory	Compulsory	Compulsory
Finance courses:					
Finance	Compulsory		Compulsory	Compulsory	
Financial instruments, institutions and markets			Compulsory		
Financial management	Compulsory	Compulsory		Compulsory	Compulsory	Compulsory
Law courses:					
Business law	Compulsory	Compulsory (combined)	Compulsory	Compulsory	Compulsory (combined)	Compulsory
Company law	Compulsory		Compulsory	Compulsory	Compulsory	Compulsory
Technology courses:					
Accounting information systems	Compulsory	Compulsory	Compulsory	Compulsory	Compulsory	Compulsory

* Table 16.5 is to facilitate comparison of the compulsory accounting and business courses across the six accredited accountancy degree programmes in Singapore. The Content column shows the types of courses in programme structure. Some of the names of courses listed in Table 16.5 have been modified or combined to facilitate the comparison and grouping of common courses, hence the actual names used in the curriculums published by the universities may vary. In addition to the courses listed in this chapter, there are other general core subjects that are not specific to accounting or business, as well as elective and optional courses, that are not listed in Table 16.5.

Notes

1 With effect from 1 January 2017, the Singapore Qualification Programme (Singapore QP) will be known as the Singapore CA Qualification and the foundation programme will be known as the Singapore CA Qualification (Foundation).
2 The Tax Academy was set up in 2006 by the Inland Revenue Authority of Singapore in collaboration with the international accounting firms of Deloitte & Touche, Ernst & Young, KPMG and PricewaterhouseCoopers, the Institute of Singapore Chartered Accountants and the Law Society of Singapore. It offers a comprehensive and structured tax education on Singapore taxes.
3 These members reside in Singapore.
4 See note 2.
5 See note 2.
6 These are the total global numbers.
7 The educational curriculum and structure of the accredited degree programmes offered by the universities are described in detail in this chapter.
8 The Council for Private Education is a statutory board established in December 2009 to regulate the private education industry.
9 They are: 1) Bachelor of Accountancy from Nanyang Technological University; 2) Master of Science in Accountancy from Nanyang Technological University; 3) Bachelor of Business Administration (Accountancy) from National University of Singapore; 4) Bachelor of Accountancy from Singapore University of Social Sciences 5) Bachelor of Accountancy from Singapore Management University; and 6) Master of Professional Accounting from Singapore Management University.
10 SkillsFuture is a national movement to provide Singaporeans with the opportunities to develop a future based on skills mastery, through driving an integrated system of education, training and career progression for all Singaporeans, promoting industry support for individuals to advance based on skills and fostering a culture of lifelong learning.
11 The information provided in this chapter is based on the programmes for the 2015/2016 academic year.

References

ACRA (2015) *About ACRA*. Retrieved from www.acra.gov.sg (accessed 16 September 2016).
CDAS (2010) *Final Report of the Committee to Develop the Accountancy Sector*. Singapore: Singapore Accountancy Commission. Retrieved from www.sac.gov.sg/sites/default/files/CDAS-FinalReport-12Apr10.pdf.
CIMA (2016) Retrieved from www.cimaglobal.com/Our-locations/Singapore (accessed 24 February 2016).
Council for Private Education (2015) Retrieved from www.cpe.gov.sg.
Institute of Singapore Chartered Accountants (2016) *Pathways to ISCA Membership*. Retrieved from www.isca.org.sg.
ISCA (2015a) *New Pathways to Widen Accountancy Talent Pipeline*. Retrieved from www.isca.org.sg/the-institute/newsroom/media-releases/2015/november/new-pathways-to-widen-accountancy-talent-pipeline.
ISCA (2015b) *Singapore CA Qualification*. Retrieved from www.isca.org.sg/become-a-member/qp/sg-qp.
Kan, F. (2015) Unlocking the future. *Accounting and Business*, 16(October).
Nanyang Technological University (NTU) (2016a) Retrieved from www.nbs.ntu.edu.sg/Undergraduate/Documents/NBS_Brochure_2016.pdf.
Nanyang Technological University (NTU) (2016b) *Bachelor of Accountancy Programme Structure*. Retrieved from www.nbs.ntu.edu.sg/Undergraduate/Bachelor_of_Accountancy/Pages/Programme_Structure.aspx.
Nanyang Technological University (NTU) (2016c) *Master of Science in Accountancy*. Retrieved from www.nbs.ntu.edu.sg/Graduate/nanyangmscacc/AbouttheProgramme/Pages/CourseSchedules.aspx.
National University of Singapore (2013) *Accountancy Internship*. Retrieved from http://bba.nus.edu/undergrad_acc_internship.html.
National University of Singapore (2016) *NUS Bulletin AY 2015/16*. Retrieved from www.nus.edu.sg/registrar/nusbulletin/school-business/bachelor-business-administration-accountancy-bachelor-business-administration-accountancy-honours.
Ngee Ann Polytechnic (2016) *Diploma in Accountancy*. Retrieved from www.np.edu.sg/ba/courses/acc/Pages/acc.aspx.

Republic of Singapore Government (2013) *Singapore Accountancy Commission Act 2013*. Retrieved from http://statutes.agc.gov.sg.

Singapore University of Social Sciences (2016) *Accountancy*. Retrieved from Singapore University of Social Sciences, http://uc.suss.edu.sg/accountancy.html.

Singapore University of Social Sciences (2016) *Full-time Programmes > The UC Experience*. Retrieved from Singapore University of Social Sciences, http://uc.suss.edu.sg/programmeComponents.html.

Singapore Accountancy Commission (2015) *ATO Guide to Practical Experience*. Retrieved from www.singaporecaqualification.com/sites/sgqp/files/ATO%20Guide%20to%20Practical%20Experience.pdf.

Singapore Accountancy Commission (2016a) *The Singapore CFO Institute*. Retrieved from www.sac.gov.sg/advocacy/singapore-cfo-institute/chapter-2.

Singapore Accountancy Commission (2016b) *Accountancy Sector Research Centre*. Retrieved from www.sac.gov.sg/accountancy-sector-research-centre.

Singapore Accountancy Commission (2016c) *Key Trends*. Retrieved from www.sac.gov.sg/insight/key-trends.

Singapore Accountancy Commission (2016d) *Singapore CA Qualification at a Glance / Overview*. Retrieved from www.singaporecaqualification.com/candidates/singapore-qp-glance/overview.

Singapore Accountancy Commission (2016e) *SAC–NP Advanced Diploma in Accountancy*. Retrieved from www.singaporecaqualification.com/candidates/sac-np-advanced-diploma-in-accountancy.

Singapore Accountancy Commission. (2016f) *Foundation Programme*. Retrieved from www.singaporecaqualification.com/candidates/foundation-programme/overview.

Singapore Accountancy Commission (2016g) *Professional Programme*. Retrieved from www.singaporecaqualification.com/candidates/professional-programme.

Singapore Accountancy Commission (2016h) *List of ATOs*. Retrieved from www.singaporecaqualification.com/candidates/professional-programme/accredited-training-organisations/list-of-atos.

Singapore Accountancy Commission (2016i) *About Us*. Retrieved from www.sac.gov.sg.

Singapore Management University (2016a) *Bachelor of Accountancy (BACC)*. Retrieved from www.smu.edu.sg/programmes/undergraduate/bacc.

Singapore Management University (2016b) *Master of Professional Accounting*. Retrieved from http://accountancy.smu.edu.sg/master-professional-accounting/curriculum.

Singapore Management University and Tax Academy of Singapore (2014) *Tax Academy of Singapore/Newsroom*. Retrieved from www.taxacademy.sg/newsroom.html.

Tan, T.M., Pang, Y.H. and Foo, S.L. (1994) Accounting education and practice: The Singapore experience. *The International Journal of Accounting*, *29*(2), 161–183.

253

Part VI
Accounting development in Asian emerging economies

Some Asian countries, such as China, India, South Korea and Singapore, are among the fastest-growing economies in the world but there are also a few countries in Asia with relatively slow economic growth and social development, owing to constraints from their political, economic and social systems inherited from historical institutional settings. However, these Asian countries have embarked on the journey of economic transition at varied paces, with various reforms measures introduced to promote economic growth and social development. Correspondingly, accounting practices in these countries have also been reformed, with significant changes or engaging in the process of accounting internationalization to different degrees, following demands or pressures from international aid agencies or donors over recent years.

Owing to their relatively small economic scales and slow economic growth and social progress, accounting developments in these Asian emerging economies have long been overlooked, receiving little exposure in Western accounting literature. In addition, some of these countries had installed different political and economic administration systems (such as Vietnam and Mongolia, which were the members of the former Soviet Bloc and had highly centralized planning economies), and their accounting practices, which departed substantially from international norms, did not receive sufficient attention from mainstream accounting studies. Thus, this part introduces the most recent accounting developments in these emerging Asian countries, including Vietnam (Chapter 17), Bangladesh (Chapter 18), Cambodia (Chapter 19) and Mongolia (Chapter 20), in order to facilitate international communities and investors to gain an understanding of the accounting practices and their current levels of advancement towards the internationalization of accounting in these emerging Asian economies, as well as to enrich the accounting literature.

Vietnam has experienced a series of periods of war in its recent history. After the end of the Vietnam War in the late 1970s, the reunited country adopted the former Soviet-style highly centralized planned economy. Vietnamese accounting was then designed to accomplish the needs of centralized economic planning and administration rather than for micro-economic decision-making, and this system remained in effect until 1995.

However, as indicated in Chapter 17, the Vietnamese government introduced the 'Open door' policy (called the Renovation) in the late 1980s, with the aim of developing a market-oriented economy and integrating Vietnam into the world market. To keep pace with the progress of the national campaign of economic reforms since the early 1990s, the Vietnamese government commenced accounting reforms and participated in the harmonization of accounting with international norms, in order to attract foreign investment for economic transition, under the financial support and encouragement of some international organizations or sponsors such as the EUROTAP-VIET project, the World Bank, the Asian Development Bank, etc. Under pressure from international institutions, Vietnam chose a two-stage model to follow regarding IAS/IFRS adoption. Thus, the Ministry of Finance of Vietnam started to promulgate new accounting standards, and the first four standards were issued in December 2001. A total of 26 new Vietnamese Accounting Standards (VAS) had been set and announced by 2005, basically following the International Accounting Standards (IAS) set by the International Accounting Standards Board (IASB) as prevailing up to 2003.

Nonetheless, the implementation of the VAS has not been effective because most accounting regulatory officials and accounting practitioners in Vietnam were used to following the detailed and rigid accounting regulations and rules in accounting and reporting practice under the influence of the traditional centrally planned economic administration systems, which had set specific rules on how to deal with accounting transactions by the use of specified charts of accounts, bookkeeping procedures and forms of accounting statements. They were not comfortable with adopting the principles-based accounting standards. As a result, the Vietnamese government had to set another set of accounting rules called the 'Uniform Accounting System' (UAS), which provides more detailed and specific practical guidance for accounting work. It is a unique phenomenon that two sets of accounting regulations have coexisted in Vietnam since the mid-2000s.

Chapter 17 outlines that there has been no updating of VAS since its issue, even though some new IAS and international financial reporting standards (IFRS) or some amendments or modifications to the existing IAS and IFRS have since been made by the IASB. Instead, the Vietnamese government has tried to adopt the new international standards by updating the UAS continuously, with the most current version of the UAS issued in 2014 to incorporate most new international accounting and reporting standards. Nonetheless, some significant differences remain between the VAS/UAS and the IAS/IFRS in accounting recognition, measurement and reporting, particularly in current practice. This chapter provides a comparison of the similarities and key differences in the accounting and reporting requirements and the practices between Vietnamese accounting standards and international standards in a detailed form, alongside an elaboration of the current legal framework of accounting regulation and statutory requirements for accounting work in Vietnam.

Chapter 18 explains that Bangladesh is a tropical country located in South Asia and is inhabited by a pluralistic population of Muslims, Hindus, Buddhists and a number of other small communities. Bangladesh was a part of British India until 1947 and became an independent country in 1971 after a long war against the government of Pakistan. Despite being a desperately poor and overpopulated country with slow economic development over a relatively long period, the Bangladeshi economy started to grow in the early 2000s, with a significant increase in GDP growth rate and expansion of agriculture, manufacturing and service industries, resulting from the opening of the domestic capital market and the government's encouragement of private-sector investment. To keep pace with its significant economic growth, the Bangladeshi government formulated a series of commercial laws to gradually improve the regulation of the accounting and auditing profession. Commencing in 1997, the national professional accounting body, the Institute of Charted Accountants of Bangladesh (ICAB), tried to recognize and accept the IAS/IFRS as the national accounting standards, which have gained mandatory status through the directives of the Bangladesh Securities Commission (BSEC). Bangladesh follows a regular approach to adopt/adapt any new accounting standards issued by the IASB, after completing a process of stringent technical review to consider their applicability in the country. The adopted IAS/IFRS are applicable to all listed companies and are subject to compliance monitoring by the market regulator (BSEC) in Bangladesh.

Chapter 18 also illustrates the development of national accounting and auditing standards as well as the convergence with international standards in Bangladesh. The national professional accounting body (ICAB) has mandated its members to follow international auditing standards (ISA, adopted as BSA) for financial statement audits in the country. However, it is noted that the quality of accounting and financial reporting remains a concern, although there is no gap in terms of the international accounting and auditing standards at present.

Chapter 19 briefly examines the accounting environment in Cambodia from the perspective of capital market regulation on accounting and auditing practices. As already pointed out by the authors, Cambodia was ruled by the French for almost 100 years and its legal system is primarily civil law: a mixture of French-influenced commercial codes. The country has gone through a long period of domestic civil war, with rapid government and political system changes in the 1970s and the 1980s, and it remains one of the least developed countries in the world.

However, Cambodia undertaken market-oriented economic reforms under the new constitution in 1993 and policies were set to restore private property rights and to abolish the price control that was installed under the former communist regime. Incentives were provided to domestic and foreign private investments. Furthermore, the Cambodian government planned to open the domestic capital market (e.g. the Cambodian Securities Exchange, CSX) in the mid-2000s and promulgated several commercial laws and regulations, including setting up a comprehensive legal framework for accounting and auditing practices. Nonetheless, owing to a short period in the reform progress towards a market economy, particularly the delay of the operation of the CSX, no formal convergence with international accounting standards has been implemented in the country and national accounting standards remain prevailing in practice, although some selected IAS/IFRS are allowed to be used by business entities on a voluntary basis. But it is expected that Cambodia will be under increasing pressure to officially adopt international accounting and reporting standards so long as its current economic reforms continue, following its urgent need for foreign investment to sustain economic growth.

Chapter 20 introduces the accounting development in Mongolia. Relatively speaking, Mongolia is a small economy in Asia and it has long been a socialist country with a formal Soviet-style centrally planned economy. Owing to its small economic scale, relying mainly on the nomadic herding industry, for a long time accounting activities were simple and crude in Mongolia. Even after the adoption of the Soviet-style economic administrative systems after the revolution of 1921, accounting has had a very limited role to play in the country, while there is almost no information about Mongolian accounting in the Western literature. This chapter examines the evolution of contemporary accounting in Mongolia from a historical perspective and describes the evolution of Mongolian accounting over three major phases: 1) the pre-revolution period (before 1921), when certain simple bookkeeping methods and records were in use; 2) the centrally planned economy era (1921–1990), when the 'memorial order form' and 'journal-order' bookkeeping and reporting systems were developed to accommodate the information needs for government's economic planning and administration; and 3) the market-oriented economic reform era (1991–present), when the Western-style accounting practices and internationally accepted accounting norms had been gradually introduced to satisfy the needs of economic transition and of obtaining international aid and foreign investment. Readers should find the introduction of Mongolian accounting development interesting as it is currently rarely exposed to the outside world.

17

Recent development of accounting and reporting practices in Vietnam

Nguyen Cong Phuong

Introduction

Vietnam is a transitional and developing country in Southeast Asia, and it was heavily influenced during the twentieth century by powerful countries, such as France, the United States, the former Soviet Union, and China. The year 1986 was a dramatic turning point in Vietnamese history as the ruling Communist Party declared an "Open door" policy (called the "Renovation"), with the aim of implementing a market-oriented economy and integrating Vietnam into the world market. In parallel with domestic reforms, Vietnam has undergone a process of largely integrating its economy into the regional and global economy. Vietnam has made important commitments to trade liberalization under various bilateral and multilateral agreements over the last two decades. It became a member of the ASEAN, as well as the ASEAN Free Trade Area (AFTA), in 1995, and joined APEC in 1998 and the ASEAN Economic Community in late 2015. In addition to trade agreements within the ASEAN framework, Vietnam has signed FTAs with the United States, Japan, Chile, South Korea, the Eurasian Economic Union, and most recently the European Union. Vietnam signed the US-led Trans Pacific Partnership Agreement on February 4, 2016.

After the establishment of the Socialist Republic of Vietnam in 1945, the French-style accounting system used by the former colonial authority was transformed in 1957 to adopt Soviet-style accounting. This traditional accounting system in Vietnam originally stemmed from a Soviet-style planned and centralized economy and existed for national economic planning and control rather than for micro-economic decision-making and remained in effect until 1995. In response to economic transition, Vietnamese accounting had been transformed from a Soviet-style accounting system to a capitalist accounting model through the adoption of the Uniform Accounting System (UAS), effective from January 1, 1996 (Ministry of Finance, 1995), in pace with the progress of economic transition in the country.

The next stage of the accounting reform, starting in 1995, was to develop the accounting system in harmony with international accounting and reporting standards promulgated by the International Accounting Standards Board (IASB), with technical and financial assistance from the EUROTAP-VIET project,[1] the World Bank, and the Asian Development Bank. Vietnam promulgated the first four accounting standards on December 31, 2001. From 2001 to 2006, 26 Vietnamese Accounting Standards (VAS) were promulgated. Furthermore, these accounting standards are based largely on the international accounting standards prevailing at the time of issue (up to 2003). Besides the issue of VAS, the Ministry of Finance has also continued to impose the UAS with follow-up amendments.[2] The latter allows the government to continue to meet the requirements of political and macroeconomic control, while the introduction of VAS testifies to the international harmonization of Vietnamese accounting in the context of economic globalization. The coexistence of the VAS and the UAS is a unique phenomenon in Vietnam.

The remaining of this chapter is organized as follows. The second section sets out the institutional settings for accounting and reporting practices in Vietnam. The third section introduces the accounting and reporting practices for company and financial statement requirements under the Vietnamese accounting regulations. The fourth section provides a direct comparison of the current Vietnamese accounting standards/practices and the international accounting and reporting standards. The final section is a brief conclusion to end this chapter.

Institutional framework of accounting regulation

Legal sources of accounting regulation

Because of its French colonial history, Vietnamese accounting preserves a legal orientation. Vietnamese accounting standards and rules are rooted in legal texts, and accounting regulation is the responsibility of the government. Figure 17.1 shows the sources of Vietnamese accounting regulation.

There is no professional organization responsible for setting national accounting standards and rules in Vietnam. Instead, five organizations are involved in the regulation of accounting in Vietnam: the Department of Accounting Policy (DAP), the Vietnam Accounting Association (VAA), the Accounting Standards Steering Committee (ASSC), the Accounting Standards Setting Group (ASSG), and the National Council for Accountancy (NCA). All of these were established by the Ministry of Finance, and the last three organizations were created from 1998 to 2000, in order to set the Vietnamese Accounting Standards. Each of the five organizations has its own functions in accounting regulation. However, these agencies are not independent of the government. Membership of the agencies is determined by the Ministry of Finance and the majority of them are staffed by accounting and financial specialists working at the Ministry of Finance (Narayan and Godden, 2000). The Vietnam Accounting Association (VAA) is

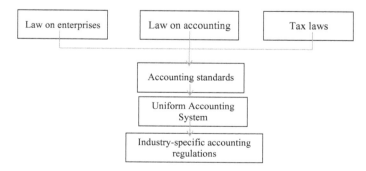

Figure 17.1 Structure of Vietnamese accounting regulation

traditionally weak and does not exercise its role as a professional body. As before, it does not play an active role in regulating accounting. According to the Law on Accounting, which was promulgated in 2003, the Ministry of Finance preserves its responsibility for setting and issuing accounting standards (The National Assembly, 2003). In order to proceed, the Ministry of Finance set up the ASSC in 1998,[3] and the NCA in 2000,[4] alongside the DAP. The ASSC is responsible for steering accounting standards. The NCA's functions include the development of strategies, policies, and other issues concerning auditing and accounting activities. The NCA is the key regulatory body for accounting and auditing arrangements in Vietnam. Its structure and functions are similar to those of accounting regulatory boards in other countries. However, the Department of Accounting Policy has also been a steering organization of the NCA since its establishment. The DAP is also in charge of exercising state management on both accounting and auditing activities.

Law on Enterprise

On November 26, 2014, the National Assembly of Vietnam approved a new law on enterprise to improve the legal framework for investments in Vietnam (The National Assembly, 2014a). The Law on Enterprise took effect on July 1, 2015. This law specifies four types of legal forms of corporation for business entities: limited liability company, joint-stock company, sole proprietorship, and partnership. A foreign entity may establish its presence in Vietnam as a limited liability company with one or more members: a joint-stock company, a partnership, a branch, a business cooperation contract, or a representative office. Foreign investors are also permitted to purchase an interest in existing domestic enterprises, subject to ownership limitations that vary depending on the relevant industry sector.

According to this law, every company established in Vietnam must comply with the VAS and the UAS. The law requires enterprises to prepare and submit truthful financial statements in a timely manner according to the regulatory laws on accounting and reporting. Companies are obliged to submit their financial statements within 30 days (for sole proprietorships and partnerships) or 90 days (for other type of enterprises) of the end of each fiscal year. Owing to the objective of protecting investors, public interest, and essentially a legal approach of accounting, several accounting obligations depend on the legal form of the company. Article 191 of the Law on Enterprises requires that, apart from reports and documents prescribed by law, the parent company must prepare more reports such as consolidated financial statements, summary of income statements of parent and subsidiaries, management reports, etc. To enhance information transparency, state-owned enterprises (SOEs) are required to give full disclosure.

In accordance with this law, the financial statements of SOEs and public joint-stock companies must be audited before being submitted to shareholders' meetings. Under the Law on Independent Audit (The National Assembly, 2014b) and the Official Letter No. 1339/ BTC-CDKT (Ministry of Finance, 2014b), annual financial statements of foreign invested entities, public interest entities (i.e., listed entities, banks, insurance companies, and financial institutions), and any other entities involved in special circumstances such as mergers and acquisitions, changes in ownership, termination, and bankruptcy, must be audited by an auditing firm legally operating in Vietnam.

State-owned enterprises are required to disclose in their annual reports basic information about the company and the company's charter; overall targets, specific targets of the annual business plan, and audited financial statements. Public joint-stock companies must prepare and submit the annual reports covering the company's business outcomes, financial statements, and report management.

Tax regulations

Most business activities in Vietnam are likely to be subject to common taxes such as corporate income tax (CIT), value-added tax, personal income tax, foreign contractor tax, etc. Taxable profit is the difference between total revenue and deductible expenses, plus other assessable income. Business taxpayers are required to prepare an annual CIT return, which includes a section for making adjustments to accounting profit to arrive at a taxable profit. These adjustments are due to several differences regarding measurement and recognition between accounting standards and tax regulations, and are generally relative to permanent differences.

Traditionally, there is a strict link between tax regulations and accounting principles in Vietnam. In other words, the UAS is driven by taxation. The dominant influence of taxation on accounting is also retained in the UAS 2006. One of the purposes of the UAS is to allow the state to control wealth distribution and determine tax revenues. The UAS is thus the essential control instrument of the tax services (Nguyen, 2002; Tran Van Ta, 2001, p. 143). Another factor that increases the link between the UAS and tax regulations is the participation of the tax authorities, as a consulting body to the Ministry of Finance, in the drafting of the UAS, so that the UAS must be a control instrument of tax services. The modifications of and additions to the UAS have so far been purported to be in line with taxation reporting. Based on this strict link, VAS and UAS compliance is being used as a basis to reassess taxes by tax authorities. The provincial tax authorities use VAS noncompliance as a reason to collect additional tax and even recover previously paid VAT refunds. Tax authorities can penalize for noncompliance through the disallowance of input VAT credits, the withdrawal of corporate income tax incentives, and changes to the method of application of corporate income tax. Thus, enterprises are advised to double-check their accounting systems, taking care to spot possible VAS and UAS noncompliance issues.

However, this link has been relatively relaxed after the issuance of the UAS 2014 (Ministry of Finance, 2014a), with a recognition of the "substance over form" principle. The UAS 2014 specifies that rules established under the UAS, such as those regulating bookkeeping and the preparation and presentation of financial statements, do not need to be applied to the determination of taxable income.[5] Notes on income tax within the financial statements do not yet present the calculation of taxable income from accounting income through adjustments.

Law on Accounting

The first Law on Accounting was enacted in 2003, to replace the Ordinance of Accounting and Statistics 1998. It provided the legal framework for accounting, auditing, and corporate reporting in Vietnam. The law prescribed the contents of accounting work and the organization of the accounting system, accountants, and professional accounting activities. Under this law, all enterprises are required to prepare and present legal-entity financial statements in accordance with the VAS. The Ministry of Finance is responsible for setting the national accounting and auditing standards.

Owing to rapid changes in business environment, Vietnam's accelerated integration into global economy and recent development of accounting internationalization, the Law on Accounting 2003 became unsuitable for accounting practices. As a result, the Law on Accounting 2015 was approved by the National Assembly and took effect from January 1, 2017 (The National Assembly, 2015). Alongside the subjects regulated by the 2003 law, this amended law provides additional regulations on accounting services and state management of accounting. In comparison with the 2003 law, the amended Law on Accounting 2015 contains the following significant changes:

1   to adopt measurement and recognition at fair value for financial instruments, monetary items denominated in foreign currencies, and assets and liabilities having frequent volatility in value as required by accounting standards;
2   to supplement the "substance over form" principle, which requires that the financial statements must fairly reflect the substance of transactions rather than their legal form;
3   to add in provision on accounting services;
4   to regulate others accounting and auditing issues such as accounting inspection, internal audit, and obligation of internal control.

Accepting the fair value and substance over form principles in the Law on Accounting 2015 allows Vietnamese accounting and reporting practice to move toward international accounting norms as well as to establish a primary legal framework for financial reporting framework in the country.

Accounting and financial reporting standards

Resulting from the continuing improvements of accounting and auditing standards, accounting and reporting practices in Vietnam have improved significantly over the years. All enterprises, excluding financial institutions and small and medium-sized entities, must now comply with the Vietnamese Accounting Standards (VAS), the Uniform Accounting System (UAS), and relevant statutory requirements, which are partially in compliance with the International Accounting Standards (IAS) and the International Financial Reporting Standards (IFRS) but contain some specific guidance and requirements that are applicable to Vietnamese conditions.

Vietnamese Accounting Standards

At abreast with the country's integration into the global economy, the accounting reform in Vietnam entered a second phase in 1995, with the technical and financial assistance of the EUROTAP-VIET project[6] and some international organizations. Furthermore, Vietnam has been concerned about transparent information and international harmonization of accounting for the purposes of further integrating its economy into the global market and attracting foreign investment, and commenced the development of accounting convergence with the IAS/IFRS in recent years. Vietnam aims to implement its commitment to harmonize its accounting system with international norms, as stated by Bui Van Mai, director of the Accounting Department at the Ministry of Finance in the early 2000s, that "Vietnamese accounting should be harmonized at 90 % with IAS/IFRS."[7] Consequently, Vietnam promulgated 26 accounting standards from 2001 to 2005, which were adopted from and primarily based on the IAS prevailing at the time of issue (up to 2003), plus additional mandatory implementation guidance known as the "circulars." Although some modifications were made to reflect the unique characteristics of the domestic accounting regulations and environment, none of the IASB's subsequent amendments to the IASs or new IFRSs issued thereafter have been updated by the VAS. The key differences between the IAS/IFRS and the VAS include terminology, applied methods, or presentation scope owing to continuing changes and amendments of IFRS. Subject to the continuing demands from the World Bank, the International Finance Corporation, and foreign investors, Vietnam is on the way to fill the gap between the VAS and the IAS/IFRS, and it is expected that a full adoption of the IAS/IFRS will be made by 2020 for listed firms in Vietnam.

Some Vietnamese companies prepare IAS/IFRS-based financial statements for the purpose of reporting to foreign investors. However, those financial statements in compliance with the IAS/IFRS are supplementary financial statements, not a substitute for financial statements prepared using the VAS. The VAS-based financial statements are the statutory and primary financial statements in the country.

Under pressure from international institutions, Vietnam chose a two-stage model to follow regarding IAS/IFRS adoption.[8] In the first stage, IAS/IFRS adoption may be superficial since Vietnam only needs an "IAS/IFRS label." Presently, IAS/IFRS adoption is in process, with various versions that are inconsistent with the IASB's prescriptions. This label would express Vietnam's intention to move toward economic globalization or international convergence, and would provide the international community with a promise of financial transparency. However, the institutional reforms in Vietnam have not been advanced enough to provide adequate accounting infrastructure (e.g., developed financial market, good corporate governance, legal protection of investors, good quality of accountants, etc.); the adoption of IAS/IFRS does not drive up the financial reporting quality.

Several studies examining the compliance of VAS with IAS/IFRS show that, overall, the VAS are aligned almost entirely with the 2005 version of the IASB standards (Adams and Linh, 2003; Anh Tuan and Guangming, 2014; Nguyen Anh Tuan and Gong, 2012; Pham Hoai Huong, 2013). For example, Pham Hoai Huong (2013) shows that the percentage of overall *de jure* convergence between the VAS and the 2005 version of the IAS/IFRS for key standards is 84 percent. This is broken down into two components: the measurement of *de jure* convergence is 88 percent, whereas the disclosure of *de jure* convergence is 81 percent. However, instead of embracing the independent accounting judgment embedded in the IAS/IFRS, the restrictive traditional accounting philosophy has been preserved so that the Vietnamese accounting system allows little scope for judgment. There is also very limited disclosure in practice, resulting in limited value to financial statement users.

Uniform Accounting System

The first uniform accounting system was introduced in 1995, resulting from accounting reform moving toward a market-oriented accounting model. After the issuance of 26 VASs by 2005, the UAS was amended in 2006 (the 2006 UAS) to update the rules of accounting recognition and measurement in light of the requirements of the VAS. To provide guidance for domestic and foreign enterprises in Vietnam to follow the 26 Vietnamese Accounting Standards being issued, the Ministry of Finance has recently issued the third version of the UAS[9] to bring up to date many accounting and reporting principles/rules adopted from IAS/IFRS, whereas the 26 VAS have not been revised and updated. This results in some conflicts (e.g., the application of fair value accounting) between the VAS and the UAS. The new UAS introduces many changes to accounting practice in Vietnam, making it more in line with the IAS/IFRS.

All companies in Vietnam are required to follow the 2014 UAS and other prevailing Vietnamese regulations and circulars. Legally speaking, the 2014 UAS provides guidance on the application and adoption of Vietnamese Accounting Standards to all types of enterprise in Vietnam, consisting of the charts of accounts and rigid formats of financial statements. The UAS includes operational guidelines on how accounts are applied to typical economic transactions and how financial statements are prepared. It focuses on the recording of transactions, rather than on recognition, measurement, and disclosure.

The securities companies are required to follow the Accounting System for Securities Companies.[10] This system provides guidance on accounting and reporting practices applicable to securities companies and related entities, regarding the use of chart of accounts, accounting methods, forms of accounting books, and methods of preparing and presenting financial statements.

Application of the VAS and the UAS

The embrace of an accounting system based on the Anglo-Saxon philosophy that focuses on a principles-based approach is only possible if accompanied by a gradual transformation of legitimating structures in the evolving social environment. Although the institutional changes in Vietnam in recent years are significant, this evolution of Vietnamese accounting does not reflect the Anglo-Saxon institutional logic. Consequently, excluding foreign invested enterprises, the VAS are not perceived to be more useful for most domestic enterprises since Vietnam lacks competent personnel and strong professional accountancy bodies to implement the new accounting standards. The code-based orientation of Vietnamese accountants has led them to prefer following specific rules, instead of general principles. Even though the VAS contain concepts and principles in line with IASB standards; domestic enterprises prefer to follow the Uniform Accounting System to record, recognize, and measure transactions and to prepare financial statements. According to a report by PwC Vietnam,[11] in practice Vietnamese authorities have been relatively relaxed in most instances with respect to the enforcement of VAS compliance.

The implementation of VAS requires a high degree of professional judgment, but the scope of professional judgment is restricted by government regulations. Lack of knowledge and experience of the IAS/IFRS is among one of the challenges for implementing the VAS in Vietnam. According to Dang Van Thanh,[12] what macro management has been accustomed to doing for a long time is setting and complying with specific accounting rules, which detail how the accounts should be applied to typical economic transactions and how financial statements should be prepared. Furthermore, according to Bui Van Mai,[13] while accounting standards contain concepts and principles designed to guide the professional application of accounting methods, Vietnamese accountants have long been accustomed to rigid rules and the majority of them do not have the competence and experience in making professional judgments concerning the use of accounting policies. Similarly, Nguyen Cong Phuong (2012) showed that only 6 percent of 191 respondents had applied the accounting standards to prepare financial statements. Most respondents replied that accounting standards are less used because: 1) they are too abstract (26 percent), 2) there are no explanations of how accounts are applied to typical economic transactions, and how financial statements are prepared from accounting and book entry accounts (27 percent); and 3) accountants lack of the competence and experience in making professional judgments concerning the choice of accounting policies (41 percent). For many accountants in Vietnam, the move to adopt IAS/IFRS involved a radical change in accounting mindset, as the IAS/IFRS are built on a different framework to the traditional Vietnamese accounting system. The previous study findings testify the main obstacles in the process of international accounting harmonization evidenced in the literature.

Industry-specific accounting regulations

To date, the actions of enterprises have been heavily dependent on the industrial sector-based policies of the state government. Many SOEs are "managed" by industrial ministers, who have the powers and functional responsibility to administer those SOEs. Consequently, Vietnam made a choice to set industry-specific regulations after the promulgation of UAS, which was justified since Vietnamese accountants had become used to following rigid and detailed rules, and the majority of them did not have the competence and experience in making professional judgments concerning choices of accounting policies (Bui Van Mai, 2001a, p. 24). As a result, the UAS includes many industry-specific accounting regulations, which provide more detailed guidance for industry-specific types of transactions.

Accounting and reporting practices

Group accounting practices

Group accounting and reporting practices appeared for the first time in Vietnam when the accounting standards regarding the groups of companies were issued in 2003. By 2014, the practices of group accounting and reporting were regulated by VAS 8 (*Financial Reporting of Interest in Joint Ventures*), VAS 11 (*Business Consolidation*), VAS 25 (*Consolidated Financial Statements and Accounting for Investments in Subsidiaries*) and Circular 161/2007/TT-BTC on additional mandatory implementation guidance of those VAS. These VAS are generally based on the equivalent IAS prevailing at the time of issuance, and they are effective at the present time. According to those regulations, groups of companies are required to prepare consolidated financial statements at the end of the financial year.

Owing to changes in the business environment and the IASB's amendments to IAS/IFRS for group accounting, the Ministry of Finance issued Circular No. 202/2014/TT-BTC in 2014 to replace Circular 161/2007/TT-BTC, to provide guidance on preparing the consolidated financial statements, whereas the related VAS were not revised and updated. The new regulation is mostly aligned with the equivalent IAS/IFRS prevailing at the time. The main changes, compared to the former regulation, are the recognition of impairment losses of goodwill alongside preserving asset amortization, correcting procedures for the consolidation of financial statements using the equity method, especially the elimination of profits or losses resulting from transactions between investors and associates in terms of the extent of the investors' interest in the associates. Although the relative VAS are not revised and updated, the new regulation brings the accounting and reporting practices for company groups in Vietnam more in line with the IAS/IFRS.

Statutory financial statements

In general, the required financial statements under the VAS and the UAS include the balance sheet, the income statement, the cash flow statement, and the notes. According to VAS 21 (*Presentation of Financial Statements*), the statement of changes in equity is part of the notes, rather than a primary component of the financial statements. Furthermore, the VAS does not require disclosure of management's key judgments, assumptions for forecasts, and sources of estimation uncertainty.

All enterprises are required to prepare financial statements annually. Parent companies are required to prepare consolidated financial statements at the end of the year. SOEs and publicly listed companies are further required to prepare full set of mid-year financial statements (e.g., interim reporting). Groups of SOEs are required to prepare the consolidated mid-year financial statements. Other companies that voluntarily prepare mid-year financial statements have the option to prepare abbreviated financial statements only. All companies are required to submit their financial statements to the tax authorities, the General Statistics Office, and the Department of Planning and Investment within 90 days of the end of financial year.

Regarding the obligation of financial statement audit, in general, the annual financial statements of enterprises must be audited once a year in compliance with related regulations and laws. Enterprises and organizations that must be audited include foreign invested companies, credit institutions established and operating under the Law on Credit Institutions, financial institutions, insurance enterprises, insurance brokerage companies, public companies, issuers, and securities trading organizations.

The audit contracts must be signed at least 30 days before the end of the financial year. The audited financial statements and auditor reports must be submitted to government authorities within 90 days of the end of the financial year.

Comparison of the Vietnamese accounting regulations and the IAS/IFRS

Although VAS have not been revised and updated since their issue even after the IASB's follow-up amendments, major changes in the recent version of the UAS make the Vietnamese accounting regulations move closer to the IAS/IFRS. Table 17.1 presents a comparison of existing accounting regulations under both the VAS and the UAS in Vietnam and the IAS/IFRS, and sets out the main differences between them at present.

Table 17.1 Comparison of Vietnamese Accounting Regulations and IAS/IFRS

IAS/IFRS	Vietnamese accounting regulations
IAS 1	According to Chapter III of the UAS 2014, the substance over form principle has been recognized since 2015. VAS 21 and Chapter III of the 2014 UAS do not require disclosure of management's key judgment. Both require an analysis of changes in equity in the notes.
IAS 2	Under VAS 2, there are several key differences regarding measurement of inventories, such as the estimation techniques of standard cost, the retail method, and the LIFO. However, under Article 23 of the 2014 UAS, these differences are eliminated.
IAS 7	There is no significant difference.
IAS 8	There is no significant difference.
IAS 10	Determination of the authorization date of the financial statements is not addressed in VAS 23. Instead, VAS 23 specifically states that the authorization date is the date when the head of the reporting entity authorizes the issue of financial statements to outsiders.
IAS 11	Both VAS 15 and UAS 2014 (Article 79) state that the recognition of revenue and cost is only made when the outcome of a construction contract can be estimated reliably and contract costs are recoverable without significant uncertainties. They do not address the treatment of revenue and costs when the outcome of a construction contract cannot be estimated reliably. Further, they provide additional guidance for contracts where progress payments are agreed in advance. For this type of contract, business entities can apply the percentage-of-completion (as determined by the contractor) method.
IAS 12	VAS 17 does not address temporary differences and deferred taxes associated with investments in subsidiaries. Nevertheless, the new regulation for group accounting (Circular 202/2014, effective from 2015) includes those temporary differences, and hence there is no significant difference between IAS 12 and Vietnamese accounting.

(continued)

Table 17.1 (continued)

IAS/IFRS	Vietnamese accounting regulations
IAS 14	There is no significant difference.
IAS 16	Measurement and recognition of tangible fixed assets are stated in VAS 3, which is based on the 2005 version of IAS 16, and in Article 35 of the 2014 UAS. Tangible fixed assets should be carried at cost less accumulated depreciation. Re-evaluation of tangible fixed assets is not allowed unless by specific approval of the government. Thus, the impairment write-down of tangible fixed assets is also not allowed in Vietnamese accounting.
IAS 17	There is no significant difference between VAS 6/2014 UAS and IAS 17.
IAS 18	Accounting for revenue is addressed in the VAS 14, which is based on the 2001 version of IAS 18, and in the 2014 UAS (Article 79). Generally, there is no significant difference between VAS 14/2014 UAS and IAS 18. Besides, VAS 14 also applies to revenue arising from other activities (called other revenue arising from extraordinary items).
IAS 19	There is no regulation that is equivalent to IAS 19. Accounting for employee benefit is addressed in detail in Article 53 of the 2014 UAS, which identifies and provides accounting guidance for only one category of employee benefits (e.g., short-term benefits such as wages, bonuses, and medical care allowances).
IAS 20	There is no regulation equivalent to IAS 20. Accounting for government grants is scattered in the standards relating to granted objects such as granted revenue, granted fixed assets, etc.
IAS 21	The effect of changes in foreign exchange rates is addressed in VAS 10, which is based on the 1993 version of IAS 21, and in the 2014 UAS (Articles 69 and 107). VAS 10 requires a differentiation between foreign operations and foreign entities. Both VAS 10 and UAS only state the determination of "reporting currency" and do not include a requirement to determine "functional currency."
IAS 23	Under VAS 16, the measurement and recognition of borrowing costs are similar to the principles of IAS 23 except that VAS 16 requires capitalization of borrowing costs that are directly attributable to qualifying assets that necessarily take a substantial period of time over 12 months, and does not state the assets that are excluded from the scope of VAS 16, such as inventories that are manufactured, or otherwise produced, in large quantities on a repetitive basis and that take a substantial period to get ready for sale. However, under the 2014 UAS (Article 54), these differences are eliminated.
IAS 24	Related party disclosure is addressed in VAS 26, which is based on the 1994 version of IAS 24. Significant differences exist relate to the required disclosure. Under VAS 26, the disclosure on related party is less detailed compared to the requirement of IAS 24.
IAS 26	There is no regulation equivalent to IAS 26.
IAS 27	Accounting treatment for consolidated and separate financial statements is specified in VAS 25 and recently in Circular 202/2014. There are key differences between IAS 27 and VAS 25 regarding the exceptions to the requirement for presenting consolidated financial statements of the parent, including postemployment benefit plans and parent's investments in subsidiaries measured at fair value through profit or loss in accordance with IFRS 9/IAS 39. Another difference is that VAS 25 allows a subsidiary to be excluded from consolidation if it operates under severe long-term restrictions that impair the subsidiary's ability to transfer funds to the parent. Those differences are not eliminated under the new regulation (Circular 202/2014). Besides, measurement of noncontrolling interest at fair value (called full goodwill method) is not allowed under both VAS 25 and Circular 202/2014.

IAS 28	Under VAS 7, investments in an associate are measured at cost if the investor does not have a subsidiary. According to the new regulation for group accounting (Circular 202/2014), any goodwill shown as part of the carrying amount of the investment in the associate is no longer amortized and is not subject to annual impairment testing.
IAS 29	There is no regulation equivalent to IAS 29.
IAS 31	Measurement and recognition of interests in joint ventures are regulated in VAS 8. Regarding jointly controlled operations and jointly controlled assets, VAS 8 adds a specific reference for Vietnam, such as business cooperation contracts (BCC). The latter is revised in the 2014 UAS (Article 44) to specify the measurement and recognition of share of the joint assets, liabilities, income from the sale, and share of expenses incurred. Proportionate consolidation is not allowed under VAS 8. The latter also does not allow to account for interests in the joint ventures at fair value as specified in IAS 39.
IAS 32	There is no regulation equivalent to IAS 32. Nevertheless, from 2011, Vietnam allows entities to elect the application of IAS 32 through issuing Circular (210/2009/TT-BTC) that provides guidance on the application of IAS 32 and IFRS 7.
IAS 34	Interim financial reporting is regulated in VAS 27 and specified in detail in the 2014 UAS (Chapter 3). There is no significant difference between VAS 27/2014 UAS and IAS 34.
IAS 36	There is no regulation equivalent to IAS 36 except that investment property held for capital appreciation and goodwill are subject to annual impairment testing as specified in the 2014 UAS.
IAS 37	VAS 18 specifies accounting treatment for provisions, contingent assets, and liabilities. Generally, there is no significant difference between VAS 18 and IAS 37.
IAS 38	Measurement and recognition of intangible assets are regulated in VAS 4 and in detail in Article 37 of 2014 UAS. According to these regulations, revaluation, or write-down for impairment is not allowed for intangible assets including land use rights; the useful life of an intangible asset for amortization period is not longer than 20 years. Besides, certain costs relating to an entity's establishment, expenditures on training activities, expenditures on advertising and promotional activities in relation to preoperation, research, and relocation of a business are allowed to be charged or deferred for no longer than three years to the income statement.
IAS 39	There is no VAS equivalent to IAS 39. However, from 2011, Vietnam allows business entities to elect the application of IAS 32 and IFRS 7 by making reference to Circular (210/2009/TT-BTC), which specifies the application of IAS 32 and IFRS 7.
IAS 40	The equivalent regulation is VAS 5 (*Investment Property*). VAS 5 is similar to IAS 40 except that fair value measurement is prohibited. Nevertheless, under 2014 UAS (Article 39), impairment testing of investment property held for capital appreciation is allowed to recognize impairment loss.
IAS 41	There is no regulation equivalent to IAS 41.
IFRS 1	There is no regulation equivalent to IFRS 1.
IFRS 2	There is no regulation equivalent to IFRS 1.
IFRS 3	VAS 11 specifies accounting for business combinations, which is generally similar to IFRS 3 (2004). Under VAS 11, combinations of mutual entities and combinations without consideration (dual-listed shares) are excluded. VAS 11 also does not address the measurement of noncontrolling interest at fair value (the full goodwill method). Goodwill is amortized over its estimated useful life of no more than 10 years after the date of acquisition. Furthermore, goodwill is subject to impairment testing under Circular 202/2014. If impairment loss of goodwill is greater than the amount of the estimated amortization, an impairment write-down must be made instead of amortization.

(continued)

Table 17.1 (continued)

IAS/IFRS	Vietnamese accounting regulations
IFRS 4	VAS 19 (Insurance Contracts) is equivalent to IFRS 4 except for the amendments to IFRS 4 as a result of the release of IFRS 7. VAS does not require a disclosure of information on insurance risk either of a sensitivity analysis and qualitative information about the sensitivity.
IFRS 5	There is no regulation equivalent to IFRS 5.
IFRS 6	There is no regulation equivalent to IFRS 5.
IFRS 7	There is no VAS equivalent to IFRS 7. VAS 22 (Disclosures in the Financial Statements of Banks and Similar Financial Institutions) is based on IAS 30, which is superseded. VAS 22 is still in effect and applicable only to banks and financial institutions. However, from 2011, entities can elect to apply IFRS 7 by making reference to Circular (210/2009/TT-BTC).

Conclusion

Vietnam is one of few countries where accounting standards (VAS) and a uniform accounting system (UAS) coexist. This differs from the Anglo-Saxon world but is comparable to the practice in China. Such a different approach to accounting developments reflects the key role of the state in accounting regulation, aimed at preserving firm governmental control while harmonizing accounting practices with international standards.

Vietnam had promulgated all of the VAS by 2005, which are aligned almost entirely with the IASB's standards prevailing at the time. Up to now, the VAS have not been revised and updated to adopt the IASB's later amendments. Therefore, there are some differences between the IAS/IFRS and the VAS. In addition, the implementation of the VAS arguably requires a high degree of professional judgment, but the scope of professional judgment is restricted in Vietnamese accounting. A lack of knowledge and experience of the IAS/IFFRS is among one of the challenges for implementing the VAS in Vietnam. The code-based orientation of Vietnamese accountants has also led accounting practitioners to prefer detailed rules instead of general principles. Thus, the VAS are not perceived to be more useful for most domestic enterprises. As a result, Vietnamese regulators have primarily revised the UAS, instead of the VAS, with the measurement and recognition rules to be aligned with the IASB's updated standards. The recent amendment of the UAS reflects a further convergence of Vietnamese accounting with the IAS/IFRS. However, considering the aspiration of Vietnam to become an integrated part of the global market, we believe that the initial technical difficulties currently faced by practitioners, and the expensive requirements for convergence with international accounting norms in Vietnam will pay off in the long-run.

Notes

1 European Union Technical Assistance Program-Vietnam.
2 2006 UAS version and the subsequent 2014 UAS version.
3 Decision No. 1563/1998 QD-BTC dated October 30, 1998.
4 Decision No. 276/QD-BTC dated March 28, 2000.
5 Article 2, Circular 200/2014.
6 EUROTAP-VIET, a Vietnam–EU economic cooperation programme, extending effective technical assistance to Vietnam, commenced in September 1995 and ended in June 1998, and boosted its capacity

for supervising the insurance market, drafting the Insurance Business Law, improving staff capacity, and developing the Vietnamese accounting system toward international standards.

7   An interview by VnExpress was released on March 27, 2003.
8   This model is noted by Tyrrall *et al.* (2007).
9   Circular No. 200/2014/TT-BTC dated December 22, 2014.
10 Circular No. 210/2014/TT-BTC, issued by Ministry of Finance on December 30, 2014.
11 Available at www.pwc.com/vn/en/publications/assets/2010_02_9_pwc_newsbriefts_vas_compliance. pdf.
12 Interview of Stocks Investment, April 12, 2009. Dang Van Thanh was the former director of the Department of Accounting Policies, Ministry of Finance, and is the president of the Vietnam Association of Accountants and Auditors.
13 Interview of Stocks Investment, dated August 10, 2008. Bui Van Mai was former director of the Department of Accounting Policies and is the vice-president of the Association of Accountants and Auditors.

References

Adams, H.A. and Linh, T.D. (2003) *Vietnamese Accounting Standards: Intent and Purpose Contrasted to International Accounting Standards.* Hanoi: ACW.

Anh Tuan, N. and Guangming, G. (2014) Measurement of formal convergence of Vietnamese accounting standards with IFRS. *Australian Accounting Review*, 24(2), 16.

Bui Van Mai (2001) The Vietnamese accounting standards in early XXI century. *Accounting Review*, 28, 3 (in Vietnamese).

Ministry of Finance (1995) *Enterprise Accounting System.* Hanoi: Ministry of Finance.

Ministry of Finance (2014a) *Circular No 200/2014/TT-BTC on Uniform Accounting System.*

Ministry of Finance (2014b) *Official Letter No. 1339/BTC-CDKT on Mandatory Audit for Enterprises and Organisations.*

Narayan, F.B. and Godden, T. (2000) *Financial Management and Governance Issues in Viet Nam.* Manila: Asian Development Bank.

Nguyen Anh Tuan and Gong, G. (2012) Vietnamese accounting reform and international convergence of Vietnamese accounting standards. *International Journal of Business and Management*, 7(10), 11.

Nguyen Cong Phuong (2012) *Global Economic Integration and Developing Vietnamese Accounting from 1995: Reality, Challenges and Prospects.* Working paper, College of Economics, University of Danang.

Nguyen, V.L. (2002) Financial, tax and accounting policies. *Accounting Review*, 36, 93–96 (in Vietnamese).

Pham Hoai Huong (2013) *De Jure Convergence between Vietnamese and International Accounting Standards.* Working paper, College of Economics, University of Danang, Vietnam.

The National Assembly (2003) Law on Accounting, N0 03/2003/QH11.

The National Assembly (2014a) Law on Enteprises, 68/2014/QH13.

The National Assembly (2014b) Law on Independent Audit, 67/2011/QH12.

The National Assembly (2015) Law on Accounting No 88/2015/QH13.

Tran Van Ta (2001) The Vietnamese Accounting in the Process of International Integration. *Accounting Review, 31*, 2 (in Vietnamese).

Tyrrall, D., Woodward, D. and Rakhimbekova, A. (2007) The relevance of international financial reporting standards to a developing country: Evidence from Kazakhstan. *The International Journal of Accounting, 42*(1), 82–110. doi:10.1016/j.intacc.2006.12.004.

18

Accounting development
in Bangladesh

P.W. Senarath Yapa and Saiful Azam

Country profile

The People's Republic of Bangladesh is a tropical country located in South Asia, 767 km long at its longest point and 429 km wide at the widest point, covering an area of approximately 147,570 square kilometers.[1] The majority of the land area of Bangladesh lies within the delta region formed by two rivers, the Ganges and the Brahmaputra. Being bordered by India to the north, east, and west, by Myanmar to the southeast, and by the Bay of Bengal to the south, Bangladesh is strategically placed at the crossroads of East and West. Bangladesh is richly endowed with arable land and natural resources and is inhabited by a pluralistic population of Muslims, Hindus, Buddhists, and a number of other small communities. Bangladesh is a lower-middle-income, developing country, with a population of 152 million. However, its adult literacy rate is 60 percent.[2]

Bangladesh is a part of the Indian subcontinent and was until 1947 ruled by the British Empire. In 1947 the Indian subcontinent was partitioned into two sovereign states (India and Pakistan), which led to Bangladesh forming a part of Pakistan known between 1947 and 1971 as East Pakistan. Bangladesh gained independence in 1971 after a nine-month-long war against the government of Pakistan. Bangladesh inherited its economic, political, and administrative structures as well as its education system from the British. The political system of Bangladesh has experienced a variety of governance structures since independence. Bertelsmann Stiftung's Transformation Index (BTI) report (2014) summarized the political transformations in Bangladesh over the past four decades by dividing its political transformations into five broad phases: 1) an elected civilian regime (1972–1975); 2) military and military-dominated rule (1975–1990); 3) democratic civilian government (1991–2006); 4) a military-backed caretaker government (2007–2008); and 5) the second democratic era (since 2009) (BTI report, 2014, p. 3).

Bangladesh emerged from its war of independence desperately poor, overpopulated, and reeling from overwhelming war damage to its institutional and physical capital (Mahmud et al., 2008). In the 1960s, the economy of then East Pakistan grew by an annual average rate of around 4 percent (Rahman and Yusuf, 2010). The liberation war in 1971 left Bangladesh on a slower GDP growth trajectory and it was not until the late 1970s that its GDP reached its prewar level. As shown in Table 18.1, the growth of per capita GDP had been slow in the 1980s, at an average of 1.6 percent a year, but it accelerated to 3 percent in the 1990s and to about 4 percent more recently. The acceleration has resulted partly from a slowdown in population growth but also from a sustained increase in GDP growth, which averaged 3.7 percent annually in the 1980s, 4.8 percent in the 1990s, and 5.7 percent since then to 2005. An average GDP growth of 6.3 percent was maintained during 2004 to 2008 (ADB, 2011), which was much higher than in previous years. After a short fall to below 6 percent in 2009 and 2010, its GDP growth picked up pace again from 2010 onwards and reached 6.1 percent in 2014. It is reported that GDP growth in 2015 and beyond is expected to remain resilient (World Bank, 2015). All broad sectors of the economy—agriculture, manufacturing, and services— have contributed to the acceleration of growth since the early 1990s (Mahmud *et al.*, 2008). Within the manufacturing sector, the growth has come largely from the ready-made garment (RMG) industry; in the 1990s, medium- and large-scale manufacturing as a whole grew at about 7 percent annually, but when the garment industry is excluded that growth was only about 4 percent (Mahmud *et al.*, 2008). The National Web Portal of Bangladesh reports that the RMG industry in Bangladesh is the second biggest in the world.[3] This indicates that the manufacturing and export base of the Bangladeshi economy has become more concentrated in the RMG sector. Per capita GDP in Bangladesh increased from $496 in 2006 to $1,096 in 2014 (World Bank, 2015). At the same time, external debts as percentage of GDP declined sharply from 24.9 percent in 2006 to 15.8 percent in 2014. There was also a downward trend in inflation during 2006–2014. Therefore, the key macroeconomic indicators of Bangladesh have remained sound.

The rest of this chapter is organized into five sections. The second section explains the regulation of the capital market. The third section discusses some issues related to accounting policymaking, while the fourth focuses on auditing standards. The fifth section provides some information about the accounting profession in Bangladesh. A summary and some thoughts on the future direction are provided in the last section.

Capital market regulation

The stock market in Bangladesh

The capital market (stock market) of Bangladesh has limited exposure to the rest of the world (Wahab and Faruq, 2012), even though investment in the Bangladeshi capital market by local investors is crucial for Bangladesh to maintain economic growth. The basic laws that regulate the Bangladeshi capital market are: 1) Securities Act 1920; 2) Securities and Exchange Ordinance 1969, as amended in 1993; 3) Securities and Exchange Commission Act 1993; 4) Companies Act 1994; 5) Securities and Exchange Rules 1987; 6) Securities and Exchange

Table 18.1 Some macroeconomic data—Bangladesh

	1980–1989	1990–1999	2000–2005	2006–2010	2011–2014
GDP growth rate	3.7	4.8	5.4	6.1	6.3
GDP per capita (US$)	210	298	351	621	939
Inflation rate CPI (% p.a.)	10.5	5.6	4.3	6.8	7.4

Source: Mahmud *et al.*, 2008; Rahman and Yusuf, 2010; Hussain, 2015.

Commission (Stock-dealer, Stock-broker and Sub-broker) Regulations 1994, as amended in 1995; 7) Securities and Exchanges Commission (Appeal) Regulations 1995; 8) Guidelines on Initial Public Offering to Local Investors; 9) Guidelines on Foreign Placement or Allotment of Securities; 10) Guidelines on Issuance of Right Shares and Guidelines for Raising of Capital by Greenfield Public Companies; and 11) Depository Act 1999. Bangladesh has two stock exchanges: the Dhaka Stock Exchange (DSE) and the Chittagong Stock Exchange (CSE), and both stock exchanges have experienced growths in trading volume and market capitalization in recent years.

The regulatory authority of the capital market in Bangladesh is the Securities and Exchanges Commission (BSEC), which was established in 1993 with a mandate to ensure compliance with capital market laws, rules, and regulations. Being attached to the Ministry of Finance (MoF) of Bangladesh, the chairman and members of the BSEC are appointed by the government. The main objectives of the BSEC are to protect investors, develop capital markets, and ensure discipline in the issuing of securities. A World Bank review noted in 2015 that the BSEC was in the process of making capital market reforms to enhance market stability. The World Bank considers these reforms necessary to establish public confidence, which will ultimately expand the sources of private-sector financing in Bangladesh. However, there is doubt on the effectiveness of financial statement monitoring tasks of BSEC owing to the lack of appropriate resources and the lack of coordination between the BSEC and dominant professional accounting bodies in Bangladesh (World Bank, 2015). Nonetheless, in line with most other parts in the world, the BSEC now requires listed companies to prepare financial statements following the International Financial Reporting Standards (IFRS) as adopted in Bangladesh (known as the Bangladesh Financial Reporting Standards, or BFRS) and requires that the statements of the regulated companies be audited in compliance with the International Standards for Auditing (known as the Bangladesh Standards on Auditing or BSA). The BSEC is also responsible for monitoring the operations of the DSE and the CSE.

The Dhaka Stock Exchange (DSE) was incorporated in 1954 as the East Pakistan Stock Exchanges Association Ltd but began formal trading in 1956. Trading activity at the DSE was discontinued for five years after the liberation war of 1971 and trading resumed in 1976. Currently the DSE is registered as a public limited company and is regulated by the Companies Act 1994, its articles of association, its bylaws, the Securities and Exchanges Ordinance 1969, and the Securities and Exchange Commission Act 1993. It currently has 250 members/dealers and 558 securities were listed as of December 31, 2015 (World Bank, 2015). The Chittagong Stock Exchange (CSE) started its operations in 1995. It is also a self-regulated, nonprofit organization, like DSE. The CSE has 269 securities listed as of December 31, 2015.

The market capitalization of DSE, the major stock exchange in Bangladesh, has increased significantly in recent years. From a low 0.9 percent in 1991, the ratio of market capitalization to GDP increased to 39.1 percent in June 2010 (Wahab and Faruq, 2012). The ratio was 24.13 at the end of 2014. Table 18.2 presents some relevant stock market information for selected years from 1986 to 2014.

However, the Bangladesh capital market has experienced a few major shocks in recent times (a severe bust was reported in 1996). Such volatility in the stock market dampens investors' confidence as investors start to question the quality of reporting by listed companies. It was reported that the capital market in Bangladesh had been in a significant downward trend, with the market capitalization of the DSE having declined drastically from about US$47 billion in 2009 to US$24 billion in 2013 (Chowdhury, 2013).

Table 18.2 The size of the capital market (DSE)

Year	Market capitalization (billion taka)	Market capitalization to GDP ratio (%)	Turnover (billion taka)
1986	5.73	1.23	0.05
1991	10.4	0.94	0.12
1996	166.04	9.98	30.14
2001	67.45	2.51	39.86
2006	315.45	7.59	65.07
2009	1903.23	30.95	1475.9
2010	2700.74	39.11	2564.11
2011	2616.73	33.23	1560.91
2012	2403.56	26.27	1001.08
2013	2647.79	25.51	952.74
2014	3259.25	24.13	1188.52

Source: Bangladesh Bank; Dhaka Stock Exchange.

Company legislation and governance

The institutional setup of corporate regulation in Bangladesh consists of six major regulators: the Registrar of Joint Stock Companies (RJSC), the BSEC, the Bangladesh Bank (BB), the Insurance Development & Regulatory Authority (IDRA), the Institute of Chartered Accountants of Bangladesh (ICAB), and the Monitoring Cell of the MoF. Each regulator operates under a distinct Act or law (World Bank, 2015). Other than these entities, the Investment Corporation of Bangladesh (ICB) and the Board of Investment (BOI) also play important roles in this respect.

The RJSC is the major umbrella regulator in Bangladesh, to which most business entities are accountable. RJSC is solely authorized to facilitate the formation of companies (public, private, foreign, and others) and keep track of ownership-related issues. The World Bank (2015) reported that 181,642 entities were administered by the RJSC (as of June 2013), of which 128,263 were companies. It is estimated that around 8,000–10,000 new companies are being registered by the RJSC each year (World Bank, 2015). The Companies Act 1994 covers most governance-related issues applicable for companies and the RJSC is empowered to ensure compliance with the regulations by these entities. The RJSC is authorized to receive/collect financial statements and other information and to inspect/investigate, where necessary, to ensure compliance with the provisions of the law. However, the World Bank has voiced its concern regarding the abilities and effectiveness of the RJSC to carry out its activities properly. In particular, the report notes:

> The effectiveness of RJSC's monitoring systems is one of the major challenges in ensuring the broader level application of IFRS that is essential to ensuring improved accountability and transparency so as to create a better investment climate. Currently, quality control inspection of financial statements is not performed. There is lack of expertise in the RJSC team and lack of facilities to examine the quality of financial statements and related compliance.
>
> *Source: World Bank, 2015.*

The Bangladeshi legislative and institutional framework for accounting and auditing services is shown in Table 18.3. The basic corporate legislation that governs the operational boundaries, responsibilities, and accountabilities of Bangladeshi entities is the Companies Act 1994, which was derived primarily from the Companies Act 1913 as adopted in the Indian subcontinent during the British rule, which was modeled on the British Companies Act 1908 (Ali *et al.*, 2004). The 1913 Act was amended several times before and after Bangladesh became independent, which resulted in the current Companies Act 1994. The RJSC is entrusted with regulatory power to administer the Act in Bangladesh. This Act requires companies, among others, to keep proper books of accounts and to prepare and send financial statements to their shareholders in order to reflect *a true and fair view* of the companies' states of affairs. These laws also require companies to verify their accounts and express opinions on them by independent auditors, as defined in the Act, within a specified time of the end of the financial year (Ali *et al.*, 2004).

The Companies Act 1994 is a prime source of accounting regulation in Bangladesh. However, other legislation has been progressively introduced in Bangladesh to fully implement the legal provisions contained in the Companies Act. For example, the disclosure of the extent and nature of Bangladesh listed companies are influenced by the BSEC Rules 1987 (Government of Bangladesh, 1987) and the accounting standards adopted by the ICAB. The ICAB, a self-regulatory body, was set up under the Bangladesh Chartered Accountants Order 1973 and the ICAB still has responsibility for issuing accounting standards in Bangladesh.[4] These regulatory bodies provide the framework for corporate disclosures. Industries such as the railways, electricity, insurance, and banks have their own distinct regulations that govern their annual reports and disclosures. Corporate disclosure is also influenced by the Nationalization Order 1972, the Banking Companies Act 1991, and the Income Tax Ordinance 1984 (Akhtaruddin, 2005). The country has an active regulator for the financial sector—the Central Bank of Bangladesh (more commonly known as Bangladesh Bank, BB). Bangladesh Bank, in addition to other regulatory bodies, monitors the compliance of relevant laws by financial institutions in Bangladesh. The BB was established via the Bangladesh Bank Order 1972. Apart from the BSEC, the BB plays an important role in monitoring corporate governance practices within the country's financial institutions. Therefore, the regulation of financial institutions seems to be stricter than that of other companies in Bangladesh. Even though a few notable donor organizations (e.g., the Asian Development Bank, ADB) identified some loopholes in the existing corporate regulatory environment in Bangladesh, the legal framework for corporate regulation in Bangladesh is akin to other countries in the region. The state-owned enterprises (SOEs) in Bangladesh are economically significant and hold a large portion of public funds invested by the state. There are 45 nonfinancial state-owned entities, 35 corporations, 112 autonomous bodies, and 66 institutions, academies, or subordinate offices in Bangladesh (World Bank, 2015). They represent a large investment of public funding. The SOE wing of the Finance Division of the MoF oversees nonfinancial entities, while financial institutions are overseen by the Banking and Financial Institutions Division of the MoF (World Bank, 2015).

Accounting policymaking

ICAB is the national professional accounting body and accounting standard setter in Bangladesh. The regulatory framework for financial reporting and audit of corporate entities in Bangladesh is governed by the Companies Act 1994, the Securities Exchange Rules 1987, and other statutes, such as the Bank Companies Act 1991. The professional responsibilities and conduct of chartered accountants are governed by the Bangladesh Chartered Accountants Bye-Laws 1973. The enforceability status for compliance with accounting and auditing standards,

Main governing Acts
• Companies Act 1994
• Securities and Exchanges (SEC) Rules 1987
• Financial Reporting Act 2015
• Nationalized Order 1972
• Banking Companies Act 1991
• Income Tax Ordinance 1984

Institutions and their main functions

Institute of Chartered Accountants of Bangladesh (ICAB)	Bangladesh Securities and Exchange Commission (BSEC)
• Approves accounting &auditing standards **[The FRC has taken over this role after the implementation of the Financial Reporting Act 2015]**	• Oversees the operations of the two stock exchanges • Administers the Securities Act and SEC rules

Registrar of Joint Stock Companies

• Administers the Companies Act 1994

Bangladesh Bank

• Administers the Banking Companies Act

• Makes decisions on monetary policy

• Determines disclosure requirements for financial institutions

Figure 18.1 Bangladeshi legislative and institutional framework for accounting and auditing services

adopted by the ICAB, emanates from these sources: being legally mandatory (force of law) or professionally mandatory (bylaw requirement) (Chowdhury, 2013).

It is reported that the Companies Act 1994 made major alternations to the financial reporting practices and disclosures of limited liability companies in Bangladesh (Ahmed and Kabir, 1995). This removed some anomalies that existed in the previous versions of the Companies Act. For example, the Companies Act 1994 requires companies to have their statements audited before their annual general meetings. Section 185 of the Companies Act specifies mandatory items to be disclosed on the balance sheets and income statements and Section 186 provides a list of information items that must be disclosed in the director's reports (Akhtaruddin, 2005). Legislative requirements prior to 1994, however, failed to indicate the actual level of corporate disclosure (Akhtaruddin, 2005).

The ICAB, as a member of the IASB, is entrusted with the task of adopting and enforcing international accounting standards in Bangladesh. The Companies Act 1994 however does not contain any provision for the mandatory observance of the adopted IAS and ISA in practice. The Chartered Accountants Bye-Laws 1973 has also not been amended to require mandatory compliance of the adopted standards by the ICAB. Hence, in the absence of any broad statutory or professional requirements, the implementation of the adopted IAS/IFRS and ISA is regarded as indicative of good, standard accounting and auditing practices in Bangladesh. Despite the adoption of the IAS and the ISA by the ICAB, there was no legal enforceability of these standards until the end of 1997. The SER 1987 (Rule 12, Sub-rules 2 and 3) were amended in 1997 such that all issuers/listed entities became required to comply with the requirements of all applicable IAS/IFRS (as adopted by ICAB) in the preparation and presentation of their financial statements, and all auditing practices are required to ensure compliance with the relevant ISA (as adopted by the ICAB) in the conduct of and reporting on the audits of the financial statements of listed entities. Hence, the IAS and the ISA, duly adopted by the ICAB as the BAS and the BSA, now have a legally enforceable mandatory status for all listed companies in Bangladesh (Chowdhury, 2013). The ICAB is one of the first national accounting standards setters in the South Asia region to start adopting the IAS/IFRS (Miazee, 2014). As of January 2013, a version of all IFRS and IAS issued by the IASB was adopted as the BFRS and the BAS, respectively, by the ICAB.

The ICAB followed a regular approach to adopt any new accounting standards issued by the IASB, after completing a process of stringent technical review to consider their applicability in Bangladesh. Once accounting standards became adopted by ICAB and gained mandatory status through the BSEC's directives, they became applicable to all listed companies. After reviewing and adopting the IAS/IFRS, ICAB labeled them Bangladesh Accounting Standards (BAS)/ Bangladesh financial reporting standards (BFRS), notwithstanding that most of these standards are carbon copies (with the same numbers) as the original IAS/IFRS (Mir and Rahaman, 2005). Once the standards are adopted, the BSEC then has the responsibility, as delegated by the government of Bangladesh, to monitor compliance with these standards by listed companies. This adoption process by the ICAB does not include other interested parties such as accounting academics, the ICMAB, the Federation of Bangladesh Chambers of Commerce and Industry (FBCCI), and general users of corporate financial statement users. A list of BAS/BFRS is provided in Tables 18.3(A) and 18.3(B):

Table 18.3(A) Adoption status of International Accounting Standards (IAS) by the ICAB as Bangladesh Accounting Standards (BAS)

IAS/BAS	Title of adopted IAS as BAS	Effective date— applicable on or after
1	Presentation of Financial Statements	January 1, 2007
2	Inventories	January 1, 2007
7	Statement of Cash Flows	January 1, 1999
8	Accounting Policies, Changes in Accounting Estimates and Errors	January 1, 2007
10	Events After the Reporting Period	January 1, 1999
11	Construction Contracts	January 1, 1999
12	Income Taxes	January 1, 1999
16	Property, Plant and Equipment	January 1, 2007
17	Leases	January 1, 2007
18	Revenue	January 1, 2007
19	Employee Benefits	January 1, 2004
20	Accounting for Government Grants and Disclosure of Government Association	January 1, 1999
21	The Effects of Changes in Foreign Exchange Rates	January 1, 2007
23	Borrowing Costs	January 1, 2010
24	Related Party Disclosures	January 1, 2007

26	Accounting and Reporting by Retirement Benefit Plans	January 1, 2007
27	Consolidated and Separate Financial Statements	January 1, 2010
28	Investments in Associates	January 1, 2007
29	Financial Reporting in Hyperinflationary Economics	Not adopted
31	Interests in Joint Ventures	January 1, 2007
32	Financial Instruments: Presentation	January 1, 2010
33	Earnings per Share	January 1, 2007
34	Interim Financial Reporting	January 1, 1999
36	Impairment of Assets	January 1, 2005
37	Provisions, Contingent Liabilities and Contingent Assets	January 1, 2007
38	Intangible Assets	January 1, 2005
39	Financial Instruments: Recognition and Measurement	January 1, 2010
40	Investment Property	January 1, 2007
41	Agriculture	January 1, 2007

Table 18.3(B) Adoption status of International Financial Reporting Standards (IFRS) by the ICAB as Bangladesh Financial Reporting Standards (BFRS)

SL #	IFRS/ BFRS	Title of adopted IFRS as BFRS	Effective date— applicable on or after
1	BFRS 1	First-time Adoption of IFRS	January 1, 2009
2	BFRS 2	Share-based Payment	January 1, 2007
3	BFRS 3	Business Combinations	January 1, 2010
4	BFRS 4	Insurance Contracts	January 1, 2010
5	BFRS 5	Non-current Assets Held for Sale and Discontinued Operations	January 1, 2007
6	BFRS 6	Exploration & evaluation of Mineral Resources	January 1, 2007
7	BFRS 7	Financial Instruments: Disclosures	January 1, 2010
8	BFRS 8	Operating Segments	January 1, 2010
9	IFRS 9	Financial Instruments	Not Adopted
10	BFRS 10	Consolidated Financial Statements	January 1, 2013
11	BFRS 11	Joint Arrangements	January 1, 2013
12	BFRS 12	Disclosure of Interests in Other Entities	January 1, 2013
13	BFRS 13	Fair Value Measurement	January 1, 2013
IFRS for SMEs		BFRS for SMEs (Small and Medium-Sized Entities)	January 1, 2013

Source: ICAB website; Chowdhury, 2013.

The adoption of the IAS in Bangladesh was facilitated by a push from international donor agencies (e.g., the World Bank and the ADB). The ICAB not only has the sole authority to adopt ISA/IFRS in Bangladesh, but it also supplies qualified accountants to carry out auditing practice. Realizing the conflict of interest in the process, a World Bank report (2003) criticized the accounting and auditing practices in Bangladesh, which made the government review the existing institutional setup and introduce a new Financial Reporting Act (FRA). After a long period since being advised by the World Bank in 2003, the cabinet of the Bangladeshi government approved the Financial Reporting Act in 2015 and set up the Financial Reporting Council (FRC) to strengthen the monitoring of accounting standards and the accounting profession. Since then all auditors and auditing firms must register with the FRC, otherwise they will not be allowed to provide auditing services in Bangladesh. Other responsibilities of FRC include: 1) to set up/adopt the accounting standards/financial reporting standards and auditing standards with the standard code of conduct for professional accountants; 2) to monitor and review the authenticity and fairness of financial reporting by public interest entities; 3) to monitor auditors with a view to maintaining high standards of professional conduct; and 4) to enforce compliance with accounting standards/financial reporting standards and auditing standards in the country. Bangladesh is entering a new phase of its accounting policymaking process, arguably a more credible accounting policy setting arrangement, after the enactment of the Financial Reporting Act in 2015.

Auditing standards

The Companies Act 1994 requires all registered companies in Bangladesh to be audited by an auditor who is a chartered accountant under the Bangladesh Chartered Accountants Order of 1973 (i.e., a member of the ICAB). The ICAB requires its members to follow ISA (adopted as BSA), effectively requiring compliance with ISA for all audits in Bangladesh (World Bank, 2015). At the same time, the ICAB is the sole custodian of the adoption and issue of International Standards on Auditing (ISA) as the Bangladesh Standards on Auditing (BSAs).[5]

The Technical and Research Committee (TRC) of the ICAB follows a stringent procedure when adopting ISA in Bangladesh to overcome any inconsistencies and to ensure conformity with domestic laws and regulations. Any particular IAPS/ISA is first considered by the TRC of ICAB, then it is critically reviewed by a nominated subcommittee comprising one or two members who undertake a stringent vetting exercise to eliminate any anomalies or inconsistencies and ensure conformity with the existing regulatory requirements. Based on the recommendations of the subcommittee and taking into consideration any necessary modifications, the TRC then formulates its recommendation to the Council of the ICAB for adoption. Once approved by the Council, it becomes a definitively adopted Bangladesh Auditing Practice Statement (BAPS)/BSA (Chowdhury, 2013).

The World Bank (2015) recognized that there was no standards gap in auditing in Bangladesh, but it raised a concern over the quality of audits currently being carried out in Bangladesh. In spite of the introduction of the Audit Practice Manual (APM) and training thereon by the ICAB, the results of reviews conducted by the relevant department of the ICAB using a Bangladesh Standard on Quality Control (BSQC) checklist revealed that a considerable number of medium-sized and small auditing firms did not follow proper audit procedures and documentation standards. In addition, some auditors were charging audit fees that were too low to allow for effective audits to be performed in compliance with the applicable standards. In some cases, even the audit report format and language revealed that either the engaging auditors did not have sufficient competency to do the audits or that they grossly neglected their duty to the public interest (World Bank, 2015). Concerns were also raised regarding the suitability of three versions of audit: one for banks, another for the tax department, and a further version for shareholders/owners.

Although Bangladesh is appearing to be more aligned with international standards in auditing, a bigger issue of audit quality in Bangladesh lies with the absence of quality auditing firms in Bangladesh. Kabir et al. (2011) report that the market size for audit services in Bangladesh constrains the bargaining power of auditing firms and thus affects the quality of audits in Bangladesh (p. 165). Many auditing firms have ownership concentrated to family members and suffer from shortages in skilled and competent auditors (Farooque et al., 2007; Siddiqui, 2010; Khan et al., 2011).

The accounting profession

The accounting profession in Bangladesh is dominated by two professional associations: the ICAB and the Institute of Cost and Management Accountants of Bangladesh (ICMAB). While financial audits are performed by members of the ICAB, the cost audits are done by members of the ICMAB. However, both organizations are under the control of the Ministry of Commerce in Bangladesh. The two institutions are run and managed by their council members, who are elected internally, and representatives from government (Mir and Rahaman, 2005). Therefore, it can be argued that the councils at both institutions are subject to (in)direct influence from the government over the development of the accounting profession in Bangladesh.

The World Bank Report (2015, para. 62) provides recent statistics on the memberships of various accounting professional bodies in Bangladesh, which are reproduced below:

> The ICAB is the largest in terms of the number of members, with 1,570 members at the end of 2013 and increasing trends in numbers entering the profession. The ICMAB has 1,080 members. Another UK-based Association of Chartered Certified Accountants (ACCA) has 103 members in Bangladesh. ACCA membership is growing fast, with 56 of its present 103 members having passed in 2013. However, ACCA is not a nationally recognized institute having no legal forms in Bangladesh and its members have to convert to be ICAB members to be licensed as auditors or accountants for public practice in Bangladesh.

The ICAB has the sole authority for training, examining, and certifying chartered accountants and for regulating the auditing profession in Bangladesh, in line with the Bangladesh Chartered Accountants Order 1973, the Chartered Accountants Bye-Laws 1973, and the directives or decisions of the ICAB Council. The ICAB is an active permanent member of several international and regional accounting bodies, including 1) the IFAC, 2) the International Accounting Standards Committee/Board (IASC/IASB), 3) the South Asian Federation of Accountants (SAFA), and 4) the Confederation of Asian and Pacific Accountants (CAPA).[6] The ICAB licenses all statutory auditors in public practice, requiring auditors to obtain practical training, an audit qualification, and sufficient prior experience and minimum continuing professional development (CPD) to meet international standards (i.e. the IAESB's International Education Standard 8 (*Competence Requirements for Audit Professionals*)). More recently, the ICAB (advised by the World Bank) has made a twinning arrangement with the ICAEW in the UK, which has resulted in significant and sustained improvement in the ICAB's training and education programs. The ICAB was accredited as a training partner of the ICAEW in 2014 and adopted the ICAEW's syllabus and examination systems to update its study materials (World Bank, 2015). On the other hand, ICMAB members intending to perform cost audits are required to obtain a practicing certificate from the institute. However, the current licensing requirements to conduct cost audits fall short of international practicing requirements (Mir and Rahaman, 2005).

The ICAB's qualification programs require applicants to complete CA studies after registering with the ICAB. As mentioned before, the syllabus of current CA studies in Bangladesh has been upgraded owing to the partnership arrangement with the ICAEW. There are two parts of CA study in Bangladesh, which have to be done simultaneously. The first part covers theoretical knowledge and the second part is practical issues. Students need to sit for examinations on several subjects in the theoretical part (depending on the level). There are three levels (knowledge, application, and advanced) in the theoretical part, containing a total of 18 subjects. The practical part of the CA studies requires students to undergo two to four years of apprenticeship practice. The duration of the apprenticeship depends on the academic level completed prior to the CA studies.

When a student successfully completes the apprenticeship, he/she can get the CA qualification. Then the student has to complete both practical and theoretical parts in order to pass the CA examinations and achieve the Associate Chartered Accountants (ACA) degree and apply for ICAB membership.

The ICAB has in recent years had difficulty attracting high-quality graduates into the accounting profession. One of the reasons, as cited by the World Bank (2015), for the reducing trend of high-quality commerce students entering professional accounting education is that the relevant government-sector services such as customs, taxes, and regulatory departments do not require finance and accounting education. A historically low pass rate of the CA qualification examinations also made the profession unattractive in society. Many potential candidates have become more interested in entering the job markets after graduation to support families rather than pursuing further long-term apprenticeships in practicing firms where the allowances paid to students is too low, while the pass rate of the CA examinations is very low (World Bank, 2015). To further complicate the situation, teaching in accounting programs at universities and colleges in Bangladesh has not been improved. As a result, the quality of accounting intakes continues to be a serious concern for the accounting profession. It has become a more crucial issue since the ICAB has adopted the ICAEW syllabus and examination systems under the twinning arrangements (World Bank, 2015).

There is also an absence of accreditation requirements in accounting education in Bangladesh. The ICMAB has faced even bigger challenges for its role in training cost and management accountants in Bangladesh. Its twinning arrangement with the CIMA in the UK has had only very limited impact. To further exacerbate the situation, the ICMAB's recent rate of admission to membership is very low, with only 157 students passing its qualification in the last four years (World Bank, 2015).

International donor organizations have always questioned the enforcement of proper financial reporting and governance framework in Bangladesh. This actually translates to low demand for professional accountancy services in Bangladesh. In addition, there is less demand for qualified accountants as the country's economic entities either are not managed professionally or are family owned firms. There is hardly any demand for professional accountants' services in SMEs, which account for 96 percent of private-sector industrial establishments and provide employment for roughly 78 percent of the nonagricultural workforce in the country (World Bank, 2015). Of the 128,263 registered companies, only about 10 percent of them submit returns with the RJSC. The same reason might have led to a majority of auditing firms being either sole proprietorships or partnerships. Karim and Hasan (2012) report that most auditing firms in Bangladesh operate from a single office and are predominantly located in the capital city, Dhaka.

The Big Four international accounting firms, as in some other south Asian countries, do not operate directly under their brand name in Bangladesh. Instead, they operate through local affiliates. The domestic affiliates of the Big Four firms are Rahman Rahman Huq (the affiliate of KPMG), Hoda Vasi Chowdhury (the affiliate of Deloitte Touche Tomatsu), A Qasem & Co (the affiliate of PWC) and S. F. Ahmed (the affiliate of Ernst & Young) (Kabir *et al.*, 2011). Two other international accounting firms are operating in Bangladesh through local affiliates: Moore Stephen and Binder, and Dijker, Otte & Co (Karim and Hasan, 2012). Apart from these relatively large auditing firms, there are a limited number of mid-sized local auditing firms. The majority of them are basically small firms with very limited auditing engagements. However, the World Bank (2015) reports the increase in the number of registered business entities at around 6 percent per year in Bangladesh. If this pace continues and a strong financial reporting framework and enforcement environment are put in place, the demand for professional accountants will increase significantly in the country.

It is found that the current recruitment criteria for financial auditors in the Comptroller and Auditor General's (CAG) Office of the government do not give sufficient attention to accounting qualifications. There is a great pressure on government training institutions to provide specialist knowledge, which has not been effective (World Bank, 2007). There are two categories of accounting officials in the public sector: 1) cadre officers in the Bangladesh Civil Service's Audit and Accounts Cadre, and 2) noncadre officers in the subordinate Accounts Services. All cadre officers are trained in the Bangladeshi civil service training academy for six months in a foundation program after appointment. The cadre officers in the training academy have to taken short courses such as: 1) accountancy, elementary to advanced; 2) book-keeping, government accounting; 3) fundamental rules of government, civil service rules, treasury rules; 4) economics, budgeting, constitution; 5) computer knowledge; 6) auditing; 7) précis and drafting, report writing; and 8) manuals, codes, rules of different audit directorates (World Bank, 2007). Apparently, current training and development programs for government accountants in the public sector in Bangladesh do not factor in the attainment of professional accountancy qualifications, which has contributed to a severe lack of skills and competence in public accounting in Bangladesh.

Future prospects

The accounting environment has experienced several reforms in Bangladesh since its independence in 1971. The economic growth in Bangladesh during the last two and half decades has brought forward the need to strengthen the role of private-sector oversight bodies. The accounting profession in Bangladesh has to reform to cater to the changing business environment. The accounting standards in Bangladesh have been converging on the internationally accepted standards and there is a reform in the regulatory oversight of the accounting profession in Bangladesh, e.g., to establish a separate regulatory body (i.e., the FRC) to oversee and regulate the activities of the profession, moving away from the traditional self-regulatory environment. However, some challenges remain to be solved in the near future.

Even though Bangladesh has made some progresses in strengthening the pillars of financial reporting systems, the statutory mechanism is yet to be defined to introduce a simplified financial reporting framework for SMEs and micro-finance entities. These entities comprise the majority of registered entities in Bangladesh. The financial reporting requirements for SOEs, some quite large in financial terms, seem to be quite relaxed at present. The challenge for Bangladeshi government is to get the reporting of SOEs to align more with international standards.

There is still a shortage of skilled staff at various regulatory bodies in Bangladesh, which has a negative effect on the regulatory oversight functions. Except for initiatives taken by the ICAB and the BSEC, no steps have been taken to strengthen the capacities of other regulatory bodies (World Bank, 2015). The accountability of SOEs has always been a question owing to a lack of skills among government accountants. Therefore, measures are needed to strengthen capacity building in public-sector accounting.

The new Financial Reporting Act came into effect in September 2015, but it remains to be seen how the accounting profession will react to the reforms in the regulatory setting in Bangladesh. The professional bodies (particularly the ICAB) have always resisted such arrangements, but support from the profession is crucial for a smooth transition from the self-regulation led by the ICAB to the FRA-led regulatory environment in Bangladesh.

Finally, the professional bodies must attract high-quality students into the accounting profession to satisfy demand from the growing economy. A coordinated initiative to improve the quality of teaching and examinations in the accounting programmes of universities is a prerequisite to achieve this goal. The ICAB might consider introducing a second-tier certification such as certified accounting technicians or a diploma in professional accounting (DPA), as such an interim certification could be particularly relevant for many partially qualified and trained students in the country (World Bank, 2015).

Notes

1 Source: www.bangldesh.gov.bd.
2 See: www.bangladesh.gov.bd, 2015.
3 See: www.bangladesh.gov.bd, 2015.
4 The government of Bangladesh enacted the Financial Reporting Act in 2015, which restrains the authority of ICAB to issue accounting standards in Bangladesh.
5 Source: www.icab.org.bd.
6 Although the responsibility of adoption and issuance of BSAs will rest with the FRC once the FRC is established under the Financial Reporting Act 2015.

References

Asian Development Bank (ADB) (2011) *Country Partnership Strategy Bangladesh: 2011–2015*. Retrieved from www.adb.org.

Ahmed, M.U. and Kabir, M.H. (1995) External financial reporting as envisaged in Companies Act 1994: A critical evaluation. *Journal of Business Studies*, *16*(1), 185–208.

Akhtaruddin, M. (2005) Corporate mandatory disclosure practices in Bangladesh. *The International Journal of Accounting*, *40*(4), 399–422.

Ali, M.J., Ahmed, K. and Henry, D. (2004) Disclosure compliance with national accounting standards by listed companies in South Asia. *Accounting and Business Research*, *34*(3), 183–199.

Bertelsmann Stiftung's Transformation Index (BTI) (2014) *Bangladesh Country Report*. Gutersloh: Bertelsmann Stiftung. Retrieved from www.bti-project.org.

Chowdhury, A. (2013) Harmonization of financial reporting and auditing practices: Bangladesh perspective. *Institute of Chartered Accountants of Bangladesh Members Conference*, Dhaka, February 23, 2013.

Farooque, O., Zijl, T., Dunstan, K. and Karim, A.K.M.W. (2007) Corporate governance in Bangladesh: Link between board ownership and financial performance. *Corporate Governance: An International Review*, *15*(6), 1453–1468.

Hussain, Z. (2015) *Bangladesh development update (April 2015)*. Washington, DC: World Bank. Retrieved from http://documents.worldbank.org/curated/en/2015/04/24323972/bangladesh-development-update-april-2015.

Kabir, M.H, Sharma, D, Islam, M.A. and Salat, A (2011) Big 4 auditor affiliation and accruals quality in Bangladesh. *Managerial Auditing Journal*, *26*(2), 161–181.

Karim, A.K.M.W. and Hasan, T. (2012) The market for audit services in Bangladesh. *Journal of Accounting in Emerging Economies 2*(1), 50–66.

Khan, A.R., Hossain, D.M. and Siddiqui, J. (2011) Corporate ownership concentration and audit fees: The case of an emerging economy. *Advances in Accounting*, *27*(1), 125–131.

Mahmud, W., Ahmed, S. and Mahajan, S. (2008) Economic reforms, growth, and governance: The political economy aspects of Bangladesh's development surprise. In David Brad & Michael Spence (Eds), *Leadership and Growth* (pp. 227–254). Washington, DC: The World Bank.

Miazee, M.H. (2014) Problems of implementing of international financial reporting standards in Bangladesh. *European Journal of Business and Management*, *6*(36), 174–181.

Mir, M.Z and Rahaman, A.S. (2005) The adoption of international accounting standards in Bangladesh: An exploration of rationale and process. *Accounting, Auditing & Accountability Journal*, *18*(6), 816–841.

Rahman, J. and Yusuf, J. (2010) Economic growth in Bangladesh: Experience and policy priorities. *Journal of Bangladesh Studies*, *12*(1), 1–22.

Siddiqui, J. (2010) Development of corporate governance regulations: The case of an emerging economy. *Journal of Business Ethics*, *91*(2), 253–274.

Wahab, M.A. and Faruq, M.O. (2012) *A Comprehensive Study on Capital Market Developments in Bangladesh*. Working paper series: WP1203, Research and Development, Bangladesh Bank, Dhaka. Retrieved from www.bb.org.bd (accessed January 23, 2016)

World Bank (2003) *Bangladesh – Report on the Observance of Standards and Codes (ROSC): Accounting and Auditing*. Washington, DC: World Bank. Retrieved from http://documents.worldbank.org/curated/en/2003/05/6561790/bangladesh-report-observance-standards-codes-rosc-accounting-auditing (accessed January 26, 2016).

World Bank (2007) *Bangladesh - Public Sector Accounting and Auditing: A Comparison to International Standards*. Washington, DC: World Bank. Retrieved from http://documents.worldbank.org/curated/en/2007/03/7606464/bangladesh-public-sector-accounting-auditing-comparison-international-standards (accessed January 23, 2016).

World Bank (2015) *Bangladesh - Report on the Observance of Standards and Codes (ROSC): Accounting and Auditing*. Washington, DC: World Bank. Retrieved from www.worldbank.org/ifa/2015/Bangladesh-FinalOutputP149852-2015-04-17%2011-17.pdf (accessed January 23, 2016).

Websites

Chittagong Stock Exchange. Retrieved from www.cse.com.bd (accessed January 23, 2016).

Dhaka Stock Exchange. Retrieved from www.dsebd.org (accessed January 23, 2016).

Government of Bangladesh. Retrieved from www.bangladesh.gov.bd (accessed January 23, 2016).

ICAB. Retrieved from www.icab.org.bd (accessed January 23, 2016).

19

Accounting environment in Cambodia

P.W. Senarath Yapa, Kerry Jacobs and C.B. Chan

Country Profile

Cambodia is an important player in South East Asia given its geographic location in the lower Mekong region between Thailand in the west, Vietnam in the east and Laos in the north. Cambodia was ruled by the French for almost 100 years and became independent in 1954 (Kiernan, 1985). The legal system is primarily civil law – a mixture of French-influenced codes from the United Nations Transitional Authority in Cambodia (UNTAC) period, Royal decrees and Acts of legislature with influences from customary law and remnants of communist legal theory, and with the increasing influence of common law in recent years. Cambodia has recently become a member of the World Trade Organization (WTO). However, Cambodia remains one of the world's least developed countries, with a population of about 14 million, a predominantly rural and agricultural economy, a life expectancy of 57 years and an infant mortality of 68 per thousand births. Cambodia ranks as one of the poorest countries in the world (World Bank, 2007).

Cambodia moved towards a market economy with the new constitution in 1993. The National Assembly approves national budgets, state plans, loans, lending and the creation, changes or annulment of taxes. Cambodia has embarked on economic reforms since the mid-1980s. In 1989, private property rights were restored and price controls were abolished. State-owned enterprises (SOEs) were privatized and increased incentives were provided to local and foreign private investments. This set the stage for the signing of the Paris Peace Accord in 1991, designed to put an end to the protracted civil wars and to assist the rehabilitation of the economy. After the 1993 general election, the newly formed Royal Government of Cambodia has formulated comprehensive macroeconomic and structural reforms and achieved some significant successes in stabilizing the economy.

The first Western accounting system was imported to Cambodia in the nineteenth century by the French to support colonial rule, so the country's legal and accounting systems developed along the lines of those in France. Nonetheless, the French did not introduce a proper accounting system in Cambodia and the Khmer Rouge regime, led by Pol Pot, destroyed most social and physical infrastructure and professionals in all disciplines (including accountants) in the country. Once Pol Pot was removed from power, the economy was rebuilt with influence from Vietnam and many Western countries and assistance from donor agencies such as the World Bank (WB) and the Asian Development Bank (ADB). Similarly, the accounting profession was rebuilt by a small number of surviving professionals. Despite the fact that Cambodia was influenced by communist regimes in the mid-1970s and 1980s, economic globalization brought about notable growth of the Cambodian economy after the 1990s.

In 2010, Cambodia's per capita gross domestic product (GDP) was US$830. Over recent years (2010–2014) annual GDP growth averaged 9.52 per cent. This growth was driven primarily by the manufacturing (13.14 percent), agriculture (6.36 per cent) and servicing sectors (9.1 per cent). Within the manufacturing sector, the clothing industry contributes significantly to export earnings and employment. Over the same period, the average annual inflation rate was about 5 percent and the average annual external debt was US$5,382 million.[1] Table 19.1 provides some macroeconomic data about Cambodia in recent years.

The rest of this chapter is organized into five sections. The second section discusses the regulation of the capital market. The third section elaborates on some issues related to accounting policy making, while the fourth focuses on auditing standards. The fifth section briefly introduces the accounting profession in Cambodia. The final section presents concluding remarks.

Capital market regulation in Cambodia

After decades of the command economy under communist rule, Cambodia began its transformation into a free market in the late 1980s. It is now integrating with regional and global markets. However, there is no well-developed capital market in Cambodia. In 2005 the Cambodian government enacted a new company law with assistance from the ADB (ADB, 2005). The law applies to partnerships and companies carrying on business in Cambodia. A partnership comprises a general (two or more partners) partnership and a limited partnership. A company can be a private limited or public limited company as prescribed in law. Each partnership or company shall file an annual declaration with the Ministry of Commerce (MoC) regarding the status of the partnership or the company.

Overview of the Cambodia Securities Exchange (CSX)

The Cambodia Securities Exchange, or the Cambodia Stock Exchange (CSX), is a joint-venture between the Royal Government of Cambodia (55 per cent ownership) and the

Table 19.1 Some macroeconomic data – Cambodia

	2010	2011	2012	2013	2014
GDP (in US$ million)	11,634	12,965	14,054	15,251	16,880
GDP growth rate (%)	9.3	10.7	8.9	8.2	10.5
GDP, per capita (in US$)	830	911	973	1,042	1,135
GDP % growth rate by economic activity					
Agriculture, fisheries and forestry	10.8	12.9	5.6	2.0	0.5
Industry	10.3	12.1	13.0	13.3	17.0
Services	2.5	8.4	9.6	10.3	14.7
Inflation rate (Consumer Price Index)	4.5	4.8	5.6	5.5	6.2
External debt (US$ million)	3,755	4,356	5,652	6,427	6,720

Source: www.nbc.org.kh/publications.

Korean Stock Exchange (KRX) (45 per cent ownership), and planned to open on 11 July 2011. However, this did not happen as scheduled owing to operational difficulties. The CSX is a private company under the supervision of the Securities and Exchange Commission of Cambodia (SECC).[2] The main objective of establishing the CSX was to promote Cambodian economic growth to drive future economic development through raising funds, forming listed companies and issuing securities such as stocks and bonds at the market. Since the stock market is a first effort in Cambodia, rigorous laws and regulations are expected to ensure the transparency, professionalism, smooth running and development of the new capital market. All of the necessary regulations and rules from the SECC and the CSX are now in place to successfully inaugurate the CSX in the near future.

Listing a company on the CSX is divided into three steps: 1) a potential company submits an application to the CSX to review its listing eligibility; 2) after getting initial approval, the company submits its prospectus, including disclosure documents and other related documents, to the SECC to apply for an initial public offering (IPO); and 3) when the IPO is approved by the SECC, the company contacts CSX to arrange listing. For the time being, only three SOEs have officially announced their listing on the CSX: the Phnom Penh Water Supply Authority (PPWSA), Telecom Cambodia (TC) and the Sihanoukville Autonomous Port (SAP). Besides these, a few foreign-owned companies and joint ventures between Cambodia and foreign investors are expected to be listed when the market is opened, followed by some family-owned companies in the near future. According to the director general of the SECC, family-owned companies will soon understand what benefits they can gain by going public, such as getting cheaper and longer-term capital through the stock exchange. Moreover, as an incentive listed companies will also get a 10 per cent discount on the income taxes they have to pay before going public.[3]

Cambodia's Law on Investment of 1994 established an open and liberal foreign investment regime. All sectors of the economy are open to foreign investment and 100 per cent foreign ownership of companies is permitted in most sectors. In a few sectors such as cigarette manufacturing, film production, rice milling, gemstone mining and processing, publishing and printing, radio and television, wood and stone carving production, and silk weaving, foreign investment is subject to local equity participation or prior authorization from government authorities. There is almost no discrimination against foreign investors either at the time of initial investment or after the investment.

According to the amended Law on Investment and its related sub-decrees, there is no restriction on shareholder nationality or discrimination against foreign investors except for investment in property or SOEs. The amended law states that the majority interest in land must be held by one or more Cambodian citizens. Pursuant to the Law on Public Enterprise, the Cambodian government must directly or indirectly hold more than 51 per cent of the capital or the right to vote in SOEs. Foreign direct investment must be registered with the MoC and investors must obtain operating permits from relevant industry administrative ministries. If a foreign investment firm would like to receive investment incentives as a qualified investment project, it must register and receive approval from the Council for the Development of Cambodia or from its subcommittee at provincial or municipal level. The application to the Council for the Development of Cambodia may be made either before or after registering with the MoC.[4]

The total amounts of registered capital and fixed assets by foreign direct investment in Cambodia from 1994 to 2013 were US$5.2 billion and US$28.14 billion, respectively. The average annual foreign direct investment inflows in terms of fixed assets between 2011 and 2013 amounted to approximately US$2.55 billion.

Legal framework for accounting and auditing

Table 19.2 shows the existing legislative and institutional framework that governs Cambodian accounting and auditing arrangements.

Accounting policymaking

The accounting regulations (circulars or *prakas*) in Cambodia are issued by the MEF. These regulations are aimed at maintaining uniform standards in the financial reporting of business entities. Table 19.3 provides the main regulations or rules for accounting and reporting in Cambodia.

The private sector consists of a sizeable number of informal or family-owned small and medium-sized enterprises (SMEs)[5] in Cambodia. Most of these SMEs have little access to local or international institutional funding or to the use of collateral for business. Therefore, accounting does not usually play a major role in SMEs. However, in 2009 the National

Table 19.2 Cambodian legislative and institutional framework for accounting and auditing services

Main Governing Laws

- Law on the Organization and Conduct of the National Bank of Cambodia (1996)
- Law on the Foreign Exchange (1997)
- Law on Banking and Financial Institutions (1999)
- Law on Commercial Regulations and the Commercial Register (1999)
- Law on the Chamber of Commerce (1995)
- Law on Commercial Enterprises (2005)
- Law on Anti-Money Laundering and Combating the Financing of Terrorism (2007)

Regulatory institutions and their main functions

Ministry of Economy and Finance (MEF)

- Approves accounting and auditing standards
- Supports ASC and AuSC activities
- National Council of Accounting (NCA)
- The Kampuchea Institute of Certified Public Accountants and Auditors (KICPAA)
- In March 2003 the KICPAA was established by the MEF.

Ministry of Commerce (MoC)

- Registration of foreign direct investment
- Maintenance of partnership and company annual declarations

Registrar of Companies

- Administers the Companies Act 2005

National Audit Authority (NAA)

- Responsible for executing the external audit function of the public sector

National Bank of Cambodia (NBC)

- Approves bank auditors
- Approves accounting and auditing standards for banks
- Determines disclosure requirements for financial institutions

Cambodian Securities and Exchange Commission (CSX)

- Oversees the stock exchange
- Administers the Securities Act
- Auditor general and deputy auditor general
- Appointed by royal decree on the recommendation of the state and approved by a two-thirds (2/3) majority of all members of the National Assembly. The auditor general and the deputy auditor generals are appointed for a term of five years

Table 19.3 Regulations for accounting and reporting

Government circulars and prakas	Approval date
Prakas on Adoption and Implementation of Chart of Accounts for Banking and Financial Institutions	25 December 2002
Circular on Daily Accruals and Amortizations for Commercial and Specialized Banks	1 October 2003
Prakas on Annual Audit of Financial Statements of Banks and Financial Institutions	29 December 2004
Circular on Multi-Currency Accounting Following Implementation of Uniform Chart of Accounts,	10 February 2005
Monthly Statement of Assets and Liabilities on Softcopy	23 June 1995
Prakas on International Transaction Reporting System,	16 January 2003
Prakas on Reporting Date for Commercial Banks and Specialized Banks,	13 September 2006

Accounting rules and reporting	Approval date
Prakas on Adoption and Implementation of Chart of Accounts for Microfinance Institutions	25 December 2002
Prakas on Reporting Requirement for Registered NGOs and Licensed Microfinance Institutions	25 February 2002
Prakas on reporting date for micro finance institutions	13 September 2006

Accounting rules and credit information	Approval date
Prakas on the accounting process for Foreign Currency Transaction	17 February 2000
Prakas on using language, currency unit, and exchange rate for accounting records and reports	13 December 2007
Prakas on Credit Reporting	24 March 2011

Source: www.nbc.org.kh/legislation/prakash.

Accounting Council of the MEF announced that the International Financial Reporting Standards (IFRS) could be applied to SMEs. As a result, all SMEs in Cambodia are permitted to use the IFRS for SMEs, although only SMEs subject to a statutory audit are required to use the IFRS. Non-publicly accountable SMEs that are subject to a statutory audit have a choice of either the IFRS for SMEs or the IFRS. The statutory audit is required when a company meets a certain threshold of revenue, asset value and number of employees (ADB, 2010).

The development of the private sector over the last decade is somewhat satisfactory when compared to the previous period of civil unrest and conflict in Cambodia. The government supports business growth in the private sector, which will create jobs if private investment expands in the future (WB, 2004).[6]

Auditing standards

With the economic and infrastructure development plans that have taken place, several other institutional developments have taken place to support financial management over the past decade in Cambodia. Among these institutional developments, the setting up of the National Audit Authority (NAA) is an important achievement in the internationalization process of accounting and auditing practice in Cambodia.

The National Audit Authority (NAA)

The Law on Auditing in Cambodia was passed by the National Assembly on 12 January 2000 and approved by the Senate on 21 January 2000. It was declared to conform with the constitution by the Constitutional Council thereafter, except for Article 40 (MEF, 2005). The purpose of the Audit Law is to establish the NAA, which is independent in its operations. The NAA is responsible for executing the external audit function of the public sector in Cambodia. The auditor general is empowered to conduct audits on accounting records, annual accounts, management systems, operation controls and programmes of government institutions in accordance with the generally accepted auditing standards and the government auditing standards. This law also mandates the internal audit function in government ministries, institutions and public enterprises.

The Public Accounts Committee (PAC)

Under Cambodian laws and regulations, before 2000 there appeared to be no independent body authorized to carry out independent reviews of all public expenditure incurred by government ministries, agencies and enterprises. The Finance and Banking Commission (FBC) performed the role of supervision over financial affairs in the public sector in an *ad hoc* fashion. However, the FBC had no official role or procedural authority for such an oversight role and its constitution has yet to be drafted. Therefore, the government set up the Public Accounts Committee (PAC), staffed by members of the National Assembly to instil public confidence on government financial operations.

The general functions of the PAC are to examine the accounts of the government and SOEs to ensure that the accounts of all entities in the public sector are kept appropriately and in accordance with the budgets and funding for the services to be charged or allocated (MEF, 2005).

The Law on Financial Management in the Public Sector

Accounting in the public sector has been under the administration of the Law on Financial Management since 2000. The law contains general provisions on the revenue and expenditure of the state budgets. The revenues of entities in the public sector are divided into current revenues, duties and taxes, non-fiscal revenue, capital revenue, internal capital revenue and foreign capital revenue, showing the corresponding amounts for the current year, the previous year and the difference between them. Expenditure is divided into general expenses, central administration, provincial administration, capital expenditure, committed credits, payment credits, domestic financing, foreign financing and repayment of loans, with further detailed amounts for the corresponding years as required (MEF, 2005).

The Cambodian accounting profession

Following independence, all Cambodian enterprises were originally required to prepare financial statements based on the French accounting model. As a result, the French companies involved in trade and mercantile activities in Cambodia would have French accountants to carry out their record keeping or accounting function in Cambodia (Chan *et al.*, 2007; National Bank, 2006). The Cambodian legal system was based on the French civil code and judges. A particular feature of the accounting profession in France during the colonial period of

Cambodia was to organize the accounting system under the *Ordre des Experts*-Comptables (OEC), which was under the control of the MEF. This association was formed in 1942 and the members of the Ordre had a legal monopoly over the practice of accounting (Bocqueraz, 2001).

A few decades after independence, accounting developments was accelerated with the establishment of the Department of Accounting within the MEF and it issued three new uniform codes of accounts for: 1) commercial enterprises, 2) industrial enterprises and 3) construction enterprises, but the three codes of accounts were combined in 1978 (Council of Ministers decision No 49 SSR, 11 April 1987).

From 1993, the MEF changed its mandates from just regulating the state and government agencies to also producing a legal and financial framework for the private sector. With the support of the French government, through the French National Accounting Council (Conseil National de la Comptabilité), the MEF started to prepare new accounting systems for the public and private sectors. It prescribed a chart of accounts (Prakas No. 012 PK-RKSHV, 7 November 1993) for both the public and private sectors and a plan for accounting rules and guidelines for all financial statements in November 1993 (Narayan and Godden, 2000), with French influence apparent in their structure, classifications and accounting approaches (Chan, 2007). Thereafter a number of other pieces of economic reform legislation were enacted to govern public-sector financial management, and the National Audit Authority (NAA) of Cambodia was formed, with the auditor general being appointed in January 2000. In 2002, French accounting recommendations were incorporated into the refined accounting rules, and a French-style professional accounting entity, the National Accounting Council (clearly modelled on the *French Conseil National de la Comptabilité*) was established as a consultative body to review accounting regulations and laws and to develop the conceptual framework and accounting standards in Cambodia (Chan, 2007).

The Kampuchea Institute of Certified Public Accountants and Auditors (KICPAA)

The development of the capital market has also resulted in reforms to the accounting profession. In March 2003, the KICPAA was established by the MEF. Although being technically independent, the KICPAA was regulated and governed by the MEF and its day-to-day operations were still directly controlled by the state (Narayan and Godden, 2000; Chan *et al.*, 2007). The KICPAA offers membership to individuals and firms and recognizes both local and international professional qualifications. The KICPAA appears to be modelled on French professional bodies such as the *Ordre des Experts*-Comptables (OEC) and on the legacies of the former Soviet-style central-planning era. The KICPAA was more like a government-controlled regulator than an independent professional body (Narayan and Godden, 2000). A World Bank report (2007) on accounting and auditing in Cambodia has criticized the competency of accountants and auditors and the capability of the KICPAA. The report claimed that the KICPAA was unable to 'move the profession forward or project its image as an effective regulator of the public accountancy profession in Cambodia' (World Bank, 2007, p. 9), and further indicated that the majority of KICPAA members held foreign accountancy qualifications, most with the British-based Association of Chartered Certified Accountants (ACCA) and some other professional associations from Australia, the UK and New Zealand. Despite over 100 qualified members being registered with the KICPAA, only 58 of them were active (and only 10 of the 15 locally registered accounting firms were active). Although most KICPAA members were foreigners (with British-based ACCA qualifications), only Cambodian citizens would be allowed to provide audit services in the country from 2010. The World Bank (2007) concluded that, although there were attempts to boost accounting qualifications and training, Cambodia's accounting profession was dominated (in terms of membership) by members of the UK-based ACCA, many business entities did not have access to professionally qualified accountants and the accountants who practised in Cambodia were not well trained or supported. However, the influence of major accounting firms in Cambodia has become more evident. By 2002, there were seven accounting firms operating in Cambodia, and three of the Big Four international accounting firms had offices in Phnom Penh: Ernst & Young, KPMG and PricewaterhouseCoopers (*The Cambodia Daily*, 5–6 September 2002). While there has been some attempt to regulate international firms by restricting the permit to offer statutory auditing or accounting work under the Cambodian accounting law,[7] it is questionable under the world trade agreements how long these restrictions can be sustained.

Accounting education

During the period of French colonization, and until about 1975, the Cambodian education system was predominantly based on the French system, divided into primary, secondary, higher and specialized technical and vocational levels.[8] To date, only one study (Seng, 2009) has focused on accounting education in Cambodia. Seng (2009) discusses Cambodia's historical and political development and the structure of Cambodian educational system. However, he ignores the British involvement in accounting education in Cambodia. At present, there are 15 public universities and about 35 private universities in Cambodia. The government has made arrangements with some public and private universities as an effort to improve accounting education through its developmental objectives (Chan *et al.*, 2007). Two universities, the Royal University of Law and Economics (RULE)[9] and Build Bright University, are working closely with the KICPAA to coordinate the accounting qualifications required by the local market. Both universities provide two-year Associate of Business Administration degree programmes. Successful completion of KICPAA examination modules enables graduates to become qualified accountants and CPAs. The lack of qualified staff to provide standard accounting education in universities and the lack of rapport with industry and business have hindered university accounting educational programmes in the country.

Not surprisingly for such a young market economy, there is virtually no properly coordinated domestic professional accounting education in Cambodia. The ACCA accounting qualification is widely accepted by Cambodian accounting and audit firms and the ACCA has sought to recruit large number of potential accounting students, including university graduates, for the Cambodian market.

Influence of the Big Four accounting firms in accounting education in Cambodia

Currently only seven major accounting firms operate in Cambodia, including three of the Big Four firms.[10] The majority of accounting staff in the international firms come from overseas and conduct audit work for subsidiaries of foreign firms located in Cambodia, as well as joint ventures and SOEs at the request of the government (Seng, 2009).

As the Cambodian university system has generally been unable to offer quality accounting degree programmes, major accounting firms in Cambodia depend on ACCA accounting and auditing training qualifications. The Big Four reported that the inflow of UK-based ACCA educational facilities in recent years had influenced Cambodia's accountancy towards a British model.

This suggests that accounting education and training in Cambodia are now driven by both the consultancy demands and in-house needs of transnationals and NGOs, with a clear preference for British-based accountancy training over the historic colonial French system. Accounting education in Cambodia can be characterized as being increasingly exposed to international influences since 1993and it has supported the country's move towards a market economy.

Looking ahead

In the area of accounting and financial reporting in Cambodia, major changes have taken place in recent decades, particularly in regard to regulatory structure and standards setting in the public and private sectors. With the enactment of various laws on accounting and auditing, Cambodia has entered a new phase of co-regulation, where accounting standards set by the KICPAA have been given legal backing. Accordingly, any business enterprise that acts in contravention of the provisions of these standards would be committing an offence in law. This may be seen as an attempt to respond to the fact that the environment in which accounting operates in Cambodia has undergone rapid development over the past decade. One of the objectives of developing a legal framework for accounting and auditing is to increase public confidence and safeguard the interests of investors and consumers.

Accounting in Cambodia is also subject to the influence of international institutions such as the International Accounting Standards Board (IASB). As a member of the IASB, the KICPAA is obliged to support the work of the IASB by informing its members of the IFRS, to work towards the possible implementation of the IFRS, and specifically to incorporate the IFRS in domestic standards. Given the current trend towards the globalization of capital markets and the importance of foreign investment to developing countries in general, Cambodia can expect to be under increasing pressure to fully adopt internationally acceptable accounting and auditing standards and to ensure that the regulatory mechanisms in place are adequate and effective for enforcing such standards.

The post-Soviet accounting rules created after the downfall of the communist regime were influenced by the French approach towards accounting regulation. There has since the early 1990s been a desire to develop a more fully formed accounting system and establish an accounting profession. While this illustrates the dominant influence of the national government and a residual influence of French colonial power, it was just a passing phase as international standards have been implemented and international accounting bodies such as the ACCA have expanded their influence in Cambodia. There is evidence that international organizations and professional bodies have played an increasing role in reshaping the accounting legal environment and the accounting profession in Cambodia despite clear regulatory efforts to promote Cambodian accountants in the area of auditing. The growth of the internationalization of accounting and auditing practices is not particularly surprising, since radical and fundamental transformations of the political and economic systems continue in the country.

Notes

1 See www.nbc.org.kh/publication, 2014.
2 SECC is an arm of the Ministry of Economy and Finance (MEF) and was officially established on 29 April 2009 (but had commenced working in July 2008).
3 See Phnom Penh Securities Plc, www.pps.com.kh/PPSUploadFiles/iv/177_en-us.pdf (accessed 28 October 2015).

4 More information about the qualified investment project process may be found at www.cambodiainvestment.gov.kh/investment-scheme/investment-applicationprocedur (accessed 15 December 2015).

5 World Bank, *Cambodia: Seizing the Global Opportunity: Investment Climate Assessment and Reform Strategy for Cambodia*, 2004

6 The World Bank, *Cambodia: Seizing the Global Opportunity: Investment Climate Assessment and Reform Strategy for Cambodia*, 2004.

7 They need to set up joint ventures with local firms or incorporate local firms as member firms in order to apply for a provisional operation licence to provide audit/accounting services in Cambodia. Cambodian accountants may form an accounting partnership with limited liability, although any new firms require approval from the MEF before they can provide statutory services.

8 The formal educational structure consists of six years of primary school (grades 1–6), three years of lower secondary school (grades 7–9) and three years of upper secondary school (grades 10–12). Before 1996 the structure was 5:3:3, and before 1985 it was 4:3:3. In pre-revolutionary Cambodia, the educational structure was 6:4:3. Therefore, while educational provision has increased in recent years, it has not yet reached the level of the period prior to the rule of the Khmer Rouge. Higher education is available at the Royal University of Phnom Penh, the Royal Agricultural University, the Royal University of Fine Arts, the Faculty of Medicine, the Faculty of Law and Economics, the Faculty of Business (National Institute of Management), the Institute of Technology of Cambodia (formerly the Higher Technical Institute of Khmer–Soviet Friendship) and the Maharishi Vedic University (an Australian-funded institution in rural Prey Veng province). Private education exists at all levels of the education system (Chan, 2007).

9 RULE was established in 1948 as the National Institute of Law, Politics and Economics. In 2003 the institute officially became a university and had almost 5,000 students.

10 Ernst &Young International, KPMG Cambodia and PricewaterhouseCoopers.

References

Primary sources

Council of Ministers decision No 49 SSR, 11 April 1987.

Ministry of Economy and Finance (MEF) (2005) *Reports on Economic Performance*. Phnom Penh: MEF Press.

Prakas No. 012 PK-RKSHV, 7 November 1993. Retrieved from www.nbc.org.kh/legislation/prakash.

www.pps.com.kh/PPSUploadFiles/iv/177_en-us.pdf - Phnom Penh Securities Plc (accessed 28 October 2015).

www.ababank.com/fileadmin/user_upload/Annual_Reports/ABA_Annual_Report_2014_English.pdf (accessed 12 October 2015).

Secondary sources

Asian Development Bank (2005) *Economic Trends and Prospects in Developing Cambodia*. Phnom Penh: ADB.

Asian Development Bank (2010) *ADB Support to Strengthen the Accounting Profession in Cambodia*. Phnom Penh: ADB. Retrieved from www.adb.org (accessed 12 October 2012).

Bocqueraz, C. (2001) The development of professional associations: The experience of France accountants from the 1880 to the 1940s. *Accounting, Business and Financial History*, *11*(1), 7–27.

Cambodia Daily (2002) Audit authority seeks hard proof of corruption. 5–6 September.

Cambodian Law on Commercial Enterprises (2009) The National Assembly of the Kingdom of Cambodia. Retrieved from www.books.google.com (accessed 28 October 2015).

Chan, C.B., Yapa, P.W.S. and Jacobs, K. (2007) The re-emergence of accounting profession in Cambodia. *Fifth Asia Pacific Interdisciplinary Research in Accounting Conference (APIRA)*, Auckland, New Zealand, 8–10 July.

Chan, C.B. (2007) The re-emergence of the accounting profession in Cambodia, Unpublished PhD thesis, La Trobe University, Melbourne, Australia.

Kiernan, B. (1985) *How Pol Pot Came to Power: A History of Communism in Kampuchea, 1930–1975*. London: Verso.

National Bank of Cambodia (2006) *Economic and Monetary Reports.* Retrieved from www.nbc.org.kh/ quarter_bulletins/bulletin%2%2021.pdf (accessed 25 July 2006).

Narayan, F.B. and Godden, T. (2000) *Financial Management and Governance Issues in Cambodia.* Manila: Asian Development Bank.

Seng, D. (2009) Accounting education in Cambodia. *International Journal of Education Research,* 4(2), 43–54.

World Bank (2004) *Seizing the Global Opportunity: Investment Climate Assessment and Reform Strategy for Cambodia.* Washington, DC: World Bank.

World Bank (2007) *World Development Report, 2007: Cambodia.* Washington, DC: World Bank. Retrieved from http://publications.worldbank.org/ecommerce/catalog/productdetail?product_id=5424413 (accessed 14 December 2007).

20

Development of accounting practices in Mongolia

*Sainjargal Banzdai, Naranchimeg Lombodorj
and Battuya Demberel*

Introduction

Accounting, as an information recording, processing, and reporting system, has a rich history within specific economic and business administration systems. However, there are few historical studies of accounting and its development in Mongolia. Researchers (e.g., Lodoi S., Tumen Ch., Jaavaa T., and Gungaanyambuu) have examined the developmental stages of Mongolian accounting, emphasizing its features, distinctions, and problems in current accounting practices. In addition, some scholars and practitioners have been studying the Mongolian accounting evolution and practices in recent years. Generally, most researchers have explained the development of Mongolian accounting in regard to the social and economic changes in the country.

This chapter illustrates accounting practice developments in Mongolia from a historical perspective. The literature divides the development of accounting in Mongolia into three major phases: 1) the prerevolutionary period, 2) the centrally planned economy era (including stages of single- and double-entry, memorial order recording, and journal order bookkeeping), and 3) the market-oriented economy era (both the initial stage and the internationalization stage). The Mongolian accounting system has changed and evolved substantially through these development phases to reflect the specific social and economic changes in the country.

Development of accounting practices in Mongolia

It is common to trace the emergence of accounting rules in ancient Mongolia with the development of the Uyghurjin Mongol script.[1] Mongolia is still known as having a historically unique way of farming and pasture husbandry practice, but little evidence has been found about its accounting practice in ancient times. Lodoi S. (2009) acknowledges that it is important to review the history of Mongolian accounting since Genghis Khan's period.[2] According to previous studies, the evolution of contemporary accounting practices in Mongolia can be divided into the following phases.

The prerevolutionary period of Mongolia

It is generally recognized that the emergence of accounting (bookkeeping) activities in Mongolia was in the fourteenth and fifteenth centuries. Prior to this period, Kublai Khan[3] (1215–1294) introduced banknotes and sent representatives to western and eastern countries not only for commercial purposes but also to study the political, economic, and monetary policies of those countries. The developments of literacy and banknote circulation enable the indication of value by physical measurement. Some researchers have attempted to explain the development of Mongolian accounting in connection to the ancient petroglyphs located in the eastern region of the country (Lodoi S., 2009, p. 29). Ancient Mongolians had certain skills in numbering and used various terminologies for digits. For instance, "*million*" is used for numbers with one to seven digits, "*dunchuur*" for nine digits, "*trillion*" for 10 digits, "*ikh nayad*" for 13 digits, "*erkhet*" for 34 digits, "*belge temdeg*" for 42 digits, and "*toolshgui*" for 60 digits.

All recording activities and estimations are closely related to the progress of literacy, therefore it is reasonable to trace the emergence of accounting (bookkeeping) records with the development of the Mongolian script and literacy. Owing to slow progress in characters and recording techniques, accounting (bookkeeping) activities were in simple and crude form in ancient Mongolia.

The centrally planned economy era

Great changes in accounting occurred in Mongolia between 1921 and 1990, when the country adopted a centrally planned economy with the strong influence of the former Soviet Union, thus bookkeeping techniques such as single- and double-entry, memorial order, and journal order recording practices emerged gradually. At the eve of the 1921 revolution,[4] Mongolia had an underdeveloped, stagnant economy relying mainly on the nomadic herding industry. After the revolution, Mongolia began to create a national system for accounting, reporting, and supervision in the early development of the country's financial and budgetary administration systems. The government established nationwide accounting guidelines and set up a simple apprenticeship system to train selected literate citizens by developing conventional custom and cooperative temporary courses. Accounting development during this centrally planned economy period underwent three major stages.

Single- and double-entry stage (1921–1940)

Immediately after the revolution of 1921, the People's Government faced great challenges relating to the formation and development of the planned economic systems in the country.

To achieve the national objectives of social and economic growth, it was essential to enhance the state treasury and maintain sound bookkeeping and control. The national economic and fiscal policies were set by the Ministry of All Affairs Policy and Implementation of Mongolian People (changed to the Ministry of Finance from 1925) and a new financial accounting system with single- and double-entry bookkeeping techniques were introduced. The establishment of large enterprises (i.e., SOEs) including the "Telephone Committee," the "Industrial Combine," and "Power Plant No. 1" made it possible to practice the modern accounting and reporting systems and to train qualified bookkeepers or accountants. In June 1924, the Ministry of Finance set up a temporary School of Customs Officers,[5] with only two instructors and 40 students, which laid the foundation of the professional accounting training system in the country. The training curriculum included several subjects such as the Mongolian language, abacus, four-digit method, customs laws, bookkeeping, and reporting procedures. This school later became the Institute of Finance and Economics, Mongolia.

Resolution II of the National Congress in 1926 authorized the establishment of an official accounting school and strengthened accounting practices. The Ministry of Finance made a decision to restructure the School of Customs Officers and established the School of Accounting, with a six-month curriculum that offered courses such as the Mongolian script, calculus, bookkeeping, accounting, bank accounting, and political studies, which started the education for accounting personnel for all state-owned enterprises.

The national currency (tugrug) was introduced on December 9, 1925, and the value of one tugrug was set as equal to 0.98 ounces of silver; the new currency system enabled or facilitated trading activities and payments and the implementation of budgetary and accounting controls at the SOEs as well as in the national economy.

On April 1, 1928, the *tugrug* was declared the national currency to be used in all financial transactions, while golden and silver coins and foreign currencies (including the Chinese currency) were no longer allowed to be used. The introduction of a national currency system facilitated uniform accounting recording (bookkeeping) and reporting nationwide.

In the early years after the revolution, different bookkeeping and reporting systems stemming from different countries were in use owing to no uniform national recording system in Mongolia, which had a long history of having mainly a pasture husbandry economy. One of these systems was the single-entry bookkeeping system, following the influence of the Chinese tradition. Under this recording system, business transactions were only recorded in chronological order in the "memory book," and were later recorded in one or only a few "journals." Finally, summary accounts or statements would be prepared.

Single-entry bookkeeping was unable to meet the needs of the then centralized socioeconomic developments in the country, so the Italian-style bookkeeping or accounting system was introduced by the government. In this system, journals, general ledgers, and subsidiary ledgers were widely used with debit and credit double-entry recording. Business transactions were then recorded in two or more accounts simultaneously in chronological order in the general journal, having more systematic accounting entries in general ledgers and making entries of systematic detailed recording in subsidiary ledgers.

The way that journals and general ledgers were recorded is the same as the old Italian system of bookkeeping, but the subsidiary ledgers had varied forms depending on the purposes and features of a variety of accounts. At this point, the journal order system (in which transactions were recorded into cash order for cash transactions and into memorial order for noncash transactions) was used to record the transaction details based on transaction source documents. Following the entries to these orders, the basic journal was recorded in chronological order and then posted to general ledgers. The Italian-style bookkeeping system provided a good instrument to trace transactions and accounting work effectively. However, the system recorded one transaction in several forms simultaneously, which increased the likelihood of making errors and increased the technical bookkeeping workload. Furthermore, the German and French accounting systems were also introduced in the country, in which memorial order records were divided into several journals such as inventory journals and cash payment journals; such bookkeeping systems allowed ledger journals to be consolidated into one document, thereafter named a general ledger.

Memorial order stage (1941–1960)

To keep pace with the progress of the centrally planned economy between 1941 and 1960, SOEs expanded significantly in number. In order to record more complex business transactions, the use of the memorial order system in bookkeeping was extended in accounting practice in Mongolia. In this bookkeeping method, business transactions were recorded in the memorial order forms upon completion and they were grouped according to the economic nature of the transactions. As shown in Figure 20.1, a memorial order form had the following content.

The memorial order form is the traditional type of double-entry bookkeeping method as used worldwide. Business transactions from source documents are first recorded in the memorial order form with debit and credit entries in chronological order. The journal entries are then entered in related journals and ledgers to produce the accounting statements. If required, the detailed recording of subsidiary accounts can be made using the memorial order entries and then various disclosures can also be produced.

Since 1940 the preparation and implementation of the five-year planning of national economic and social development has been introduced, which requires a sound performance evaluation and effective use of public resources. The need for enhanced accountability has called for more effective and advanced accounting and reporting systems. During this period, several regulatory tools, such as the Charter of Rights and Obligations of Stock-keepers, the Regulations on General (Senior) Accountants, the Rules on Accounting and Reporting, the Accounting Documentation and Recordkeeping Rules, the Rules on Cash Transactions, the Planned Accounts for Industry, Agriculture, Construction, Trade, Transport and Communication Sectors, and the Guidance for Balance Sheet Formation were all drafted and implemented.

Generally, SOEs had to use the memorial order system. Before this stage, business accounting records made by enterprises and organizations were kept with various types of accounts and bookkeeping methods owing to a lack of an integrated accounting system. Professor Dambadorj L. has noted that more than 300 accounts were in use and handmade sheets were common as printed sheet recording did not exist at all (Lodoi, 2009, p. 141). To facilitate the bookkeeping

---

Organization Name:

Memorial Order No:

19.....year .... Month

Bureau: ....tugrik from.............credit account to ......debit account and ....tugrug from.............credit account to ......debit account etc.

Figure 20.1 Sample of memorial order form recording

Source: The Ministry of Finance of Mongolia, *Brief History of Accounting of Mongolia,* 2011, p. 19.

process, the state cooperative association developed the diary recording method and published 10 more books and forms for accounting and reporting, which became the origin for the journal order system that emerged later.

In 1949, Tumen Ch. and Yorkov A.A., both training instructors from the former Soviet Union, jointly published the first edition of the *Essentials of Accounting* in Mongolia. A number of other translations of Soviet accounting textbooks also became available in Mongolia.[6] In the late 1950s the government decided to launch an advancement programme for the qualification of accountants and evening schools for the accounting education programme were set up at the College of Finance and Economics and the Faculty of Economics at the National University of Mongolia. The Institute of Economic Studies was established in 1956 following the decisions of the Central Party Committee and the Cabinet of the Ministers, and it started to enroll students for the accounting major in the 1960s, which initiated the start of the formal accounting education system in the country.

Journal order system (1961–1990)

This period includes a systematic development of accounting practices in light of the progress of economic planning and administration in the country. Originally the journal order method came from Europe, developed in the former Soviet Union in the 1930s, and was introduced in socialist countries from the 1950s. Historically, the system was in use from the 1960s in some industry sectors and became used widely in all sectors in Mongolia. The Ministry of Finance cooperated with the former Soviet Union to introduce the journal order system in accounting work. Comrade Molom Ts. and Tumen Ch. were sent to the Soviet Union by the Mongolian government in 1961 to study the journal order accounting system. They held meetings with Bezrukhih P.S., the director of the Accounting Department, and the Ministry of Finance of the former Soviet Union and discussed the possibility of adopting the journal order system developed there by Fiznichenko. After three months of tailor-made training, they returned home and the system was introduced in Mongolia in 1962.

The Fourteenth Congress of the Mongolian People's Revolutionary Party addressed the importance of eliminating the burdensome settlements that existed in the accounting systems of the time and formally introduced the journal order accounting system to improve accounting and reporting practices. In 1968, to enforce the Party Congress's resolution, the Ministry of Finance developed template accounts with fewer than 99 codes for the journal order accounting system, under the supervision of Liushin, a specialist from the former Soviet Union, with experts from related administrative ministries (i.e., Markhaaj and Tumen Ch.). The planned chart of accounts was used until 1990.

The journal order system consists of more than 10 kinds of journals, over 10 types of subsidiary journals, and other clarification journals. Many advantages were observed in the journal order system over the previous memorial order system, such as eliminating repeated recording for a transaction. Under the journal order system, bookkeeping work was needed to record one or two numbers in one journal; these were then carried over to journal order forms from the subsidiary journals and posted to the general ledgers from the journal order forms. Trial balancing was then made based on the balances of accounts. Many uniform accounting textbooks, training program handbooks, materials, and professional study guidelines were published for training accounting students and professionals nationwide after 1960. The journal order system was adopted for all industrial sectors except the agriculture sector and lasted until the early 1990s.

The memorial order or journal order system, as different forms of double-entry bookkeeping instruments, enables the classification and summarization of accounting data at varied aggregation levels and is used for preparing financial statements. The main differences in data processing procedures in the journal order system and the memorial order are:

1   Under the journal order system, accounting transactions are grouped by similarities within a smaller number of accounts and for recording journal entries in a special form of the journal order being developed; and

2   Credits are entered in the journal order forms and debits of the accounts recorded in the forms called general accounts, classifying the transactions by a preset chart of accounts. The benefits of the journal order system include easy posting for transaction records, reducing the risks of recording errors, and enhancing the chance of systematically generating accounting data in terms of preset accounts.

Market-oriented economy period

Mongolia shifted to a market-oriented economy after 1990. The accounting practices stemming from the centrally planned economy became outdated. It became necessary to reform the accounting and control systems, as well as their methods and procedures and professional training systems that had been adopted and implemented several decades beforehand to accommodate the new economic administrative systems. This development period can be divided into the initial stage (1991–2001) and the internationalization stage (from 2001).

Initial stage (1991–2001)

The new constitution of Mongolia, adopted in 1992, declared the recognition of democracy in Mongolia. The centrally planned economic system was abandoned and the country started to embark on reforms to shift to a market-oriented economy. The changes in economy required the modification of accounting regulations and practices. To bridge the gaps, the Ministry of Finance initiated the reform of accounting regulation systems and methods in 1992 and submitted a draft accounting law to the parliament of Mongolia. The Accounting Law was approved on 8 February 1993. Owing to a lack of legal expertise of domestic experts to implement the new law, the government sought support from international organizations and donor countries.

The implementation of the international accounting standards (IAS) was then highly appreciated and accepted by international financial institutions, which all supported the internationalization of Mongolian accounting. Arthur Anderson LLP, a Big Five international accounting firm, was designated by the World Bank in 1993 as an implementing agent to improve accounting and auditing systems in Mongolia. The accounting system reforms produced the following outcomes within the framework of the reform support project:

1   The project improved the skills of accounting professionals nationwide and accountants of the larger corporations, enhancing their awareness of the IAS;

2   Accounting education programmes and curriculums at colleges and universities had been reviewed and improved within the project subcomponent;

3   The accounting and auditing development strategic plan up to the year 2000 was made, maintaining positive communication with international organizations to seek funding support and to ensure the effective implementation of the development strategy and continuing reform initiatives; and

4   The full adoption of IAS in their accounting systems was required for large SOEs and national corporations such as Gobi, APU, and the National Trade Development Bank.

As a result of these reform activities in 1994–1997, the accounting systems of more than 50 large companies had been restructured with the support of international and domestic professional experts. In 1995 the Ministry of Finance issued the *Manual for Accounting Accounts*, *Guidelines on Preparation of Financial Statements* and *Instructions on the Forms of Recording Accounting Journals for Business Entities*.

During this period, a few international agencies made direct influence on accounting reform in Mongolia. For instance, the Asian Development Bank introduced several supportive projects: the Improvement of Accounting and Auditing Systems in Mongolia in 1996–1997 and Competence Building for Mongolian Accounting and Auditing Professionals in 2002–2004, which contributed significantly to the development of accounting and auditing practices in line with the progress of the market-oriented economy in Mongolia. Within the framework of these projects, multistage training on financial accounting, cost and management accounting, auditing, and accounting information systems for accounting professionals, as well as training of educators to teach new accounting methods, were provided; supporting activities were sponsored for the Institute of Certified Public Accountants of Mongolia (MICPA) to move toward joining the International Federation of Accountants (IFAC). International professional organizations also provided consulting services for the preparation of the draft Audit Law in the country.

Furthermore, the implementation of the new laws and international requirements was beneficial for the development of the accounting profession in Mongolia. Numerous popular Western accounting and auditing textbooks on international accounting and auditing standards and practices were translated into Mongolian, contributing positively to training Mongolian accounting professionals. Therefore, the decade between 1991 and 2001 can be considered the early stage of the internationalization of accounting and auditing in the country.

Internationalization stage (since 2001)

When the country embarked a switch from a formal centrally planned economy to a market-oriented one, reform was demanded in the accounting systems that had been in use for public enterprises since 1990. To adopt the new accounting systems, the World Bank and the Asian Development Bank carried out several projects to provide technical expertise and consulting services to assist the implementation of the generally accepted accounting principles and the international accounting standards, including the following activities within the framework of those supportive projects:

1   To formulate a legal framework for implementing the new accounting systems through new accounting and auditing laws and to develop instructive sample procedures for carrying out accounting work and preparing financial statements;
2   To improve public awareness of new accounting systems and modification of accounting curriculums at colleges and universities as well as offering retraining for accounting professionals;
3   To monitor and evaluate the implementation outcomes of accounting reform projects and strategic development plans step by step; and
4   To establish the Institute of Certified Public Accountants of Mongolia, the Association of Independent Audits, and professional committees or nongovernmental institutions that can enable the expansion of international cooperation and receive consulting services and expertise from foreign professionals and organizations.

For instance, in 2002, the Law on Management and Financing of Budgetary Institutions was enacted with the assistance of the World Bank under its "Fiscal technical assistance project." This law required all budgetary entities to produce accrual-based financial statements in accordance with international public-sector accounting standards (IPSAS). In addition, the World Bank project implemented in 2007–2009 addressed the need to strengthen auditing capacity. In fact, the main components of the project required the Mongolian government to develop guidelines for audit quality control, and to organize workshops and consulting services for auditing firms in the country.

The implementation of economic administration system reforms in 1991–2001 contributed significantly to the introduction of new accounting and auditing systems in Mongolia. However, some domestic and international scholars reported that the primary objectives of those reform projects had not been achieved completely as actual accounting and auditing practices still fell behind the requirements of the new systems being introduced. The main reasons for the failure were:

1 The objectives were not flexible: the reform initiatives aimed at the adoption of the international accounting standards did not fully consider the historical traditions of the Mongolian bookkeeping system and the competence of Mongolian accounting professionals;

2 Business enterprises in the country were relatively small and their needs for transaction data may differ considerably from their international counterparts, while the characteristics of the public sector and small and medium-sized enterprises had not been reflected in the internationalization processes; and

3 Professionals in small and medium-sized enterprises possessed poor knowledge of international accounting and auditing standards and there was a lack of sufficient guidance to address the needs of these groups.

Thus, several new initiatives or actions were introduced to tackle these problems step by step, which included: 1) amendment of the accounting and auditing laws in line with domestic circumstances and development progress; 2) introduction of international standards with consideration of the scope and scale of business operations, both public enterprises and small and medium-sized businesses, and serving the public interests; and 3) preparing guidance on the application of international standards with the involvement of professional bodies in policy formulation and management to establish national committees for developing domestic standards.

In 2001, the Mongolian parliament made a substantial amendment of the Accounting Law of 1993, which was the legal basis for regulating accounting work. In addition, the amendment of the Audit Law in 2007 played a significant role in regulating the activities of professional accountants (certified public accountants, CPAs) and professional organizations. The amended laws led to promoting accounting and reporting practices in accordance with the IAS or the IFRS, reforming public-sector accounting, developing independent audits, establishing state internal audits under the Ministry of Finance, and improving the capacity of the MICPA as a main professional body. In addition, the system of forensic accounting and the improvement of accounting education have been witnessed.

The government declared 2001 the Year of National Accounting Investigation, to review the process and the results of the introduction of the International Accounting Standards (IAS), and the next the Year of Accounting Improvement, to reinforce the new accounting and auditing systems being introduced. Since 2002, the Department for Accounting Policies at the Ministry of Finance has issued a number of guidelines and procedures for the implementation of international standards:

- Amended accounts templates for business enterprises that were introduced by the minister of finance in 2000;
- Manuals for filling the primary documentation for all types of enterprises and organizations in 2002;
- Manual for analyzing financial reports of business enterprises in 2002;
- Manual for accounting forms and methods for small entities in 2002; and
- Procedures on the use of monitoring accounting software in 2006.

The Ministry of Finance, with the cooperation of professional bodies, published new accounting standards modeled on the IAS and guidance on the practical application of the standards in 2003, 2005, and 2011, and compliance with the standards has improved substantially in recent years. Besides the formulation and implementation of national accounting policies in Mongolia, the Ministry of Finance has also been in charge of the development of external auditing, but it has delegated some responsibilities to the MICPA. The Audit Law, amended in 2007, sets up the legal environment for developing auditing services and has contributed to the establishment of accounting firms and an improvement of the quality of accounting and reporting of public entities.

The adoption of the International Financial Reporting Standards (IFRS) on corporate financial reporting in the past years has produced visible outcomes with notable changes:

1 The introduction of the IFRS has been reflected in the accounting education curriculums at universities;
2 The Big Five international accounting firms have opened their branches in Mongolia;
3 More than 130 auditing firms with over 3,600 CPAs are in place nationwide;
4 The accounting functions of nongovernmental professional organizations such as the MICPA, the Mongolian Institute of Certificated Appraisers, and the Mongolian Association of Certified Tax Consultants have been established; and
5 Mongolian corporations have successfully launched their IPOs on international stock exchanges.

Even though accounting is perceived as the process of recording past events, business forecasting, the provision of timely and relevant information to various stakeholders, and transparent reporting are getting more popular in practice. The recent application and enforcement of the IAS and the IFRS have advanced, however the adoption of the standards with consideration of domestic business development, scope of business activities, and governance practice remain to be improved, as the translation of the international standards in a fully understandable manner into the native language is essential.

Although the Accounting Law of 1993 and its amendment in 2001 outline Mongolian public accounting policies and establish legal regulation of financial reporting by business entities, the further development of the profession and accounting practices was prompted by the Parliamentary Assembly of Mongolia in June 2015, when the following amendments were made:

- Public entities and organizations must adopt the IFRS, and International Standards of Auditing (ISA) must be followed in financial statement audits;
- Small and medium-sized enterprises should comply with the IFRS for Small and Medium-Sized Enterprises. Although these entities are not required to take a mandatory financial audit, ISA must be followed when a financial investigation is required;

- Public entities are required to comply with the IPSAS; and
- The responsibilities for translating international standards, preparing the conceptual framework, and developing guidelines are assigned to the nongovernmental professional organizations (such as MICPA).

As a result, the introduction of international auditing standards in Mongolia has been conducted. This has involved several stages and ongoing improvements have been made to strengthen the further growth of accounting internationalization in Mongolia.

Conclusion

Accounting in Mongolia has evolved continuously in light of specific social and economic changes in the country. This chapter examined the development of Mongolian accounting practices since the fifteenth century. According to previous studies, the evolution of contemporary accounting in Mongolia can be divided into three development phases. The first phase is prerevolutionary period, commonly defined as the fifteenth to the nineteenth century, when some bookkeeping activities existed in a very simple and crude form. The second phase refers to the period of the centrally planned economy, when some modern bookkeeping or accounting techniques or methods, such as single- and double-entry recording, memorial order recording, and journal order bookkeeping practices, were introduced in the country in 1921–1990. Mongolia began to establish a nationwide system for accounting, reporting, and supervision as the early development for the administration of the country's fiscal and budgetary organizations and SOEs when the country moved to the former Soviet model of economic planning and administration. The third phase started in 1990, when the country redirected toward a market-oriented economy. Mongolian accounting systems have undergone significant reforms since 1991. The Mongolian parliament enacted the Accounting Law and the Audit Law to lay down a legal foundation for the changes in accounting and auditing practices in Mongolia. These laws, with their subsequent amendments, mandate compliance with international standards on accounting, financial reporting, and auditing, thus accounting and reporting practices should be in accordance with international standards. Reform of public-sector accounting and the development of independent auditing have become the reality. Several international financial institutions (e.g., the World Bank) and professional bodies (e.g., the IFAC) have contributed significantly to the recent development of accounting and auditing in Mongolia.

The internationalization of Mongolian accounting advances gradually and the application of the IAS or the IFRS has progressed steadily over the last two decades. However, the adoption of the international accounting and auditing standards with consideration of the domestic conditions, the scope of business activities, and governance practices remains a major issue to be coped with for the effective enforcement of international standards in the country. We believe that adoption of international standards in a fully understandable manner in the native language is essential for the further development of Mongolian accounting.

Notes

1 The Mongolian Uyghur alphabet as Mongolian vertical script was an early development of the traditional Mongolian alphabet system around 1204.
2 Genghis Khan (1162–1227), born in Temüjin, was the founder and the Great Khan (emperor) of the Mongol Empire, which became the largest contiguous empire in history.

3 Kublai Khan (1215–1294), was the fifth Great Khan of the Mongol Empire, reigning from 1260 to 1294.
4 The Mongolian Revolution of 1921 was a military and political event by which Mongolian revolutionaries, with the assistance of the Soviet Red Army, expelled Russian White Guards from the country and founded the Mongolian People's Republic in 1924.
5 See the *108-Volume Scientific Book Series of Mongolia*, Vol. 34 (edited by Professors Dorj T., Dagvadorj D., Luvsandorj B., Sereeter Ch., Enkhtuvshin B., and Sainjargal B.) Ulaanbaatar, 2010, p. 190.
6 The translated textbooks include *Industry Accounts Balances and Analysis* by P. Savichyev and I. Ivanov, which was translated by Lkhamsuren M. and Khojoo D. in 1956, *Operational Analysis of Industry*, translated by Tumen Ch. and Zanabazar L. in 1957, and *Financial Operational Results Analysis for Industries*, by Lkhamsuren L. and S.M. Miroshyenko in 1959.

Bibliography

Accounting Development Fund (2003) *Some Older and Younger Accountants Memories and Thoughts.* Ulaanbaatar: ADF.

Agvaan, N. (1995) *Improved Accounting.* Ulaanbaatar: Press of Ulaanbaatar Railway.

Bolormaa, B. (2014) *To Methodology for the Adoption for IFRS in Entities.* Thesis, Ulaanbaatar, Mongolia.

Bolormaa, B., Jaavaa, T., Tsolmontuya and Myagmarjav (2015) *Profession, Formation and Analysis for Accounting of Mongolia.* Monograph, Business School of National University of Mongolia, Ulaanbaatar, Mongolia. Munkhiin useg Press.

Dorj, T., Dagvadorj, D., Luvsandorj, B., Sereeter, C., Enkhtuvshin, B. and Sainjargal, B. (2010) *108-Volume Scientific Book Series of Mongolia: 34th Volume.* Ulaanbaatar: Mongolian Academy of Sciences.

Erdenebileg, S. (2003) *Throughout the Double-Entry History.* Thesis, Ulaanbaatar, Mongolia.

Lodoi, S. (2009) *Accounting Development Pathway.* Ulaanbaatar: Huh Sudar.

Ministry of Finance (2011) *Brief History of Accounting of Mongolia.* Ulaanbaatar: Ekimto.

Rinchin, M. (1996) *History of Financial Department of Mongolia.* Ulaanbaatar: Ekimto.

World Bank (2008) *Report on the Observance of Standards and Codes: Mongolia Accounting and Auditing.* Retrieved from www.worldbank.org/ifa/rosc_aa_mongolia.pdf.

World Bank (2009) *Report on the Observance of Standards and Codes: Corporate Governance Country Assessment.* Retrieved from www.worldbank.org/ifa/rosc_cg_mongolia_09.pdf.

Index

Page numbers in **bold** refer to tables; those in *italics* refer to figures or images.

For Product Safety Concerns and Information please contact our EU
representative GPSR@taylorandfrancis.com
Taylor & Francis Verlag GmbH, Kaufingerstraße 24, 80331 München, Germany

www.ingramcontent.com/pod-product-compliance
Ingram Content Group UK Ltd.
Pitfield, Milton Keynes, MK11 3LW, UK
UKHW011454240425
457818UK00021B/822